MW01061903

GREENWICH VILLAGE, 1920–30

CAROLINE F. WARE

Greenwich Village

1920-1930

A COMMENT ON AMERICAN CIVILIZATION

IN THE POST-WAR YEARS

Foreword by

Deborah Dash Moore

UNIVERSITY OF CALIFORNIA PRESS

Berkeley • Los Angeles • London

University of California Press
Berkeley and Los Angeles, California

University of California Press, Ltd.
London, England

© 1963 by Caroline F. Ware

Foreword © 1994 by Deborah Dash Moore

Library of Congress Cataloging-in-Publication Data

Ware, Caroline Farrar, 1899–
    Greenwich Village, 1920–1930 : a comment on American
  civilization in the post-war years / Caroline F. Ware.
        p.   cm.
    Includes bibliographical references and index.
    ISBN 0-520-08566-3
      1. Greenwich Village (New York, N.Y.)   2. New York (N.Y.)
  —Social conditions.   I. Title.
F128.68.G8W25   1994
974.7'1042—dc20   93-35953
                                                                           CIP

Prepared under the auspices of Columbia University Council for
Research in collaboration with Greenwich House.

This book was was originally published by Houghton Mifflin Company
in 1935 in the United States of America, and is here reprinted
by arrangement. HARPER COLOPHON edition published 1965 by
Harper & Row.

Printed in the United States of America

9   8   7   6   5   4   3   2   1

The paper used in this publication meets the minimum requirements of
American National Standard for Information Sciences—Permanence of
Paper for Printed Library Materials, ANSI Z39.48–1984. ∞

CONTENTS

PART III

INSTITUTIONS

LIST OF CHARTS

FOREWORD

More than half a century after its initial publication, Caroline F. Ware's brilliant account of Greenwich Village in the 1920s endures as a provocative and challenging analysis of the multicultural urban character of American civilization. Ware's disturbing and insightful study deserves not only to enter the vocabulary of American community studies, as Middletown has, but also to serve as a touchstone for contemporary efforts to understand the American city. Ware grasped, as few have since, that in the daily struggle to earn a living, build a home, and raise children in one multiethnic New York City neighborhood lay the social processes that would produce a common American culture. Americans, she warned, ignored their cities and the immigrants who lived in them at the peril of their future as a nation.

Ware published her pioneering study of New York City's famous —and infamous—Greenwich Village in 1935, in the midst of the New Deal era of social reform.[1] In it she explicitly addressed pressing issues of city life that engaged reformers in Washington, including poverty, crime, slums, public health and education, immigrant acculturation, machine politics, and urban development, as well as a host of concerns reformers ignored, like street culture, family patterns, and sexual mores. "The story is not primarily concerned with America's bohemia," she announced in the book's second sentence, ". . . nor can it be told through the famous names of those who have lived and worked within the Village" (3). Yet her book initially attracted attention not for its penetrating portrait of American urban society but because it examined New York City's controversial neighborhood for avant-garde artists.

Greenwich Village's international reputation as a center of sexual and artistic experimentation preceded Ware's study. Indeed, the Village retains its reputation to this day, despite the rise of such alternative neighborhoods as SoHo and the East Village. In the 1920s, the "Brevoort crowd" of writers like Sinclair Lewis, Nina Wilcox Putnam, Rose O'Neill, and Edna St. Vincent Millay formed the public image of Greenwich Village, along with the "long-haired men and short-haired women" who frequented its many speakeasies and nightclubs.[2] Most reviewers of Ware's book gravitated immediately to those sections that discussed the mores of the "Villagers," the young people from the South and Midwest who came to the Village to escape the constricting norms of America's "Middletowns." Only after devoting attention to these highly visible and intriguing rebels did reviewers note Ware's thoughtful analysis of the "local people," most of whom were Italian immigrants and their children, the second generation.

The literary critic Malcolm Cowley observed that *Greenwich Village* contained new material, "some of it pretty close to being sensational." He cited the surprisingly frank terms Ware used to discuss the sex lives of Villagers who didn't bother to pull the blinds, as well as her revelations of links between politicians and criminals. Although Cowley noted perceptively that the chapter on the Italians "gives a better idea of immigrant psychology than anything else I have read," he condemned the book for not presenting what he considered the real drama of Greenwich Village: the rise during the 1920s of artistic champions of individual salvation, self-expression, and escape from society, and their subsequent decline into psychological despair when they discovered that they could neither adjust to society nor escape its pressures.[3] The reviewer for the *New York Times* was so absorbed by the book's "frank, fearless, sociological" approach to the Villagers that he misread Ware's study as an account of "Greenwich Village as a Melting Pot," a notion Ware explicitly rejected.[4] Even John Palmer Gavitt's review, "The City Wilderness," begins with a discussion of the Villagers' state of mind and praises Ware's "admirable candor." Gavitt, however, grasped the poignant plea to America that Ware put into the mouth of a second-generation youth in the last chapter.[5] The critical story here was not the lifestyle of the famous and would-be-famous but the agony of the second generation and what it portended for the future of the American city.

The first republication of the volume, in a paperback edition in 1965 at the peak of the "War on Poverty," reiterated the significance of Ware's study for a nation concerned with urban problems.[6] Riots exploded that summer, especially in Watts, Los Angeles, riveting attention upon American cities and raising questions about where

American society was heading after the civil rights movement and
several decades of urban renewal projects. The Report of the
National Advisory Commission on Civil Disorders, published in
1968 following several more summers of increasing urban violence,
concluded ominously: "Our nation is moving toward two societies,
one black, one white—separate and unequal." It called for "the
creation of a true union—a single society and a single American
identity."[7] The Commission's disturbing vision of polarization in
the nation's cities and its plea for a unitary society and culture
echoed Ware's own foreboding conclusions. "What new patterns
may develop," she queried, "to replace the rampant individualism
which finds few outlets in the urban life of twentieth-century America except in predatory action or escape?" (424). Ware found little
hope for the future either in the predatory culture of young second-
generation Italian men or in the escapist values of male and female
Villagers. In both cases, traditional norms and social patterns had
been cast aside in favor of American individualism. "The most
diligent search," she wrote, "brought forth no evidence that the
direction of social evolution in this community was toward a social
order for twentieth-century America, but only that it was away
from the social orders of the past" (422).

Ware's sober assessment of the corrosive character of individualism pervades the book, aptly subtitled *A Comment on American
Civilization in the Post-War Years*. Looking at a decade of enormous
social change that included immigration restriction in 1924 and
ended in the catastrophe of the Great Depression, she persistently
asks what common values Americans share. She peppers her brief
concluding chapter with questions designed to raise the consciousness of her American readers—pleas as relevant to contemporary
ghetto life as to that of sixty years ago. "We have no one that we can
look up to," say the "articulate and inquiring young people." Surely
the painful absence of role models continues to plague adolescents
growing up in urban slums. "How can we rely on the schools when
we don't believe that they understand the real problems which we
have to face?" is a question that could easily come from any city
public school child today. "But tell us, do we ever actually get that
'American standard of living,' or must we just hope for a 'break'?"
Doesn't this materialist dream still tempt the poor and working
classes, with its promise of a decent home and job and the dignity

and sense of self that come with them? And what of the anger when the promise is broken? Finally, and most poignantly, the children of immigrants wonder if "we'll ever really get by as Americans, or are we bound to stay 'wops' and 'kikes' for the rest of our lives?" (423).

Ware offers no answers to these legitimate and demanding questions about the disjunction between the promise of pluralism and the reality of intergroup relations pockmarked by prejudice and segregation. She finds no alternative to racism, poverty, and greed in the experimental and temporary lifestyle of the Villagers; their escapist individualism does not produce an urban vision that might point toward a common future. Nor does she place much faith in a unity stemming from the acclaimed friendliness, informality, and freedom of the Village. Though she admits that she was unable to explore the effect of popular culture, particularly movies and music, as a potential source of shared values and experiences, she does note that local people and Villagers do not read the same papers, nor do Villagers attend movies with the same frequency as local people. Had Ware pursued the issue of popular culture, she probably would have uncovered the same divergences that she found in virtually all aspects of neighborhood life. Only the small Irish community maintained a measure of cultural continuity, through its religious and political institutions. Thus Ware's portrait of Greenwich Village during a troubled decade raises real doubts about the possibilities of creating a viable urban culture in America. Its initial republication during the heyday of suburbanization refocused the attention of urbanists upon enduring problems that had not suddenly appeared with the migration of African Americans to the nation's metropolitan centers.

When Columbia University's Council for Research in the Social Sciences asked Caroline Ware to conduct a community study of Greenwich Village, she was a young professor of American history at Vassar College, her alma mater. Columbia's offer came in 1931, the year she published her first book, *The Early New England Cotton Manufacture,* a slightly revised version of her Harvard dissertation. Ware's study of industrialization won the prestigious Hart, Schaffner & Marx prize for the outstanding book in economic history in 1929. Later generations of labor and social historians have recognized how her innovative and comprehensive approach to her subject anticipated their intellectual agendas.[8] An observer might have thought it bold of Ware to leap from the mill towns of nineteenth-century New England to the ninth ward of twentieth-century New York City with its contradictory reputations as working-class neighborhood, immigrant slum, and avant-garde bohemia, but Ware brought to her contemporary inquiry skills she had acquired during her training as a historian. The opportunity to study Greenwich Village gave her a chance to implement ideas she had just started to articulate about the practice of social and cultural history.

Ware's awareness of the interrelationship of class and culture as it was inscribed on the urban landscape first developed during her childhood in suburban Brookline, but her understanding of history took shape at Vassar. During her undergraduate years at Vassar she studied with Lucy Maynard Salmon, who had "a profound intellectual influence" on her. She learned from Salmon the value not only of looking for historical sources in kitchens and backyards, women's traditional arenas, but also of applying her historical understanding to contemporary social change. As Ellen Fitzpatrick observes, "Salmon never used the term 'culture' in her teaching," but she urged students "to examine the fabric of everyday life." After a summer internship doing social work in New York City between her junior and senior years, Ware turned toward an academic career without abandoning her concern for social responsibility. In 1922 she joined the first tutorial staff at the Bryn Mawr Summer School for industrial workers; there she encountered working women and heard their intellectual and activist concerns. The following year at Oxford gave her the experience of being an alien in another culture. By the time she arrived at Harvard, Ware was ready to make the unorthodox choice of anthropology as her "outside" field for her general examinations, a decision that reflected her independence as well as her growing interest in social and cultural history.[9]

Ware's choice of anthropology placed her outside the profession of sociology. Although she was acutely aware of developing theories of community studies at the University of Chicago, sociologists did not reciprocate an interest in her work.[10] She admired Robert and Helen Lynd's first study of Middletown, published in 1929, and even cited it in the preface to the paperback edition of *Greenwich Village*. By contrast, Harvey Zorbaugh's *Gold Coast and the Slum* (1929) and its depiction of a "Little Sicily" did not serve Ware as a model. She eschewed the "guilt by association" tendency, common to sociological studies of Little Italies, to view immigrants within the framework of urban pathologies.[11] Despite her clear concern with problems facing American cities, she refused to reduce her study to a theoretical exploration of "group and class in the life of Italian-Americans" or "the social structure of an Italian slum," the subtitles respectively of Herbert Gans's *Urban Villagers* (1962) and William Foote Whyte's *Street Corner Society* (1943). Her own subtitle defined her subject as American culture, not industrial pathologies, immigrant subcultures, or even urban communities. *Greenwich Village, 1920–1930* transcended common categories of contemporary scholarship on cities and immigrants.

Ware used what she called the "cultural approach to history." Her review of *Middletown in Transition,* the Lynds' second study, emphasized that historians could learn much more from this study than its predecessor because it focused on the process of change while maintaining its concern with the "culture pattern" of the community. Ware urged social historians to pay attention to the inarticulate and to those processes common to all times and places: making a living, making a home, rearing children.[12]

The republication of *Greenwich Village* in 1965, as academic interest in cities exploded, fueled in part by their manifest problems, brought Ware to the attention of a growing cadre of young urban historians. They particularly appreciated her historical analysis, her sensitivity to social and residential changes within Greenwich Village, and her insights regarding not just immigrant accommodation but second-generation patterns of acculturation as well. Ware's focus upon "Italian immigrants and their children, Irish longshoremen, truck-drivers, and politicians, Jewish shopkeepers, Spanish seamen, and a remnant of staid old American and German citizens" made sense to scholars increasingly conscious of how ethnicity determined the fabric of city life (3). However, the renewed interest in her study did not prompt Ware to return to urban history. After editing a volume on *The Cultural Approach to History* that emerged from a conference of the American Historical Association in 1939, Ware had turned to contemporary issues in international development and social work. "It would be many years," Fitzpatrick observes, "before American historians explicitly embraced the intellectual imperative laid down by scholars such as Ware."[13]

The decision to again reissue *Greenwich Village* nearly sixty years after its first appearance reflects renewed appreciation for this classic of urban history scholarship as well as a desire to introduce it to a new generation of students. As Ware noted in her preface to the paperback edition in 1965, "The study was undertaken when methods of social research were less refined," yet the book remained "relevant and timely, for many of the processes which it reveals and the problems on which it throws light" endure. It is worthwhile reiterating Ware's assessment, especially at a time when immigration (albeit not on the scale of the pre-World War I period) has filled American cities once more with substantial numbers of foreign-born parents and their children. But a demurral from Ware's self-critique is also required. Although she undertook the study at a time when there were few similar works to serve as model and guide, her methods of social research do not lack refinement. Rather, they are both rigorous and innovative. Her mastery of a diverse array of sources, from real estate deeds to rapid transit turnstile receipts, from census records to participant observation, indicates an extraordinary sophistication and refinement. *Greenwich Village* challenges contemporary students of urban life with its formidable methodology, not just its brilliant synthesis and disturbing conclusion.

Ware supervised a team of researchers working out of a small office on Jones Street in the Village. Her administrative abilities and collaborative skills allowed her to gather materials quickly, to formulate the intellectual questions, and to order the whole into a cohesive narrative. The book appeared just four years after she began her research. Although it bears her name and reflects her vision, *Greenwich Village, 1920–1930* is a model of collaborative scholarship. Ware worked with college students and graduates who were residents at Greenwich House, a large, well-established settlement house, as well as with local young people. She evidenced particular sensitivity in her choice of interviewers, taking care to choose insiders when she thought it valuable to reach ordinary men and women and outsiders when she sought to elicit more extended explanations from various elites.

Her note on method in Appendix A specifies the two cardinal principles she followed: first, "a fundamental and genuine respect for the people and institutions studied and a determination to view them first and foremost in their own terms; and, secondly, the assumption that all types of material, whatever their source and form, may shed light on a problem if they are regarded as evidence and are subjected to the tests and criticism which all evidence demands."

Here is Ware's credo as a cultural historian, a credo that guided her research and shaped the final outcome. Without ever losing sight of her own interpretive framework, she lets the reader hear and see the residents of Greenwich Village in their own terms. Nowhere does she do this more incisively than when she juxtaposes the Italian immigrants' portrait of the bohemian Villagers with the Villagers' image of their immigrant neighbors. The clash of cultures and values that occurred daily in the streets vividly appears in the pages of the book, from the Villagers' explicit dislike of the smells of Italian cooking and the sounds of children at play to the Italians' cool disdain for the Villagers' meager food purchases and willingness to spend foolish sums on rent. In each case, Ware's genuine respect for the people studied makes the cultural differences real even as it encourages empathy.

Ware begins her study with an examination of Greenwich Village's gentrification, although the term did not exist then and the process it describes—middle-class reclamation of a working-class neighborhood through remodeling old buildings, raising rents, promoting and speculating in real estate; and constructing new apartments—was not generally recognized. The chapter "Old Houses and New People" deftly links the residential reconstruction of the Village to forces of urban growth, including construction of rapid transit lines, relocation of industry, and expansion of suburban housing in the outer boroughs. She emphasizes the significance of ethnicity in defining the social groups of Greenwich Village, but by starting with the area's changing physical character and the corresponding mobility of its population Ware not only highlights the importance of class but also demonstrates how variously class position is inscribed on the urban landscape. Middle-class Irish and Italian families chose very different types of housing from the more recent arrivals, the middle-class nonethnics or Villagers. From the very beginning of the study, culture and class intersect; Ware uses both independent variables in her analysis. Indeed, Part I, "Community," covering the history, population, economy (including a perceptive discussion of the impact of bootlegging upon local Italians), occupations, ethnicity, and physical attributes of Greenwich Village, would be sufficient to satisfy many urban history scholars as a perceptive account of the neighborhood.

However, Ware is interested in something more than a portrait of Greenwich Village in the 1920s, and Part I, for all its insight, serves largely as a prelude to the heart of the book, Part II, "People." Here her training in anthropology, especially the use of informants as cultural interpreters and guides, becomes evident. She begins this section by rejecting the sociological theory of neighboring and community. Living next door to one another, she argues, does not make people into neighbors—that is, into individuals who share a similar point of view and way of life. As she will argue in her concluding discussion of the family, primary face-to-face groups in Greenwich Village do not sustain a common culture. The acids of urbanism, particularly rapid mobility and physical disintegration, erode possibilities for community, neighborhood, and family, and thus threaten cultural bonds that link individuals and ethnic groups. Ware argues that the passionate presumption in favor of neighboring stems from "the assumption of American democracy that community of interest is identical with common residence, and that interest groups and social classes do not exist" (81).

Despite this American bias to reify neighboring, Ware concludes that Greenwich Village was not a neighborhood except in a very limited sense. Italians, Irish, and Villagers—the three main social groups in the area—each sent their children to different schools despite their physical propinquity. Stores usually catered only to one group, since the Italians' propensity for bargaining could not easily be accommodated to the Villagers' desire for a fixed price. Although each group had its own middle class, ethnic ties proved stronger than class associations. Even in the realm of casual contacts on the streets or in the stores and speakeasies, individuals rarely crossed the divide separating their groups, especially the powerful split between local ethnics and Villagers.

Ware trenchantly observes that "those who talked about the neighborly atmosphere of the Village in the same breath praised its freedom, the absence of a norm of behavior such as would be maintained by public opinion in a functioning neighborhood" (86). Indeed, Mary Simkhovitch, one of the founders and leaders of Greenwich House, argued in 1935 for a nebulous unity in the neighborhood that expressed itself in a "certain informality and freedom." "I do not mean the 'bohemian' freedom," she hastened to explain, but a freedom "evidenced by the homely custom of shopping without bothering to put on a hat. This friendliness has in it powerful elements of cohesion," she asserted, that "are producing an emergent common life."[14] Ware does not deem these relatively superficial characteristics sufficient to justify speaking of Greenwich Village as a neighborhood, given the profound separation she uncovered among its different groups. She prefers to characterize this freedom as tolerance of privacy, "the chance to live unhampered by what one's neighbor thought, and to be free from making contacts because of mere propinquity" (86).

A strikingly similar vision animates a book that points to the Greenwich Village of the 1950s as the ideal neighborhood even as it proclaims its freedom and the anonymity of its residents. In *The Death and Life of Great American Cities,* Jane Jacobs refers repeatedly to the streets outside her Village apartment to illustrate a healthy urbanism and public culture. Describing the beauties of Hudson Street's daily pedestrian ballet—the crisscrossing patterns of individuals pursuing their mundane activities—Jacobs waxes lyrical in praising "the tolerance, the room for great differences among neighbors . . . which are possible and normal only when streets of great cities . . . [allow] strangers to dwell in peace together on civilized but essentially dignified and reserved terms."[15] By 1960 the concept of neighborhood has changed so radically that the absence of neighboring and shared culture that Ware noted is considered instead by Jacobs as tolerance of privacy. Ware's description becomes an account of the virtues of urban public community.

Ware does not let her disturbing conclusions regarding the corrosive character of social change during the 1920s color her discussion of ethnicity. She resolutely resists the dominant views of local social workers (as well as the popular stereotypes of her era) that portrayed Italian immigrants, the majority population in Greenwich Village, as victims of the slums and interpreted their behavior as expressing a culture of poverty. Rather, Ware adheres to her historian's credo and vividly describes Village street culture on its own terms, as an urban product of the second generation, a type of working-class behavior formed during Prohibition when alternative venues for male socializing did not exist. The young men hanging out on the block did not share their values with their parents or, Ware hints, with second-generation Italian youngsters living in exclusively Italian sections of the city. Ware notes the influence of the local Irish on the Italians as models for becoming American suggesting a complex process of acculturation occurring outside formal institutions of the area. She also clearly depicts the local youths' disdain for Villagers and predatory attitude toward women, even describing sexual assaults on women who unwittingly strayed outside the street culture's prescribed boundaries of proper behavior.

If ethnicity, not class, formed the most fundamental and inescapable social division among local people, within each ethnic group gender similarly defined identity. Ware never mistakes Italian men for all Italians or Irish men for the Irish, nor does she reduce women to mothers, focusing exclusively upon their home activities. She pays attention to women in the family and to girls at school, to women at work and at leisure, to women's attitudes toward health and medicine and to their religious beliefs and behavior. Gender bisects the local community and Ware uses it as a category of social analysis—providing, for example, a gendered account of generational conflict between Italian immigrant parents and their children.

One of the most salient areas of cultural change was courtship, as demonstrated in Table VIII. Virtually all Italian young people rejected arranged marriages and the corresponding notion that girls and boys should not associate with each other unless engaged. Ware observes that the central interest in marriage for girls was the home, but even Italian girls no longer subscribed to the idea that large families were a blessing. Thus, Italian norms that viewed families primarily as kinship units rather than household ones succumbed to romantic notions of love and the American bourgeois ideal of marriage. By introducing a gendered analysis of acculturation, Ware discovered that generational conflict occurred most often over familial values, particularly those involving female behavior. Like the neighborhood, the family suffered from disruption caused by the relentless individualism of American life that undermines the ability of parents to transmit their culture. The continuity that registered in a child's ability to speak Italian or in preference for an Italian neighborhood or even in enduring superstitions hardly outweighed the conflict apparent within the family.[16]

Yet these changing attitudes did not flourish in a vacuum nor were they mere abstractions. Ware repeatedly returns to the physical character of the neighborhood, describing its parks and stoops, churches and stores. The boundedness of young Italian women's lives emerges from her pages in the circumscribed paths they trace daily from home to school and later to work, in the limited friendships that develop from evening strolls on the street or visits to church meetings. One can see, too, the young men lounging around the candy store or speakeasy, for Ware notices their posture and the creases in their fashionable clothes. Her use of participant observation makes the daily interactions of the neighborhood come alive. Were one suddenly dropped back into the Greenwich Village of 1930, with Ware's book as a guide one could easily recognize the tea rooms and speakeasies and understand why the Italian grocer put the slightly burned rolls into the Villager's bag.

Several topics covered in *Greenwich Village* anticipate future interests of urban historians. Ware's attention to leisure, for example, matched some of the concerns of contemporary social workers, but her approach invites comparisons with such recent histories of leisure-time activities as Kathy Peiss's *Cheap Amusements*.[17] Ware contrasts the largely homosocial leisure world of young unmarried Italian women with the Villagers' explicitly heterosocial public leisure pursuits. Though Ware devotes less attention to the bohemian lifestyle, she incisively notes the significance of casual sex and illegal liquor for Villager socializing. She also observes the bitter contradictions of the new freedom for young women and their vulnerability to exploitation. Ware's concern with the impact of American individualism upon Italian families reflects her view that these rapid changes profoundly disrupt ethnic group life. By contrast, such recent historians of immigration as Virginia Yans-McLaughlin, Donna Gabaccia, and Miriam Cohen, reinterpreting these changes, stress the resiliency of Italian women and continuities in family ethnic culture.[18] Ware's treatment of health care and the impact of health professionals, especially outsiders, on local people raises issues of acculturation and power that have been explored by many historians of medicine. She argues that the public health authorities, more than the public schools, influenced core behaviors and values of local people. Finally, Ware's sensitivity to Italian Catholicism and its religious customs suggests the influence of her anthropological interests and anticipates the recent fascination among scholars of religion, as well as historians and anthropologists, with the Italian *feste* and street religious culture.[19]

Her provocative penultimate chapter on family brings her study to the source of a common culture. Here Ware not only synthesizes earlier material presented on Italian, Irish, Jewish, and Villager families but draws it into a typology. Ware develops three family models:

patriarchal, bourgeois-romantic, and experimental-individualistic. As she describes the structure, values, and meanings for men and women of each model, she also demonstrates how Italian immigrants were moving away from the patriarchal toward the bourgeois-romantic even as the Villagers were fleeing the bourgeois-romantic for the experimental-individualistic family. In each case, Ware assesses the goals and functions of the family type, finding that none truly fulfills its own values. Each possesses fatal flaws and glaring inconsistencies that undermine its viability. This sober analysis, rather than romanticization of an earlier era, provides the basis for Ware's conclusions regarding the atomistic future of American civilization.

Yet behind the probing questions in her conclusion regarding the American future lies Ware's conviction that a new common culture pattern can develop if only Americans will accept the pluralist possibilities of their multiethnic urban society. Despite all the differences separating Villagers from local people, and Irish from Italian from Jew, despite the fact that living next door does not make people into authentic neighbors, despite the corrosive and destructive force of poverty and prejudice, Ware's account of Greenwich Village points to common aspirations and struggles. The ordinary social processes of earning a living, making a home, and raising children hold the potential to produce a common American culture if we Americans will pause long enough to listen to each other, to understand and respect our differences, and to become real neighbors. Ware saw the future not in the Middletowns of the American heartland nor in the artistic community of Village intellectuals but in the chaotic diversity of the American metropolis. Despite her pessimism, her study of Greenwich Village during a tumultuous decade can be read as an eloquent plea to Americans to embrace their cities and forge a common culture.

DEBORAH DASH MOORE

[1] Caroline F. Ware, *Greenwich Village, 1920–1930: A Comment on American Civilization in the Post-War Years* (Boston: Houghton Mifflin, 1935).

[2] See Kenneth Campbell, "Topics: The Village of Other Days," *New York Times*, 27 March 1965, 26, col. 3.

[3] Malcolm Cowley, "Muddletown," *The New Republic*, 15 May 1935, 23.

[4] R. L. Duffus, "Greenwich Village as A Melting Pot," *New York Times Book Review*, 5 May 1935, 4.

[5] John Palmer Gavitt, "The City Wilderness," *The Saturday Review*, 25 May 1935, 13–14.

[6] Caroline F. Ware, *Greenwich Village, 1920–1930* (New York: Harper & Row, 1965).

[7] U.S. Riot Commission Report, *Report of the National Advisory Commission on Civil Disorders* (New York: Bantam, 1968), 1, 23.

[8] I am indebted to Ellen Fitzpatrick's excellent article for Ware's intellectual biography. See Ellen Fitzpatrick, "Caroline F. Ware and the Cultural Approach to History," *American Quarterly* 43 (June 1991): 185–189.

[9] Fitzpatrick, "Caroline F. Ware," 179, 180.

[10] The only citations to Ware that I could find were by historians, especially urban and immigrant historians. Maurice Stein's survey of community studies, *The Eclipse of Community: An Interpretation of American Studies* (New York: Harper, 1964), moves effortlessly from Zorbaugh to Whyte, ignoring Ware because, one assumes, she was not part of the Chicago school of urban sociologists.

[11] Robert Harney and J. Vincenza Scarpaci make this point in their introduction to the volume they edited, *Little Italies in North America* (Toronto: The Multicultural History Society of Ontario, 1981), 2. Among the sociological studies that fall into the trap of guilt by association with urban pathologies are Harvey Zorbaugh's *Gold Coast and the Slum* (1929), William Whyte's *Street Corner Society* (1943), and Herbert Gans' *Urban Villagers* (1962).

[12] Caroline F. Ware, review of *Middletown in Transition* by Robert and Helen Lynd, in *American Historical Review* 43 (January 1938): 426–427.

[13] Fitzpatrick, "Caroline F. Ware and the Cultural Approach to History," 173–174; quote on 193.

[14] Mary Kingsbury Simkhovitch, "The Village," *The Nation*, 29 May 1935, 635.

[15] Jane Jacobs, *The Death and Life of Great American Cities* (New York: Vintage, 1961), 72.

[16] Ware's emphasis here diverges sharply from that of such social scientists as Nathan Glazer and Daniel Patrick Moynihan who argued for continuity and a strong familism among Italian ethnics in New York City in *Beyond the Melting Pot: the Negroes, Puerto Ricans, Jews, Italians and Irish of New York City* (Cambridge, Mass.: MIT Press, 1963), 186–201.

[17] Kathy Peiss, *Cheap Amusements: Working Women and Leisure in Turn-of-the-Century New York* (Philadelphia: Temple University Press, 1986).

[18] Virginia Yans-McLaughlin, *Family and Community: Italian Immigrants in Buffalo, 1880–1930* (Urbana: University of Illinois Press, 1982), 220–221; Donna Gabaccia, *From Sicily to Elizabeth Street: Housing and Social Change among Italian Immigrants, 1880–1930* (Albany: SUNY, 1984), 100–102; Miriam Cohen, *Workshop to Office: Two Generations of Italian Women in New York* (Ithaca: Cornell University Press, 1993), 3–4, 8.

[19] For example, Robert Orsi, *The Madonna of 115th Street* (New Haven: Yale University Press, 1989).

PREFACE
TO
THE PAPERBACK EDITION

Greenwich Village 1920–1930, a study in social change, was written in the early 1930s at a time of depression and in a pre-war and pre-atomic world so different from that of today that the present generation has difficulty in imagining it. The study was undertaken when methods of social research were less refined and there was little background against which to project a study of change in a segment of urban life, except the work of the University of Chicago group of sociologists and the Lynds' pioneer study of *Middletown*.

Nevertheless the book as it is reissued is relevant and timely, for many of the processes which it reveals and the problems on which it throws light are with us still, and the manner in which some were handled in the 1920s and 1930s has a significant bearing on American life today. The fact that sections of the book have been included in compilations of readings or have been reproduced for student use and for the training of teachers and social workers testifies to the continuing relevance of the material and the issues treated.

As the British social analyst Richard Titmuss has pointed out, those social processes which impair the ability of people as parents to give basic security to their children have repercussions in the personality formation of succeeding generations, long after the disorganizing or destructive conditions have passed. *Greenwich Village* examines a sample of America's past population of immigrants, who had come at the rate of a million persons a year in the peak years before World War I, at a time when they were striving to find a place in American urban life during the bootleg era. It catches the older, American-born children of this mass migration just as they were coming of age, facing the rejection of depression and joblessness, and thereafter the trauma of war.

These were the ones, usually, who "Americanized" their younger brothers and sisters and often their parents. The processes glimpsed in this study hold clues to the roots of many of our stubborn social problems today.

The study documents a number of problems which the anti-poverty program is now highlighting: the failure of education where the poorest schools, and often the most discouraged teachers, are provided for the children who need to be treated with the greatest skill and understanding; the gulf in assumptions and views of reality between those who offer social services and those for whom these are designed, with the tendency to reach only those for whom the gulf is narrow and to miss those most in need; the issue of whether and how people of the neighborhood may participate in planning and acting on their own behalf.

We are struggling today with the counterpart of the cultural gap defined by the Italian neighbor who told the settlement house worker, "My people understand two things, force and kindness; when you treat them in terms of persuasion and fair play they think you are weak and disloyal".; or the bewilderment and distrust of the mothers who tried to respond to the instructions of the "ladies" from that outer world, only to find themselves charged with "begging tendency" when they kept coming back to the family welfare agency, just as they had been told to come back to the health center; or the plaint of the teen-agers, "When do we get that American standard of living? Do we ever become real Americans or do we remain 'wops' and 'kikes' for the rest of our lives?" The permanent issues of the relation between promise and reality and of intergroup relations in a pluralistic, open, urban society are here.

So, too, are a variety of institutional problems: differing roles of the churches, the political mechanism with its interplay of party loyalty and ethnic identity, the thin line between the underworld and legally ordered society, the pervasive hand of the real estate interests pulling the stops on the community's life.

Perhaps the book is most "dated" by the element which gave Greenwich Village its reputation, the "Villagers," for they do indeed belong to a different era of sophistication, bohemianism and the revolt of the younger generation. But the beatniks and the far-out fringe have changed mainly their style; anonymity and absence of status remain features of urban life; and the social incongruity of neighborhoods composed of those who can afford to live well in the central city and those trapped there—the "gold coast" and the "slum"—is still with us, often enhanced and made official by the juxtaposition of luxury apartments and public housing in programs of urban renewal.

One could wish that the study might be brought up to date, not so much by a re-study of the Greenwich Village neighborhood as through a look at the lives of those who made up the Village in the 1920s and 1930s. This is the human fruit of the social conditions and changes here reviewed.

CAROLINE F. WARE

May, 1965

ACKNOWLEDGMENT

ALTHOUGH this study appears over a single name, many students, members of Greenwich House, research assistants and others aided in the collection and preparation of material. Acknowledgment is due, especially, to the following people for substantial contributions to particular chapters: To Grace Fabricant, Chapters IV, VIII, XIV; Aurelia Ricci, John Gobetti, Charles Adorro, Vincent di Stephano, Michel Rubino, Jo Monica, Chapter VI; Mary Alice McInerny, Chapters VII, IX, X; Prospero Melendez–A., Chapter VII; Norman Creese, Chapter X; Sophia M. Robeson, Chapters XI, XIII; Andrew Steiger and Frank Kaplan, Chapter XII; Paul Wueller, Appendix C; Robert Kantz, Ruth Shallcross, Howard Myers, Appendix D. Alice Chase helped throughout the study. Archie Bromsen's assistance on many sections of the manuscript was invaluable.

Thanks are also due to the Committee for its oversight and guidance, to Mrs. Simkhovitch of Greenwich House for her generous co-operation, and to Conyers Read for criticism of the manuscript.

CAROLINE F. WARE

WASHINGTON, D.C.
February, 1935

PART I
COMMUNITY

GREENWICH VILLAGE
1920–1930

I. THE VILLAGE IN AMERICAN CULTURE

THE story of Greenwich Village during the post-War decade is a chapter in the history of American culture — the chapter which shows the inherited pattern of American social life repudiated by many to whom it was traditional, and without sufficient vitality or relevance to mould the lives of immigrant newcomers. The story is not primarily concerned with America's bohemia, New York's Latin Quarter of 'long-haired men and short-haired women,' artists and pseudos, speakeasies, night clubs, and haunts which the tabloid press likes to describe; nor can it be told through the famous names of those who have lived and worked within the Village, from Aaron Burr and Tom Paine to Max Eastman, Alan Seeger, and Maxwell Bodenheim. The 'Greenwich Village' of national and international fame appears, in these pages, as only one aspect of the life of the territory long known as Greenwich Village. Italian immigrants and their children, Irish longshoremen, truck-drivers, and politicians, Jewish shopkeepers, Spanish seamen, and a remnant of staid old American and German citizens made up the majority of the population and, in combination with their more famous neighbors, gave the life of this community its social texture. All of these elements have their place in the evolving pattern of social life in America. In Greenwich Village they can be studied under conditions which show, in extreme form, many trends of recent years — conditions characteristic of the central sections of older American cities.

The basic pattern of American culture was formed during the colonial period and emerged in the early years of the nineteenth century. Essentially agricultural and mercantile, individualistic, mobile, and dominated by Protestant ethical values, it has never been fundamentally reconstructed. In the early nineteenth century, dominant groups in all parts of the country — merchant shippers of New England, gentlemen farmers of New York, merchants of Philadelphia, and planters of the South — all lived according to the social pattern which had been established during the colonial period. The westward movement carried this pattern in its various forms into new territory, where it was subjected to the modifying influences of the frontier.

In the course of the nineteenth century the pattern has been worn thin; it has stiffened or it has become warped with the passing of years. But it has not assimilated any important divergent institutions. Its momentum has remained that of the founding fathers. The W.C.T.U. on the one hand, and the genteel tradition on the other, represent distorted and vacuous versions of the pattern which the New England Puritan and the Jeffersonian gentleman handed down to a country in which industry was to dominate an ever-increasing part of the energy and wealth of the population.

Most especially, American culture has never assimilated industrialism. Where the factory could be ignored or where its workers could be regarded somewhat as retainers or tenants, the dominant pattern could survive its impact. In the small New England mills, the employers who had a strong sense of responsibility did not find their way of life disrupted by the factories which they owned; in part they ignored and in part they patronized. Similarly, the factory worker, coming from the farm into a small mill, could carry his social code into his new economic situation so long as he still retained a measure of connection with his land, and while his role in the factory resembled that of the independent artisan. But the increasingly proletarian aspects of industrialism, and the actual gulf between employer and employee which cut across political democracy, could not healthily be ignored. The traditional social code of the employing class became ever emptier until it reached the stage of the New England Brahmin. At the same time the doctrines of agrarian individualism became less and less relevant to the actual conditions of a growing mass of workers and gave little social coherence to their lives. The spread of industry and the growth of cities during the nineteenth century thus constantly reduced the area in American life to which the traditional culture pattern was appropriate. But the pattern could still survive because there remained a large field of activity — farming and small business — within which it continued to apply.

During the twentieth century, the process of industrialization has been greatly accelerated. Even had there been no intervening major calamity, this generation or the next might well have seen the complete collapse of the traditional American economic and social structure; the advent of the European War hastened the collapse. The years with which this study deals — the interval between the World War and the World Depression — saw the serious disruption of the culture pattern of the nineteenth century.

In the War and post-War years, Greenwich Village became a symbol of the repudiation of traditional values. Here congregated those for whom the traditional pattern in which they grew up had become so empty or distorted that they could no longer continue a part of it and submit to the social controls which it imposed. Many who were drawn to the Village came to seek escape from their community, their families, or themselves. Others who did not altogether repudiate the background from which they had come sought to reconcile new conditions with whatever remained of their traditional ways. In this effort they had to struggle without the support of a well-established community to sanction their efforts, or clear standards of behavior to guide them.

Greenwich Village was, at the same time, the home of a group of people to whom the American tradition was both unfamiliar and irrelevant — a large body of Italian immigrants. While immigrant groups at all times have had to meet difficult problems of adaptation, the Italians of this community were confronted by a social situation, not only foreign to their own social experience, but so lacking in coherence itself as to offer little guide to their adaptation. They were exposed to the traditional pattern of American culture as it was taught in the schools and elsewhere, a pattern which clearly did not fit the community which they actually knew. American life as they saw it conducted, either in the movies or by those representatives of the American community who were their neighbors, did not correspond with the official standards.

The most culturally coherent group in the community was the Irish population which had made its own distinctive adaptation to American city life a generation before. That adaptation rested on the maintenance of their own basic cultural institution, the Catholic Church, and the moulding of the American political system as they found it in the city into a form which became distinctively their own. In the post-War period, both Church and political system stood well established and firm in their city environment. The Irish pattern offered a more coherent form to guide the adaptation of the Italians than did that of the old Americans. Not only did the Irish, as immigrants, also occupy a non-dominant status, but the Catholic Church brought their pattern closer to the Italian experience and their realistic political approach seemed to meet urban conditions.

Others in the community included a few old American families born and reared in the locality who clung wistfully to the shreds of the old American culture pattern, and scattered representatives of other immigrant groups whose problems resembled those of the Italians and Irish.

In each of the social groups which lived in this community during the post-War decade, individuals were thus faced by fragments of conflicting culture patterns and conflicting principles of social organization. Under these conditions they were forced to make their social adjustments in terms of themselves as isolated individuals rather than as parts of coherent social wholes. The result was a great weakening of social controls and an almost complete absence of community integration.

The process of city development which brought these various peoples together within the area of Greenwich Village reflected the conditions left in the wake of a rapidly expanding metropolis. During the hundred years prior to 1920, the district passed through the stages of development characteristic of the ordinary process of city growth — the succession of inhabitants of lower and lower economic levels; the invasion of industry with the accompanying growth of industrial slums; the departure of heavy industry to find cheaper land in the suburbs; and the expansion of the central business section into the area.

To this well-known type of city growth, there was added in the post-War years the latest stage in urban development — a residential backflow from the periphery of an overgrown city or from its suburbs to reclaim areas near the business heart of the metropolis. This residential backflow has been observable elsewhere on Manhattan, and in such sections of other old cities as the back side of Beacon Hill in Boston where houses and streets have been reclaimed from the slums for high-class residences. It has arisen from causes characteristic of the unplanned, dynamic American city.

The institutions of this community, with the exception of the Catholic Church and the political clubs, were as confused in their interrelations as were the individual inhabitants. The Protestant churches as parts of the old American pattern lost not only most of their membership but also much of their validity for the community. The public, parochial, and progressive schools put forth three divergent efforts to mould the younger generation. The welfare agencies operated according to varying interpretations of human behavior, functioning with increasing technical proficiency, but not always with an awareness of the social scene within which they worked. These conditions of cultural confusion were intensified by the conflict and instability which are present in every community, the procession of the generations and the development of new technology.

A study of the dynamic interrelations within this community presents acute problems of analysis — the danger of oversimplifying what is, by definition, a complex situation; the impossibility of isolating for laboratory study factors whose essential quality is their interplay with others; the difficulty of seeing clearly and stating intelligibly situations in which a coherent pattern is lacking and conduct does not fit traditional categories. The following study is inevitably fragmentary and inconclusive. On practically no point has the evidence been sufficiently full and definite to give the force of certainty to generalizations based upon it. Available material has rarely been in a form which was easy to compile and compare. The small numbers involved in all the statistical data made such data useful only to confirm or to challenge the non-statistical material. The results, like those of every study, have been partly shaped by the process of selecting and framing the subjects upon which evidence has been sought. Every process of selection throws certain aspects of a situation into relief and leaves others in shadow. A kind of distortion is bound to result when implicit assumptions are given articulate expression. Yet the very factors which stand in the way of a complete and conclusive study make the Greenwich Village of the post-War years a challenge to those who would understand the forces that are shaping contemporary American culture.

II. OLD HOUSES
AND NEW PEOPLE

1. HISTORICAL BACKGROUND

GREENWICH VILLAGE owed its physical form and many of its social characteristics to a succession of developments extending over a hundred years. Its distinctiveness, and the fact that even by 1930 it had not fully become an indistinguishable part of the city, went back to the early nineteenth century, when the independent and thriving village of Greenwich lay a pleasant afternoon's drive beyond the outskirts of New York City. Its streets had already been laid out on a diagonal to the axis of Manhattan before the checkerboard street plan was drawn for the island in 1811, and they remained an evidence of the Village's identity and a source of confusion to visitors when the boundary of the city had moved far beyond the Village to the north.

The houses which still made up the greater part of the buildings in the locality in 1930 dated from the years when the Village was suddenly and swiftly transformed into an integral part of the expanding city during the 1820's and 1830's. In the midst of the yellow-fever epidemics of 1819, 1822, and 1823, the panic-stricken city populace swarmed into the Village and made it into a boom town. 'On lots but lately overgrown with woods,' noted a traveler in September, 1822, 'are now erected stores occupied by the principal merchants of the City... many of them put up in 24 hours.'[1] Each time that the panic subsided, many of the refugees

[1] Riley, Henry A. *Some Reminiscences and Events of a Life of Three Score Years and Ten,* MS. diary, vol. I, p. 217.

remained; the hastily constructed frame buildings were supplanted by the solid brick dwellings which gave the area its characteristic appearance a hundred years later. A newspaper editor predicted in 1825 that 'in three years' time, at the rate buildings have been everywhere erected during the last season, Greenwich will be known only as a part of the city and the suburbs will be beyond it.'[1]

From 1825 to 1850, the Village was the residential section into which people of substance moved as the expansion of business pressed them up from the south. The potter's field was turned into a park — Washington Square — in 1827 and was soon surrounded by the dignified and capacious residences of New York's elect. In 1833, the building of New York University brought still another element into the vicinity. During the decade from 1825 to 1835, the population of the Village and the Washington Square region doubled and doubled again in the next fifteen years.[2]

In physical structure, the Village of 1850 had assumed the general lines which it was to retain until the second decade of the twentieth century. Stores lined the two streets which remained the shopping centers of the neighborhood. The solid rows of brick dwellings were broken only occasionally by the yard in front of a set-back house or by a frame building. Scattered through the blocks near the waterfront, a few industrial establishments gave a lower tone to this section and presaged its later industrial development. One block only was still undeveloped — all that remained of the farm upon whose fields the Village had originally arisen.[3]

Thereafter, the expanding city passed the Village by. Along Fifth Avenue and Broadway, to the east of the Village, the city advanced northward up the island, and one area after another passed through the familiar sequence of country, suburb, residential fringe, high-class residential, business, or slum. The Ninth Ward, as Greenwich Village came to be known, was subjected to none of these influences, for its diagonal streets blocked

[1] Editorial in *Commercial Advertiser*, quoted in Denison, L., and Fischel, M., *Villages and Hamlets Within New York City*, New York, 1925, p. 18.

[2] *Census of the State of New York for 1865*, p. xxiv.

[3] *Real Estate Atlas of Manhattan, 1852.*

the through avenues and the main line of city development followed other routes. For the next half-century it remained a quiet backwater, undisturbed by the strong current of city life which flowed past its wealthy, fashionable eastern district or its poorer western edge.

Its detachment from the rest of the city saved it from the fate of the other, once fashionable, downtown sections — from degeneration into a slum peopled with poverty-stricken immigrants. In recognition of its uniqueness in this respect, the Village was known through these years as the 'American Ward.' Although there were 11,000 foreigners, 32 per cent of the population, in the Ninth Ward in 1875, no other ward in the city contained so small a proportion of foreign-born inhabitants.[1] It was the American element, moreover, which appeared to set the tone of the neighborhood. In 1893, a magazine writer could still attribute 'the cleanliness, moral and physical, of the Village' to the fact that it 'distinctively is the American quarter of New York. A sprinkling of French and Italians is found within these limits, together with the few Irish required for political purposes; and in the vicinity of Carmine Street are scattered some of the tents of the children of Ham. But with these exceptions the population is composed of substantial, well-to-do Americans.... As compared with the corresponding region on the east side — where a score of families may be found packed into a single building, and where even the bad smells have foreign names — this American quarter of New York is a liberal lesson in cleanliness, good citizenship, and self-respect.'[2]

But an area so central, so convenient to industry, adjacent to docks, and separated from the East Side slums only by a few blocks of factory buildings, could not escape forever from the invasion of the tenement, and its occupant, the foreigner. Toward the close of the century, the substantial, middle-class complexion of the 'American Ward' was rudely destroyed by the erection of tenements which spread from two directions — the waterfront on the west and the factory and Negro areas to the southeast — encircling, invading, and finally overrunning the Village in the clos-

---

[1] *Census of the State of New York, 1875*, p. 21.
[2] Janvier, T. 'Greenwich Village' in *Harper's Magazine*, vol. 87 (1893), pp. 356-57.

ing years of the nineteenth century and the early years of the twentieth.

The waterfront had always been a distinct part of the Village, increasing in importance as its piers, and those lying immediately to the north, became the principal Manhattan terminus for transatlantic and much coastwise shipping. In 1895, the shipping population of the Ninth Ward was double that of any other ward in the city.[1] Some of the earliest of the local tenements had been built before 1880 along the waterfront and adjacent streets. In the last two decades of the century, tenement construction in this section was general, while the area immediately to the north was built up even more solidly into a longshoremen's quarter. In 1897, a new waterfront parish was cut off from the old parish of the ward, relieving the better established of the local Irish and other Catholics from the necessity of rubbing shoulders with the newer and poorer element.

Meantime, a second tenement invasion was transforming the Village on its southeastern edge where lay one of the principal Negro quarters of the city. The ward adjoining the Village on the south, known as the 'Negro Plantations' when it was still farm land,[2] contained nearly a quarter of the Negro population of the city in 1865[3] and was the source from which Negro families filtered north until they reached Washington Square. This, even more than the waterfront, was the section from which tenements spread into the Village, but the new quarters were not primarily built to house the Negroes. While the colored people constituted an entering wedge, they were followed and finally supplanted by Italian immigrants, spreading west from their East Side centers. It was the 'invasion' of the latter which effectively transformed the lower part of the Village from a 'liberal education in cleanliness, good citizenship, and self-respect' into a slum area, more like the tenement city of the East Side than like the middle-class 'American Ward.' In the last decade of the nineteenth century, and the early years of the twentieth, the blocks to the south of

<hr/>

[1] New York City Department of Police, *Census of the City of New York, April, 1895*, New York, 1896.

[2] Map printed in *Harper's Magazine*, vol. 70 (1885), p. 842, entitled 'Plan of the Bogardus Property.'

[3] *New York State Census, 1865*, p. 9.

CHART-I

RESIDENTIAL SPACE

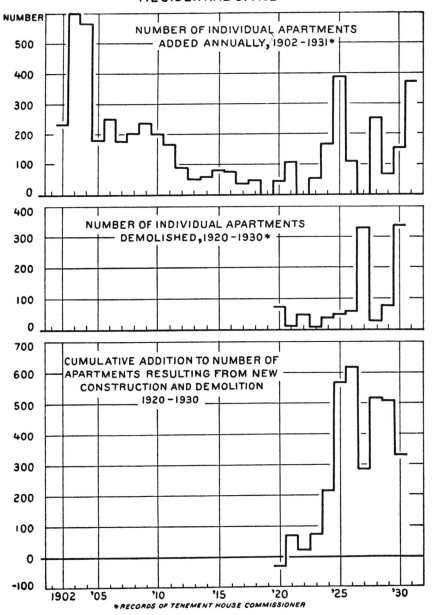

NUMBER OF INDIVIDUAL APARTMENTS ADDED ANNUALLY, 1902-1931*

NUMBER OF INDIVIDUAL APARTMENTS DEMOLISHED, 1920-1930*

CUMULATIVE ADDITION TO NUMBER OF APARTMENTS RESULTING FROM NEW CONSTRUCTION AND DEMOLITION 1920-1930

*RECORDS OF TENEMENT HOUSE COMMISSIONER

Washington Square were, one after another, rebuilt with six- and seven-story tenements.[1] By 1910, half of the inhabitants of the section were Italian-born and over eighty per cent were of foreign birth or parentage.[2]

Such a transformation of the outer portions of the Village could hardly leave its core untouched as a middle-class American neighborhood. During these years of transformation, the inevitable tenement appeared in the heart of the Village — a single building here, a row of buildings there — until scarcely a block remained without its six- and seven-story structures and its supply of two-, three-, and four-room flats. By 1901, there were tenement accommodations in the Village for upwards of five thousand families, and an equal number in the immediate vicinity.[3] In 1902 and 1903, two settlement houses chose the very center of the Village as appropriate sites for neighborhood social work serving Irish, Negroes, and Italians. Clearly the tenement invasion had done its work.

The area was well located for an industrial population, for it occupied a strip only half a mile wide between the waterfront and the blocks of industrial loft buildings that ran like a spine up the middle of lower Manhattan. Moreover, with the decline in land values within the area brought on by the emigration of homeowners and the entrance of tenements, the Village itself became attractive to industry. To the few industrial establishments that had always existed near the waterfront — an old brewery, some small iron works, and the remains of coal and lumber yards that had been there since before 1850[4] — new factories were added, especially near the waterfront, but also on virtually every main and side street in the area. In the first decade of the twentieth century, the further deterioration of property values brought by these industrial establishments gave every indication that the district would go the way of other downtown sections and be wholly transformed into an area of factories and industrial slums. But

[1] Cf. Chart I, p. 12.

[2] *Materials for Demographic Study of the City of New York, 1910, Sanitary Areas*, 35, 37.

[3] Records of Tenement House Commissioner showing 'old law' tenements; De Forest, R., and Veiller, L., ed. *The Tenement House Problem*, 2 vols., New York, 1903, vol. I, p. 201.

[4] *Real Estate Atlas of Manhattan, 1852.*

before this transformation was anywhere nearly complete, the trend was checked.

It is difficult to appraise and to assign to any one cause the influences which rescued the Village from its descent and saved it for a future of international fame. The migration of heavy industry from the center of the city to cheaper land on the outskirts which set in after 1912 halted the drift of industry into the area. More importantly, the district offered many advantages for reclamation when conditions in the city produced the need for a residential area near the city's center. Even while the immigrant invasion and the process of industrialization were still going on, the arrival of a few residents of a new type — artists, journalists, professional people of small means seeking attractive, convenient city dwellings at small rent — marked the prelude of the residential resurrection of the Village.

During and after the War, the residential reclamation of the Village reversed the trend which had been in process since the late nineteenth century. The downward movement of property values ceased. The few remaining owners who had not yet sold their family homes and moved uptown held on to their property as an investment and some stayed on as residents. Properties became too expensive for factory sites. After 1910, tenement building ceased and the only houses built in the next decade contained five- to seven-room apartments at substantial rents. In 1916, the residential future of the heart of the Village was assured when the city's Zoning Commission, acting on representations, among others, from real estate dealers, settlement workers, and residents with a stake in the district's development, set apart the central blocks in the Village for residence. The heart of the Village was 'saved' — but not its outer sections. Both the waterfront and the blocks south of the Square were left open to industry, their future to be determined by economic rather than by political influences.

Throughout the hundred years from the time when Greenwich Village was a boom town to the years covered by this study, none of the successive changes in the Village was complete. Middle-class home-owners survived the tenement invasion; industry did not wholly supplant residence; much of the tenement population stayed on when the process of reclamation was well under way, and factories continued to operate, though the tenement section was remodeled for high-rent occupants. Many of the old Americans who gave the Ninth Ward its American reputation mingled with the German and Irish newcomers; the latter did not disappear when the Italians took possession; and the Italians, in turn, remained the largest element in the community when the Village and the apartment houses were filled with artists and Babbitts. It was these remnants of successive stages in the Village's history which gave to the district much of its confusion and its heterogeneity.

2. RESIDENTIAL RECONSTRUCTION

In the years after the War, the isolation from the city's main line of development, which had kept the Village a unit and a backwater, was completely destroyed, and its physical unity was broken, by the rapid-transit lines which fed it and traffic thoroughfares which cut it up. The West Side Subway, opened in 1917, brought the Village within a short ten-minute ride of Wall Street to the south and Times Square to the north and into convenient touch with the remote regions of Brooklyn, upper Manhattan, and the Bronx. Simultaneously, the wide swath of Seventh Avenue, a by-product of subway construction, was cut through the heart of the community and brought a rush of swift traffic between upper and lower Manhattan to the places where narrow, crooked streets had maintained privacy. The ugly scars left by buildings partly torn down, the expulsion of the occupants of houses demolished to make way for the avenue, and the barrier of traffic between the east and west halves of the neighborhood destroyed much of the social unity which had characterized the old Ninth Ward. Between 1926 and 1930, still further demolitions made way for another traffic artery one block east of Seventh Avenue, for a new subway, and for a railway viaduct and terminal. The opening of the Holland vehicular tunnel, the principal route off the island of Manhattan to the west, brought an ever-growing stream of through traffic down the Village's avenues to the tunnel entrance immediately to the south.

By 1930, the Village was one of the most 'passed-through' and accessible sections of the city. Its main thoroughfare had all the earmarks of a country highway with twelve gas stations, four automobile repair shops, three automobile supply stores, and a sprinkling of lunch-wagons and eating-places distributed along its three quarters of a mile of length. The surface avenues, elevated lines, trolley, subway, ferry, and Hudson River tubes which entered or passed through its half-mile of width made accessibility rather than isolation the locality's chief characteristic. The local music school was counting on the Bronx for a large proportion of the children in its clientèle, and the groups which congregated nightly to enjoy the 'atmosphere' of the Village so generally came in by rapid transit from outside that their meeting places were dubbed by observing neighbors 'where Bronx meets Brooklyn.'

No one coming into the Village in 1930, without a knowledge of its past, would have been likely to recognize, in the narrow strips of dwellings with half-demolished edges exposed along the traffic lanes, the Village which had been described forty years before as maintaining 'its independence in the very midst of the City of New York... in the resolute spirit of another Andorra... submitting to no more of a compromise in the matter of its autonomy than is involved in the Procrustean sort of splicing which has hitched fast the extremities of its tangled streets to the most readily available streets in the City Plan.' [1] Those residents who continued to visualize the old 'neighborhood' had not fully erased from their minds' eyes the picture of the unbroken physical unity of the past.

The social texture of the Village in the post-War years was largely the product of its residential reconstruction. The back-flow into the Village grew out of two conditions which brought at the same time a residential revival to other parts of the city — most conspicuously to the east Forties and Fifties. As the city's high-class residential district expanded northward up the island, it was blocked when it reached the edge of Negro Harlem. In the face of the impossibility of erecting fashionable apartments within the bounds of this Negro city, or of dislodging so large an entrenched population to make way for white residence, the realtors had to turn to other sections of Manhattan — to the fringes where slums had always flanked the narrow ribbon of fashionable residence, and back downtown to the wastes of lower Manhattan.

At the same time, the problem of transportation to work became

[1] Janvier, *op. cit.*, p. 339.

more and more acute for those who had followed the city's metropolitan growth onto Long Island, across to Jersey, and north into the Bronx and Westchester. Such of these as had been drawn by the migration of factories to outlying regions were not bothered by the problem of commuting, but an increasing proportion of the population was engaged in business activity as New York became the financial and commercial hub of the country and declined in relative industrial importance. The choking of transit facilities with rush-hour crowds exacted a high price in time and energy for the advantages of living in the suburbs or on the city's edge. From 1917, when the West Side Subway was opened, to 1930, the number of subway passengers carried by the Interborough Rapid Transit Company in a year increased by 139 per cent.[1] The Regional Plan of New York found the West Side Subway, in 1921, already carrying a rush-hour load amounting to nearly four times the seating capacity of the trains and called attention to the 'extreme seriousness' of the situation in view of the rate of increase in traffic.[2] The volume of subway travel continued to increase thereafter at a fairly even rate, reflecting the growing congestion to which commuters were subjected.

Of the various possible places to which realtors might have turned when pressed by the *impasse* of Harlem and the discomfort of the subway rush, the Village offered certain distinct advantages. Lying midway between the financial and the shopping and amusement centers, it met the desire for convenience. Through all the changes of the nineteenth century and the early twentieth, moreover, a few families of social standing had continued to live around Washington Square, furnishing a nucleus similar to that on Beacon Hill in Boston or Rittenhouse Square in Philadelphia around which a reclaimed residential district could more easily be developed than in a section which had become wholly devoted to business, or which, like the lower East Side, consisted of a great expanse of uninterrupted slum. The artists who had discovered the studio possibilities of the row of stables back of the mansions on the Square, when the advent of the automobile had made these quarters cheaply available for men instead of beasts, constituted

[1] *Annual Reports of Interborough Rapid Transit Company*, 1917–30.
[2] Regional Plan of New York, *Regional Survey of New York and its Environs*, New York, 1928, vol. IV, pp. 51, 52.

a second nucleus. The district was known, too, through one of the settlement houses whose residents in the first decade of the century numbered many persons later prominent in a wide range of social endeavor. Some of these became attracted to the neighborhood while at the House and made their homes in the vicinity after leaving. With so favorable a location, and with these several residential nuclei already established, the real estate agents who undertook to develop a residential reputation for the Village found their work half done.

The physical possibilities of the area, moreover, were good. In spite of its proximity to the center of the city, land values in 1920 were relatively low. Land ranged from $360 per front foot to $1400.[1] Only the properties around Washington Square, along Sixth Avenue, and the thoroughfare of Fourteenth Street were assessed at over $720 per front foot. The great bulk of the property ranged from $400 to $650.[2] To find equally cheap sites in 1920, it would have been necessary to go to the lower East Side which was a larger tenement area and much less accessible, to the waterfront blocks on either side of the island, or to Harlem. The many small houses which had survived from the middle of the nineteenth century were easily transformed or easily torn down to make way for high-class apartments. Few pieces of Village property contained valuable improvements. For the district as a whole, buildings added on the average only 17 per cent to the value of the land. On two thirds of all the lots in the Village in 1920, the building constituted less than a quarter of the combined value of land and building. The Village thus lay 'fallow,' an area relatively easy to acquire — except for the fact that much property was held in twenty-five-foot lots that could not be used for apartment building — easy to rebuild because of the absence of edifices difficult to remove, and easy to make attractive to the public.

The reconstruction of the Village for residence began in earnest around 1915 [3] with the remodeling into small apartments of single-family houses which had stood in the Village since the middle of the nineteenth century. In 1924–25, the building of new apart-

[1] One corner property was assessed at $2040. Cf. map, Appendix G.
[2] New York City Department of Taxes and Assessments, *Tentative Land Value Maps, 1920.*
[3] *New York Times,* May 23, 1915.

ments supplemented the remodeling of houses as the supply of the latter was rapidly becoming exhausted. By 1928, remodeling had spread from single houses to tenements and in a number of buildings three- and four-room 'cold-water flats' were transformed into one- or two-room up-to-date apartments. In 1929 and 1930, construction was begun on a number of fifteen- to eighteen-story, skyscraper apartments which advertised the latest details of high-class apartment style.[1]

The remodeling and building of houses and apartments was accompanied by changes in the type of population, in part a cause and in part a result of such changes. In 1920, the population of the district was 54,643,[2] more than 90 per cent of whom could be classed as tenement dwellers and the rest as of a higher income and social group. By 1930, the number had dropped to 38,045,[2] and less than 80 per cent were tenement-dwellers. Most of the higher income group were to be found in the upper or central part of the neighborhood, and the tenements were concentrated in the lower part, especially south of Washington Square and in the direction of the waterfront. But the reclaimed area was not confined to one section of the Village, and those who moved into both remodeled houses and new apartments found themselves next door to old factories and to tenements.

The new element which made the Village its home during these years was composed of types which changed as the process of reclamation gained momentum. The first remodeling of single-family houses was accomplished with a relatively small investment as few improvements were included, and the resulting apartments were offered at low rentals. These apartments were advertised to the public on the basis of charm and quaintness rather than of convenience, and they attracted people with taste, but no money — artists, writers, and poorly paid professional people. As the Village became better known and more popular, the inevitable followers of any artist community came apartment-

[1] New York City Tenement House Commissioner, Records of dwellings containing three or more families.

[2] *U.S. Census.* Figures for 1920 published in *Materials for Demographic Studies of the City of New York*, edited by Cities Census Committee; those for 1930 supplied directly by the U.S. Census Bureau. Hereafter referred to as *U.S. Census, 1920, 1930*. All population and other statistical data compiled for the area covered by six census tracts, sanitary areas 65, 67, 69, 71, 73, 75. Cf. Table I, Appendix F, p. 462.

hunting, but their requirements for comfort were greater and their purses were fatter and better able to pay for more improvements. Greater investment in improvements on the part of the realtors and higher rents, therefore, characterized the later phases of re-modeling. Instead of the cold-water tap in the hall, hot water and baths had to be furnished with each apartment and steam heat superseded the open fireplace or the gas log. A remodeled house, however, could never achieve the last-minute modernity of a newly built and equipped apartment. So a measure of the old discomfort and quaintness was retained and offered as an attraction to apartment-hunters. Some houses had not been remodeled up to the heat and hot-water stage by 1930, yet even these shared the high rents which accompanied the improve-ment of other houses.

The higher rent level established during the 1920's made the more extensive remodeling of tenements appear as a good invest-ment to owners and dealers. When people were anxious enough to live in the Village to pay $50 to $75 a month or more for one- or two-room apartments, the investment necessary for tenement remodeling seemed likely to yield a good return. In 1929 one of the city's largest realtors judged the area ripe for a high-class residential development, bought up the few sites so situated at irregular street intersections that tall buildings would not violate the zoning ordinance, and started to introduce the latest Park Avenue apartment style.

An exact index of the rent increases which encouraged and then reflected the successive stages of reconstruction could not be compiled because the complete lack of standardization in re-modeled buildings made comparison virtually impossible. In-formal evidence, however, mounts up to indicate the reality of rent increases in the remodeled houses and apartments. Con-stantly recurrent is the statement that rising rents are forcing artists and intellectuals out of the heart of the district to the water-front fringe or away from the Village altogether. Already in 1917 the low level of Village rents was being denied.[1] In 1922, artists had organized to deal with the rent problem and were blaming bourgeois intruders for causing rents to rise. According to the 'chairman of the rent committee of the American League of

[1] *New York Times*, March 8, 1917.

Artists' in 1922, prices for studio apartments 'have gone up so that the poor artist who is struggling to make a start is being driven out.' [1] 'Rents have been multiplying chiefly, it is alleged, by the competition of bourgeois people who know nothing of art, but like to wear flowing ties and live in the midst of temptations.' [2] In the following year, the *New York World* warned artists: 'The Village must expand — if it won't go nonchalantly, high rents will push it.' [3] In 1927, the *Christian Science Monitor* announced that the exodus of the artist had been virtually completed when it headlined before the nation, 'Greenwich Village Too Costly Now For Artists To Live There: Values Increase So That Only Those Who Can Write Fluently In Check Books Can Afford It: One Room and Bath Cost $65.' [4]

The complete change in the type of apartment offered and of the class for whom it was built was well represented in the prospectus of an elaborately equipped, high-rent building completed in 1931 and advertised as 'planned and built with the definite purpose of meeting the ideas of those who respond to the flavor and appeal of the "Village" with its nearness to everywhere and everything.' The equipment noted in the advertisement included 'sunken living rooms, woodburning fireplaces, frigidaires, over-size rooms, bath for every chamber, terraces, ornamental railings, immense closets, decorated kitchens, dining alcoves, dressing rooms, dining foyers, RCA radio outlets.' These attractions provided 'comforts and conveniences new, desirable and necessary,' and at the same time offered 'a "studio" atmosphere that makes for attractive and unconventional furnishing.' Except for the 'studio atmosphere,' little remained to suggest the type of reconstruction to which the Village had been subjected during the earlier stages of its rebuilding.

On the residential rebuilding of the Village, a total of some $18,000,000 was expended from 1920 to 1930.[5] This sum provided for converting approximately ten per cent of the local tenement

---

[1] *New York Times*, September 17, 1922.

[2] *Ibid.*, September 19, 1922.

[3] *New York World*, March 4, 1923.

[4] *Christian Science Monitor*, August 29, 1927.

[5] Based on estimated expenditure stated at time of applying for building permit and reported in *Real Estate Record and Builders' Guide*, New York, 1920-30.

flats — 970 out of a total of about 9600 such flats in 1920 — from residences renting from $5 to $10 a room to apartments at $25 a room or more. Some 1360 new apartments were added by the construction of new apartment houses (excluding 376 apartments in three large houses finished in 1931), with rents resembling those in remodeled tenements. Two hundred and eighty single-family houses which had previously been used by at least three families were remodeled, as well as an undeterminable number used as lodging houses or by one or two families.[1]

The result was not only to transform the area from a low-rent to a higher-rent section of the city, but to produce and mix together on the same blocks two essentially different types of dwellings, with a wide difference in rents, in the type of living which they presumed, and in their occupants. The rent structure of the Village in 1930 showed a conspicuous absence of middle range dwellings — those from $40 to $60 a month. There was a relative absence of the highest-rent[2] and lowest-rent dwellings as compared with the whole of the city — of those renting for over $100 or under $20 a month — and a greater proportion in the $20 to $30 class on the one hand and the $75 to $100 class on the other.

If $50 per month in 1930 be selected as the dividing rent between the one half and the 'other half' of the city's population, the Village is found to be still more largely a low- than a high-rent area. Sixty-one per cent of the Village dwellings rented for less than $50 as against 58 per cent in Manhattan, 56 per cent in the whole of New York City, and 25 per cent in the high-rent section of the upper West Side. Comparison with the corresponding area on the lower East Side, however, shows how far from a thoroughly low-rent region the Village had become, for on the East Side 96 per cent of the flats rented for less than $50.[3]

By 1930, the families in the Village were distributed among the types of local dwellings in the following proportion:[4] between 60 and 65 per cent[5] occupied tenements; approximately 10 per cent

[1] Records of New York City Tenement House Commissioner.
[2] Partly because Village apartments were almost uniformly small.
[3] U.S. Census, 1930. Cf. Table II, Appendix F, p. 463.
[4] A larger proportion of the *population* was tenement-dwelling than of *families*, since the tenement families were larger than those in apartments.
[5] Could not be estimated accurately without knowing the percentage of vacancies in different types of buildings.

were housed in remodeled tenement or factory buildings usually containing apartments of one and two rooms with modern equipment; another 10 per cent occupied newly built apartments which ranged from the 'white-collar' type built around 1925 to the elaborate, 'liveried-doorman' affairs of 1930. About 15 per cent were to be found in the twelve hundred single houses, most of which had been built before 1850. These houses were used as everything from cheap lodging houses to handsome single residences. The bulk had been reclaimed to some extent, and more than half would fall into the upper division. A small proportion, not over three per cent, of the local families found accommodation in the few, large, 'walk-up' apartments which had been built around 1910 for a definitely middle-class clientèle. These were the buildings occupied by the more prosperous members of the earlier Village population who could afford to leave the tenements, but did not care to leave the neighborhood. They were not part of the process of reclamation, and were not attractive to the newcomers. A few residents lived in hotels of different grades, ranging from waterfront hostelries and a large, fifty-cent 'flop house' through old-fashioned 'family' hotels to high-class apartment hotels.

3. MOVEMENT OF POPULATION

While a new population was accompanying real estate development into the Village, the old tenement-dwellers were on their way out. Their movement was partly forced by eviction from buildings slated for reconstruction, but largely it was a voluntary movement, corresponding to that from other parts of lower Manhattan, and it left more tenement vacancies than were needed to accommodate the people put out by demolition and remodeling.

During the post-War decade, a tremendous working-class exodus depleted lower Manhattan and brought a corresponding phenomenal growth to the outlying boroughs of Bronx, Brooklyn, Richmond, and Queens. Great sections of the lower East Side were almost deserted. School after school on lower Manhattan, which in 1920 had been running double sessions, was consolidated with other schools, while Queens schools were packed to overflowing twice a day.

Those who remained in the Village in 1930 were inclined to attribute the migration of their neighbors and the tremendous population decline to the forced removal of those who had lived in demolished or remodeled houses. But careful scrutiny of the available evidence indicates that voluntary migration, starting before and continuing after the principal volume of demolition and remodeling, was the primary cause of population decrease. An effort to estimate the extent of the population displacement which resulted from tenement remodeling and new building yielded a figure amounting to only 13 per cent of the difference between the population of 1920 and 1930. Since this figure was arrived at by most conservative means, 10 per cent was probably nearer the fact and 15 per cent would certainly be an outside estimate for the part of the population decline attributable to tenement remodeling.[1] The demolition of houses containing less than three families, and not, therefore, appearing among the demolition records of the Tenement House Commissioner, would account for some of the rest, but not for any large number. Although the birth rate declined rapidly until deaths exceeded births in 1930, this was not a cause of actual population drop, since there was an aggregate excess of births over deaths from 1920 to 1930 amounting to 4 per cent of the 1920 population.[2]

[1] Estimate of change in population due to:

	Increase	Decrease
Excess of births over deaths, 1920–30	1856	
Demolition of tenements (a)		3960
Erection of new apartments (b)	2205	
Remodeling of tenements (c)		2133
	4061	6093
Total decrease in population 1920–30		16,598
Net estimated decrease from above causes		2,032
Unaccounted for by above causes		14,566

(a) Allowing 4.25 persons per apartment as indicated by an average of baby and child clinic records from 1921 to 1929. This is the highest average found in any of the samples examined. Number of apartments affected by demolition and remodeling from records of Tenement House Commission. Ten per cent allowed for vacancies. A conservative figure in view of assertions by real estate dealers that they could house thousands of families. No accurate data on vacancies available.

(b) Allowing 1.8 persons per apartment as indicated by 212 questionnaires from sample of apartment and remodeled tenement dwellers. This is the lowest average found in any sample examined. Ten per cent allowed for vacancies.

(c) Population displaced computed by method (a) less new population by method (b).

[2] Figures supplied by the New York City Department of Health.

The rise in tenement rents may have been the cause of removal for some individual families. Up to 1929, those who stayed in their flats were theoretically protected from having their rents raised by the emergency rent laws passed during the housing shortage after the War. But a landlord could add to the rent to cover 'improvements,' he could evict when he wanted to remodel on the ground that such remodeling was necessary to salvage his investment, and he was not restricted by the law in dealing with new tenants. In the sample houses studies in 1930, families which had been in the house for a number of years were paying a substantially lower rent, while there were frequent reports of individual cases in which the rent of a flat was radically advanced when the old tenant moved out. The best index of rentals which could be prepared from available materials showed an increase of approximately 40 per cent in the rent per room between 1921 and 1929 — from an average of $5.50 per room to $7.65 per room.[1]

For the vast majority of those who moved, rising rents, in and of themselves, can hardly have been a determining cause. The movement of these years was not in search of lower rents but of better homes, and local rent increases frequently reflected improvements made by landlords in the effort to hold those who were dissatisfied with their living conditions. Social agencies testified that some few of their clients had left in order to take advantage of the much lower rent scale on the East Side, but these were the exceptions. The main stream of migration consisted of those who were better rather than worse off, and it flowed up and out rather than deeper into the heart of the slums. Though by itself illiteracy is not an accurate gauge of economic or social status, it offers supporting evidence that the exodus drew selectively the more successful. While the proportion of illiterates in the population of New York City dropped from 6.2 per cent in 1920 to 4.5 per cent in 1930 and among the foreign-born from 13.8 per cent to 10.7 per cent, the proportion in the Village increased in these years from 7.2 per cent to 7.6 per cent of the total population and from 14.0 per cent to 19.4 per cent of the foreign-born.[2] The increase in the proportion of foreign-born, and especially

[1] Based upon records of families attending two clinics.

[2] *U.S. Census, 1930*; based on population over ten years of age.

Italian, men between 1920 and 1930 suggests that families rather than single people were the chief ones to move.[1]

The living conditions from which so large a proportion of the population sought escape were far from satisfactory according to generally accepted standards. Of the total of 11,065 households in the Village in 1930, 40 per cent to 45 per cent were housed in the so-called 'old law' tenements, built before 1901 and condemned as unfit for habitation by the Tenement House Law of that year. A few of these — at most one per cent of the total households — resided in flats of the 'railroad' type, where only one of the three or four rooms in the flat opened to the outer air, the interior rooms remaining windowless and dark. The latter type of house was infrequent, as tenement-building had not reached the Village to any extent before 1879 when the 'railroad' type was prohibited by law, and several of these had been selected for remodeling, presumably because they were hardest to rent. Most of the 'old law' houses were of the typical 'dumbbell' type which met the requirements of the law of 1879 by having each room open onto the 'outer air'; i.e., onto a well usually from three and a half to six feet wide or about seven feet at its narrowest and twelve feet at its widest points when two 'dumbbell' houses adjoined.

In these houses, built on lots twenty-five feet wide, the rooms were small and, on the lower floors of six-story buildings, dark. Typically, each floor contained four flats, two four-room flats in front and two three-room flats in the rear. A toilet at one or both ends of the hall was shared by four or two families. There were no baths and the only running water was in the kitchen sink. The largest room in each flat was at most eleven feet wide by twelve to fourteen feet deep, often less. The other rooms were from nine to six feet wide and less than ten feet deep. Closet space was almost never provided and every room was habitually used for sleeping. Even where the family was small, these quarters were dark and congested. When the family was large, or when winemaking was added to the functions of the home, living was decidedly cramped. Basements in these buildings were so far be-

[1] *U.S. Census, 1920, 1930:*

	1920	*1930*
Foreign-born men per 100 foreign-born women in Village	123	132
Italian-born men per 100 Italian-born women in Village	119	135

low the minimum for decent living that their occupancy was forbidden altogether by the Multiple Dwelling Law of 1929. The application of this law was, however, postponed and in 1930 the basements of many of these houses were still tenanted.

By the Tenement House Law of 1901, the further erection of the 'dumbbell' type of tenement was forbidden and conditions laid down which eliminated the worst features of the older houses. Additional requirements for light and air did away with the narrow air well in favor of an open court, and a toilet had to be provided inside each flat. These 'new law' tenements, containing three- and four-room flats, housed some twenty per cent of the families of the neighborhood in 1930. With larger rooms, more light, and private toilets the occupants of these houses had distinct advantages over those who lived in older buildings. Both types of houses were commonly provided only with cold water.

In the effort to hold their tenants, landlords made a number of improvements during these years. The first two requisites, electricity and 'white sinks,' had been introduced into most of the houses of the district by 1930, but they were still new enough so that 'white sinks' were frequently specified on 'to let' signs. Hall toilets were still general, and were the feature of local housing about which the local mothers' clubs were most agitated. Hot water, baths, and occasionally even steam heat had been supplied. Houses with heat and with baths were in full demand in 1930, while the percentage of vacancies in the more poorly equipped houses was high. Except for the few houses built around 1910 there were no large flats to satisfy the local demand for 'five and six rooms for decent families at a reasonable rent.'

All testimony agrees that the major part of the 16,000 persons who disappeared from the census rolls between 1920 and 1930, and of the additional number whose places were taken by new people moving into the area, went to the same places as other former residents of Manhattan — to the outlying boroughs and to New Jersey. A random sample of 240 school transfers showed the distribution to have been:

Brooklyn........ 19%	Bronx............ 15%	N.Y. State............ 4%
New Jersey...... 16	Long Island....... 7	Elsewhere in U.S....... 11
Manhattan...... 16	Staten Island...... 3	Foreign countries...... 9

The scattered membership of an Italian society which had been made up of local residents showed roughly the same distribution, with Brooklyn farther in the lead and the Bronx containing more than Manhattan.[1] The principal local furniture mover who, at the height of this exodus, transported six to eight families a day out of the tenement neighborhood, emphatically insisted that they had all gone to South Brooklyn — 'Take it from me, I know them all and I carried them there.' But all other evidence points toward a general dispersion into all the outlying regions rather than a wholesale migration to a single district.

There is little to indicate that the bulk of those who moved did so because the industries in which they had been employed had shifted to outlying parts of the metropolitan area. Although it is virtually impossible to trace any substantial number to their new homes, the samples which could be found, and the character of those who remained, pointed very strongly to the relative unimportance of place of work in determining place of residence.

A very large part of the population living in the area in 1930 rode to work on one of the rapid-transit lines. On the three lines carrying 80 per cent of all the travel in and out of the district, the number of persons who dropped their nickels in subway or elevated turnstiles between 7 and 9 A.M. amounted to half of those reported by the census as being gainfully employed.[2] With allowance on the one hand for those who started to work before 7 or after 9 A.M., those not going to work at all on the days used as samples, and, on the other hand, for children riding to school, the proportion would still be large. Obviously, the desire to save the cost and energy of commuting had not controlled the decision of many local residents as to where to live.

Those who were employed in the district, on the other hand, rode in to work on the same transit lines. A canvass of industrial plants in 1930 revealed the fact that all of the larger plants and most of the small ones — 60 per cent of the number of plants re-

---

[1] Addresses in 1930 supplied by society's doctor.

[2] Figures from fares at subway and elevated entrances in district supplied for a typical week day in November and May annually, 1924–31, by the I.R.T. Not an accurate indication of persons from the area because of use of same subway stations by residents of contiguous areas. Adjusted for Fourteenth Street express station on northern boundary by including only one fourth of the fares there collected. No adjustment made for southern station.

porting, involving a much larger proportion of the number of employees — employed workers practically all of whom lived at a distance. Of the rest, only a few — 12 per cent of the whole — stated that their workers were predominantly drawn from the locality, while the remainder drew from both near-by and at a distance. A number greater than the total of those employed in factories left the area by rapid-transit lines between 5 and 7 P.M. In the absence of a measure of the total number of persons employed in the district in other than factory jobs, it is not possible to judge what proportion of all industrial workers were included in this body of subway and elevated-line travelers.[1] From this volume of travel it appears that rapid-transit lines rather than proximity had come to be the determining factor in distributing residence in relation to work,[2] for the bulk of the six thousand industrial workers employed in local factories in 1930.[3]

It was not possible to trace a large number to their new residences to discover whether they had followed their place of employment. But out of a sample of fifty families,[4] only two gave work as their reason for moving and all except eight commuted to work. Only one of the eight who did not commute was a factory worker. The rest had stores, business, or a trade. Of the forty-two who commuted, six came back to the Village to work. Small though this sample is, it lends support to the evidence from other sources.

A search for better living conditions appears to have been the dominant motive of those who left this part of the city. The stock phrase 'to better themselves' — 'Isn't that why everybody moves?' asks an Italian woman in Brooklyn — meant a higher

[1] Fourteenth Street omitted altogether because of shopping center there. Stations at southern edge serve a number of industrial buildings lying south of the district.

[2] This does not answer the question entirely as the evidence of those interviewed clearly indicated. Residence may be chosen because the subway ride is relatively short or against the traffic — a prime consideration asserted by the largest proportion of new residents interviewed or questioned.

[3] Must be discounted for the possibility that workers in local plants, particularly women (30 per cent of total), may commute while the head of the family works near the place of residence.

[4] Random sample made up of 16 Brooklyn residents found by following up school discharges, 28 residents of Long Island, Brooklyn, New Jersey, and the Bronx found by consulting the janitors of various types of houses and by tracing the former occupants of some remodeled tenements, and 6 individuals found through miscellaneous contacts.

material standard of living, more especially a better house. Half of the sample of fifty gave a better home as the sole or principal reason for their moving, and most of those in the sample who had been evicted by remodeling or demolition had moved out when they could not find quarters which suited them at reasonable rentals in the Village. Five specified more fresh air as their sole or chief interest and seven sought a better neighborhood. Among the latter, three Irishmen declared respectively that the Spanish element had ruined the Irish neighborhood, that the neighborhood was no longer a safe place in which to raise a daughter because of the mixed nationalities, and that the bohemians 'going around half clothed, practically nude, I would say,' had made it an unsuitable neighborhood in which to bring up children.

Of the fifty sample families, all except two improved the quality of their housing by the move. In the Village, most had lived in 'cold-water flats' without either hot water or steam heat. Only one of thirty for whom a detailed description of household equipment was available [1] had moved to a cold-water flat. For twenty-one, hot water was a new feature, while eight had had hot water in their Village flats. Only three of the houses outside of the Village were without steam heat. In the Village, only three had had steam heat. Baths, similarly, were innovations for twenty-three out of thirty. Clearly, those who moved improved their standard of living in the process.

This improved housing, however, was achieved at a price. Comparison of the rents paid by this group before and after moving demonstrated the fact that quality of housing rather than absolute rent was responsible for the exodus. None of the fifty paid less rent after the move. Twenty-eight paid higher rent, thirteen purchased their new homes. Five continued to pay the same, in one case for less good quarters. Four did not report their rents. The average rent paid in the Village by the twenty-two reporting exact rent figures was $28. After the move, the average paid by this same twenty-two was $41.

As people moved away, many tenements stood vacant. In 1928, one of the local real estate agents stated that he could find accommodation in the neighborhood for 2000 families at $6 to $10

---

[1] It is clear from the general information about 18 more than these were not without hot water and baths after moving.

a room.[1] Landlords continued to add improvements even after the depression had begun. Higher wages in the mid-years of the decade, a rapidly rising standard of living induced by advertising and installment selling campaigns, and the pressure from grown children to move to better quarters turned the bad housing of the lower West Side from an accepted condition of life into a reason for moving to newer neighborhoods.

Few of those who left their tenements in the search for better quarters moved into the reclaimed dwellings in the neighborhood, for these were designed for quite other types of residents and the rents were away out of their reach. The less expensive of the new houses accommodated a very few of the more prosperous old residents, politicians who had reason to remain in the neighborhood, business men with factories near-by, doctors, and some of the more prosperous storekeepers.

While some 20,000 of the tenement population were moving out in search of better quarters, approximately 4000 residents of the new type came in to occupy the newly constructed or remodeled houses. The great bulk of those who were in the neighborhood in 1930 had moved to the district because of its convenience to their places of work and play.

Fifty-nine per cent of the sample of 212 people replying to a questionnaire gave convenience as the most important reason for living in the Village. This was equally true of married and of single people. Another 12 per cent listed convenience second among their reasons for moving.

The type of available apartments was responsible for a number of others. Fourteen per cent gave it first place — both families with children who found apartments in small houses with back yards or gardens and single people looking for small, compact places — and 21 per cent mentioned it second. Eight per cent mentioned the attraction of low rentals, but a number vigorously protested the suggestion that rents were low and declared they were there in spite of rents, not because of them. Although 12 per cent came because of friends, 6 per cent because of the 'atmosphere' of the neighborhood and 2 per cent for other miscellaneous reasons, the indications are that the vast majority — 80 per cent of the sample — were attracted to the locality for

[1] *New York Tribune*, March 25, 1928.

physical rather than for sociological reasons. Over a hundred interviews confirmed this conclusion for the group living in the Village in 1930.

Those who moved in came from all over the United States. It was the current impression in the locality that a very large proportion had come from the South. Superintendents describing the occupants of their buildings specified Southerners. A local doctor asserted that a large proportion of the newcomers whom he served were Southerners. Democratic political leaders called attention to their fortuitous gain in Democratic enrollment because of the traditional Democratic affiliations of the new apartment-house residents from the South.

The sample investigated, however, showed 10 per cent to have been born in the South as compared with 23 per cent in the Middle West and 35 per cent in the East, outside of New York City. Thirteen per cent had been born in New York and 5 per cent on the West Coast. Fourteen per cent were foreign-born, in Canada, Europe, Central America, and Asia. Of those who were American-born, 35 per cent had been born in metropolitan communities — 16 per cent in New York City and 19 per cent in other cities of over half a million inhabitants. Sixteen per cent came from rural communities of less than 2500 inhabitants and another 12 per cent from small towns between 2000 and 10,000. The rest had been born in small and medium-sized cities.

Neither the tenement population which remained nor the apartment-dwellers who moved in were stable in their residence. Among the old American and Irish families who had stayed in the neighborhood through all its changes, there were home-owners who clung tenaciously to their residences. Many of the Italians bought houses, but as investments rather than for residence. In a few select parts of the Village, made-over houses were bought by newcomers. All these, however, were the exceptions. In 1930, only 2.0 per cent of the families in the Village owned their homes. The comparable figure for Manhattan was 2.5 per cent.

Among the tenement population, the habit of moving was fairly general. It was the custom of some families to move every year in order to get clean, freshly painted rooms, since it was harder to get the landlord to keep an occupied flat in condition than it was to find a vacant flat which had been made attractive for new tenants. Families moving in and out of houses, sometimes only a few doors away, were a constant sight; trash of the sort which only appears at moving time — floor linoleum, bed springs, broken-down furniture — kept local children supplied with playthings. The condition of moving was an accepted state. On the other hand, a canvass of representative tenements showed a large proportion to have lived in the same house for years. Out of a sample of 425 families and single residents, 53 per cent had been at the same place for five years or more, 30 per cent for at least ten years, and 6 per cent over twenty years. For the better houses in the more mixed part of the Village, the period of residence was shorter than for the tenements in the heart of the Italian section, indicating that moving, within the Village as well as outside, has been motivated by a quest for improvement.

Among the newcomers, especially the young, single men and girls, constant moving was taken for granted. Many houses did not require leases. Others reported that they were used to having tenants skip their leases and go away even when they had signed a contract for a year. Second-hand furniture dealers reported a steady business fitting out newcomers and buying back the same furniture in a short time. Janitors described their cellars as full of cheap furniture which had been left behind by tenants who found it cheaper to abandon their painted tables and chairs than to pay for moving them. Out of the sample of 165 who answered the question — a sample which may have been weighted in favor of the more stable element which was interested enough to take the time and trouble to answer — 41 per cent had moved on the average of at least once in two years during the previous ten years.

4. CHARACTER OF POPULATION

The net result of the movement of population during the post-War years was to reduce the congestion of the district, partially to change its economic character, to increase the proportion of native to foreign stock, and to raise the age level.

The decrease in population, which amounted to 30 per cent between 1920 and 1930, did not begin with these years. From 1910 to 1920 there had already been a decrease of 19.3 per cent.[1]

[1] Cf. Table III, Appendix F, p. 464; Chart II, p. 34.

Relative inaccuracy of the state census figures for the inter-census years makes it difficult to determine accurately the year when the decline set in. The figures for 1905 and 1915 show a large increase from 1900 to 1905 and from 1905 to 1910, and a sharp drop from 1910 to 1915 which reduced the district's population below that of 1900. Between 1915 and 1920 they show a substantial gain, followed by an even more precipitate drop from 1920 to 1925. Even allowing for very considerable understatement in the 1915 figure, it appears that the district changed from an expanding to a declining neighborhood when the building of new tenements ceased and the War cut off the supply of new immigrants. The change certainly antedated the post-War trek toward the suburbs.

Decline in numbers greatly relieved the congestion of the area. In 1905, three local blocks had been numbered among the 123 blocks in the city whose population exceeded 750 persons per acre. In 1925, these three blocks were reported as containing 458, 516, and 454 persons per acre respectively. The census tract to the south of Washington Square had constituted in 1910 the eleventh most densely populated tract on Manhattan and the nineteenth in 1920. By 1930, its 1920 density had been cut in half.[1] While the decline in population removed certain of the most intense social problems of the locality by thus relieving congestion, it also gave a definite psychological tone to the community where the state of mind of the district and the problems of its institutions were conditioned by dwindling numbers.

The new residents were, on the whole, of a higher economic status and they substantially raised the income level of the community. By 1930, 3065 men and women were listed as engaged in 'professional and semi-professional service,' 14.5 per cent of all the gainfully employed in the Village as against 8.7 per cent in Manhattan and 6.7 per cent in New York.[2] Every sample of new residents — those responding to questionnaires, those interviewed, and those who sent their children to a local progressive school — showed a preponderance of professional workers, with the various literary and artistic branches of the professions most strongly represented.

The tenement population worked chiefly as truck and taxi

[1] Laidlaw, W., ed. *Population of the City of New York, 1890–1930*, pp. 208, 209.
[2] Cf. Table VII, Appendix F, p. 466.

CHART–II

INDEX OF POPULATION CHANGE BY NATIVITY GROUPS, 1910–1920–1930*

GREENWICH VILLAGE COMPARED WITH MANHATTAN AND NEW YORK CITY

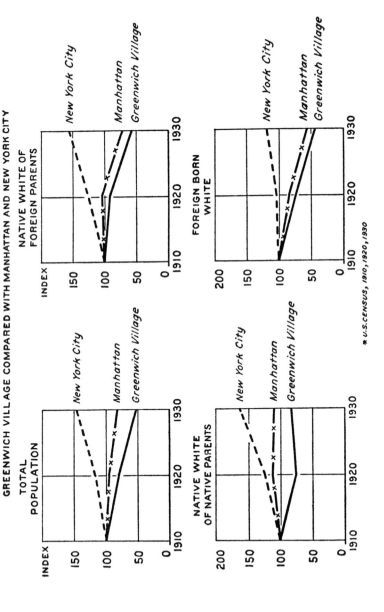

TOTAL
POPULATION

NATIVE WHITE OF
FOREIGN PARENTS

NATIVE WHITE
OF NATIVE PARENTS

FOREIGN BORN
WHITE

* U.S. CENSUS, 1910, 1920, 1930

drivers, longshoremen, and skilled artisans, with a number engaged in common labor and most of the women employed in factories. Two samples of the tenement-house population in 1930,
and a sample of blocks in the heart of the Italian section, nearer
its edge and on its fringe, in 1925 all showed a large proportion of
skilled workers, a substantial number in small businesses and a
few in the clerical, professional, or executive ranks. The clerical
workers were chiefly drawn from the younger generation.

The occupational range of new and old residents overlapped
only in the clerical occupations and, very slightly, the professions.
Whereas the occupational scale of the old residents went from
common labor up to clerical work with a few in the professions,
that of the new residents began with clerical work and mounted
into the high ranks of executives.

The old and new residents were less sharply divided with respect to income than occupation. Clerical workers, and the less
successful artists and writers, earned no more than the skilled
artisans or white-collar workers of the other group. The income
of the small business men among the older population frequently
compared favorably with that of the professionals among the new
residents. Although the bulk of the old population represented a
definitely lower income level than the bulk of the new, there was
considerable overlapping.

An attempt to estimate the effect of the decade's developments
upon the proportionate distribution of incomes in the locality
yielded the rough results indicated in Table IV.[1]

The presence of the new residents increased the proportion of
native stock from 17.7 per cent in 1920 to 28.4 per cent in 1930.[2]
The Village was beginning to regain its status as the 'American
Ward.' The relative increase in those of foreign parentage as
compared with those of foreign birth reflected, of course, the cessation of immigration and the increasing number of American-born
children in the immigrant community.

As between the nationality groups represented, however, there
was little important change, not only from 1920 to 1930, but in
the ten years previous as well.[3] Italians remained overwhelmingly dominant, with the Irish occupying second place. Substantial decreases in the proportion of Irish and Germans were

[1] Page 36.   [2] Cf. Table III, Appendix F, p. 464.   [3] Cf. Chart III, p. 38.

TABLE IV. ESTIMATE OF INCOME DISTRIBUTION, 1920, 1930 [1]

LOCAL PEOPLE	1920	1930	VILLAGERS	1920	1930	1920	1930
Lowest Down and out Inadequate income Temporarily down	12%	15%	*Lowest* Bohemians Poor artists Temporarily down	40%	10%	15.0%	13.5%
Low Middle Low income Large family One or two low-paid workers	40%	35%	*Low Middle* Low clerical Irregular employment	10%	20%	37.0%	30.5%
Middle Artisan Shopkeepers Several in family working	40%	40%	*Middle* Salesmen Better clerical Lower professional	40%	35%	39.5%	38.5%
Upper Middle Property-owners Good stores or other business Medium bootlegger	7%	7%	*Upper Middle* Professional Real estate Business	9.5%	25%	7.0%	12.5%
Upper Prosperous bootlegger Prosperous business Prosperous politician	1%	3%	*Upper* Business Successful professional	.5%	10%	1.5%	5.0%

[1] This is a very rough estimate, based for 1930 on a combination of rentals and samples of persons interviewed or recorded. It was impossible to secure an accurate record of income distribution because no tax returns are available, difference in methods of expenditure make such common indices as rent very inadequate, differences are so much more a matter of family composition than of occupation or earnings of the head of the family, and there is no way to take account of such supplements to incomes as are derived from illegal activities, from relatives, or from gambling, which was nearly universal. The data for 1930, moreover, were gathered shortly after the depression had set in and the 1920–1930 trend had begun to be reversed. As the progress of the depression leveled out the differences here indicated and reduced many more to a common proletarian status, income differences had less and less importance.

The estimates for 1920 are even more inexact than for 1930. They are based on changes in the proportion of the population made up of old residents as against Villagers, changes in the wage rate for the most prevalent occupations, and changes in the age distribution of the families. Among the Villagers, they rest on the change in the type of Villager as described by those who had been in the area for a long time and in the type of building and rentals provided for them.

partly balanced by increases of Italians and, slightly, of Jews. The small colonies of Spanish and Lithuanians dwindled. But on the whole the twenty-year record is one of relative stability in the ethnic composition in spite of the heavy movement of population. The constancy of the ethnic composition introduced an element of stability into the otherwise unstable and heterogeneous community. Here there were none of the kaleidoscopic successions of nationalities that have characterized some sections of Manhattan and other Eastern or industrial cities — only a gradual decline of the older relative to the newer group.

The reason for this relative stability lay chiefly in the anomalous character of the district. From the point of view of immigrant population, it was neither an area of first settlement nor of second settlement, but something in between. Neither Irish nor Italians, nor any others had been accustomed to find their way first to this section upon entering the country. The Irish originally came into the district from the East Side. For them, in the late years of the nineteenth century, it was definitely an 'area of second settlement' to which the more successful and ambitious moved from their East Side center. With the advent of the Italians, however, the district lost its status for the Irish as an area of second settlement.

At the same time, it did not become a first-settlement district for the new Irish who came out: the upper East Side rather than the Village took the place of the older first-settlement area on the lower East Side. The Italians, first coming in as an overflow from the East Side, did not abandon their East Side settlements, but retained these as first-settlement points for new arrivals. Nor did other immigrant groups find the neighborhood available for mass settlement. A comparatively small section, with relatively high rents for a tenement neighborhood and diverse in its population and accommodation, is not the sort to offer facilities for new arrivals. Neither the very poor-grade, low-rent houses like those which owed their existence on the East Side to the constant stream of new arrivals,[1] nor a deteriorating district of one-time fine residences, made the Village a characteristically favorable area for first immigrant settlement. Individual families did come to occupy some of the very dilapidated and cheap dwellings

[1] *Regional Survey of New York and its Environs*, New York, 1929, vol. II, p. 57.

scattered through the district, but these were as likely to be run-down families of older stock as the very recent immigrant arrivals.

Offering, thus, neither the attractions of an area of second settlement nor the cheapness of an area of first settlement, the Village remained from the time that the Italians took possession of it a stable district as far as its ethnic composition was concerned. Such small shifts as are recorded in the relative proportion of different foreign stocks reflect primarily differences in the rate at which the several groups left the area rather than differences in their coming in.

The change in age composition by the combination of population movements and declining birth rate was more marked than any ethnic shift except that represented by the increase of native stock. Distinctly, this became more an adult's community.[1] In each succeeding age group, from the youngest to the oldest, the proportionate decrease from 1920 to 1930 was less than for the younger group. Whereas there were 62 per cent fewer children under 5 in the neighborhood in 1930, there were only 17 per cent fewer persons over 45.

Percentage Decrease in Greenwich Village Population, 1920–1930 [2]

Under 5	62.0 per cent	15–20	27.4 per cent
5–9	52.0	21–44	22.6
10–14	41.7	45 and over	17.3

The full significance of the shift only appears, however, when the figures are examined in detail. In the first place, the shift in the age structure of the district differed with respect to the several nativity groups. Among the native stock, decrease in the lowest age groups — under 10 — was proportionately less than among those of foreign parentage, presumably because of the presence of young third generation Italian children on the one hand and, on the other, the fact that a number of new residents came to live in the Village because there were houses which provided yards for their young children. For those of foreign parentage on the other hand, the group from 15 to 20 showed a relative increase, clearly the children of the great 1900 to 1910 invasion. The relative increase in the proportion of persons in the twenties and thirties was characteristic of the native stock especially — young

[1] Cf. Table V, Appendix F, p. 465.   [2] *U.S. Census, 1920, 1930.*

CHART- III

CHANGE IN FOREIGN STOCK OF SELECTED NATIONALITIES AND OF NATIVE STOCK 1910 –1930*

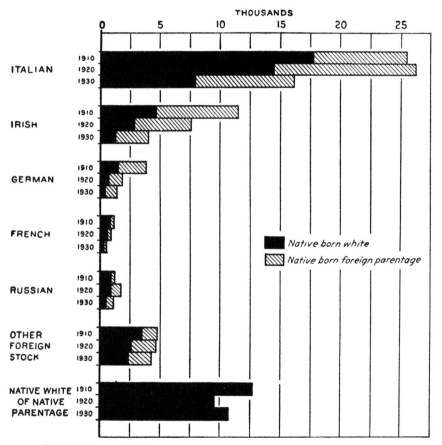

* U.S.CENSUS, 1910, 1920, 1930; NWFP, 1910 INCLUDES ONLY THE NATIVE BORN, BOTH OF WHOSE PARENTS WERE BORN IN THE SAME FOREIGN COUNTRY; NWFP, 1920 ESTIMATED FOR EACH NATIONALITY

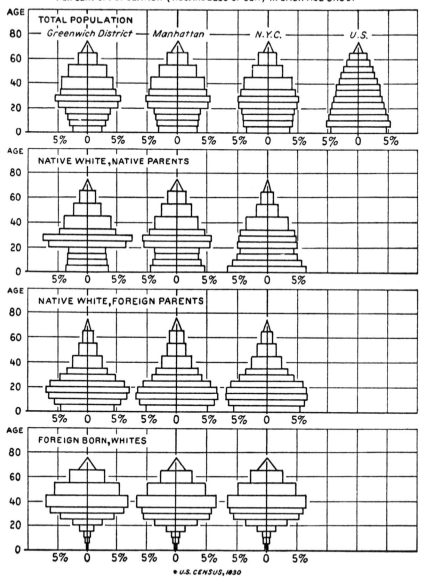

CHART-IV

AGE DISTRIBUTION-1930*

PER CENT OF POPULATION (REGARDLESS OF SEX) IN EACH AGE GROUP

* U.S. CENSUS, 1930

men and women coming to live alone in the city — but also of those of foreign parentage. The foreign-born, on the other hand, showed their greatest proportionate increase in the years after forty-five.

Chart IV shows the age distribution in 1930 resulting from these shifts. In comparison with Manhattan and New York City as well as with the United States, the whole district in 1930 contained an abnormally large proportion in the twenties, with a very small proportion in the lowest age group and a large proportion over 45. The charts of the separate nativity groups, however, show unmistakably how the population pyramid for the total population is actually a composite of the very different pyramids of the different nativity groups. For the native stock, the tremendous concentration in the twenties is most striking. The foreign-born and their children were concentrated respectively into age groups twenty years apart — from 30 to 45 and from 10 to 25 respectively.

If the evidence is scrutinized in yet greater detail, still other factors are apparent. With respect to the different sections of the area, quite marked variations in the age structure of the different nativity groups are apparent and indicate social differences that are important for the study of these years. The native stock in the predominantly tenement neighborhood was greater in the youngest than in the other age groups under 20, showing the presence of third generation children of young second generation Italian couples. A very large proportion were in the 20 to 30 group, 30 per cent of the native stock in these sections falling between those two years, and reflecting the presence of single Villagers in the 'bohemian' quarters and also the homeless, casual laborers residing in a large, cheap hotel. In the section of greatest remodeling, the distribution among the younger age groups was more irregular and the concentration in early adult years more evenly spread from 20 to 35. In the waterfront section, there was a relatively large proportion of children from 6 to 20, presumably the children of the second generation Irish families who antedated the Italians by at least half a generation.

Difference between parts of the area is most noticeable in respect to those of foreign parentage. In the Italian tenement section, the proportion was greater in each succeeding age group up to 20, and then became less by correspondingly even steps, partly because the oldest children of the bulk of the Italian settlers were, in 1930, not over 20 and to a less extent because many of those in their twenties who had married had moved away. In the re-modeled section, most of those of foreign parentage were between 20 and 30 — children of earlier and more successful Italian mi-grants who had moved into this section from the blocks farther to the east and children of the Irish. In the waterfront, on the other hand, the greatest proportion was from 5 to 9, with a smaller number in each older age group. These were the children of the Spanish and, to some extent, the other scattered nationalities of the region, who came in about ten years later than did the Italians, from 1910 to 1915 instead of from 1900 to 1905. In all sections, the foreign-born were concentrated into the 35 to 45 year age range.

The age structure of the several groups in the locality revealed by these figures was essentially the product of population move-ments which were episodic in character rather than steady in their drift. Each separate social group which entered the area came within a fairly short period of time and was more or less homo-geneous in age composition at the time when it arrived. The result was that in 1920 and in 1930 each of these groups presented its distinct age pattern. Although figures for 1920 were not avail-able for comparison with 1930 by detailed age groups, the fact that essentially the same people of foreign birth or parentage who were there in 1930 were already there in 1920 makes it possible to re-construct for these groups a rough picture of their age distribution in the former year by moving the whole age pyramid back ten years. Except for the moving-out of young people at the time of their marriage, neither migration nor death was a sufficiently selective factor to alter radically the age structure between the earlier and the later dates.

The Irish group during these years consisted of three genera-tions — the remnant of really old people, born on the other side, who had come to the district as young people fifty years before; the children of these people raised in the district during the last decade of the nineteenth and the first few years of the twentieth century; and, thirdly, the children of the latter, the older of whom were beginning to marry and move away in 1920 while the younger were still in school in 1930. Along with these was a mere scattering of those who had not moved out on marriage and who were starting to raise their families in the neighborhood. The study of the Irish must, therefore, be couched largely in terms of the middle generation, the parents of grown and nearly grown children — with some consideration for the youngsters in their teens and the very old.

The Italian group, by contrast, was made up of persons who emigrated as young people between 1900 and 1913. Some few were already here in the 1890's. Some very few came out as young people after the War. But most of them were raising young families when the War broke out. During the post-War decade, the oldest members of these families reached maturity. By 1930, some had married and moved away, some very few were starting their own families in the neighborhood, and the big element in the community had become the single young people between 16 and 23 with an oncoming group between 10 and 15. The Italian group must be studied in terms of this young, second generation element and of their parents — somewhat younger than the middle group of Irish, ranging between 35 and 50 in 1930. The few old people — parents who were brought out by children who had established themselves here, or remnants of the very few early settlers — and the young children of American-born mothers completed the group.

The age composition of the Jewish group corresponded very closely to that of the Italians. Coming to America — and this neighborhood — at approximately the same time, their older children, by 1930, were graduating from or entering college. This group was, thus, also to be described in terms of middle-aged parents and young people.

What remained of the Lithuanian settlement had also come in the same period as Italians and Jews. Its older children were marrying toward the end of the period. The younger children were in their teens and the parents between 40 and 50. Neither younger couples, nor old, nor yet very young children were to be found in the remnant of this community.

The Spanish group was perhaps ten years younger than the Italian, Jewish, and Lithuanian. Its older children had not yet reached the marriageable age, or would not have were it not for the tremendous superabundance of men that made it hard for a girl to remain single to the end of her teens. It was, therefore, characterized by parents in younger middle age and children of school age, rather than by the age distribution of either Irish or Italians.

The German group was the oldest of any. Except for a very few young third generation children, its younger members were in their late thirties and the parents in their sixties.

The ranks of the new residents were annually enlarged by young people in their twenties, with a slight trend toward an older group in the new apartments which only the prosperous could afford.

During these years the number of men in the district exceeded the women by a substantial but decreasing proportion, representing a definite contrast in this respect to Manhattan and the whole of New York City, where the sexes were very nearly equal, with women slightly in the lead in 1920 and men in 1930. The preponderance of men was due in part to the waterfront, with its overwhelmingly male population of seamen and longshoremen, and in part to the large excess of males among the foreign-born immigrants. The latter excess was greater in 1930 than it had been in 1920, indicating that it was families who moved out of the district, while the single men remained. Among the newcomers of native extraction, women predominated. The ratio of men to women among the native stock fell from 101.3 men to 100 women in 1920 to 91.4 men in 1930. In the Italian group, the sex ratio for the Village resembled that for Manhattan and New York City in 1910 and 1920, 129 and 119 respectively, showing it to have been a representative section of the Italian population. In 1930, there were 135 foreign-born Italian men for every 100 Italian-born women. At all times the other foreign-born elements in the population, Irish, German, Russian (Jewish), and French, contained a larger proportion of men than did the same group in Manhattan and the city.[1]

Single people made up a larger proportion of the adult population of the locality than they did for Manhattan or for New York City. In 1930, they constituted 48.2 per cent of the men and 40

---

[1] *U.S. Census;* sex ratio by nationality groups not available for Manhattan and New York City in 1930, but Greenwich Village ratio for 1930 higher than the 1920 ratio for each group in Manhattan and New York City.

per cent of the women of the Village as compared with 38.5 per cent and 31.8 per cent for the men and women respectively in New York City.[1]

In general trend, the population of Greenwich Village reflected the changes of all Manhattan from 1920 to 1930, but in every case the trend characteristic of Manhattan appeared in Greenwich Village in an exaggerated form. While Manhattan declined 18.2 per cent in total population, Greenwich Village declined 30.4 per cent. While for Manhattan the proportion of the total population which was under 21 dropped from 35.2 to 29.5 per cent, in the Village these younger age groups dropped at a faster rate, from 37.1 to 28.7 per cent. The proportion which native stock bore to the total population increased for Manhattan from 17.0 to 21.0 per cent, and for the Village from 17.7 to 28.4 per cent.[2] While Manhattan's birth rate fell from 24.8 per thousand of the population to 21.0, that of the Village declined precipitately from 22.7 to 12.1. Although the death rate of the Village declined while that for Manhattan did not, the differential between births and deaths in the Village dropped much more. Whereas for Manhattan the excess of births over deaths fell from 10.3 to 5.1, the Village's excess of 6.1 in 1920 turned into a deficiency of 1.4 births per thousand as compared to deaths in 1930.[3]

These shifts arising from a declining birth and death rate, the cessation of immigration, and the increased proportion in the upper age groups were not unique to Manhattan, but, except for Manhattan's stationary death rate, were characteristic in a less degree of the entire population of the country.

The result of all these changes, both before and during the post-War period, was to juxtapose types of dwellings and types of residents in such a way as to give to the Village the thoroughgoing heterogeneity which is characteristic of areas in process of reclamation or of disintegration. A description of the block upon which the office of the study was located — close to the center of the area — will give a miniature picture of the Village's complexity and confusion in 1930.

In this block were seven single houses of the 1840 type, six of

[1] U.S. Census, 1930. Cf. Table VI, Appendix F, p. 465.   [2] U.S. Census, 1920, 1930.
[3] New York City Department of Health, Annual Report, 1920–30, for Manhattan. Births and deaths for Greenwich Village furnished directly.

which had been made over into apartments, while the seventh remained a low-grade rooming house; five tenements — four of which had been built before 1879, and one between 1880 and 1900 — had, by 1930, been remodeled into one- and two-room apartments renting at $55 to $65 a month. Two large, four-story houses on the front and back of a lot had been turned into semi-housekeeping, furnished apartments of one and two rooms renting from $75 a month up. Seven 'old law' tenements presented various degrees of improvements — some of the cold-water-toilet-in-hall type, some with bath, and some with steam heat installed in 1930. A large, 'new law' tenement in which heat had been installed in 1929 completed the residential buildings on the block.

Among them were distributed three factory buildings, making such diverse things as feather mattresses, children's toys and Italian ice cream, an old stable used for storage, and one of the buildings of a settlement house. A representative supply of retail shops included two groceries, a tobacco and candy store, a Chinese and a French hand laundry, a barber shop, an ice dealer's cellar, an Italian men's café, a tea room, and the workshop of a wrought-iron craftsman. A quota of speakeasies of various grades, never fewer than three, added the remaining touch.

The block opened at either end onto streets which were typical of widely diverse aspects of the Village. One was the main business street for the tenement population — lined with pushcarts and with stores selling Italian food, dry goods, cheap jewelry. The other was the thoroughfare from the subway to the night-club and tea-room section, appropriately lined with shops selling peasant smocks, antique jewelry, gifts, and second-hand books. On the corner at the first end was an old-fashioned apothecary shop with patent medicines as its usual window displays and no soda fountain. The corresponding corner at the other end contained a drugstore whose principal feature was its fountain and lunch counter and whose displays featured cosmetics and contraceptives. Directly opposite one end of the block was an ice-cream parlor, the hang-out of the local Italian young men. Opposite the other end was a tea room with striped awnings and a 'quaint' name.

Here in a nutshell was a record of the changes which had come over the Village, and an evidence of the physical confusion which laid the foundation for its social diversity.

III. BUSINESS AND WORK

1. LOCAL BUSINESS

IN ADDITION to those who made Greenwich Village their
home, a daytime working population of upwards of six
thousand emerged from the subway in the morning, filled
the sidewalks and patronized the lunch counters at noon, and
left at five o'clock for the journey home. Hardly had these departed when a second type of outsider began to arrive, the patrons
of the tea rooms, speakeasies, and night clubs, who came to the
Village in search of amusement and made certain of the streets
their own during the evening and night. Neither industrial worker
nor amusement-seeker was an integral part of the life of the community, but both contributed to the setting within which the life
of the local residents was led. Local residents, in their turn,
derived their living either from the small shops of the locality
or from employment in other parts of the city.

Although the Village had ceased to be primarily an industrial
district by the time of the War, factories employing some 6750
people were still located in the area in 1930. These were chiefly of
two types: (1) remnants of industries which had been located here
previously — of heavy industries which had moved onto the cheap
lands of industrial suburbs leaving only scattered plants behind,
and of the needle trades which had migrated during and after
the War from their center just east of the Village to the mid-town
area, leaving the poorer shops behind; and (2) service and maintenance industries, chiefly job printing and electrical equipment,
which had lately moved in.[1]

[1] Cf. Table XXVIII, Appendix D, p. 454.

The latter were the product of the second type of rebuilding which transformed the Village during these years — the construction of large, up-to-date office and loft buildings on the southern edge of the area. As the financial and business district on the lower tip of Manhattan expanded, it spread north, reaching the section immediately south of the Village by 1924. Here and on the southern most blocks of the Village, tenements were demolished on a wholesale scale to make way for new buildings, and not simply sporadically torn down or altered as they were on most of the Village blocks.

Comparable figures for 1920 are not available to show whether the new industries which occupied these buildings brought in more workers than went out with the older type of shop. The evidence of the fares taken in at the subway and elevated entrances from 5 to 6 P.M. indicated that the number employed in 1930 represented roughly the volume of employment during the second half of the decade.[1] The contrast between the workers in the new and old plants — skilled printers, engineers, and office workers as against needle workers and heavy labor — and the larger proportion of local people in the old shops, however, suggest a substantial change in the type of worker and in the proportion drawn from outside the neighborhood.

Workers in the newer plants, and many in the older type as well, were drawn from the whole metropolitan area. Brooklyn was the place from which workers were most frequently said to come, but an examination of the direction of subway travel during the 5 to 6 rush hour showed, from 1924 to 1930, that twice as many went home to upper Manhattan and the Bronx as entrained for Brooklyn.[2] A comparable record of the rush-hour fares of those commuting from New Jersey was not available, but since travel to Jersey[3] by ferry or tube constituted 20 per cent of all the travel[4]

[1] Information furnished by Interborough Rapid Transit Company for a typical week day in November and May, 1924–30.

[2] Perhaps an underestimate for Brooklyn, since workers living in the part of Brooklyn not reached by the subway line running through the Village may either have walked across to the other subway line or, if they could afford two fares, may have ridden uptown and changed at Times Square.

[3] Local passengers only. Commuters holding combination railroad and ferry tickets would add a considerable number.

[4] Since presumably relatively few residents of the Village went to work in Jersey, a larger

out of the area at all hours of the day, it is fair to assume that a substantial part of the working force was drawn from there.

A large proportion were skilled men who, in 1930, made up half of the local labor force.[1] On the basis of statements of managers as to the national origins of their employees, roughly 25 per cent of the 1930 workers appeared to have been Italian, 11 per cent German, 8 per cent Irish, and 12 per cent Jewish. The rest, except for a few Spanish, French, Greek, and Swedish workers, were not distinguished by their employers as being of any distinctive stock. A quarter of the local plants, chiefly the smaller ones, employed Italians exclusively. A few others expressed preferences for German, Jewish, or American employees, but most stated that they had no policy of seeking workers of any particular ethnic types.

In the new and growing industries, work conditions were distinctly good. These — the printing trades and telephone equipment shop employing 55 per cent of the workers of the district — were housed in high-ceilinged, cement-floored, fireproof structures which could be kept clean and sanitary and furnished plenty of light and air. But the dying and departing industries showed in 1930 a combination of all the factors constituting 'bad working conditions.' In these trades — garment, millinery, fur, artificial flower, and food industries — the shops which remained in 1930 were the dregs of the industry, those which had been too weak to join the migration to the midtown center to compete on equal terms with the rest of the industry, and which

proportion of the total Jersey fares represented workers returning from, rather than going to, work. Some who did not work actually within the area came in by elevated and then boarded the ferry, however. Information furnished by Delaware, Lackawanna and Western Railway and Hudson and Manhattan Railway Company.

[1] Distribution of 6750 employees of manufacturing establishments in Greenwich Village shown by a canvass of these establishments, October, 1930:

Men — Skilled	49 per cent	
	Unskilled	19	
	Office	3	
	Total		71 per cent
Women — Skilled	5	
	Unskilled	15	
	Office	7	
	Total		27
Unknown			2
			100 per cent

survived only by sweating labor on low piece rates and saving rent by using otherwise abandoned lofts. Such loft buildings, located mostly alongside of the elevated structure on the eastern edge of the district, were ancient, three- to five-story brick buildings with worn, rickety, dark, wooden stairs, low-ceilinged, narrow, dark rooms with small windows only at the front and rear of the building, dirty wooden floors, inadequate plumbing, and no suitable means of escape in case of fire. Some of the old buildings which housed the remains of heavy industries near the waterfront were as bad. Such local shops were regarded by the rest of their respective industries, and especially by the organized labor groups in these trades, as menaces to the standards of the respectable parts of the industry. In the neighborhood, they were known for their sweatshop conditions of work.[1]

In the artificial flower and needle trades, home work was given out. When the former was a flourishing industry and the latter was centered locally, a great deal of home work had been done in the neighborhood. Two hundred and ninety-eight of the tenement houses in the district, approximately 60 per cent of the local tenement buildings, were licensed for home work in 1930.[2]

The amount of home work greatly decreased between 1920 and 1930. Although in the latter year one could still see women sitting on the stoops on warm days making flowers or setting out in the early morning to deliver large boxes of completed flowers to the shops, flower-making was far less universal than it had been. Work was scarce and piece rates shockingly low. An occasional style flurry boomed one type of handmade ornament or another — feather novelties had a temporary resurrection while this study was in process — and women rushed for this work, but by 1930 home work on flowers and feathers brought at best a meager and uncertain supplement to a family's income.

More of the home work in 1930 was put out by the garment shops, principally men's dress coats to be hand-sewn and some babies' clothes to be embroidered. Even this work was scarce, however, and the women who got it considered themselves lucky.

[1] All material on working conditions derived from a study of 48 plants employing women to which an investigator went in the guise of a job-seeker, and from information secured from trade union headquarters.

[2] New York State Department of Labor, Division of Home Work Inspection. Bulletin listing licensed tenement houses, 1930.

They kept the place where they secured work secret from their neighbors — sometimes even trying to conceal the fact that they were doing home work at all — lest their neighbors should get the work away from them. Yet piece rates were so low as to net only a few dollars a week, perhaps three or possibly five dollars, from constant labor.

Practically all of the Village residents who were employed in local factories worked in the 'remnant' plants. Although the local people spoke emphatically of the low standards of these places and of their unwillingness to work in them, the small marginal shops, especially in the needle and artificial flower trades, were found to contain a much larger proportion of local workers than did the newer and better shops which drew workers from a wide radius. Probably the very irregularity of work, combined with the fact that these shops gave out home work, made them rely on neighborhood workers rather than on those from a distance. The shops of this sort visited in 1930 were found to contain mostly older Italian women or very young girls. The majority of the Village's residents, however, were not local factory workers and were not directly touched by the fate of local industries or of those who worked in them.[1]

Much closer to the life of the community were the local docks and the various service industries and retail trades, all of which furnished employment to local residents and some of which were patronized by them.

Shipping activity along the local waterfront and the trans-atlantic piers to the north had always been an essential feature of the neighborhood, chiefly because of the employment which it offered to dock workers. Crews were not locally recruited, all the local lines carrying steady crews with little turnover, except when the place of an occasional ship jumper or incapacitated seaman was filled at this end of the run. During the time — twelve hours to four days — that the various ships were in port, the crews lived aboard, but went ashore to patronize the speak-easies, poolrooms, and cafés that lined the waterfront. Some made their way into seamen's boarding houses. These, as well as many

[1] Cf. Odencvantz, L. C. *Italian Women in Industry*, New York, 1919, for account of Italian women workers from this locality, most of whom worked in near-by factories and two thirds of whom were under 21 years old.

of the waterfront cafés and poolrooms, were kept by and for Spanish people, although only one of the lines running boats out of the local piers reported a large proportion of Spanish in its crews.

In contrast to the crews, the longshoremen were not only re-cruited locally, but were newly recruited each time a vessel needed to be loaded or unloaded. The method of hiring men for a given job of loading or unloading was by the usual one of the 'shape' — i.e., the waiting men crowded around the hiring boss who tossed a brass check to those men whom he chose to hire for the particular job. This method of employment meant that when men went to the docks in the morning they could not know whether or not they would have work that day. If they did not get a check in one of the eight o'clock 'shapes,' there was the chance that they might in one of the noon 'shapes,' or, failing then, in a four o'clock one. This uncertainty, and the necessity of reporting for work at three different times in a day, made it necessary for longshoremen either to live near the docks so that they could go home for four hours after failing to get work, or to hang around waiting, often all day long. Longshoremen, especially those less certain of getting work, continued to live in the neighborhood when workers of other types were moving away.

The docks within the Village area belonged to lines engaged in the coastwise or river trade, or to railroads which carried freight cars from terminals in Jersey to the Manhattan piers to be un-loaded. Three of the coastwise lines brought in southern products for local distribution or transshipment and carried out mixed freight. Two others ran small vessels carrying job lots of freight to and from the Connecticut shore and the Hudson River towns. A total of approximately 35 vessels of various sizes, carrying crews aggregating about 2000 men, put out from this group of piers each week. Approximately 1000 longshoremen handled the loading and unloading of freight in 1930. In contrast to the trans-atlantic lines, where the volume of freight fell off heavily after the War, these coastwise lines continued to handle a fairly con-stant volume of freight and to run their regular vessels with little variation. But changes in the method of handling freight, and the drop in volume on the Atlantic lines, seriously affected the work of local longshoremen.

During the War, longshore work had been a flourishing trade. There was no waiting around, much overtime, a strong union, good pay, and extra rates for handling munitions, which sometimes meant as much as $80 or $90 on a Saturday night. But bit by bit the volume of work on the docks decreased, there was less to be handled on the transatlantic lines, machinery cut the number of men on a given job in half, pay went down, the union had been broken as far as the coasting trade was concerned, and by 1930 the chance of getting work was small, and that of making a decent living by it smaller yet. Irish had been the chief longshoremen in the years before and through the War — both the greenhorns, fresh from Ireland, and their sons, derisively known as 'narrowbacks' by the brawny immigrants. In 1930, they were still numerous on the transatlantic docks, where the union remained powerful, but on the Village piers their places had been taken by newer immigrants and, especially, by Negroes. The latter did not live in the neighborhood, but came in for the 'shapes.' Local Italians, Poles, Lithuanians, and Spanish worked with the Negroes and assorted West Indians and Central Americans, generally known as 'Cubians.'

Although hiring was only for the duration of each job, the shipping lines all reported that they had a certain group of men who always came to their dock and from whom each gang was regularly picked — sometimes on the basis of the most efficient, at other times in an effort to spread the limited amount of work among those who had worked for the line in the past. The hiring boss, having full power to choose at will, was in a position to give all the work to a certain few or to distribute it. As the volume of work decreased, competition became greater and it became increasingly difficult for men to get work on docks where they were not known by the boss.

The result was embittering and demoralizing to the workers of the area. The hiring boss was accused of having favorites: those who got work regularly had uncomplimentary names for the 'shenangoes' — the floaters always trying to get work who were accused of getting in the way of men who were working and of starting trouble; the Negroes and Spaniards were violently hated for ruining a decent trade and undercutting wages which the union had achieved; Negroes complained that the union discriminated against them. Italians reported that, though they were technically admitted to the union, they could not so much as use the 'longshoremen's rest' maintained by the union because the place was full of Irish ready to run them out. Efforts to organize the local docks brought strong-arm methods on both sides which resulted in 1930 in a series of three murders, including that of a union organizer, in a week.

Meantime, men went to the 'shapes' day after day and came away with no job; one or two days a week, perhaps, there might be pay to bring home; some men were found in 1930 who had gone to the docks three times a day for months and months, always hoping, and hoping only. By 1930, the once proud calling of longshoreman had become a beggar's trade. Though local residents still worked on the docks when they could get a chance, the water-front no longer furnished a principal source of employment or had any but a depressing effect on the community's life.

The cessation of immigration after 1921 had brought a further blow to the waterfront by destroying the thriving hotels and 'gyp' stores which co-operated, with their system of runners, to rid both arriving and returning immigrants of their surplus cash. In the heyday of immigration, two or more of these 'gyp' stores in each waterfront block carried on a legitimate business in overalls and work clothes with the local dock workers and vied with each other in the ability to secure from the immigrants fabulous prices for suits which were hopelessly faded, out of style, or even lacking a sleeve. After 1921, these stores continued to thrive for a time on sales to prosperous returning immigrants, equipping them to make an impression on their home villages by a veritable network of watch chains across their vests and an array of fountain pens — 'I sent a man who couldn't write his name home to Portugal with five in a row,' boasted a 'gyp' store salesman — sticking out of their breast pockets. But by 1930, all but a very few of these stores had gone and the remaining ones were reduced to a meager legiti-mate business, while such of the hotels as survived were chiefly patronized by a few retired old men who had been around docks or ships all their lives and wanted to end their days on the water-front.

The various parts of the local amusement industry — cabarets, tea rooms, and speakeasies — were partly operated by local people and partly by outsiders, they gave employment to local residents, and they were more or less closely interwoven with various aspects of the community's life. Tea rooms and cabarets differed essentially in the fact that the latter were almost purely business ventures, while the former were frequently run to serve a definite social function as well. They resembled each other in their common effort to capitalize some aspect of the Village's reputation. The district became a center for speakeasies, both because of the Village's reputation which drew patrons and of the presence of local residents particularly well equipped to operate a liquor industry, especially an illegal industry. The cabarets were the business ventures of outsiders, though some of the earliest cabaret proprietors had been among the early backflow of residents who discovered the Village. The tea rooms were chiefly in the hands of people who had come to live in the Village and who identified themselves with their patrons sometimes to the point of being unable to talk about them with detachment because of their emotional feeling about 'their people.' The speakeasies were operated by the local Italians and constituted the chief industry, which not only was located in the Village, but was owned and manned locally and brought profits to the community.

At the beginning of the period, it was primarily the tea room which brought to the Village outsiders seeking amusement and excitement. In the mid-years of the decade the cabaret had risen to prominence if not to first place. By the close, both had been eclipsed by the speakeasy.

The tea rooms were numerous throughout the decade — forty would be a conservative estimate (depending somewhat upon definition) for any one time. Though some continued to operate throughout the decade, their life was frequently short — 'I've been here quite a while, nearly five months,' reported one proprietor — and they ranged all the way from those which featured good food and taste to those which served little besides 'atmosphere.' They drew upon the artistic or intellectual side of the Village's reputation, using local celebrities as baits and gaining their clientèle by advertising their well-known steady customers. So-and-so was to be seen or heard at such-and-such a place. The tea rooms really belonged to the bohemian stage of the Village and the proprietors were capitalizing essentially the spirit of bohemia. They were patronized by both local residents and up-town or out-of-town amusement-seekers, some of the former furnishing the attraction for the latter.

The cabarets drew on the Village's exotic reputation rather than its intellectual or artistic fame. They had little direct connection with the locality, except as a few of the girls who lived in the neighborhood acted as hostesses. They had no reason to continue to operate when they ceased to be a business success.

Characteristically, the Village cabarets sold 'atmosphere' rather than the glitter and nudity which brought high profits to midtown night clubs. Those who patronized them got their thrills by being served in the atmosphere of a pirate's lair, a jail cell with waiters in convict stripes, amid the topsy-turvy decorations of a 'nut club,' or by trying to mount an old-fashioned high bicycle at a county fair and dancing among the overalled hayseeds of a village barn.

Cabarets began to come into the Village shortly before 1920. They reached their heyday in the middle of the decade and then entered a decline as the Village became too well known and ordinary to be sought for a really exciting evening and its attractions were eclipsed by the rising fame of Harlem. Village cabarets were relatively low-priced and were patronized more by college boys and girls out for a good time and less by 'sugar daddies' with chorus girls than were the midtown night clubs. By 1930, the Village reputation was no longer a sufficient attraction to draw patrons, but the district had become sufficiently a night-club center for some places, which did not feature the Village at all, to be established there. In 1930, the most crowded of the cabarets was a newly established, disreputable edition of Harlem, located some distance away from the Village's cabaret center.

The economic importance of the night clubs to the Village was not great. About half of the wages and payment for supplies went to local people — the rest outside.[1] Cabaret patrons had no dealings with other local trades, except to buy liquor on the way in or to tip the small boy who opened the taxi door. Between 1921 and 1924, the property-owners' association regarded them as bad for land values, and engineered a police drive to 'clean up' objectionable places.

[1] From canvass of cabaret proprietors.

Their patrons came almost exclusively from outside of the locality. Four places in 1930 had some slight local patronage, one because it had been in operation since the early years, was a cross between a cabaret and a tea room, and had a group of patrons who had used the tea-room part for years as a meeting place and a 'pick-up joint.' This place, however, depended upon outside for its chief patronage and did its advertising in smart metropolitan magazines and in the railway stations of suburban Westchester. Two other places received some local patronage because they served good dollar dinners before their night-club clientèle arrived, while the fourth had a Lesbian reputation and used some local girls as hostesses and attracted a few others as patrons.

The cabaret did, however, bring onto the Village streets a collection of irresponsible people whose effect upon the local youngsters was regarded with some apprehension by social workers and the crime prevention division of the police.

If accurate information could be secured, it might well be found that the principal industry of the Village in the later years of the decade, both in terms of the numbers of residents engaged in it and the income brought from it, was some form or other of bootlegging. Obviously, no such detailed information could be secured, and it was only possible to trace the exodus of the old saloon and the development of the new industry from small and disreputable beginnings until it became the leading and most respected industry in the locality with its business standards and practices, its political protection, and its high- and low-class patronage.

In the manner of similar districts, especially those inhabited by Irish, the Village of pre-Prohibition days had been liberally supplied with old-fashioned corner saloons. Most of these had had Irish proprietors, except for a few Germans whose beer gardens resembled the 'gin mills' of the Irish. The proprietors of these saloons had been leading citizens, frequently politicians — a third of the 57 saloonkeepers in and near the Village of whom a record could be secured had been in politics — prosperous and respected in the local community. Their places were rarely visited by such of the new residents as came to live in the district before Prohibition, and, of course, they attracted no trade — except that of the factory workers within the locality — from other parts of town.

With the coming of Prohibition, practically all of these old saloons went out of business. In fact, most closed prior to the national act in response to wartime Prohibition. In the 57 which have been traced — either within the area or similar 'places' in the immediate vicinity — the proprietors retired with a competency, they sent their children to college and into politics, the professions, or the Church; if they had not done so previously, they moved to a comfortable home in a good neighborhood; perhaps they took a trip to Ireland. All but two were in comfortable, often wealthy, circumstances. Only five of these old saloonkeepers or their sons continued to carry on the liquor business either in the old or in a new locality. The post-Prohibition liquor industry was a new business with new people, new methods, and a new clientèle.

Immediately after the advent of Prohibition, little liquor was sold, and that mostly of bad quality by the more lawless element. These ran the first of the local speakeasies, dingy, 'hole-in-the-wall' places, stowed away with utmost secrecy and entered only with knock and password by those who were known. To enter one of these places and to drink exorbitantly priced stuff of very doubtful origin — alcohol at $40 a gallon, gin at $5 or more a quart — was to run no insignificant risk. Patrons for the most part were not from the immediate locality, but were persons from uptown and the suburbs who wanted to taste the wild life of Greenwich Village. Local Irish and bohemians lacked the prices asked, and the Italians still preferred their homemade wine to bad whiskey or gin.

The repeal of the New York State Enforcement Act in 1923 gave a tremendous stimulus to local industry. Here as elsewhere the Italians had always made their own wines. Now that wine became a marketable product, Italian grocers added it to the products which they offered for sale, and restaurant-keepers who had in the past served wine with their dinners made a feature out of the wine. Individuals, mostly Italian, but, especially in the waterfront speakeasies, some Irish, German, and Spanish as well, became liquor-sellers exclusively.

But the business of selling liquor was still a rough proposition. One of the most reputable dealers in the district made a practice of setting up customers to drinks until they were in a condition to buy much more than they meant to and kept a taxi at the door ready to take such customers as emerged drunk down to the waterfront to be robbed. The quality of the liquor was still very doubtful, and prices fantastic. Only the daring entered speak-easies to buy. Deliveries were a dangerous business.

In 1930, this same house had its steady and eminently respect-able customers — local and non-local, Irish, new residents, politicians, teachers, professional and business people. Its liquor was regularly subjected to chemical tests before being sold. Prices were moderate and were being forced lower by acute competition. The only relic of its earlier character which it retained was kept as a souvenir, and 'just in case' — a piece of half-inch steel cable, at one end doubly thick and dipped in lead. 'Never hit a guy in the head with this,' the visitor who was shown the 'souvenir' was advised. 'You'll split him open like a dropped watermelon. Hit him on the shoulder or the back. It's safer.' The proprietors of this and similar establishments were among the most highly regarded of local residents, admired for the succession of new and each time more handsome cars, regarded as a good matrimonial catch by neighborhood girls.

The sale of liquor had become a very extensive and reputable occupation. Every sort of store — grocer, cigar store, barber shop, bootblack, etc. — sold some form of the prohibited beverage. According to the opinion of one of the oldest and best established of the Italian delicatessen storekeepers, none of the grocers on side streets and few of those on the main shopping streets could make ends meet in 1930 without the income from their wine or other liquor. To discover all the places which sold liquor in 1930 would have been an utter impossibility. 'Do you want to go into every store in the Village?' inquired a young man who had the reputation of knowing the industry pretty well. When asked for a list of places, he produced some thirty addresses and added, '*and* every Italian barber, bootblack, cigar store, and grocer.' 'Times certainly are different,' remarked one housewife. 'In the old days you never would have thought of buying your wine at the fish store.' In the fall of the year, truckloads of grapes might be seen being unloaded in front of tenements or stores, the remains of mash purpled the gutters, and women grocery-store keepers apologized for the condition of their hands as they weighed their vegetables. The number of liquor producing and distributing establishments in and near the Village was placed by the local police in the thousands in 1930.

Though the sale of hard liquor had also become widespread, it was somewhat more specialized than the sale of wine. Whereas in the wild days the alcohol used had been of doubtful origin and quality, the later supply was mostly standard stuff. Except for the drinks sold for consumption on the premises, bottled hard liquor to take out was handled by a relatively small number of well-established dealers. The chief competitors here were not the miscellaneous grocery stores and barber shops, but, newly developed near the close of the period, the 'cordial shop' — fly-by-night affairs, renting a store on Friday, setting carpenters to work and being ready for business by Saturday night, here today and there tomorrow — operating on a minimum of capital and constituting a pest to the well-established bootlegger whom they undersold.

Liquor for consumption on the premises was sold chiefly in two types of places, Italian restaurants operating behind more or less securely locked doors, or wide open with liquor sales sometimes limited to known patrons, and bars closely resembling the old-fashioned saloon except that the liquor was cut, prices high, women usually admitted and prominent, and locations less conspicuous. Even to canvass such places was an impossible task. A sample of 100 of the better known, more substantial, and centrally located places, 44 of which were visited in the fall of 1930, yielded, however, a certain amount of descriptive data. Though the sample was small, the highly competitive character of the industry made it reasonable to suppose that other less well-known places would be forced to adopt similar measures to stay in the business.

This sketchy sample showed certain distinctions between the Italian restaurants, the bars, and the places selling liquor to take out. Apart from a very few of the purveyors of bottled liquor, the Italian restaurant, catering to a respectable, partly uptown clientèle, appeared to be the oldest, averaging four years in business. The newest were the 'cordial shops,' all less than a year old, while the bars were either unstable or of recent origin, and the tendency of stores to add liquor to their other lines appeared to be growing. The restaurants were the most numerous and depended upon uptown clientèle for a quarter to a half of their custom, while, except for one very large bar where two thirds of the patrons were non-local, the bars catered more to local people. By 1930, however, competition had taken much of the profit out of the restaurant-speakeasy business. In order to attract patrons, restaurants of this type had lowered the price or improved the quality of their meals to the point where their table tended to be far superior to what could be purchased at a similar price in a place not serving liquor, the proprietors counting for their profits largely on the sale of liquor. The customer who failed to order wine was regarded reproachfully by the waiter. If he should comment on the excellence of the food, the waiter would hintingly tell him, 'The boss, he lose money on this dinner.' One proprietor was reputed to be taking a daily loss of $20 on the food which he served in order to sell his drinks.

The bars visited were those patronized by the residents of the Village or by outsiders. Catering to the local population were also characteristic places — Spanish poolrooms, seamen's boarding houses and cafés, longshoremen's hangouts, and the Italian men's cafés. These had retained their pre-Volstead aspects, except for the fact that those run by Irish and especially those for longshoremen were to be found in back kitchens instead of on conspicuous corners. A few old-style saloons, so called and so operated, survived among certain of the Irish groups, semi-political hangouts, true to the old type of men's saloon. Their patrons and proprietors had a hearty contempt for the newfangled speakeasy bars where women were as constantly present as men. The principal political clubs had, of course, places in or near the clubhouse.

The great majority of speakeasy proprietors were local residents, as were, with few exceptions, their help. Both they and their help were Italian, except for some of the Irish barkeepers who not infrequently dated from pre-Volstead days and had come back into the business while their old employers, the saloon proprietors, retired. Out of 44 places of all sorts, which were visited, 34 were operated by local residents, 8 by persons whose residence was not discovered, and only 2 by individuals known to live elsewhere. In these 44 places, the total number of employees was approximately 200, the number per establishment varying from an average of 5.5 in the various types of restaurant to 3.5 at the bars. There was no possible way to estimate the total number of persons engaged in the local business at any time or gaining any or all of their income from it. It can certainly be said, however, that the liquor business in one form or another was the chief new source of employment or income for residents of the area — especially the Italian residents — during the second half of the decade.

As far as the retail distribution of liquor was concerned, the business was in the hands of small individual proprietors. Back of these individuals stood the more highly organized parts of the industry. The manufacture of wine, like the retailing of all spirits, was also organized on a highly individualistic basis. Hard liquor, likewise, was compounded by the bootleggers out of alcohol and essences as an individual enterprise. Alcohol, in turn, came from two sources, individuals who operated private stills — one of the local hardware stores kept copper stills on display in its window — and wholesalers who either operated larger stills or secured access to government or other supplies and passed them along to the bootleggers.

Among all these parts of the business, the basis of operation in 1930 was a strictly business one. The old days when the industry had no standards were passed. To be sure, bills were sometimes collected at the point of the gun since they could not be collected by law. The means taken to eliminate competition might be drastic, though no direct notice of such came to the attention of this investigation. Even violent measures, however, had become part of the recognized business code. A group of girls were heard to discuss the proprietor of the bar where the brother of one of the girls worked. One of two partners had left that bar and set up for himself a short distance away on the same street. It was too bad, they said, because the first partner would be sure to 'give him his,' and after all he was a nice man — but what could he expect when he set up in competition like that?

The regular bootleggers handled wine and hard liquor only, leaving beer to be sold over the bars. In contrast to the wholesale alcohol and whiskey business, the beer business was entirely monopolized for this as for other areas, all retailers securing their supplies from the same source.

Although the industry was an illegal one, by 1930 it had become practically as open and aboveboard as a legitimate trade. An Italian woman might give a stranger whom she encountered in a grocery store a card to her husband's place, urging her to bring her friends. Apartment dwellers received almost daily advertisements from new dealers, especially cordial shops, containing price lists for gin, rye, and Scotch with the announcement that 'We pay protection. We defy all. Local and federal immunity.' [1]

The amount expended for protection could not be discovered, but the form of the protection was well known. In the early days of the industry, before the repeal of the State Enforcement Law, both federal men and local police superiors received their 'envelopes' — cash fees, commonly $50. Common patrolmen were kept friendly with occasional presents of liquor or small fees and were paid therewith for warning proprietors when the federals were around. Jealousy between local and federal branches of the enforcement service helped to protect all dealers except those who did not 'come across.' Cases were on record in which the local police refused aid when federals raided one of their local customers.

After the repeal of the State Enforcement Act, the local police, formerly the more serious problem of the two, were no longer a problem, and only the federals continued to collect their 'envelopes.' The latter made such a good thing of it that on at least one occasion gangsters masqueraded as federal men and shook down a number of the local bootleggers, until the real federals came around to warn dealers not to pay protection to the fakes. It remained necessary, however, to keep both local police and local politicians friendly as a guaranty of immunity from enforcement of the civil code which was incidentally violated in the course of doing business. The police and politicians, therefore, continued to receive their 'packages' — i.e., liquor — and, in the case of restaurants, entertainment for their guests at the proprietor's expense or even meals sent to the station house. Regular contributions to the political clubs took the additional form of 'advertisements' in the program of the club's annual banquet.

All this was accepted as part of the cost of doing business — contributions in kind being preferred to those in money because

[1] Cordial shop advertisement, received by mail, February, 1932.

of the feeling about any liquor stocks that their value was uncertain so long as they might be seized, while the value of money was well known. Those who were regular in their payments counted on being warned before a raid so that they could remove all their valuable stores from the premises. They counted, too, on being able to make life more disagreeable for any hostile policeman whose beat included their location than the latter could make trouble for them. It was the boast of one establishment that when a young and zealous member of the force had attempted to annoy them by giving tickets for automobile parking, speeding, loitering, littering the street, excessive noise, etc., they 'had him transferred so far out in the jungles that he could go hunting rabbits on his beat.' Indignation was expressed only when payment was made so that a raid would not be conducted and the raid was made just the same. Padlocking was met by immediate migration to a new location in the vicinity.

Periodically, of course, a nervous panic swept over the industry as the policy of the prohibition force was changed. But on the whole, the business jogged along, all the family turning to and working, paying protection, fighting competitors, advertising to the public, its most successful members swanking around in fine cars, and bringing to an increasing proportion of the local population a supplementary income and a supplementary prestige.

Like the liquor business, service industries and retail trades were an integral part of the life of the community as the factories were not, the majority of the stores being owned and operated by local residents, employing local labor, and serving one group or another of the local residents. Most of the cafeterias and lunch rooms relied for a portion of their trade — sometimes a large portion — on the daytime factory and business population. Half of the fifty canvassed in 1930 reported that their busiest time was at noon, and another third were equally busy at noon and at night. A small group of antique jewelry, Russian blouse, and gift shops which lined the route from the subway to the night clubs catered to the evening amusement-seekers. Though the gas stations served transients chiefly, all but two of the twenty-one garages housed neighborhood cars or trucks. The rest of the four hundred or more neighborhood shops depended on neighborhood patronage.

One group of these shops had come in to serve the new apartment population, the other had been part of the old neighborhood. A few stores — some groceries, delicatessen, or shoe repairing shops — drew their custom from both old and new residents, but most served either one type or the other predominantly. It was not only that the apartment people furnished the principal demand for dry cleaners and hand laundries, while the barber shops and clothing stores were predominantly patronized by local people. The style of store, quite as much as its products, varied according to the group served. 'I decided long ago,' explained an Italian delicatessen-storekeeper, 'that I couldn't be both an American and an Italian store. My Italian customers wanted to take their time and bargain. The Americans wanted quick service and a fixed price. I had to choose — so I made my place an American store.'

The chief types of store to come in with the apartments were tailoring, dry cleaning, and hand laundries. Ninety per cent of the establishments of these types in the district in 1930 had come in during the last ten and the majority during the last five years.[1] A canvass of stores in 1930 revealed a larger number of tailoring and cleaning shops than of any other type of store. The stores which disappeared with the moving-out of tenement dwellers were chiefly the clothing stores. Eighty per cent of the clothing stores still operating in 1930 had been in business there for over ten years. At least twice as many such stores were doing business locally in 1920 as in 1930.

The stores especially designed to serve the apartment dwellers found the neighborhood an increasingly favorable one for business. Those which had served the old residents on the blocks which were in process of reclamation found it difficult or impossible to adapt themselves to the new. Only a very occasional greengrocery or delicatessen store succeeded in adapting its wares and its displays so as to attract the newcomers. The butchers chorused their stock complaint about the 'two chops' which were all that the apartment people ever bought and most of the old grocers eked out their diminishing regular income with liquor sales. Although having to meet the competition of chain stores, none blamed the chains for their economic distress, but all attributed it to the popu-

[1] From canvass of stores, 1930.

lation shift. The stores which handled durable goods — clothing, furniture, musical instruments, jewelry — found themselves suffering not only from the departure of their old customers and the fact that the apartment residents habitually shopped for this type of goods in the midtown shopping center rather than at the neighborhood store, but from the tendency of those of their old patrons who remained in the locality also to do this type of shopping in the midtown area.

All types of stores and shops combined to employ something over fifteen hundred people, in 1930, as proprietors or workers, distributed among more than four hundred shops. The shops were typically small, averaging two and a half employees per store. Tailors, grocers, barbers, delicatessen, clothing, and beauty shops all averaged less than two employees per shop. Bakeries, garages, restaurants, and drugstores hired from four to six workers on the average and employed among them more than half of those engaged in service or retail trade in the locality.

The largest number of stores were, naturally, kept by Italians, who operated three quarters of the groceries, meat and fish markets, bakeries, barber shops and shoe repair shops. Americans and Jews ran the next largest number, the Americans concentrating on lunch rooms, drugstores, garages, and beauty parlors, while the Jews ran the majority of the clothing, tailoring, and laundry businesses. A scattering of Germans, chiefly in food stores, and a number of Armenian tailors and grocers who had no connection with the neighborhood outside of their trades, accounted for most of the rest of the local business, apart from an occasional Greek restaurant, French pastry, or Chinese laundry.

The storekeeper's status in the community depended in part on his type of store. Those who served the apartment population gained no local status thereby, whether they resided locally or kept their residence outside. Among the more prosperous of the old storekeepers, a number had moved to Brooklyn and commuted to work, while others had stayed, declaring that their property was not safe in the neighborhood unless they were there to watch it. On the whole, it was the smaller, less pretentious of the shopkeepers who retained their local residence, and, with few exceptions, they were not distinguished from their neighbors by either their wealth or social position.

2. WORK AND INCOME

The greater part of the Village population was dependent for its livelihood on no local activity, industrial, longshore, mercantile, or other, but was employed in miscellaneous occupations throughout the city. Three quarters of the gainfully employed in 1930 were engaged in service trades, transportation and communication, trade, and professional or semi-professional activity — all types of work which involved scattered employment rather than mass labor. Only a fifth were employed in manufacturing.[1]

As a result, Village residents were not bound together, as are employees of one mill or workers in a single trade, by work contacts or common work experience. Earning a living was a matter of catch-as-catch-can, not of following a fixed course or occupying a fixed place. Diversity of occupation, the small proportion of the population which worked in the locality, and the fact that the most usual type of job was largely self-directing rather than subject to the regimentation of an industrial plant and the watchful eye of a foreman, were all factors inimical to economic solidarity. When men and women came home from work, they did not bring home with them any common knowledge of the conditions in the shops which they had left. The longshoremen were the only substantial element in the community whose work groups carried over as social groups.

In these circumstances, class consciousness was almost completely absent among the industrial workers of the locality. The people of this community were not 'workers' in any self-conscious sense, conscious of occupying a place in the economic system. Trade-union membership was, and had always been, small, and trade unions played no important role in local life. The longshoremen on the transatlantic docks were organized, but not those who worked for the local, coastwise lines after the strike of 1921. Some of the seamen were organized, but not the Spanish who occupied the local seamen's boarding houses. There were truckdrivers' unions, but none for the taxi drivers, and few of the truck drivers from the locality belonged to unions. The barbers of this section of the city had not been organized, though an effort had been made by a local group to introduce a union. The union

[1] *U.S. Census, 1930.* Cf. Table VII, Appendix F, p. 466.

of Italian tile-layers was the only one with sufficient local membership to maintain a local office. For the rest, a scattered membership of masons and carpenters and a handful of food and garment workers completed the roll of organized workers in the locality. Printers were organized in nineteen of the local near-by shops, and a number of these lived in the neighborhood.

'Labor' interest had never been sufficient to bring out a crowd for any sort of local labor meetings. The local neighborhood house held such meetings from time to time over a period of years without arousing interest or support. Only after the depression had deepened and unemployment had become chronic and widespread did the appeal for joint action meet with any substantial response. Class consciousness was not traditional to the Italians and Irish of this neighborhood as it was to the Germans and Russian Jews of the East Side, nor was it bred by American experience.

The sharp distinction between the business class and the working class that was found in the Middletown study was not characteristic of this community, where occupational lines were not clearly drawn, the same family contained a wide range of occupations, and families changed their economic status radically with the addition of children's earnings. The white-collar worker among the new residents was as far from the Italian and Irish stenographers as from their sisters who worked in clothing factories. The single girls who lived in the remodeled houses were just as inaccessible to the Italian bank clerk as to his brother the taxi driver. The Italian business man was as likely to marry the daughter of an Italian workman as an Irish girl at his own economic level. Social divisions ran through this community along other than economic lines, primarily.

In the economic experience of this community, it was not economic so much as political power which created the most obvious economic problems — it was not the 'bosses' who stood in the way of an adequate living for the workingman, so much as those who had the power to exact some sort of toll or withhold some favor.

For the many people who depended upon the sale of liquor at least to supplement, if not to furnish, their incomes, the enforcement of Prohibition was a major economic problem as well as a political one. The 'federal men' were the real economic enemies, the butt of that widespread resentment reserved, in more class-conscious circles, for the exploiters of labor. Legitimate business, too, was under obligation to, or in danger from, the politicians. A storekeeper's profits depended in part upon his sales and in part upon how much protection money he had to pay — and the presumption always was that part, at least, of the protection money found its way into the politicians' pockets. A landlord's income was partly determined by his rents and partly by his taxes, which were at least believed to vary substantially with difference in political contacts. A pushcart owner considered it the better part of wisdom to remain a loyal Democrat, lest some excuse be found for revoking his license.

The political club was assumed to be the best aid in securing employment, not only on city jobs, but in private industry as well. Other organized methods of finding employment were virtually nil. A study of the job histories of a hundred persons who were unemployed in December, 1930, showed that these had always found jobs in the past through friends, relatives, or the chance reading of signs. Employment agencies in the locality were confined to the placing of hotel help, and other city-wide agencies were expected either to cheat those who applied or to be of no use. None compared in efficacy with the pull that could be exercised by local political leaders. The Irish, with their preference for civil service positions, were, of course, especially interested in the jobs which were directly at the disposal of politicians. The Italians, by 1930, had begun to look increasingly in the same direction. From a number, the question, 'What does American citizenship mean to you?' brought the answer, 'A city job.' Since the whole political system was thoroughly accepted as the inevitable *status quo*, it is easy to see how economic forces were obscured by the political influences which bore so obviously upon the economic position of local residents. In these circumstances, it is not surprising that a common economic interest was not the basis for local organization.

Some difference in status did go with specific occupations, especially among the Irish, who recognized a clear occupational hierarchy from common labor via longshore work and truck driving, through the building trade to the civil service, with politics, law, the Church, and business, especially real estate at the top.[1] Although more income tended to go with more highly regarded occupations, this was by no means universally the case, and type of work was rated on the basis of social standing rather than income.

The Irish young people were reluctant to reveal their father's occupations when they were low in the occupational scale. They were on the defensive about their own occupations as well, feeling the limitation of status which their own jobs entailed and always thinking in terms of the occupational group above them. In describing the neighborhood, moveover, the Irish consistently thought in terms of the better rather than the lower occupational groups which were represented. In spite of the fact that a large proportion of the Irish boys were taxi drivers and automobile mechanics, a group of Irish mothers commented that the trade training of the continuation school was more suited to the 'foreigners' on the East Side than to 'the kind of jobs held in this neighborhood.'

The occupational preferences which prevailed among the Italians carried little in the way of distinctive status. The more ambitious Italian families retained a strong desire to place their boys in professional occupations — especially as doctors — and to secure a professional man as a son-in-law. Cases were found where very high dowries had been offered if a marriage could be arranged with a professional man. Parents abandoned their prejudice against clerical work on the chance that by working in a professional man's office a girl might get a professional husband. A number of families were found who put direct pressure on their children to become professional workers, especially doctors, and made considerable sacrifices in order to make this possible. Both social workers and prominent Italians reported that it was frequently the parents who had ambitions in this direction while the children were indifferent.

Apart from the pressure toward professions, the Italian group recognized little social advantage in one job over another and showed slight interest in steering their children into any particular line of work. Respect for craftsmanship had been reduced by 1930 to a gauge of security — a man with a trade might function any-

[1] Cf. below, Chapter VII.

where, whereas one whose occupation depended upon particular local conditions would be less flexibly and securely placed. As one mother expressed it to her son who was working as a mechanic and delivering for a bootlegger at the same time, 'Stick to your trade. You could be a mechanic in China, but where else could you be a bootlegger?' Even this much respect for the skilled trade was waning. It was the observation of social workers that whereas ten years before Italian families tried to send their boys to a trade school, in 1930 a few tried to have them learn stenography, while most left them to drift into any occupation whatever.

Among the younger generation, there was some distinction in status between the white-collar and the industrial worker. The glorification of the 'white-collar' job which beset America during these years did not pass this community by. The young people tended to fall into groups according to whether they were office workers or industrial workers, but groups did not keep strictly within these lines. It was usually possible to say of any group of young people, 'These are mostly office workers,' or, 'These are mostly factory workers'; but the fact that it was always necessary to include the qualification 'mostly' indicated that the division was not sharp.

The chief advantage accorded to clerical work was that conditions of work were pleasanter and, for girls especially, there was greater opportunity to meet a higher class of people. It was in these terms that the desirability of clerical as against factory work was consistently described. Girls were ready to do anything in their power to meet a higher class of men, and the 'college man' was the ambition of the local girl. There was always the possibility, as they learned from the movies, that they might marry a millionaire. It was with this possibility in mind that one large group of young girls expressed their desire to become movie actresses. Others, older, and with more freedom of action, sought out exclusive beaches in the summer time in the hope of a successful, high-class pick-up. When a clerical worker at a local clinic married one of the doctors, the clinic was besieged with applications for jobs, and parents who had been doubtful about permitting daughters to work there began insisting that they get clerical training on the chance of their getting in. The possibility of marrying one of superior status was, certainly for the girls, the strongest element in the drive toward clerical work in preference to shop work.

It was, thus, what clerical work might lead to rather than the work itself which carried social status. Of itself it did not give a girl sufficient superiority to affect her eligibility. To the young men, the categories 'office worker,' 'shopgirl,' 'home girl' distinguished types which were more or less distinct. The office worker was assumed to be more refined than the shopgirl who worked in the ten-cent store or in a factory; she was presumably a 'higher type.' But when it came to individual girls, the consideration was of minor importance. If a girl had the normal requirements of good looks, sociability, and a family that did not insist that she be home too early in the evening, she could be sure that being a 'shopgirl' would not seriously stand in her way. A girl did not spoil her chances of a good match by working in a factory, except as the men whom she had the opportunity to meet at work were less desirable.

In the case of men, the job, quite naturally, made more difference, and had more to do with status. But it was a subordinate consideration in any ranks below the professional, except as special prestige was attached to some occupation, such as bootlegging. It was of sufficient importance, however, so that boys made their job sound as nearly like white-collar occupations as possible. The 'clerks' who turned out to be 'shipping clerks' — i.e., the boys who loaded parcels onto trucks — were characteristic cases.

As between members of the same sex, the difference between clerical and industrial occupations was a measure of personal character rather than of social status. Because the pressure to enter the white-collar rank was so strong from school and other sources, it had become almost synonymous with ambition. The white-collar worker was one who had stayed in school or had gone to night school, thus setting himself apart from the others who 'took just any job' when they got out of school and did not have the ambition to go on. Those young people who regarded white-collar workers more highly than those in industry assumed that the former possessed ambition, refinement, and seriousness, in contrast to the careless, take-things-as-they-come attitude attributed to those who had not sought to follow the white-collar gospel. Girls in offices looked upon the 'low type' who 'just go into shops' as lacking in taste and ambition. It was in these terms, rather than in terms of social classes, that lines were drawn.

Nowhere, however, were occupational lines clearly drawn, for the same family might contain a wide range of occupations. A family did not take its status from the occupation of the father where working children were at different occupational levels. Among the Italians, especially, the occupational gap between parents and children was frequently very great. There was, consequently, a tendency for the children to disassociate themselves socially from their parents or for social status to be independent of occupation.

One occupation had come by 1930 to carry such social prestige as to place it in a class by itself — namely, bootlegging. Anything which had to do with bootlegging or the operation of a speakeasy gave status to those who participated, especially among the younger Italians. The only type of independent business in which the younger Italians were interested in engaging was the liquor business. To work for a bootlegger conferred a measure of prestige. One person so engaged reported that all the girls 'fell for him' as soon as they found out his occupation. A girl whose younger brother had just taken a job in a speakeasy was worried for fear he would go back on his own girl and get his head turned now that he was working in a speakeasy, because the girls were already beginning to go after him. Another girl confessed that she would give anything to get her hands on a good bootlegger for a husband. The enthusiasm for persons engaged in this business was partly based upon the idea that anyone so engaged must be rich. The young bootlegger just quoted reported that he did not have to spend money on girls because they assumed that he had it and he, therefore, did not have to show off. Those who were close to the trade, however, were quite sure that it carried a prestige value beyond the assumption that the trade was lucrative. Even the neighborhood fear of being a 'sucker' yielded to the eagerness to do errands for a bootlegger with or without pay. The glamour of an illicit and somewhat dangerous calling held a powerful attraction. Those girls who haughtily talked about the other girls who 'fell for the kind of guy that you and I wouldn't tumble for' seemed, from the evidence at hand, to be in the minority.

Difference in income had even less effect on social status than difference in occupation — except at the extremes — for, among the old residents, such differences were chiefly the result of differences in the number of workers in a family in proportion to the number to be supported out of the family income.

With the exception of the few professional men, some shopkeepers, and the bootleggers, difference in income between one wage-earner and another was so slight that the economic status of families could not vary widely if it depended upon the earnings of any individual member. During most of the period studied, the number of family members who were working was a more important consideration than the number supported. When, in 1930, the problem of unemployment became acute, the number to be supported started to loom larger than the number who could work. Even at this time, however, a number of possible workers in the family increased the possibility that someone would have a job and the whole family would not go breadless. Families were consistently described as well off because 'they are all working for it,' or poorly off because only one member — father, mother, or child — was working.

The range of wages for the majority of the population was not great. The mass of factory, white-collar workers, skilled trades, and small businesses received wages of $20 to $35 per week with little variation from 1921 through 1930. Women factory workers earned less; skilled craftsmen and small business men made more, irregularly, and, in the case of small-store keepers, with the aid of the labor of other members of the family. The difference of $15 a week between the upper and the lower range of the general wage level was not such as to make a radical difference in living standard or social status. A few more mouths to feed, a slightly better flat, a little more sickness or irregularity of work, and the differential would disappear. It was never easy to maintain a family on the wage of the general run of inhabitants of this locality, and those heads of families whose earnings were not supplemented were able to provide little more than the bare necessities, if that. Home work by mothers, though usually bringing in only $3 to $5 a week, often meant the difference between being able to make ends meet or not, and the decrease in home work available was seriously felt by families whose position above the subsistence level depended on this slight supplement. It was when the children became old enough to go to work, or the mother went out to work, that the situation of the family changed, and extras could begin to be provided.

How completely a family's status might change was well illustrated by a family of six children, three of whom, in 1930, were of working age. In 1920, the children of this family came to school inadequately clad and went to bed hungry. They lived in the cheapest flat they could find, paid the rent when they could, and scraped along as best they might on the father's inadequate earnings, which never amounted to more than $18 a week. In 1930, this same family presented a very different picture. The oldest boy was an electrician, working steadily at his trade; in the evenings, he made deliveries for one of the local bootleggers, making an additional $10 a week by this means. The second brother was running a small gas station from which he brought in about $18 a week. The daughter was working in a factory, and the little brother, still in school, was making his two or three dollars a week opening taxi doors for the patrons of speakeasies. The father was still conscientiously earning his $18, but instead of scraping along in a meager flat they were living in one of the best of the houses that contained any Italian families — the only other Italian occupant, in fact, was the well-to-do landlord — paying what was for the local Italians the phenomenal sum of $70 rent per month.

The change in position of this family had nothing of the unusual to it, except, perhaps, the fact that it remained in the neighborhood. In many ways it was a thoroughly typical family. The parents had come from the south of Italy at the height of the migration to the district, had come directly to the neighborhood, and had here remained, moving about from block to block, but never leaving the district. At the time of arrival, the parents had been young people in their twenties — corresponding in age to the bulk of immigrants; their children had been born in the years when births in the neighborhood were at the maximum. The six who survived were more than the average, but far from unique. The parents were of no special background or capacity. The children varied in their intelligence and seriousness. None of the three older went through high school, but the younger were intending to. They entered obvious occupations and made fair, but in no sense extraordinary, earnings. The only 'break' of a special character was having the bootlegger for whom the older brother worked help to set up the younger in his modest gas station. Otherwise the story of this family might have been the story of any ordinary Italian family in the neighborhood.

The change in the proportion of the family which was earning, in the many families whose age composition resembled this one, added substantially to the income level of the community during these years. It was a common generalization in 1930 that the area had become much more prosperous than it had been ten years before. In part this generalization, made by teachers, social workers, real estate dealers, and individual residents, merely reflected the temper of 'prosperity' which characterized the boom years; in part it arose from the impression of prosperity lent by the gains of those who had gambled successfully in the stock of the Bank of Italy or had become the *nouveaux riches* of the liquor traffic; in part it reflected the higher standard of living made temporarily possible by the popularity of installment selling and the fact that the younger generation was wearing silk stockings along with everybody else. There were some in the neighborhood who realistically discounted these factors and insisted, 'Nobody but the bootleggers are making anything in this neighborhood. Times haven't been good for the workingman since the War.' But behind the external semblance which, unquestionably, gave an appearance of prosperity relative to 1920 which was in excess of the fact, and in spite of the fact that there was little change in wage rates to permit a higher standard of living, there was a real change in status for that great group of families whose children had, during the period, reached working age and begun to contribute to the family income.

A large proportion of such families had moved out by 1930, using the children's earnings to pay the first installments on the house on Long Island. Some unfortunates, described with a little malice by their old neighbors who had 'had the sense' to stay in the neighborhood, found themselves saddled with a house in a strange neighborhood for which they could not pay when the children on whose earnings they had counted married and used those earnings to set up for themselves. The wise ones commented knowingly, 'What did they expect? Of course the girls wanted a better house to receive their friends in so that they could make a good match.' To the extent that the more prosperous left the neighborhood, the increase in family income was not reflected in the income of the local community.

In general, the addition of children's earnings did not shift the social standing of the families in the locality as it changed their income level. The families which moved out secured a new status, often based on income, in their new communities, and they tended to look down upon those 'poor relations' who remained in the district instead of moving to 'better' neighborhoods. But among those who remained, a better income made little social difference. While still penniless, the family described above felt superior to other families in the house who did not keep their house and their children clean, or whose clothes were not well patched. In other families the father continued to hang around the café with his cronies, though his new income permitted more selective company.

Among the younger generation, some distinction was made between those who could afford to go out of the neighborhood for their pleasure, who had money in their pockets with which to entertain girls, to attend fights or to ride around in a car, and those who had no spending money and had to hang out on the street corner or wherever they could stay for nothing. But this difference did not cut very deep. The outstanding example of the boy with more money to spend was completely 'one of the boys' and hung out with the rest in the local candy store when he was not otherwise amusing himself. Those who lived in the better houses adopted the characteristic aloofness which distinguished these houses from the more gregarious tenements. But only if a family became distinctly well-to-do, by the fortunes of the stock market or by business activity, did it really sever its connection with its poorer neighbors and then it rarely remained in the neighborhood.

The social indifference to economic status, in spite of the terrific stress placed by the local community on the money-making drive, rested on the widespread assumption that economic advance came from 'getting the breaks.' To these immigrant groups, possession of wealth carried none of the moral sanction which the old American tradition conferred upon it. Those who had money were simply assumed to have had the 'breaks.' Such 'breaks' might come to anyone, and if they did, it was important not to be so stupid as to fail to take advantage of them. But it did not reflect any particular glory on anyone that he had luck on his side. Correspondingly, poverty carried no social stigma.

In these circumstances, gambling was a general and accepted way of making, or trying to make, money. The district abounded in men who were ready to place any sized bets, from five cents up, on anything. Horses, prize-fights, ball games, lotteries, 'numbers' — almost anything would do to bet on. The poolroom where one of the tough groups hung out was supplied with a ticker to report racing results for those who bet on the horses. During the stock market boom, some of the younger men started to play the market instead of the horses. The number of straight gambling places, and whether or not they had increased, was not ascertained owing to the difficulty of locating them and, frequently, their fly-by-night character, but several places were well known and certain of the big gambling proprietors of the neighborhood were famous for their political prominence.

The state of the gambling art and the size of the stakes fluctuated with the condition of the times. When times were good and work steady, the pot at the regular Saturday crap game on a certain block was reputed to have run into several hundred dollars; when times got worse, this was cut, and as most of the players became unemployed, the stakes decreased proportionately. But though bad times and unemployment reduced the stakes for which it was possible to gamble, the depression increased rather than decreased the tendency toward gambling itself. The harder it became to make anything in the ordinary course of work or business, the more attractive became the accidental windfall which gambling might bring, and even men who had never bet or gambled began to bet on 'numbers' in the feeling that there was nothing better that one could do with a quarter than to take a chance on really making some money.

This tendency for gambling to increase as times got worse confirmed one of the reasons for the universality of gambling in this neighborhood — the difficulty of making a reasonable living by regular means. The trend of these years brought out ever increasingly the disparity between the standard of living which could be purchased with the wages of local workers and that which the press, the movies, and the school indicated as desirable. In the face of this fact situation, the American tradition that the lowest could rise to the top became merged with the gambling impulse, and each individual believed that only a 'lucky break,' and certainly not the traditional virtues of industry and thrift, would transform him from a slum dweller into the owner of a house with a two-car garage.

In the old American tradition, the possession of wealth has been taken as a measure of virtue. Although the Puritan belief that material success was evidence of election has long since lost its theological basis, the social attitudes that went with that belief have survived. The man with money has occupied a position of leadership in American life based less on his economic power than upon the moral advantage which wealth has given him, while poverty has been accepted as the sign of laziness, lack of thrift, or lack of capacity.

In this community, the acquisitive drive was no less intense than under the Puritan theocracy, but it lacked all moral implications. Possession of wealth, consequently, did not confer leadership. While the rich man was respected for the power which he could wield and was envied for the expenditure in which he could indulge, he was not assumed to have wisdom or virtue, his advice was no better than the next man's though his automobile might be, and any of his potential admirers or followers might any day be standing in his shoes. In fact, a great amount of wealth carried quite the opposite connotation, for it was taken to mean not only that its holder got the 'breaks' but that some unsavory action was involved as well. All large sums of money were presumed to be in some way or other tainted.

The economic life of the old residents of this community was thus characterized by an economic drive which carried with it neither social organization nor moral sanction, but contributed to the individualizing and disorganizing influences in the community.

Among the new residents, many consciously repudiated income differences as a basis for social organization. Their occupational differences were reflected in their social life in so far as they represented common interests, and some of the artistic pursuits, especially, carried a measure of prestige. But though the newcomers were largely drawn from the group for which the gospel of work, thrift, and acquisition rested on moral grounds, many had come to the Village to escape from communities whose social values were measured in money terms. Their life here represented an effort to subordinate the economic to the cultural — in extreme cases reaching the point of complete economic irresponsibility.

PART II
PEOPLE

IV. THE SOCIAL NEIGHBORHOOD

1. BREAK UP OF OLD NEIGHBORHOOD

IT HAS long been the presumption that living near-by makes
people into 'neighbors' — that it either moulds them to a
common pattern or brings them together and gives them, in
spite of personal differences, a common point of view as members
of the same 'neighborhood.' The 'neighborhood' has, in fact,
been very dear to the heart of the sociologist as being, with the
family, the primary face-to-face group which is 'fundamental in
forming the social nature and ideals of the individual.'[1] It has
held an important place in the American culture pattern largely
because of the assumption of American democracy that community of interest is identical with common residence, and that
interest groups and social classes do not exist.

Where a community has been subjected, as Greenwich Village
has, to physical disintegration and to the juxtaposition of diverse
elements, the effectiveness of the neighborhood as a functioning
unit is put to the acid test. The evidence of this community indicates that where such forms of urbanism as can here be seen
are at their height, the neighborhood very largely ceases to be a
basis for social intercourse and a formative influence on the lives
of its residents. Only selectively did 'neighbors' in Greenwich
Village know each other, identify themselves with the 'neighborhood,' and engage in common activity, either informally or formally. The social code enforced by the public opinion of the neighborhood group was effective only upon the element which led its
life in the street.

[1] Cooley, C. H. *Social Organization*, New York, 1925, p. 23.

Thirty or more years before this study was made, the Village was, according to the testimony of the survivors, a genuine neighborhood. All agreed that Yankees, Germans, and Irish got along together, that each block was more or less like a big family, that neighborhood affairs were the great events of the year, and that the neighborhood encompassed the lives of its residents. With due allowance for exaggeration on the part of those who looked back fondly to a departed age, evidence is strong that before the arrival of the Italians the area could, not too inaccurately, be considered a neighborhood. The changes in buildings and in people, the movement out of the area and the type of apartment population which came in, together with the influence of rapid transit, movies, the press, and the radio, all tended toward making the neighborhood less and less of a social unit. Association on a geographical basis was relegated more and more to the less ambitious, to those with fewest material or other resources. Such neighborhood sentiment as the newcomers felt and expressed was a negative sort of tolerance rather than the consciousness of being part of a social unit for activity or for social control. In 1930, the few old-timers, whose neighborhood feeling was a carry-over from the days when the area more nearly resembled a social as well as a geographical unit, were still talking in neighborhood terms, but their words were hollow echoes of an earlier date and appeared incongruous in the face of later-day diversity and disintegration. Virtually all the conditions which would favor neighborhood relationships were absent. The physical basis for neighborhood was restricted to very small areas by the presence of wide traffic lanes.

When the children east of Sixth Avenue had to cross two major arteries to reach their school, it seemed to their parents that the distance which they were required to go, even when it was only six short blocks, was excessive. Once such traffic barriers had been introduced, the qualifications for getting about and across them were the same as for going greater distances, and the advantages of physical proximity were lost. The local music school pointed out that it was easier for some uptown children to come for their lessons than for many of the neighborhood children a few blocks away. If they could get into the subway near their homes, they had no traffic artery to cross when they got out and only had one avenue to cross to get back into the uptown subway entrance. Even within the small areas between arteries, neighborhood relations were impeded by the diversity of housing facilities and of residents.

By 1930, the area presented a picture of physical confusion. Of the 100 small square blocks in the district, 7 were purely industrial, 10 purely low-class residential, 6 purely high-class residential, and 75 were a mixture of high- and low-class residential or of residence and industry.[1]

The distribution of the different types, or combinations of types, moreover, did not remain constant. Although there was some concentration in the building of new apartments near Washington Square and remodeling proceeded further in certain blocks, the process of substituting high for low rent dwellings proceeded most irregularly. In four cases a group of houses was remodeled together as a unit so that the physical provision for neighborhood relationships was made possible by the change. On more than half the blocks remodeling changed the type of resident, and on another quarter industry supplanted residence and inhabitants were expelled or demolitions to make way for public improvements scattered the population to the four winds. Where houses were remodeled from low to high rent dwellings, especially on the fourteen blocks where multi-family tenement houses were transformed, old neighborhood contacts were broken by the enforced emigration of low-rent-paying families from the block. The new element which intruded into the block found no neighborhood group ready to absorb it, but rather a population, economically and socially distant, indifferent or hostile to the newcomers' arrival.

[1] Even the blocks of similar mixtures were not segregated. In the 6 census tracts the grouping was as follows:

| | Census Tract No. | | | | | | Total |
	65	67	69	71	73	75	
Industrial...........................	0	1	6	0	0	0	7
Low-class residence..................	1	4	1	0	2	2	10
High-class residence.................	2	1	0	2	1	0	6
Low-class and industrial.............	5	3	8	1	1	10	28
High-class and industrial............	0	0	0	4	0	0	4
Low-class and high-class.............	7	6	0	3	14	3	33
Low-class, high-class, and industrial...........	0	3	0	3	3	1	10

In its turn the new element made the continuance of old neigh-borhood relationships difficult because these had to be carried on under alien eyes and often in the face of complaints against dis-pleasing conduct. The new residents, among themselves, could not easily live a neighborly life with their own kind if they would. Under the necessity, to their way of thinking, of avoiding contact with their slum 'nigh-dwellers,' they lived their own lives apart except where a small group in a few adjacent houses formed a nucleus. 'We live on an Italian block,' explained a resident of a mixed street, 'so the children, of course, can only play in the yard.' And in their tiny yard behind three small houses, flanked on the other sides by factories and the back windows of Italian tenements, a small group of children and their parents huddled in unneighborly seclusion.

The end of the Village's isolation removed a primary influence toward neighboring, and the exodus of so many families from the district not only broke up many old associations, but also brought outside contacts to those who remained in the area. Many of the latter found the district empty and lonely. 'Now that my friends are gone,' observed one woman sadly, 'I just sit in my room and listen to the radio and watch out of the window what goes on in the street.' At the same time, connection with the friends and relatives who formerly lived in the locality gave them a metro-politan outlook which dwarfed their neighborhood interests.

There is no measure of the extent to which the adventures of radio and screen favorites here took the place of the affairs of the family next door as a preoccupation. Unquestionably, however, the various forms of commercial entertainment did their part both to break up the old ways in which the neighborhood used to spend its leisure and to shift the focus of people's thought. In-creasingly, neighborliness became an accompaniment of a low income level. Those who could afford little commercial amuse-ment were forced to get from each other as much recreation as they could, from gossiping on the stoops or from exchanging news in the cafés. With increased prosperity, especially of the Italians, during these years, the number forced to rely on the neighborhood for their amusement was reduced.

By 1930, lack of neighborly contacts had become one of the signs of social superiority and of sophistication. Those who lived in the better of the low-rent quarters characterized their houses as the kind where 'everybody doesn't know about your affairs.' The younger, more prosperous, or more Americanized women, especially, were apt to maintain the attitude, 'Oh, I keep to myself. You get along better that way than if you are familiar with your neighbors and they know all about what you are doing.'

The newcomers who entered the district in these years were the worst sort of members of a 'neighborhood' group. Neighborhood relationships do not grow overnight. They are predicated upon a measure of identification between the individual and the place where he lives, and rest upon at least quasi-permanent residence. The new type of resident did not come to the Village for a home, but rather for a temporary resting place. One Villager aptly phrased the point of view of this element, in stating that 'the Village is an ideal place for a home; there are so many good restaurants.' With no expectation of even relative permanence, with no home feeling or home activity susceptible of expansion into neighborhood feeling or neighborhood activity, the shifting apartment-house residents had none of the prerequisites of neighbors.

Those among the newcomers — with the exception of the first group to discover the locality — who talked about the Village as a neighborhood revealed by the sense in which they used the term how essentially unneighborly they were in their point of view. At the most they felt that personal isolation was not quite so great here as in some of the other apartment-house regions of the city, a feeling frequently prompted by the presence of small houses in contrast to mammoth apartment buildings, and by the greater informality on the streets or in restaurants. More often they registered by the term the presence of like-minded people in the vicinity rather than actual contact. The interviewer soon came to expect such comments as, 'Neighbors here tend to be like myself, professional people who like civilized living and who do not feel that wealth is the only index of that. The sense of an educated, thinking group with standards and background make me willing to live here.' 'Uptown is the *milieu* for the moneyed people; the Village attracts intelligent people. The proportion of people who know how to think, discuss and exchange ideas is much greater in the Village than elsewhere.'

Those who had been in the Village for some time — the same who felt it to be a community because of the presence of like-minded people — were inclined to agree that this condition was departing. 'Formerly the Village was enjoyable,' they complained, 'because it was a neighborhood where educated people of moderate means or income could live decently. Now it has been ruined by real estate exploitation.' 'The old Greenwich Village contained earnest, intellectual, cultivated people who were making a real effort to attain the fine and lovely things in life. A great many of the present occupants are living here just to be smart.'

Most characteristically, however, those who talked about the neighborly atmosphere of the Village in the same breath praised its freedom, the absence of a norm of behavior such as would be maintained by public opinion in a functioning neighborhood. New residents of all types stressed social tolerance as the distinguishing feature of the locality, noting that it extended beyond the anonymity characteristic of metropolitan situations and included the tolerance of friends and acquaintances as well as of strangers. As one young woman quaintly observed, 'The Village is especially kind to persons in any way failures. Here, too, queerness is not pointed out and, unless too exaggerated, is tolerated, sympathized with, and overlooked. Many broken hearts find healing in the Village atmosphere of equality and tolerance.' Another, seeking to be accurate in defining what she had in mind, specified, 'Privacy, perhaps more than freedom, is what I mean.' The live-and-let-live point of view appeared to be quite universal, for the strongest praise of this attitude came quite as much from those whose conduct was thoroughly conservative as from those of unconventional tastes. What to the new residents made the Village a 'neighborhood' was the negation of neighborliness, the chance to live unhampered by what one's neighbor thought, and to be free from making contacts because of mere propinquity.

Formal organization of the community on a neighborhood basis was sponsored from one of three sources, social workers, real estate agents, or persons seeking to exploit the Village. A group which for a number of years had borne the name 'neighborhood association' still survived in 1930. This group, originally organized with a civic purpose, had worked for improvement in the public services provided in the locality. Under the leadership of the head of the neighborhood settlement, it had been influential in such measures as securing the erection of public baths and gymnasium, the conversion of a public pier into a recreation ground, and the guarding of street crossings used by school children. It continued to exert some civic pressure during the post-War years, and saw its long struggle for a public swimming pool crowned with success in 1930. Its membership was drawn almost entirely from social workers and the old neighborhood groups, including a very few Italians who had been among the first to come into the community, a handful of the new element drawn from the first ones who discovered the district, and chiefly the old-time Irish and the remnant of old American and German elements. At its annual dinner, some prominent politician habitually reminisced about the old days, one of the old Germans and one of the neighborhood social workers spoke, and perhaps a local real estate agent was heard. This association represented the continuing effort of those who had known a genuine neighborhood to maintain the activities and retain the social atmosphere of that time.

The second form of neighborhood organization existing during the period was furnished by the taxpayers' associations which appeared from time to time. In the high-rent district around Washington Square, a flourishing taxpayers' organization — flourishing enough to maintain a paid secretary — represented the property-owners in their efforts to get assessments reduced or to improve the neighborhood. In 1920, it had been engaged in fighting, with the aid of the police, the Village's growing reputation for iniquity. In 1930, it was still on the job. A similar organization existed in the center of the new apartment and remodeled section of the Village itself, led by the man who owned or was agent for much of the property in the vicinity. The function of both these organizations was limited — working as they were toward the specific end of improving their real estate investments. From the real estate point of view, conditions calling for action of some sort were numerous. The property-owners throughout the period were trying to hasten the process by which the district became transformed from a slum into an apartment area. Their services to the 'neighborhood' were, as a result, not always in the interest of the people who made up the community, especially on such a problem as whether to provide play streets for children at the expense of the rental value of the property on such streets.

To the neighborhood association and taxpayers' groups were added those individuals or groups which sought to build up the idea of the Village as a neighborhood in order to exploit this idea for some end. Of such a character were the perennial attempts to publish local newspapers and magazines. These ranged all the way from nearly illiterate gossip sheets to ultra-literary efforts, but they all presented the common characteristic of stressing the fact that the area was a 'neighborhood.' The type of neighborhood pictured or assumed varied, of course, with the kind of circulation which the paper sought. If it sought the substantial, well-to-do element, there was no neighborhood in the city so full of home-owners and prosperous citizens; [1] if the literati were addressed, the neighborhood was the home of that free and irresponsible intelligentsia that had given the Village its fame; if the voter was sought, it was a neighborhood of 'folks' who were interested in who was keeping company with whom and what a 'good time was had by all' on an outing at Coney Island.

Those who published the various local papers knew as well as anyone that calling the area a neighborhood did not make it one. A confession of one editor told the story. After he had expounded how wonderful it was that here in the heart of the city one could find a real neighborhood, he was asked just what his racket really was. 'I want to make the paper look like a good little thing,' he replied, 'so that I can sell stock in it and get out.' Some of these papers were sponsored by real estate dealers, others by politicians 'selling the Village small-town newspaper stuff, and they like it. Plenty of names of locals, from obits to social activities, and they all like to see themselves mentioned.' Some were just the efforts of somebody who had 'always wanted a paper of his own' and thought that he might be able to whip up enough sentiment to make a go of one here, or who had a pet idea to promulgate. Others were the media for literary 'self-expression.' They came and went throughout the years under review, some lasting several years, more a few months. One of the 'Home News' type, was read fairly generally by the Irish and pre-Irish residents during

[1] By carefully selecting the right blocks, they could quote figures to show a high percentage of home-ownership in comparison with the rest of Manhattan.

the time when it was published. One of the literary sheets acquired some reputation outside of the Village. But few residents in 1930 would take these publications seriously, either the sheets which had died or the new ones which were being started. They were regarded as 'nothing but real estate copy,' 'a printer's effort to drum up trade,' 'another of those literary attempts.'

The organization that strove most consistently and honestly to function as a neighborhood body was Greenwich House — a neighborhood settlement which had conducted recreational, educational and health activities for thirty years. In all its work it stressed again and again the idea of 'neighbors.' In its early days it had succeeded in identifying itself with its neighbors, then chiefly Irish, by maintaining informal, personal relations and taking part in the neighborly social life characteristic of that time. At the close of the War it had moved into larger and more institutional quarters in order to house the many activities which had been started informally to serve the interests of the neighbors and which had grown in size and in technical quality. During the post-War years it saw the community which it served losing more and more its character as a neighborhood, and it recorded in its 1929 annual report that the locality had become a cross-section of a heterogeneous city. To meet these new conditions it maintained a variety of services designed for a variety of groups.

The House itself constituted a center for the performance of certain neighborhood functions, primarily those which fell in the category of social work. For some time it housed the local office of a district nursing service and an agency for the care of cripples, and was the place where the probation officer met the juvenile delinquents who were on probation and the parole officer met those from the district who were under his supervision. It offered its building as a meeting place for groups of social workers and for such local organizations, drawn from any element in the community, as would use it. Its individual workers served as leaders in civic and welfare activities. But changes in the community expanded the social area which the House served. The more specialized and highly developed of its activities, especially in art and music, became widely known and drew from all over the city, while at the same time the people of the locality enlarged their contacts and became less dependent on this or any other specifically local institution.

Although by 1930 the 'neighborhood' in the old sense had dissolved, the neighborhood idea was constantly being revived, either by those who hoped to profit from keeping the idea alive, or by Greenwich House, which continued to feel that even under the later conditions the effort to retain something at least of the neighborhood spirit added a humanness to city life and stimulated civic betterment.

Even after 1930, two new developments bore witness to the persistence of the neighborhood idea — 'Greenwich Village Week' and the organization of a 'Civic Association.' Both were supported by groups which had earlier 'neighborhood' experience. The 'Week' was sponsored by Greenwich House, seconded by one of the newspaper editors who had staked his chance for profits on persuading the Village that it was a neighborhood. It was supported by the local shopkeepers, especially those, like the tea rooms, which depended on outside patronage and relished publicity. Libraries, schools, and churches were induced to participate, though the principal of one school complained at wasting school time training the children for a 'neighborhood' performance because, she said, they always sang to empty air on these occasions, for nobody turned out to hear them. It got Greenwich Village into the press and may have contributed hope to some who wanted to start local newspapers. The shopkeepers found it worth the dollar subscription which they invested. The same group that attended the functions of the neighborhood association turned out for a banquet.

The Civic Association represented a consolidation of other interested groups — the old neighborhood association, the taxpayers' bodies, the real estate interests, the neighborhood house, the local historical society. It formed committees for neighborhood betterment which immediately encountered the old problem of whether real estate values or social conditions were to be 'bettered' — whether children's play should be made safe or streets made quiet. By these 'neighborhood developments,' too, the bulk of the population remained untouched.

There were no leaders to whom the neighborhood looked to represent the whole community. To the community, the term 'leader' meant political leader. These were assumed to be in the political game for what they could get out of it and were recognized as leaders of their own political clubs rather than as leaders of the neighborhood.

Those of the social workers who had been in the neighborhood for some time looked upon themselves as neighborhood leaders, and functioned in that capacity on civic issues. But few evidences were found to indicate that, except in rare instances, a large proportion of the local residents looked to these workers as their own leaders rather than as persons who were doing something for them. The priests and at least one of the Protestant ministers exercised a real measure of leadership for their own parishes. The other Protestant ministers, however, shared the 'for-but-not-of' position of many social workers as pastors of either mission churches or churches reaching a tiny fragment of the community. In only one of the schools was there anything suggestive of neighborhood leadership to be observed. Lay leaders looked to by all the community could not be found.

The use of neighborhood facilities and the existence of informal personal contacts are perhaps better indications of a functioning neighborhood than formal organization. On these points, the evidence was fragmentary and largely negative. Among the new residents there were a few who had been there a number of years who liked to boast that they 'never went above Fourteenth Street' — their friends, their shopping, their work, and their entertainment all were local. These were, emphatically, the exceptions. Among 198 of the new residents who answered the question as to which neighborhood facilities they used, less than half patronized anything except food stores, restaurants, and movies. In respect to these, moreover, the fact that only 83 per cent patronized local food stores, for which one would expect 100 per cent patronage, is as clear an indication of non-dependence on neighborhood resources as the much lower proportion using other facilities. Those services involving social rather than purely business relations were the least patronized — in fact, they hardly touched this group. One person used the neighborhood house, five a local clinic, six — i.e., 3 per cent — the local schools; 12 per cent attended church, and 32 per cent used the public library and voted. The things for which a neighborhood is almost universally used were far from receiving the patronage of the new residents.

In each case the patronizing of local stores and such slight contact with social institutions as existed was greater among married than single people or those from broken marriages. But though the preponderance of single people in the Village had much to do with the absence of neighborhood relationships among this element, the following table clearly indicates that even the married group did not depend on the neighborhood.

Patronage of Neighborhood Facilities by New Residents

	Married Persons (51 cases)	Single, Widowed, Divorced, Separated (147 cases)
Food stores	96 per cent	78 per cent
Restaurants	84	72
Movies	74	50
Library	40	30
Voting	35	32
Church	12	12
School	6	2
Clinic	6	1.5
Neighborhood house	2	0

The evidence of this table was amply reinforced by statements in over one hundred interviews. The average 'Greenwich Villager' of 1930, particularly the single person, tended to go out of the Village as much as possible. Everything except his actual dwelling place seemed to pull him out of the community. The only important exception — the proportion of cases was not ascertained — was in the patronage of speakeasies. Except for these, young people only used the Village for recreation as a last resort. If their purses could stand it, uptown they went, to movies, dancing, theater, and restaurants. The use of the Village by Village residents was apt to be evidence of lack of funds. Those who found recreation there came from outside.

Among the tenement residents the use of local facilities was very much more general. Except for a few Jewish housewives who traveled to the East Side in order to patronize Kosher stores, food continued to be bought locally. For other products, the trend of these years was toward more and more patronage of city in preference to neighborhood stores. Clothes were bought increasingly in the Fourteenth Street department stores and then at

Macy's in the mid-town shopping center. The 'living-room suites' of furniture which represented for many their rising standard of living were more often bought uptown on the installment plan than from the neighborhood furniture dealer. For entertainment, Times Square and Coney Island beckoned the younger people especially. Here, too, lack of money dictated the use of the neighborhood.

To most of its inhabitants, both newcomers and those who had lived there for many years, the Village had thus ceased to be a 'neighborhood' in anything but name. At the most it was a community within an ethnic, an interest, or an economic group and a memory of a more homogeneous time. At the least it was a subway entrance, a hat rack and a bed. At the most it was a group of social workers thinking in community terms for a community with which they had never succeeded in fully identifying themselves and of a few individuals who had made much of hypothetical community relationships in order to bring profit to themselves. It was a 'low-class' neighborhood from which the more ambitious of the tenement dwellers sought escape and against which even the housewives — who lived more within the locality than anybody except the children — locked their doors, priding themselves on not being the kind of people who had to do with their neighbors. It was an area in which the conditions favoring neighborhood relationships became increasingly few and the alternatives to such relationships increasingly numerous.

Yet to the outside world Greenwich Village had a reputation and an entity which other parts of the metropolis did not possess. A common reputation and a sense of identification with the locality is one of the usual attributes of a functioning neighborhood, producing the kind of loyalty which brings out an entire town behind the local baseball team, since the team's success means prestige for the residents. A common reputation may do much to overcome dissimilarities of economic or social status and to create a neighborhood sense.

The reputation of Greenwich Village, however, hardly served this purpose, for it was very largely manufactured and imposed from without rather than being a *bona-fide* reflection of those who resided or had resided in the area. Before the district was 'Greenwich Village' in its new incarnation, it was the Ninth Ward.

To many of the old residents it remained 'the Ward.' At no time since it ceased to be 'thè Ward' did it constitute for these residents an area with an entity of its own. Some learned to call it 'Greenwich Village,' although they were quite likely to be confused as to its boundary and to explain that 'what they call "Greenwich Village" runs from the Battery up to perhaps Twenty-Third Street.' To others it was just the 'neighborhood.' To the Italians, in distinction from the other Italian settlements, it was the 'West Side' or the 'lower West Side.'

The newcomers were the ones to be most generally aware of the Village and its reputation. Among more than a hundred who were interviewed, scarcely one failed to offer some reaction, however varied, to the reputation of the Village and to reflect a consciousness of it as an entity.

The reputation which the Village enjoyed during these years was not a single one, but a series of different reputations falling roughly into two more or less competing groups, those which featured 'atmosphere' and 'charm' and those which stressed freedom, exoticism, intellectuality. Each, moreover, successively reflected a current climate of opinion. Real estate dealers, property-owners, and business people were the most active publicists for each of the reputations in turn.

First to be featured was the Village's 'colonial charm.' The metropolitan press, local news sheets, and even books containing specially prepared historical accounts and illustrations, called attention to its quaint corners, its high-ceilinged rooms, and its handsome old doorways. One of the first corporations formed to rebuild old dwellings in an 'attractive manner' announced that its members knew the district's charm and sought to retain it,[1] and the successive remodeling of other groups of red-brick houses was featured, with stress on the same element of 'charm.'[2] The state of public opinion which created the enormous market for antiques, led museums to open American wings, and made a fetish of the 'early American' style, created excellent advertising copy for Greenwich Village. Shops dealing in antiques, hand-wrought jewelry, and peasant wear moved into the locality to make the most of this kind of local fame. As demolitions and rebuilding proceeded, the typical press article about the Village be-

[1] *New York Times*, May 23, 1915.   [2] *Ibid.*, March 28, 1920.

gan to be devoted to the passing of old landmarks — effective reminders of the quaintness which had been proclaimed.[1]

When the 'early American' reputation had more or less run its course, and the combination of cheap rents and attractive surroundings had brought a group of artists and thinkers to the locality, the artistic and intellectual features were the next to be stressed. The development of this reputation coincided with the burst of original American expression which followed the close of the War and the Village spokesmen claimed credit, not only for such of the successful writers as had struggled in poverty in Village garrets, but for the many intellectuals from other places who gravitated to the Village when passing through or visiting the metropolis. From a 'charming bit of early America,' the district became the 'cradle of modern American culture.'

This was the phase out of which the tea rooms made the greatest capital, advertising that famous characters were their patrons and could be seen at their establishments. The fact that many of the intellectuals at the time were living in furnished rooms or non-housekeeping apartments made them frequent patrons of eating-houses, which in turn became their hangouts or informal clubs. Trailing behind these were the 'pseudo' tea rooms, where 'poets' recited their verses by candlelight, and the gullible or curious absorbed 'art.' These places made the candle positively a Village symbol.

These dimly lighted, 'arty' dens helped to carry the Village's reputation on from its intellectual to its bohemian stage. In the early 1920's, the Village was the Latin Quarter of New York, America's bohemia, where flourished free love, unconventional dress, erratic work — if any — indifference to physical surroundings, all-night parties, crowding, sleeping where one happened to be, walking the streets in pajamas, girls on the street smoking, plenty of drink, living from moment to moment, with sometimes a pass at creative work but often not even that. Girls from conventional homes could spend a daring evening in the Village and might screw up their courage to ask, in wide-eyed awe, 'Do you *really* believe in free love?' More adventurous young people were attracted to the Village by the lure of the excitement and daring of bohemian life, and especially by the opportunity for sex

[1] *New York Times*, October 31, 1920.

experience and experiment. This new phase corresponded with the burst of 'flaming youth' which made the elders' hair rise on end in the mid-twenties.

Because the most picturesque and most easily capitalized, the bohemian became the most tenacious of all the reputations which the Village acquired. The bohemians were conspicuous. Sight-seers could see them, and sight-seeing buses added the Village to their nightly routes. One of the Catholic priests found that he created a sensation whenever he met a tourist bus, 'the guides have just told them what a den of iniquity Greenwich Village is and they almost lose their eyes at a religious walking around the streets.' Cabarets joined in the effort to make money out of the Village's exotic flavor. The tea room or studio which had served in the last phase as a place featuring artistic atmosphere, now developed into a 'pick-up joint.'

As sex taboos broke down all over the country, and sex experimentation found its way to the suburbs, the Village's exoticism could no longer rest on so commonplace a foundation. Again, the shift of current interest supplied a basis for a new phase in the Village's reputation. When public attention had been called to homo-sexuality by the suppression of 'The Captive' and 'The Well of Loneliness,' the Village became noted as the home of 'pansies' and 'Lesbians,' and dives of all sorts featured this type.

As the conventional form of unconventionality called increasingly for violation of the liquor law, it was not surprising to find speakeasies concentrating in and becoming distinctive of the locality. By 1930, the gangster was added to the Village picture and sight-seers were assured that they could observe notorious underworld characters in the appropriate speakeasies.

While each of these successive characters was attributed to the Village by publicity agents backed by real estate men, restaurant-owners, and antique dealers, others set up a counter-current in an attempt to put down the more extreme of these reputations and to win fame for the area on other counts. By 1920, a tax-payers' association was already conducting a clean-up campaign to establish the respectability of the district. The houses of prostitution which had been located south of Washington Square were raided and the property facing the Square was developed for high-class residential use. Certain of the tea rooms and night clubs were also raided at the instigation of the same group. As the Village had never been an extensive red-light district, it did not take much to clear out the actual disorderly houses. From this time on the same association made consistent and repeated efforts to achieve respectability for the area. With the construction of up-to-date apartments in 1929–31, the victory of respectability seemed assured. But the exotic reputation persisted. While the conservative press in 1931 was carrying articles on the passing of the old Village landmarks and the extent of building activity, the 'wicked Village' still was good copy for the tabloid press.[1]

The changing place of the Village in the eyes of the respectable public was reflected in the type of article which described it in the *New York Times*:

The Old Village
1913–1915 — Old home week, Greenwich Village Fair, children's concerts, flower show, housing problem.

Plans to Remodel Old Houses
1915–1916 — Village charm, demand for houses, good investment.

Bohemia, the Tea Room, the Cabaret
1917–1919 — Controversy over 'poseurs,' Village morality; lists and descriptions of tea rooms, news of raids; drama in the Village.

Cleaning up the Village
1920 — Police report of reforms.

News of Real Estate Ventures
1921–1923 — Houses bought for remodeling.

Remains and Memories
1920–1924 — Landmarks, bits of old Greenwich, quaint touches.

The Battle of the Tea Rooms
1921–1924
    1921 — The local population protests.
    1922 — The taxpayers' association gets into action
    1924 — The taxpayers' association reports the 'vicious element routed.'

[1] *New York Evening Graphic*, September, 1931. Series of articles on Greenwich Village.

Improvements

1923 — Real estate developments now described as 'improvements.'

Organized Reminscence

1923–1927 — The Greenwich Village Historical Society organizes, unveils monuments, celebrates anniversaries.

Is Art in the Village Dead?

1923–1931 — Recurrent special articles on actual or potential artistic revival, especially 1923, 1927, 1931.

News of Building Operations

1924 ff. — Apartment building, etc., reported in real estate section of paper.

Commercialism in Art

1925 — Controversy over commercialism in Village theaters.

Historical Interest

1926–1928 — Feature articles on aspects of Village history.

The Village is No More

1927 ff. — Crescendo through 1930.

Wistful and Wishful

1931–1932 — Village urged to retain its atmosphere; surviving traditions sought out.

Art is Still Here!

1932 — Notices of sidewalk art market.

Those who sought to capitalize the changing reputation of the Village were, of course, most aware of its existence. The new residents included those who agreed that the Village had charm and regretted that the construction of apartments was destroying it, those who either relished or resented its reputation for bohemianism, some who defended or refuted its claim as an intellectual center, and some who insisted upon its essential respectability. Out of a small sample of fifty who expressed themselves directly on whether or not they were glad to see the building of new apartments, twice as many expressed regret as satisfaction. Only a few were wholly indifferent to its fame or notoriety. The ones with a most nearly 'neighborhood' attitude were the professional or artistic people who had lived there for some time and had known most of the other residents of the same type in the days when their number was few, who had been attracted by the 'colonial' charm, resented the stamp of bohemianism, and, to some degree, identified themselves with the community as they conceived of it in these terms.

To the old residents this changing reputation was of no concern except as a few young men who had gone to college felt that, although they did not actually know any of the artists, they liked to live where there were artists and intellectuals around. A common reputation, clearly, did not make the Village into an effective neighborhood, for it reflected the interest of exploiters rather than of residents; those residents who were most aware of it were the newcomers to whom the neighborhood meant least, while the old residents, who retained a measure of real neighborhood spirit, were hardly aware of living in 'Greenwich Village.'

While the Village as a whole was ceasing to function as a neighborhood, individual blocks retained somewhat more of the qualities of neighborhood units. By 1920, the blocks where the Irish resided had already lost some of their distinctive qualities, while the Italian blocks were still largely made up of people from the same province of Italy. In 1930, many blocks were thoroughly mixed as the result of remodeling and of mobility. Shorter residence on a block worked against the block's functioning as a neighborhood unit. The more varied a block's residents, the greater likelihood that they had lived there for a comparatively short time. For the Italians, a canvass of residents on sample blocks in 1930 showed that where most of the people on the block were born in the same province, a large proportion of them had lived on the same block for twenty or thirty years. On the blocks more newly occupied by Italians, or blocks which were thoroughly mixed, shorter residence was combined with greater provincial and national diversity.

Where people moved to a new block there appeared to be a tendency for former associations to persist rather than for new connections to be made. In the groups of all ages found hanging around one block on which there had been considerable remodeling, present residents were hardly more numerous than those who had formerly lived on the block, but who now were scattered through the neighborhood and as far away as Brooklyn. This was especially true of groups of older boys, but even the children continued to play upon their old block after their families had moved and women came back frequently to hobnob with their old neighbors. It was not possible to discover how long a period of residence it took to bring people into association with residents on a new rather than a former block, but there were some indications to suggest that it might not be wholly a matter of time. Where the old block had constituted a close group and the new one did not, new block associations were slow to be made. This was conspicuously true among the Irish, where people who had been on a block for only two years reported that they were still strangers, and talked about their former place of residence as 'their block.'

Though block units had ceased to be neighborhoods in their total composition, especially those blocks which were mixed, they still tended to constitute quasi-neighborhoods for those who had resided long at the same place, and for the children who played on the street. For the young children who were commonly subject to the restriction that they should not leave their block, the block association was the only possible one. All children's play groups continued to be principally made up on a block basis with the addition, in older groups, of those who formerly lived on the block. Interblock games were still played, and occasionally resulted in block fights, but the fights between blocks that used to be the rule had practically disappeared. The only form of block solidarity which survived was loyalty to the play gang which usually represented a block and frequently took a street for its name.

For older boys, the block was less likely to determine their associates — in fact, the latter were most apt to be drawn from those who had been block neighbors when younger. Among twelve street groups of older boys, for each of which the addresses of from five to ten members were known, two drew exclusively from a street block or the houses immediately around the corner, three from within a radius of three blocks, two from a wider local radius of five or six blocks, while five contained members from Brooklyn, Long Island, or the East Side. Thirteen per cent of the 125 boys in this sample came from outside the Village.

Girls frequently stated that they did not want to marry the boys from their blocks because they had known them always. They complained of how 'fresh' they were, always stopping to exchange words or blows with them as they sat out on their stoops in the evening. Though the boys took liberties with the girls on their own block, they nevertheless had a certain amount of pride which made them the protectors of these girls. One Italian girl, who had more freedom than most, reported that she could always come home at any time of night because the boys on the block not only would never molest her but would see that she was not molested, and the same report came from other girls on other streets. To this extent, the reputation of a block was bound up with the reputation of the individual. It did not extend at any time to the apartment-house occupants, but was confined to the occupants of unreclaimed dwellings.

Such general forms of block organization, however, as the block parties which the political organizations used to stage had entirely disappeared by 1930. Outstanding individuals were not looked to as leaders of those blocks and did not bring any particular fame to the block neighborhood. Though the women were usually acquainted with people in the neighboring houses, they, too, kept their old connections after they had moved and were quite as likely to know people whom they met shopping in the pushcart markets as people on their own block, and much more likely to associate with relatives. As for the men, their groups, though frequently drawn from the neighborhood, were not apt to be drawn from the particular block. At the carpenter's shop or the café, the saloon or the political club, the cronies with whom they hung around were no more likely to be residents of their own than of near-by blocks. It was, thus, for the children almost exclusively that the block retained its pre-eminent importance in 1930 as a social unit.

An attempt to discover how much the residents of one sample Italian block knew about the others of their own kind on the same block showed other selective factors. The children who lived at one end did not know the children who lived at the other, and

never played with them. Certain families, most of them interrelated, living in scattered houses through the block and the adjoining blocks, knew each other. A resident of one house who had
always lived there could go through the house telling what kind of
people lived in each apartment, but some were not known personally. In the other houses on the same block, only those who
played in the streets or who were related were known to each other,
and there were those who professed to know nobody and to take
care not to be known. In fact, the block constituted a social unit
for those children who played in the street and those of the young
people who had been children on the block. Those who were not
permitted to play in the street were no more a part of their block
than if they had lived anywhere else. A large proportion of the
children on the street came from large families for whom there was
no room in the house or whose parents could make no other provision for them. The average number of children in the families
of children who constituted street play groups or older hang-
around groups greatly exceeded the average family size reported
or discovered by other methods of sampling. Neighboring appeared to have become partly an accompaniment of family size.

Where an appearance of neighborhood unity was found, it
frequently turned out to be at least reinforced by, if not actually
based upon, blood relationship. An exact examination of the
family relationships upon individual blocks could not be made.
Among the children, however, who were the principal ones to associate on a block basis, a great deal of interrelationship was
found. In fact, on the block most intensively observed, only three
families of children were identified who did not have any relatives
on that or the next block. Though this may not have been the
whole count, and certainly was not if the children who did not
play on the street were included, it indicates that, among the
Italians at least, neighborhood groups were apt to be also family
groups.

For the new residents, block residence meant nothing at all —
except for a few especially created block neighborhoods, and even
in the latter, neighboring was deliberately avoided. Because this
part of the city was one of the few places where small houses with
back yards were still to be found, the possibility of transforming
a group of old houses into a garden community presented itself.

In 1920, a row of houses on one street backing on a corresponding row on a neighboring street were thrown together into a garden community with two back yards in between. Subsequently other such communities were created, the largest comprising thirteen houses. A careful examination of one of these revealed the respects in which the little self-conscious neighborhood units were or were not social neighborhoods.

This group of houses had everything favorable to the development of a real neighborhood. It was planned as a co-operative enterprise, to provide a situation in which white-collar and lower-paid professional workers could secure advantages for both parents and children. Its social organization clearly demonstrated that those who moved into the reclaimed Village not only did not make good 'neighbors,' but were positively averse to neighboring as a form of social intercourse, and repudiated, at least for themselves, the values supposed to lie in this type of association.

The contract for the members of this community was framed by the original group of purchasers with a view to encouraging a community where parents could have the freedom and variety typical of urban life and where their children would have the advantages generally found only in the suburbs — space in the home, space outdoors for unsupervised play, and free relations with other children. Its provisions related only to such points as necessitated joint action — requiring every house-owner to contribute his yard for the common garden, to pay maintenance fees for the garden and refrain from building additions which would reduce its size, and to share in the expense of a central heating plant. Some of the houses were owned by their occupants, some rented on long leases, and the rest turned into apartments.

The group which came to live in these houses was homogeneous in taste and social attitude and ready to co-operate in the necessary business arrangements. They were cultivated, interested in their families, appreciative of freedom and space for their children, and in agreement on educational matters. They provided their own nursery school for their pre-school children and sent those of school age to the same local progressive schools. They administered the garden through a committee.

But with all their common interests, common tastes, and practical co-operation, they consciously resisted the tendency for their community to become a 'neighborhood.' Entering the arrangement because they were anxious for the benefits which it would confer on their children, they feared lest it become a 'colony.' They did not want to feel that the person next door would have a social claim. They hoped to avoid the easy intercourse typical of suburban communities and to prevent the group from becoming a 'Main Street' neighborhood. Their only interest in group living was the fact that it facilitated the solution of problems faced by families with children in an urban situation. By conscious effort they kept the group free from the practice of neighboring. There was no back-and-forth visiting. They were not even all acquainted. Except for co-operation on all problems that demanded joint action, the members of the group led the same sort of social life that they would have led if they had not lived in a garden community.

Single tenement houses, containing twenty or forty families, and apartment houses, containing even more, were as large units as many small village neighborhoods and, in the case of some tenements, functioned socially in much the same way. The higher the rent for a house, the less the likelihood that residents would be acquainted with each other. In a cold-water flat, people were more apt to know each other than in a better house and it was more the code to be neighborly, unless the latter house had been occupied by the same people for a great time. The sharpest line was drawn when the entrance door was locked. People, regretting that certain houses were no longer as 'good' as they used to be, distinguished the time when the door used to be locked. Tenement-owners, planning to 'improve' their houses, talked about installing the lock. With a locked door went less familiarity than with an open entrance. There were exceptions to this generalization, some houses of the same class having a reputation as houses where people knew each other, while in other similar houses on the same block, usually with more varied occupants, most people were not acquainted. Though types graded into each other, one could say, with reservations, that the social line between a tenement and an apartment house was the line between a house in which neighboring took place and one in which it did not.

The houses occupied by the new residents were little more neighborly than their blocks. In the new high-class apartments, people did not know each other. Of the people from those apartments who were interviewed, none knew anyone else in the same house. When two girls went the rounds of the new apartment houses built during the 1920's, ostensibly apartment-hunting, most of the renting agents either informed them that of course in that kind of house people did not know each other or else they looked surprised at being asked if the girls would meet people there. When they told the girls that they would be able to meet people, there was usually a conscious attempt to give the impression of bohemianism. Even in the smaller remodeled houses, people seldom knew each other. Only in houses which contained not more than four or five apartments whose occupants had been there for some time were people known to each other in the same house.

The social quality most common to all types in this community had become, by 1930, the habit of ignoring the other human beings encountered in daily living. Imperviousness to human contacts was one evidence of the district's extreme urbanism. In so far as Village residents thought of the area at all as a community or a neighborhood, they thought in terms of the members of their own social group. As the shift in population and the process of reclamation brought increased diversity, less and less was left of the geographical basis for social living.

2. TWO SOCIAL WORLDS
'LOCAL PEOPLE' vs. 'VILLAGERS'

Socially this community lived in two distinct social worlds. The first world was the world of the local people, mostly tenement dwellers who made up the basic population, to whom the community was home, and whose behavior patterns constituted the basic pattern of the community. The second was the world of those who came to reside in Greenwich Village without becoming a part of the locality, the backflow whose social patterns had been built up elsewhere, whose social contacts remained far-flung, to whom the locality was a mere place of residence, and who did not mesh with the basic population. The distinction between these two worlds was as sharp as is frequently the case in a suburban community where the commuting element lives in a world of its own distinct from that of the non-commuters, or where a summer colony of outsiders enters a community but maintains a social existence wholly distinct from that of the natives. Between 'local people' and 'Villagers' the gulf was and had always been wide and virtually unbridged. Although they lived side by side on the same blocks, even, very occasionally, in the same houses, they were strikingly unconscious of each other.

They were, moreover, unable even to think intelligently about each other because of the fundamentally different terms in which each group built its picture of the other. In a homogeneous or integrated society, one in which relationships are fixed and a common form of behavior is accepted, even people at different economic or social levels can think about each other with more or less understanding. Though the code of behavior of the English tradesman and the English gentleman are at variance, such variance is not of the kind to preclude understanding. The gentleman knows when a tradesman is being a good tradesman and respects him for it, knowing his code. The tradesman knows when the gentleman is being a good gentleman, and respects him in turn. Neither feels called upon to act like the other or to judge the other in his own terms. Both speak the same language on enough common points, as Englishmen, to make communication possible.

Between local people and Villagers no such common basis existed. In the first place, the position of neither group was static or fixed. In the second place, neither had a recognized place within the frame of reference of the other. In the third place, there was no common code known to both according to which they could communicate and think about each other. Each, consequently, thought of the other in his own terms, and set him down as what he himself would be if he lived in that way.

The gulf between the two worlds was caused by difference of education, social background, wealth, and social standards. Each of these factors in turn reinforced the others. Between the older generation Italians, a quarter of whom were still illiterate in 1930, and the Villagers, of whom a large proportion (54 to 60 per cent of samples investigated) were college-bred or professionally trained, the gulf was clearly inevitable. It was easy for the Villagers to set all of the Italian community down as ignorant, especially since many could not speak English and most did not speak it well. The Irish, too, although not illiterate, represented a lower level of education — rarely, in the group that remained in the neighborhood, more than grade school for the older generation — and thereby were separated from the Villagers by the same educational gap. In a group to whom literate culture meant less, such differences in education might have been of minor social importance, but for a large proportion of the Villagers literature, art, and music constituted their vocation or principal avocation. These interests raised a barrier against the uneducated which little except outstanding talent could surmount.

Actual difference, however, was not the whole story, for the second generation Italian, Jewish, or Irish young people, even with college or at least high-school educations, were nearly as completely disregarded by Villagers as were their parents. As far as most of the younger element were concerned, the Villagers were factually correct in assuming that the level of education was low. In spite of a tendency to continue in school longer, the majority of the local boys and girls did not go beyond the first year of high school in 1930. But the educated element among these younger people was no nearer the Villagers than was the mass. Though educated, they were often not cultivated, their speech was rough as were their manners — the code of the street did not tolerate an air of refinement — and they were, therefore, ignored as a class. It was irrelevant to social relations in this community that some of the local boys and girls were better informed than some of the Villagers who ignored them. The latter had only the solace of returning scorn with scorn and of reflecting, as one of the more articulate did, 'Those people think that we have no thoughts, that we are ignorant scum. Some day we will show them. It is we who will be on top.'

While the Villagers felt the social gulf largely in terms of education, the local people were more strongly aware of differences in occupation and income as grounds for that gulf. Although many of the Villagers were less well-to-do than a substantial proportion of the local people — a situation that was, on the one hand, increased by the rise in prosperity of the local element during these years, and, on the other hand, was decreased by the building of better-class apartments for people with more money — it was assumed by the local people that all Villagers, except the out-and-out bohemians, were 'wealthy.' Correspondingly, the Villagers, equally undiscriminatingly, assumed that all the local people were poor. This mutual assumption rested partly on difference in occupation and partly on difference in standard of living. As in the case of education, occupational overlapping did not draw the groups together socially. Though the number of white-collar workers among the younger of the local population increased and a larger proportion of Villagers were drawn from the same white-collar ranks, greater occupational similarity did not bridge the gap. In their relations with each other, these young white-collar workers of both groups took their status from their parents' position rather than from their own jobs.

Standards of living, and the social values that went with them, were the most conspicuous surface manifestations of social differences. Money was handled in a different manner by the two groups. Among the local people, the one crime against oneself and society was to be a 'sucker' — to get less than one's money's worth. In their observation of, and dealings with, the Villagers they had ample opportunity to discover grounds for scorning them on this count. The high rents which the Villagers paid condemned them from the start. The local population generally lived in tenements with a minimum of modern improvements and considerable crowding. Among Villagers with families, the aim, at least, was a room for each child; among the local people a bed for each child was usually an impossibility. It was not simply that one group had more money to spend, but that they spent it very differently with an entirely different sort of budgeting.

To the local people, $35 a month for an apartment for a whole family was high. To the Villagers, $50 for one or two people was low. The fact that the very houses where the Villagers were paying $50 to $75 were nothing but made-over tenements where the former occupants had been paying $20 to $25 helped to make the payment of such rents seem to reflect a warped sense of values. The Villagers, whose living standards called for a minimum of decency, condemned their neighbors wholesale for living in squalor — i.e., in the only houses which the incomes of most of the local families could encompass. Well-grounded disgust with the type of tenement house in the neighborhood was translated into a condemnation of the people who lived in such houses. When the

Villagers were asked what they disliked about their Italian neighbors, they frequently revealed this attitude in the ready answer, 'the way they live.' In this condemnation, the Villagers were quite undiscriminating, for they entertained an all-embracing contempt for tenement living without distinguishing between those who had money and the choice to live differently and those who did not.

The local people's sense of values made them critical of the Villagers' high rents on two counts, first because the latter were letting themselves be gypped — surely they could find something decent to live in at a reasonable price — and second, because of their choice to pay high rent in preference to other forms of expenditure which their critics regarded as more important. Even while classing the Villagers as 'wealthy,' the local people registered the fact that they skimped on food whenever they were pinched, and they derided them for starving themselves. Their conclusions about the habits of the Villagers were well founded. Among the Villagers interviewed, half stated that they would put expenditures on such things as rent, books, and theaters ahead of food, and many of the rest only replied that they could not do so because their food allowance was already at an irreducible minimum. The food standards of the Villagers were often below what the local people regarded as a level of decency, just as the latter's living quarters fell below the standard of decency set by the Villagers. The difference in these values, like many differences between local people and Villagers, reflected their respective backgrounds even more than their immediate position. The Villagers, especially that very large proportion who came from out of town, had lived in homes characterized by a modicum of space, air, light, and warmth. Since city housing was proportionately much dearer than city food, the irreducible minimum in housing, judged from the standards to which the Villagers were accustomed, was only met by a severe tax on their incomes, while food remained flexible. They had, moreover, rarely faced actual hunger or starvation. The local people, on the other hand, had often known the meaning of hunger and would not knowingly repeat the experience.

Physical standard of living was only one element in the whole set of values which differed radically in the two worlds. In their fundamental attitudes toward money, sex, and the institution of the family, as well as countless minor aspects of their social lives, the assumptions of the two groups were in conflict. With the passage of years and the process of Americanization, some of the differences had begun to disappear. But in 1930, these had only been importantly reduced with respect to the small, educated element among the local people and the newer of the white-collar Villagers. 'They have moved from the foreign press to the American tabloids,' observed a local college student of his local neighbors. 'But they aren't yet on the plane of the *New York Times*, and when they get there the distance between the *Times* and the *New Republic* will remain to be traveled before the attitudes of local people are like those of the Villagers. It's a long way.' Where the two groups differed in basic social assumptions, it was frequently one side only, and not always the same side, which was aware of the difference.

Almost without exception, the various types of Villagers agreed in setting a relatively low social value on money for its own sake. It was this more than any other single cultural value which had made the great bulk of Villagers leave home communities with whose standards they were not in sympathy. For the local people, in direct and violent contrast, the money drive was the great outstanding fact of life. By spending money carelessly in purchasing groceries or liquor, the Villagers earned the hearty contempt of those from whom they bought. It had become a matter of unconscious habit for one storekeeper systematically to put her less good articles — cans with the labels torn, rolls that were slightly burnt — into the packages for the Villagers — 'the people you can put things over on' — rather than in the orders for her Italian customers. The bootleggers had little respect for any of their customers, but only the ones who came in with 'I can get this for $2 at Jack's. What kind of a price can you give me?' were entitled to even a modicum of regard. That a person could afford to be a little careless — to pay an extra dollar a month for his liquor — was of no importance. If he had been gypped, that was all there was to it. The Villagers were unconscious of the contempt meted out to them on this score.

As a corollary of the money drive, the local people took it for granted that everybody was out for himself or for his family. Conduct based on any other motive was inexplicable. Disinterest-

edness was part of the code of at least a substantial part of the
Villagers, while it was an unknown quality to the local people.
This difference stood in the way of any contact between the two
groups where self-seeking was not the basis, making the local
people sharply suspicious of any gesture of the Villagers. It
complicated the relations between social agencies and their clients,
for the social workers' motives had no place in the latter's social
code, while the social workers in turn were baffled by and indignant
at the people's tendency to exploit the agencies. Neither group
in the community was directly aware of the contrary assumption
on the part of the other, but each interpreted actions of the other
in the light of his own assumption. To the Villagers the Italians
were 'grasping' — to the Italians the Villagers were 'crazy.'

Differences in attitudes toward sex contributed a generous
share of misunderstanding and confusion. Here, again, contempt
was chiefly on the side of the local people, but the Villagers were
more aware of how their assumptions differed. To the Italians,
there were two kinds of women, the good and the bad, the virgin
and the prostitute. You married the first and you 'laid' as many
of the second as you could get by hook or crook. Although the
Italians differed on the basis of their education and Americanization as to the circumstances, if any, in which they would refrain
from taking advantage of a girl, they were agreed in assuming that
whatever happened would be the girl's responsibility rather than
the man's. If a boy got a girl into trouble, the fault lay with the
girl's father who had not protected her. It was quite safe to make
advances to a married woman because, if her infidelity was discovered, it would be she who would suffer the husband's wrath
and not the other man. The Irish were more ready to lay responsibility on the man and were less single-minded in regarding
a woman as simply a source of physical satisfaction and in classing
all as 'good' or 'bad.'

On the basis of these assumptions, the local people's estimate of
Villager girls were simple. They were loose. They were 'kept
women.' 'How else could they live in these apartments? You
know what a girl can earn.' A little peeking into windows where
blinds were frequently not drawn was enough to confirm the
generalizations. The Villager men were envied their good-looking,
well-dressed 'women,' and the idea that they all had money was

supported by the presumption that they did not get girls like that for nothing. To the Italians, living among the Villagers was almost like living in a large-scale disorderly house; to the Irish and others, it was only somewhat less so. No wonder the local people regarded the Villagers as a menace to the decency of their neighborhood and to the morals of their children.

For their part, the Villagers were indifferent to the attitude of the local people. Armed with their own ideas about Freud, about 'bourgeois morality,' or about the independence of women, the Villagers went calmly on their way without the slightest concern for what interpretation the local people might place on their conduct. When the neighbors in desperation called in the police, and insisted that at least the shades be drawn, the Villagers expressed surprise that their conduct had been offensive. Since the sex life of the local people was led less conspicuously than that of the Villagers and the latter were, in any case, less noticing and curious about their neighbors than were the former, the Villagers did not take the trouble to notice sex attitudes of the local people. When they thought about the subject at all, their generalizations about 'all Latins' fitted the Italians, and their ideas of middle-class respectability most of the rest.

In their attitudes toward the institution of the family, the two groups were poles asunder. The Villagers condemned their tenement neighbors because they had 'too many children.' Next to their noise and dirt, this was the most frequent source of complaint. Correspondingly, the local people accused the Villagers of living only for themselves and not taking on the responsibilities of raising a family which was everybody's responsibility and one of the principal reasons for living. In this clash of assumption were combined two tenets of the Villagers, first that child-bearing was a matter of choice, that parents had no business to have children unless they could afford to rear them, and that the low-class, poor people like their neighbors had no business having a large family; and, secondly, that the end of life was the individual rather than the family group and that, therefore, child-raising did not fall as a natural responsibility upon all, but was an alternative to other forms of activity. They were familiar with the view, held by the older generation, at least, among the local people, that children were sent by God, and must be accepted as his gift with the faith that He would provide. They condemned this attitude as evidence of ignorance and of economic irresponsibility.

While these major clashes of assumptions, and the psychological gulf growing out of them, were much more acute between the Villagers and Italians than between Villagers and other local people, certain areas of incomprehensibility divided the others, especially the Irish, from their new neighbors. For the Villagers, the Irish interest in politics was very hard to imagine. To the former, Tammany was a synonym for evil; to the Irish it was the road to success or at least to jobs. In the Villagers' eyes, the political machine was an utterly rotten compound of graft and corruption. The Irish took it for granted as 'just the way things work.' This was the point on which Villagers and Irish were the farthest apart.

The Catholic Church and what it stood for was an added source of social distance. Few of the Villagers were Catholics. Many were wholly irreligious. Both Protestant and Catholic churches of the locality described the apartment dwellers as a 'godless' crowd, and among the Villagers questioned the great majority (71 per cent) did not attend church. The close adherence of the Irish to the Catholic Church was, thus, to the Villagers, an incomprehensible evidence of ignorance or medievalism, while to the Irish the Villager 'atheists' were steeped in sin. Most of the Villagers, coming from Protestant backgrounds, shared the characteristic Protestant difficulty in understanding the Catholic position. But the more profound gulf was between the religious and irreligious, between those to whom religion was meaningless and those for whom it was not only the most basic of assumptions but the major social institution in their lives.

Social habits did not separate Villagers and Irish to the degree that they did Villagers and Italians. Though the Irish looked askance at the behavior of the Villagers, deploring their lack of family life, and though they raised their eyebrows at girls who smoked on the street, and were very dubious of their new neighbors' morality, they were sufficiently used to American habits not to set every Villager girl down as a 'loose woman.'

To the Villagers, in their turn, the Irish were not wholly mysterious. Some had had Irish cooks or nursemaids in their youth; others Irish schoolmates. There was no language barrier as there was with the Italians. Except for the high place in the Irish social hierarchy given to a political career, the Irish social scale closely resembled the old American, and though many of the Villagers repudiated this scale, they were aware of it and could recognize it. But while the psychological gulf between Irish and Villagers was less than between the latter and the Italians, the social gap remained unbridged.

When each side expressed itself articulately about the other, it voiced a compound of dislike of specific external forms of behavior and an interpretation of that behavior in terms of its own attitudes. The Italians summed up their view of the Villagers in the current statement, 'They are too free with themselves. They have no respect.' The Irish were quite clear that 'It's crazy, I call it, living in made-over stables. There's no other name for those people, they're nuts.'

The Villagers expressed their objections to those ways of their neighbors which impaired the attractiveness of the locality as a residential section. They objected to dirt and smell — to the dregs of the wine barrel on the sidewalk; the banana peels hurled out of the window; the odor of garlic; the litter habitually tossed on the streets where, in warm weather, people lived out-of-doors and where there was rarely a rubbish can; grimy children whose play space was the gutter. Almost more strongly, they disliked noise — the children at play, the scolding of the women, the vendors peddling their wares — all the human sounds characteristic of congested living. The adults were too gregarious, always congregating on the stoops and chattering. The children were frightful. The few people to whom these sounds and sights meant vitality and local color were the tiny minority. Most took it for granted that the community should be geared to their taste. From their point of view, the problem of their relation to the local people was simply that between a higher and a lower standard of living. Many complained that when they moved in they counted on the neighborhood being 'cleaned up' soon. Those who bought houses on this assumption, in particular, found the failure of the area to be rapidly and completely transformed from one type of district to the other particularly distressing to their pocket-books as well as to their peace.

On the side of the local people, the relationship was not quite so simple, for it involved the invasion of what they regarded as their home by people whose advent threatened or effected their eviction, whose higher social status and superior Americanism made it impossible to ignore them, but whose standards of conduct were at variance with those which the Irish and Italians wished to impart to their children.

There was no evidence that years of living in an Italian community had any effect on the Villagers' attitude toward 'foreigners' in general or Italians in particular. Among a sample of forty-five Villagers representing a variety of local types who came in contact with Italians on their blocks, not the slightest correlation could be found between their attitudes toward intermarriage with Italians and their observation or dislike of them as neighbors. The completely negative character of this evidence suggested that the irritation and conflict produced by physical juxtaposition in this community did not cut through to the underlying prejudices and tolerances of those who came to reside here. The fact that the Villagers almost all entered the area as adults meant that their point of view was originally shaped elsewhere, while the social gulf between them and their neighbors prevented any observations they might make of the latter from being incorporated into their point of view. Interrelations between Villagers and local people in this community tended to reflect rather than to mould attitudes — at least for the Villagers.

Time had brought some very slight modification of the psychological gulf between the two groups on the side of the local people, but none on the side of the Villagers. For the latter, the gulf was, if anything, widened by a change in type of resident. The first type of Villager was closer to the local neighbors than were the later types. Although some who first moved in sought only cheap rents and convenience and regarded the local population as necessary, noisy nuisances — if they regarded them at all — many of the earlier type had been attracted to the locality partly because of its picturesque charm and they regarded their neighbors with a broad, though distant, human sympathy. They recognized themselves, moreover, as the intruders into a community which had its own social standards.

Among the newer type, few signs of such appreciation were found. The butcher, the baker, the laundryman, and the pushcart owner were little more than so many animated jobs. Though in 1920 neither group really crossed over into the other's world, but only dallied on the edge of it, some members of each group had the opportunity to distinguish some members of the other group as persons and to find some slight basis of understanding. In the new Village, with its apartments and made-over tenements, filled with people who were there first and often exclusively for convenience and who felt that the area belonged to them, such bridgings of the gulf were very few and far between.

On the other hand, the younger generation among the local people had come to look upon the Villagers only partly with contempt. By 1930, envy had crept in to temper their scorn, and such envy was the first step toward moving them into the same sphere. In the first place, the younger element had learned to distinguish between the 'bohemians' and the 'professional people.' It was the latter whose superior education, nicer homes, better-looking girls — even the greater social freedom of their way of life — were not only tolerated but coveted. When the question, 'What do you like about the new residents?' was put to 144 Italians, the answers of the older and younger groups were strikingly different. Among the older people, two thirds liked nothing. Among the younger, all except one liked something — their education and freedom, their artistic and literary interests, their better homes, their dress, their originality. None feared their moral influence in undermining the institution of the family as their parents did. 'You really do envy them,' acknowledged one youth, 'and it's your defense reactions that make you despise them. When you're standing outside the delicatessen store and they walk in without even seeing you — well, you resent it, because you're jealous of them; they have more than you — more money, more education. You'd be sore at them for being condescending if they spoke to you, but you do wish they'd notice you.'

At the same time that the local men and girls were becoming somewhat more tolerant of the Villagers' social ways, resentment against them on economic grounds was rising. The first Villagers did not constitute an economic threat to the residents of the locality, however much they might be ignored or heartily condemned as moral menaces. With the wave of remodeling of houses in 1925 and especially the remaking of tenements after 1928, the Villagers became a direct danger to those who desired to remain in the neighborhood. While many had not wanted to remain and had moved away, those who stayed on were attached either by necessity or choice. It was, therefore, not surprising to find them indignant at the Villagers. 'They have money. They can live anywhere. Why do they have to take our homes away from us?' The old storekeepers, with only one or two exceptions, were unanimous. 'They have ruined business, buying nothing but a box of crackers or a can of beans.' Economic fear reinforced moral indignation and helped to prevent the gulf between local people and Villagers from being bridged.

Actual contacts between local people and Villagers were few and far between. Even when they lived in closest proximity and encountered each other daily on the same street, they would pass literally without seeing each other. This was somewhat truer of the Villagers than of the local people, for the latter were more likely to be hanging around or sitting on stoops, noticing and passing remarks about everybody who went by. Out of ninety Villagers questioned directly on this point, two thirds never greeted any of the local population when they met them on the street. In the places patronized primarily by local people, the presence of a Villager was conspicuous. 'They stick out like a sore thumb when they are shopping from the pushcarts — asking the name of this and that — trying to like Italian food.'

Business contacts were few, hurried, and involved only the group of local shopkeepers. The great mass of local Italians and Irish who engaged in unskilled labor, truck-driving, factory work, or skilled trades had no personal dealings with the Villagers whatever. Contact between Villagers and local professional people was almost equally scarce. With the introduction of electric refrigeration, even the iceman had been eliminated. Delicatessens and drugstores, cleaners and laundries, restaurants and speak-easies, and, to some extent, groceries were practically the only kinds of local businesses which were patronized by the Villagers. And here efforts to make contacts on the part of Villagers were countered with indifference or scorn. The casual, friendly relations between storekeeper and customer — the kind which existed be-tween the local storekeepers and their local customers — were repulsed as evidence of condescension on the infrequent occasions when some of the Villagers made a move in this direction. 'You know the kind — that make a fetish of trading at the same store, thinking "This is Mary. She's a good soul" — asking after her health — has she any trouble — can they help her — and all the time paying more than they would have to pay at the chain store across the street. Mary pays no attention — just says "yes, yes," and goes on with her work. You don't earn the respect of people by being condescending and at the same time a sucker.'

The principal place of contact was in the speakeasies, but even here any effort at social contact was met with contempt. 'The more you talk to the bootlegger, the less he thinks of you.' Nothing earned greater scorn than to talk Italian. 'You don't like people who try to turn native.' One speakeasy proprietor, who 'considered himself a gentleman,' but had to have some conversation with his patrons in letting them in through the locked door, was so annoyed at their efforts in Italian that some Jewish boys on the block taught him a Yiddish phrase which would express his real sentiments toward these customers. His response to the hated 'Buon giorno' was, 'How are you, signor? May you drop dead, signor.' It delighted his neighbors to hear him call after a departing patron, 'Good-bye, signor. May you drop dead, signor.'

And yet it was in business more than in any other field that contacts between local people and Villagers arose. Religion did not bring them together, for even the few Protestant Italians had separate ministers and separate congregations within the English-speaking churches. In a very few cases, new Catholic families moved into the new apartments and, by taking an active part in the affairs of the principal Catholic church, became associated with the Irish element. For the most part, however, the few Catholics among the Villagers merely went to church to hear Mass and left, making no contact with any of the rest of the parish or even with the priest. Except for a few high-up politicians who had moved into one of the new apartments built by a local political figure and largely occupied by Tammany politicians, the Villagers did not enter politics sufficiently for any contact to develop there. The local district captains, in fact, took non-voting on the part of the apartment-house dwellers largely for granted and relied for a showing at the polls almost entirely upon the old local element.

The Socialist local, on the other hand, was composed of a wholly white-collar group.

Some of the facilities of Greenwich House were used by a few Villagers — its pottery instruction, music school, Italian class, professional women's gym class — and a few Villagers patronized its nursery school and its clinics. The House encountered the difficulty, however, in offering its services to Villagers, that many of the latter associated it with the local people and never thought of using it themselves. Except for a few who took part in a theater group, moreover, even the use of the House was unlikely to lead to social contact. The House found its efforts to get the parents of its nursery-school children together obstructed by the fact that they came from both groups and were hard to mix. If it invited Villager women into a group made up of local mothers, it ran the risk of having its invitation regarded as an insult. Those few of the local boys at the House who tried to get to know the Villager girls who came there neither succeeded in their efforts nor added to their prestige among their fellows. They even came to feel that the residents at the House, often young college men and girls, were inaccessible to them, though they, also, had been to college. 'If you want to dance with some of the boys,' a college boy who patronized the House advised an investigator, 'go and stand with the girls, not with the residents. It takes an awful lot of nerve to ask one of the residents to dance.'

As civic interest lagged in the post-War years, as the 'community spirit' fostered during the War died down, and as the old group of socially minded Villagers was supplanted largely by the self-centered or the indifferent, the efforts of the House to serve as an amalgamating force between the two major groups in the community encountered insuperable obstacles.

Children, the ever-present source of contact in communities where differences are less marked, were here no link, for the children of Villagers were not permitted to play on the street. Only at the progressive public school, and through the Parent-Teachers' Association connected with that school, had the two groups been brought together. Once in a while, one of the Villagers might take an interest in the children on the block — an artist who taught them to do something with paint, a young man who set them to making model airplanes out of fruit crates, a woman who invited some of the little girls up to her apartment. But for the vast majority of the Villagers the children were simply a source of noise and torment.

In the informal social life that went on in the apartments and homes of the respective elements of the community, there was no crossing of the line. The local boys looked through the unshaded windows with envy at the gin and the girls which adorned the parties given by the young Villagers. They cast especially covetous eyes upon the attractive girls whom the New York University fraternity men brought to their fraternity houses, saying, 'What we couldn't do to them!' But they never expected to get in on such parties and they never molested such girls or the Villager girls who lived in neighboring houses. Only when a person stepped out of his own sphere did contact take place. If a Villager girl should stray into an Italian men's café alone, stay too long, fraternize with the boys, and get too drunk, she could not be too surprised to come to in an empty apartment with a crowd of boys taking advantage of her in turn. Such episodes, however, were rare. Yet the fact that they occurred, and the comments of the people on the block, 'She got what was coming to her,' indicated the circumstances in which the two planes might impinge on each other.

Rarely did any of the local boys or girls stray into the tea rooms, cabarets, or hangouts of the Villagers. By their parents, such places were assumed to be dens of iniquity, 'free love, and God knows what else,' and it did not even occur to most of the local girls to enter. Those very few who so ventured did so at the risk of serious trouble at home if they were discovered. A local Jewish college girl defied the local code and adventured with one of the local Italian girls into some of the tea rooms. When the Italian girl's father discovered where they were, he came to the tea room and made a furious scene, taking her away. On another occasion the Jewish girl's father came after her and ordered her to leave the tea room and to stay away.

Rather than visit the Village cabarets, local girls and boys would go to the Times Square section and patronize one of the cheaper of the Chinese 'dine and dance' places on Broadway. Even the girls who had greater liberty than most reported that their parents would absolutely prohibit their going to a Village cabaret. When a crowd of local young Italian men had made a large winning on a punch-ball game, or perhaps a successful stick-up, they sometimes celebrated by hiring dress suits and 'crashing' a cabaret. The 'crashing' consisted not in getting in without paying, but in paying their way to where they felt that they did not belong. This feeling of not belonging in places patronized by Villagers or by people from outside extended even to some of the drugstores and lunch counters. Though the two groups swung their legs at the counter of the same diner and pushed trays in the same cafeteria, certain of the conspicuously located drugstores were only entered by local boys and girls with the feeling of being intruders, while in the candy stores where the latter drank their ice-cream sodas the Villagers were not at home.

Both Villagers and local people were practically unanimous in asserting that personal relations between individuals in the two groups were virtually non-existent, except for the members of the Parent-Teachers' Association and the children at the progressive public school. A few scraps of evidence, however, suggested that contacts might have taken place more often than came to light. Though isolated episodes, they qualify the general statement that the social gulf between local people and Villagers had always been and remained complete. A handsome young Italian bootlegger's assistant was asked by a Villager girl to deliver some gin, which she could easily have carried home herself. When he arrived, she invited him in, gave him drinks, danced with him, and ended by sleeping with him. A young man who owned a dog reported that by means of this dog he had picked up acquaintances with some of the Village women dog-owners. One case was found where a local Italian boy was invited to a Villager's party — in one of the few houses occupied by both Villagers and local people. The Villager, a young clerical worker, was in the habit of giving allnight or two-day parties with a great deal of gin, and girls and men from uptown. At one of these parties one man was lacking, and an Italian boy from downstairs was invited up. When the girl who fell to his lot for the night demurred, the host told her that after all it was his party and he could bring in whom he chose. One or another of the local boys would occasionally pick up one of the Villager 'fairies,' sometimes to make a little money off him, sometimes to rob him.

When the two social worlds impinged on each other, it was more likely to be in conflict than in contact. Though the prevailing attitude of each group to the other was one of indifference touched with contempt, active clashes occasionally arose. These were acute when the first of the Villagers began to move in. Those who bought houses found themselves faced with an almost hopeless struggle to protect their property against the depredations of children — to keep the windows whole and the vestibules free from scars and filth. One of these reminisced bitterly about the early days and enumerated the others who had come in when he did, but who had been unable to stick it out and had gone away. Around 1920, it was the local residents who were the aggressors, attacking the intruders who had come into a neighborhood which was eminently theirs. With the progress of remodeling, the tables were turned. By 1930, the Villagers regarded at least certain parts of the district so thoroughly as theirs that it was they who took the offensive in seeking to interfere with the habits of the natives. Again, the children constituted the point of conflict. Between February and June, 1931, the police of the precinct which contained twenty-three mixed blocks responded to calls from the new residents of seventeen of these blocks to assist them against the local children. Complaints against the children specified vandalism, hoodlumism, or simply ball-playing or hanging around the steps. They represented in a mild form the running battle between two groups trying to live different kinds of lives on the same blocks.

On block after block, episodes revealing conflict were reported. On one block the superintendent of a newly remodeled apartment house stated firmly, 'This is a quiet street. We have had some trouble with boys playing ball out here, but we have chased them and have got the police after them. Where are they to play? We don't care — in front of their own houses, but *not* here.' The house next door was occupied by 'those boys.' It was a corner house facing on a thoroughfare with a trolley-line and on the quiet side street. The side street presented an ideal play situation, and the boys got up a petition, signed by all the local people on the block to have the street closed and made a play street. The Villagers not only refused to sign, but countered by calling the police to chase the boys. The sympathies of the police were with the boys.

'Where else are they to play? — But what can we do? The complaint comes in and we have to answer or the property-owner will make trouble.'

This was not an isolated instance. On another block, one side of the street had been remodeled; the other side had not and was occupied by Irish. A new resident summoned the police daily to chase the children at play. She called them 'gangsters' and cuffed them when she could lay hands on them. An Irish mother protested, 'This is a decent street. I done my best to raise my children right. I can't let the little ones go onto other, tougher blocks where they'll learn wrong and I won't be able to keep my eyes on them. Why haven't they the right to play in front of their own homes?' She accused the woman of having pull because her husband was a lawyer. The woman, in turn, complained that the police were Irish and favored the children. The Irish mother retorted with counter-charges of the things that her daughters had to see through the upper windows across the street. 'How can I bring them up decent with that sort of goings-on right under their eyes and those nuts that call themselves artists not even taking the trouble to close the blinds.'

On still another block the situation became acute. The noise of the children, the remarks passed by young men loafing around the candy store, the shouts of the women and the cries of vendors all combined to make tenants of the remodeled houses move out, making apartments almost impossible to rent and forcing one realtor into bankruptcy. People who had hoped that the street would be 'cleaned up' when they moved in felt that the situation had gone from bad to worse. 'This street seems to get rougher and rougher,' they complained. Again the protest was not one-sided. A group of young people, coming out very drunk from a midnight party in one of the new apartments, offended a group of Italian card-players on the opposite stoop until the latter resorted to action. One of the merrymakers was knocked out completely and the rest sought refuge indoors. When the party finally broke up at 3 A.M., the revelry of home-goers was the signal for tenement windows to fly up and buckets of water and garbage to come hurtling down.

Even on quiet streets where remodeling had become almost complete, minor differences produced irritation if not conflict. A woman complained of the Italian who kept the speakeasy that she shouted so in talking with her friends, that 'it's almost like living in the slums. I am nearly ready to move on account of it.'

The failure of the gap between local people and Villagers to be narrowed in spite of years of juxtaposition was the most striking evidence of the complete distance and difference of their two worlds. Other factors during the period contributed strongly to making the local people aware of much in the background of the Villagers of which they had earlier been unaware. Partly through formal education, much more through the things which they saw in the movies or read in the tabloid press or heard over the radio, the horizon of the native population was tremendously expanded in the direction of a new familiarity with the backgrounds and modes of conduct familiar to the Villagers. It was striking that, through all the evidence of the widened horizon which was found, there was no indication that the actual lives of their neighbors had contributed to this widening. It was rather the impersonal, general, cultural sources from which such knowledge of other standards of living and other ways of behavior had been drawn.

Beyond the worlds of both local people and Villagers was still a third world, very much nearer to the former than to the latter — the underworld of gang life. Although most of the local people lived relatively law-abiding lives, the wall which separated them from the underworld was a thin one which might at any moment be broken through. To the Villagers, except for a few newspapermen, gangdom was a more or less remote area. For the local people, it was just around the corner. A young Italian barber, helping to build up an independent union, would find himself guarded by some 'East Side material' while a West Side gang took charge of the leaders of the rival union. All types of local storekeepers had the experience of being forced to pay protection, and, in such businesses as coal, ice, or laundry delivery, forced to keep out of the territory which 'belonged' to rival interests. Although the general run of retail liquor distributors in the locality were not part of the criminal element, the liquor traffic was a link between the ordinary life of the community and the underworld. The possibility of crossing over into the world outside of the law, ever present in the lives of the local people, carried them still farther away from the Villagers than did the other aspects of their lives.

No division within the ranks of the local people or in those of the Villagers compared in completeness with the gap between the two. Though an Italian might not speak to an Irishman or a business man might not associate with a laborer, each was conscious of the other and lived his life in terms of the presence of the other. The laborer looked with envy on the prosperous man and would emulate him if he could. The business man noticed the laborer sufficiently to feel his superiority. At least within very wide boundaries, certain common standards of values and commonly accepted patterns of behavior obtained.

It did not occur to either local people or Villagers to include the other group in their social hierarchy. When the Villagers distinguished among themselves as to the groups with whom they associated and the types of behavior which prevailed, it never seemed necessary to them to note any distinction between themselves and the local people, this was taken so completely for granted. Villagers interviewed almost always had something to say about other groups among the Villagers, pointing out to the interviewer that they did not all do thus and so. Never once did they make any comment upon the local population in a manner to indicate that they included the latter in at all the same category as themselves. The only exception was the social workers, and they, of course, did not identify themselves with their clients or the patrons of their institutions. In an editorial on a complaint of some of the local people against the Villagers, the *New York Times* recognized how deep-seated were their differences. 'It is to be noted that the complainants describe themselves as "residents of that part of the old Ninth Ward now prominently featured as Greenwich Village." By that phrase they proclaim their position in the ancient feud which has been going on ever since artists began to infest Washington Square and the old residents began to lift the scornful nose. Preferences in that struggle depend on congenital differences of opinion; the whole human race might be divided into the Ninth-Warders and the Villagers.' [1]

The social relationships here described were not unique to Greenwich Village. The backflow of population was an urban development likely to become more characteristic of metropolitan centers. The two worlds of commuter and non-commuter have

[1] *New York Times*, June 4, 1921.

become familiar to suburbs. Immigrant newcomers have been penetrating into disintegrating middle-class communities in all types of cities and towns. Situations in which the same community contains separate, non-integrated social realms instead of a clear social hierarchy are likely to become increasingly characteristic of urban life.

V. LOCAL PEOPLE

1. ETHNIC GROUPINGS

AMONG the local people, the most fundamental social division was the ethnic one. More than economic barriers or geographic divisions, ethnic lines cut across the local population so firmly that for practically every aspect of local life the several ethnic groups had separate institutions and distinctive ways and were more or less firmly separated from each other by social barriers. Though these lines were not, and had never been, hard and fast, and though they varied in their intensity and inclusiveness for different ages, degrees of education and economic levels, they were inescapable.

The Italians, comprising over half of the population of the district, had come nearest to imposing upon the whole area their own social characteristics. The Irish were less ethnically distinguishable from the other English-speaking people at a similar economic level, but they, too, were conscious of themselves as a group and possessed distinctive habits. Though few in number, the Jews stood out clearly. The Spanish colony had so lost in membership as to have been almost eliminated, but it still supported its own institutions and had little to do with anybody else in the community. The scattered remnant of Germans had been cruelly reminded of their national origin during the War. Even the mere handful of families who survived from other groups were still distinguishable in 1930. The original old American families had retained enough sense of themselves as a group to be able to supply the names of the families who really 'belonged.' In 1920, three Negro blocks had been all that remained of what was once the principal Negro settlement in New York. By 1930, two 'Negro houses,' dilapidated tenements under the elevated, housed all the Negroes except janitors or seamen who were left. The Lithuanian settlement, which had been sufficiently strong and cohesive to organize a church in 1909, had nearly disappeared by 1930, but the church continued to function. The French settlement, which had been large enough around 1900 to furnish talent for French plays at Greenwich House, was reduced to a few houses containing some of the French waiters in the lower Fifth Avenue hotels. The scattering of Polish, Austrian, and Scandinavian families represented the remains of groups that had never had the coherence of the other ethnic elements in the community.

Ethnic divisions among the local population in the community arose as a matter of historical development. Because each group represented an inroad into the area at a different time and under different conditions, the ethnic label carried more than a strictly ethnic implication. To the Irish the 'Guineas' were not only 'foreigners' but newcomers. They were the ones who 'took their neighborhood away from them.' Even in 1930, thirty years after the Italian mass invasion, the older Irish still regarded the Italians as intruders.

The original difference in economic status which distinguished the penniless immigrant at the time of his arrival from those already in the community survived as a social attitude even after the difference had factually disappeared. Although during these years the relative economic position of Italian and Irish was almost reversed by a combination of hard work, saving, and bootlegging on the part of Italians and the decline of the longshore trade and selective migration among the Irish, the latter continued to look upon the former as poor immigrants. When they recognized the economic realities of the situation, it was to comment, 'You would be surprised how well off some of them are,' or else, 'No wonder they get ahead. They will grab anything.'

The social origins of the immigrant groups still further reinforced the ethnic line. Because most of the Italians and Spaniards were peasants at home, they were accorded in this community the status of peasant immigrants, and the son of a professional Italian, as far as non-Italians were concerned, was tarred with the same brush as the rest of the group as long as he remained in it.

The passage of time had worn off the sharp edges of the ethnic groupings, but had not destroyed their basic relevance. No other division cut across so many lines and was, itself, cut by so few. To analyze the community in other than ethnic terms in 1930 would have been difficult, for each alternative category would have had to be broken down into ethnic subdivisions. To have done so in 1920 would have been virtually impossible. Though the cessation of immigration, the Americanization or standardizing influences of the schools, the tremendous growth of the popular press, and the widespread impact of radio and movies all tended to reduce differences and to destroy the rigidity of ethnic lines, the process of standardization had only touched the outer surface. Ethnic lines were blurred but not blotted out, ethnic differences lessened but not eliminated. Under all the veneer of movie-minded, ten-cent-store Americanism, ethnic groupings remained fundamental to the mass of the population of this area, still determining both the culture patterns and the social structure of the local community and producing those social habits which continually called attention to differences. The smell of Italian cooking was a constant reminder frequently commented upon by the Irish neighbor. A young man was not allowed to forget that the girl whom he wished to take out was Italian when he found that she could not come, or that he must deliver her home again by ten o'clock or earlier.

Between the principal ethnic groups which made up the local population, Italians and Irish, relations ranged from violent antagonism to indifference, with some little contact and a tendency over the years toward less bitterness at least, if not toward more cordiality. Far from living in a different world as did the Villagers, the Irish were very much of the Italians' world, occupying the same houses, the same jobs, and the same streets. In a very real sense the Irish community, rather than the world which the Villagers represented, was the 'America' to which the immigrant Italians came. Their ways, in so far as the Italians could observe them, were 'American' ways. They occupied a higher position on the same plane rather than an altogether different and distant plane.

In their first impact, the clash between Irish and Italians resulted from fundamental economic competition. When the Italians began to invade the Village, they were a direct menace to the homogeneity and the residential quality of the area. Some of the better-class Irish met the invasion by moving to other parts of the city, while the rest retreated gradually westward, slowly abandoning block after block to the newcomers.

In this situation, it was not surprising that active conflict between Italians and Irish should arise. In the first stages, the fight came mostly from the Irish side, in resistance to the invasion of foreigners. Gangs of Irish boys did their best to prevent Italian children from using the public library by lying in wait for them and destroying the books. Interblock fights with bricks and stones were not uncommon. The Italian boy knew which streets it was good for him to walk on and he also knew the consequence of walking on the side of the park which the Irish had set apart for themselves. One street was, for many years, the no man's land where the major fights between the 'Wops' and the 'Micks' were waged — fights not always confined to youngsters.

Such active conflict subsided during the decade. The Irish retreat, during the later years, was faster than the advance of the Italians, the intervening space being occupied by a wedge of Villagers. As a result, it was on the 'better' streets and in higher-rent houses that the two came together in 1930 — a fact which combined with the toning-down of even the rougher streets to make active conflict rare. Moreover, 'Americanization' and long residence in the community had earned for the Italians a higher status than that which they had occupied a decade before — and therewith greater tolerance. Nevertheless, conflict between the two ethnic groups had not entirely vanished.

Some active economic conflict remained chiefly on the docks where the Irish longshoremen, once the aristocracy of the laboring population in the locality, had lost their position in handling the coastwise trade to lower-paid labor, Italian, Spanish, and Negro. Here the conflict was bitter and acute. But for the most part the two principal groups revolved within their respective economic and social spheres, simply retaining a consciousness of difference and a readiness to call 'Wop' or to break up an argument with 'Aw, you're Irish. Dumb Irish. There's no use arguing with you.' On the whole, relations between the two groups had been reduced by 1930 to a state where the Irish either feared to lose their power and prestige or else accepted the state of affairs with apathy, and where the Italians combined their newly developed confidence and lurking jealousy into a mixture of defiance, criticism, and tolerance.

The Irish continued to regard the Italians as 'foreigners' and the Italians to resent the superiority of the Irish. An Irish priest confessed his distaste at having to marry the nice Irish girls of his parish to the 'greasy Wops'; an Irish attendance officer aroused the ire of a parent by addressing her truant offspring as a 'Guinea bastard'; a political leader acknowledged his fear that the rising Italian element in the club might oust the existing Irish leadership. To the Italians, the Irish were still the ones who got all the favors and held desired and privileged positions. They thought of the change in the position of the Italian community in terms of the fact that 'the Irish can't lord it over the Italians the way they used to.'

The Italians directly questioned found it much easier to state what they disliked about the Irish than to name anything about them which they liked. The most general accusation was drunkenness — whiskey alone *vs.* wine with meals. Stubbornness, pugnacity, and, especially, stupidity were the stock phrases in the Italian's vocabulary reserved for his Irish neighbors. 'Did you ever hear of an Irishman with an idea in his head? You don't mind the girls so much. After all, you judge a girl by a different standard.' Sociability and good-natured humor were the saving graces of the Irish disposition which a number of the Italians who were questioned were ready to acknowledge. The merits of an individual Irishman had to outweigh the handicap of his nationality. An Italian defending his political leader could make his point no stronger than by declaring, 'Now he's Irish, and me and you, Tony, we're Wops, but you've got to admit...'

The principal contact between the groups came in politics, where the Irish had taken steps to prevent the loss of their mastery.[1] The fact of their common religion did little to bring the groups together, for a separate Italian-language parish had been formed when the Italian colony was still young. Some intermingling had taken place in the southern geographical parish of the district during the period when the one national group was

[1] Cf. Chapter IX.

supplanting the other, but this parish had become almost solidly Italian by 1920. The remaining three parishes retained their Irish character. Many of the Italians were such indifferent Catholics, moreover, that the Irish hardly regarded them as co-religionists. In the one Irish church which was attended by a number of Italians, they were resented by the Irish because they did not contribute proportionately to the support of the church.

In school, too, the two groups hardly met, for the Irish filled the parochial and the Italians the public schools. Before the Italians came in, the Irish had filled the public as well as the parochial schools, but they withdrew from the former under the impact of the Italians, and after the closing of the one elementary school in their section of the neighborhood in 1930, those remaining in public school were very few. Most Italians, much less faithful in carrying out religious precepts, sent their children to parochial school only when the latter was more conveniently located. The one parochial school in the center of the Italian district was entirely Italian, though the sisters were Irish. In 1929, a new school, in charge of an Italian order, was opened by the Italian church and was drawing pupils by the fact that it was distinctively Italian. The children of the two groups thus met only in one predominantly Irish parochial school convenient to a large section of the Italians which in 1930 was about one-eighth Italian and seven-eighths Irish.

Among the children on the street, violent clashes had become much fewer with the change in the street code, but as late as 1929 an Irish youngster was killed in a gang fight waged with bottles, bricks, and hatchets when the Irishers undertook to beat up the neighboring Italian crowd for molesting one of their smaller fellows. Most block gangs continued to be made up principally of distinct nationalities, largely because blocks were fairly homogeneous in residence. Such mixing in street groups as was found in 1930 appeared to be on the basis of individual accomplishment rather than a disregard for ethnic differences, for where an individual of a different nationality was found in a group, he was apt to be the leader or an otherwise outstanding member. This was true not only of Irish and Italians but of Jewish, Spanish, and colored boys as well. Of the 36 street play groups investigated in different parts of the district, 20 contained only one nationality.

Of the 16 mixed groups, 8 were of primarily one nationality with a single additional member who had some particular quality of distinction. Two Italian groups were led by Negroes and one was led by a Jew. Of the 8 truly mixed groups, 4 contained three or more nationalities, 2 were Irish-Italian, 1 Irish-Jewish, and 1 Russian-Spanish. A group of Irish girls admitted two Italians to their membership only after a hot debate.

Such intermingling as took place among children did not appear to carry over beyond early adolescence. Among the 16 older street groups studied, 11 contained a single nationality and 4 more were predominantly either Italian or Irish, with only one or two of the other nationalities among them. One group only out of the 16 was truly mixed. As soon as boys began to associate with girls, they reported that they quickly fell back within their own groups.

At Greenwich House, there was intermingling between part of the original Irish clientèle and the Italians who made up an increasingly large proportion of the membership. Children's groups and boys' athletic teams were thoroughly mixed. The young people, especially girls, and the adults who were brought together at the House were drawn from a distinct element among the Italians, and, to a lesser degree, among the Irish. The Italian girls who came to the House came primarily from the more Americanized homes rather than from those families which were absorbed within the Italian group, clung closest to the Italian church, or patronized one of the other centers because it had an Italian staff. The Italian girls at the House knew little about the general run of girls in the neighborhood, had few friends among them, and tended to refer to them as the 'low' type of girl. The boys were a less selected type, but they represented a level of education above the majority of neighborhood boys, and, partly for geographical reasons, were rarely drawn from the heart of the Italian community. Italian women patronized the clinics and sent their children to nursery school, but few joined in social activities, where the mothers' clubs were primarily Irish. The House contained no men's clubs, but it offered its hall from time to time for meetings of Italian societies.

The Irish had long been closely associated with the House and made up its staunchest clientèle. Though their relative numbers declined, and though some families lost interest in the House when it became predominantly Italian, a nucleus of remaining Irish constituted part of the several House groups. Some differences of interest, such as a greater interest in intellectual activities and in discussion on the part of the Italians, made the paths of Irish and Italians diverge even within the House, and some of the groups which had been formed outside and had come into the House as clubs were made up predominantly of one or the other group. But at dances, and in the groups composed within the House, the Irish and Italians who attended mingled freely.

Some contact resulted where different nationalities lived in the same houses on certain blocks. In such cases as were found, however, the Irish woman tended to keep apart from her neighbors, either ignoring them or maintaining a superficially friendly but conscious distant relationship, finding that 'it's better to keep to yourself and never enter an Italian argument. They're bound to turn on you all together even if you have taken one of their parts. They're jealous of you as an American, though you may not have any more money.' The fact that in most of the houses containing both Irish and Italian it was the code to keep more to oneself prevented common residence from leading to much contact.

The extent, nature, and results of intermarriage would throw the strongest light on the subject of contact between ethnic groups and the process by which the gulf between them was bridged. Data on this subject, unfortunately, could not be secured, for marriage licenses recording the nationality of parents were not filed according to locality, but were lumped with the rest of New York's millions; churches kept only a record of intermarriage between Catholics and Protestants, not between two different Catholic groups; and even if one were willing to guess from the names appearing on the parish registers, the records of the local churches would not show the most usual form of intermarriage, that between Italian boys from the locality and non-Italian girls from outside the neighborhood who would be married, of course, in the bride's parish.

Attitudes toward intermarriage ranged all the way from the Irish woman who reported that her daughters knew enough to stick to their own kind and to refuse to dance with Italian men at the political club, to the family in which the German-American wife of an Italian had to ask her daughter what kind of men and girls her own children had married or had gone with, and whether her grandchild was baptized Catholic or Protestant. Both these positions were extreme, but the view of the majority appeared to lie somewhat nearer the first than the second attitude as far as the Irish were concerned. Out of twenty-five Irish persons expressing themselves directly on the question of intermarriage, eighteen were emphatic in asserting their objections to having a daughter or sister marry an Italian, though some realistically added 'if we could help it.'

Objections on this score were stronger on the part of the Irish than the Italians, for they looked upon themselves as social superiors, not to be demeaned by marriage with a 'foreigner.' Among the older Italians questioned, however, 41 per cent objected to intermarriage with the Irish. On the Italian side, the objection did not carry over strongly into the second generation. Only 12 per cent of the younger Italians questioned were opposed to the idea, and some of the Italian boys interviewed even expressed a definite preference for Irish over Italian girls, though such expression of preference did not mean that they would necessarily succeed in marrying one or even really want to.

A sufficient amount of intermarriage between Irish and Italian had actually taken place to be the subject of comment and of general knowledge. Among the fifty Irish interviewed, all knew cases of intermarriage between Irish and Italians. The same was the case when a group of Italian boys at one of the local hangouts was questioned. The parochial school of the parish where most of the contact took place reported the presence of 25 children of mixed marriages out of a total of some 700. The Irish priests reported an increase in the number of Italian boys whom they had married to Irish girls and a number of individual cases came to light in the course of this study. The birth records of the area for 1930 showed out of a total of 186 Italian-born fathers, 31.2 per cent married to wives who were not born in Italy, and out of 146 Italian-born mothers, 12.3 per cent married to men born elsewhere. This indicated little, since it revealed only nativity and not ethnic stock and there was nothing to indicate that these Italian-born fathers were not all married to American-born women of Italian extraction. Nor were comparable birth records available for earlier years. Birth records revealed nothing about inter-marriage in the second generation.

According to the ready generalizations of local residents, Ital-ian men marrying Irish girls were the most frequent. Italian girls had much less opportunity to make contacts outside of their own group than had the men, and hence more rarely married other than Italians. Some very few cases of Italian-Jewish couples were known in 1930, but always one or the other had come from another part of town. Occasional Italian-German and Italian-Polish mar-riages had taken place.

Though the volume could not be measured, it was apparent that intermarriage between Italians and others, especially Irish, had been taking place, probably in increasing volume. It was not, however, a new phenomenon, for some of the first of the local Italian immigrants had Irish wives. It may, indeed, have been more common in the days before the mass Italian immigration. The cultural results of intermarriage could not be discovered with-out extensive case studies. There was considerable evidence to point toward the fact that whenever such marriages had not worked out satisfactorily, nationality differences — 'That's what you get for marrying someone who's not your own kind' — were readily held to blame.

There was some slight indication that the less alien member tended to take on the more alien culture, rather than *vice versa*. The evidence on this point was most fragmentary, but certain factors definitely contributed toward such an end. Since the com-munity was predominantly Italian, the pressure to adopt Italian ways and at least to understand the Italian language was strong; the closeness of the Italian family group led to the incorporation of in-laws into the group and made a high degree of adaptation necessary in order to preserve peaceful and friendly relations; the dominance of the Italian man in the family and the fact that it was usually the Italian man rather than the girl who married out-side the group helped to maintain Italian standards; the greater distinctiveness of Italian customs and the social stratification of the community along ethnic lines made the Italian element in the mixture the distinguishing one and tended to pull the family down to the social level of the Italians rather than up to the social level of the Irish.

An Italian-Irish family in this community thus tended to take the status of the Italian rather than of the Irish. An Irish woman who had married an Italian in her home community on Long Island and subsequently moved into the Village where he had been raised was keenly and painfully aware of these pressures. 'When we were on Long Island,' she said, 'he seemed like one of us. But here I see now how Italian he is and how much closer he is to his family than to me.' Her parents took the children out to Long Island as much as they could to keep them from growing up Italians.

The years lessened the gap between these principal ethnic groups though they did not narrow the gulf between local people and Villagers. Though the Italians continued to regard the Irish as pig-headed drunkards who acted as if they owned the earth, and the latter still looked upon the Italians as dirty, foreign Guineas who had ruined a good neighborhood and were out for all they could get, they had enough in common to understand each other in at least some respects. Occupying a similar economic status and living in the same type of houses, their living habits were not unlike. Though the Church played a different role in the two groups, the fact that both were Catholic gave a primary basis for *rapprochement*. Most especially, the fact that many of the Italian ideas about Americans were drawn from the conduct of the Irish among whom they moved and who dominated the neighborhood gave them common standards to the extent that the Italians adopted Irish ways. Yet the fact remained that Irish-Italian relationships in this community rested on so precarious a foundation that sympathy was not easy to maintain in the face of the ever-present consciousness that the others were different, and not always desirably different.

From the beginning, Jews and Italians lived side by side in the district with comparatively little friction. To be sure, it was the code in the public schools for the Italian majority to pick on the Jewish boys, probably as much because they were likely to be good at their lessons and classifiable as 'sissies' as because they were Jewish. They were free, also, to call 'Jew boy' not only at the Jewish child, but, on at least one occasion, at a Jewish teacher who strayed onto an Italian block. A large proportion of the Italians questioned — 70 per cent of the older and 49 per cent of the younger groups — said they objected to intermarriage with Jews, and family battles had arisen over such intermarriages when they did take place. Nevertheless, these differences did not prevent a sympathetic attitude and never led to the kind of open clashes that used to characterize difficulties between Italians and Irish — possibly for no other reason than that the Jews had always been few in number. A number of Italians interviewed gratuitously offered the generalization that Italians got along well with the Jews — better, in fact, than with the Irish or old Americans — and none were at pains to assert, or even ready to admit, the opposite proposition. Some pointed to the amicable relations between Jews and Italians at work; others mentioned the regard in which the local Jewish shopkeepers were held and the extent to which they were accepted on the street where they lived with Italians; others called attention to the Italian boys who went with Jewish girls. A number of Italians who had moved away selected a Jewish section of the Bronx in preference to an Italian or any other type of neighborhood.

Since the Jews of this district had always been a scattered minority living among the Italians, they necessarily occupied the same houses, attended the same public schools, their children played together, and they had dealings with each other. They were drawn together, too, by the treatment which both received from the dominant American and Irish elements. Latin and Semitic immigrant newcomers of the same period shared a position of inferiority in the face of entrenched 'Nordic' domination. Years of common residence and of common experience in rebuff made them increasingly sympathetic. Together they were excluded from much in American life which they sought. Some few might have had contact with exclusive schools which 'do not take Jews and Italians.' More had applied for jobs where 'Jews and Italians are not wanted.' Still others had been members, or sought to be members, of trade unions where officials disliked 'Jews and Italians,' whom they regarded as bad workers, always out to get something for themselves. As the two largest minority groups in the city, the Jews and Italians found themselves coupled together and excluded by those who occupied desired positions or held the keys to social and economic advancement.

But for all the similarity of experience which brought Jews and

Italians near together, their fundamental difference of religion and the racial separateness of the Jews kept them in some respects farther apart than Italians and Irish. The Jews, long acclimated to the position of a minority group living its own distinctive life within a larger community, never forgot the line which separated the Gentiles from them, or the fact that their neighbors, the Italians, belonged on the other side of that line. All Gentiles were inferior, but to the Jews of this district the Gentile population with which they came in contact was especially inferior. Traditionally devoted to education, the local Jews could not fail to look down upon the Italians and the low-class Irish, a large proportion of whom were indifferent to educational benefits. In the local schools the Jews were used to being the bright ones, making up the rapid advancement classes, going on to high school and continuing in college while most of their Italian friends dropped by the way. Taught to rely on their wits rather than on their brawn and not to fight back, the Jewish boys rated as sissies. Neither on the street nor in school, nor, more especially, at home, were they allowed to forget their difference. They must earn admission to street groups by their skill at ball; when they got home, it was again and again impressed upon them that they were not to be like the 'Irish bums' or the 'Wops.' Rough language and conduct picked up on the street was described as 'the way the Goys act,' and condemned as unworthy of a Jew.

At an earlier age than the Italian or the Irish child, each of whom started his career in an environment predominantly composed of members of his own group, and much earlier than the Jew of a Jewish neighborhood, the Jewish child of Greenwich Village learned that to be a Jew was to be different. Instead of adhering closely to the pattern of behavior which he found about him, he was taught from the first that he must act differently, and as soon as he began to notice the conduct of his neighbors he realized that their rhythm of life differed from his — the Sabbath, food, Christmas which was nothing to him and the High Holidays which were nothing to them. Whatever his later experience, the Jew raised in this community had had impressed on him in his early years a consciousness of difference which the Jew of the Bronx did not have.

While to the Jews the Italians remained low 'Goy,' the latter in turn regarded the Jews as forever outside the pale. The highest compliment they could pay to the individual Jew whom they had taken into their group was, 'You're one square Jew.'

It was hard to distinguish any indications that this basic gap had been in any way actually lessened. The Jews among the local population of the Village were no less conscious of their Jewishness than they had been a decade before. Though they had dropped many of their observances, the Jewish families of the neighborhood still remained consciously and self-consciously Jewish. The slight decrease in Jew-baiting reported at school seemed to reflect a decrease in the roughness of the school rather than an increase in tolerance, and the Jewish youngsters in school in 1930 insisted that they had to face the same scorn and dislike as their older brothers had found. Jewish children joined in Irish and Italian play groups because they were too scattered to form block groups of their own, but the young people, with very few exceptions, either hung around together or spent their time in the Jewish neighborhoods of Brooklyn or the Bronx.

Between Jews and Irish there had always been less harmony than between Jews and Italians, for the former resented the superiority which the Irish maintained but the Italians could not assume. Only those who entered politics found it expedient to come to terms with the Irish. The most conspicuous of these went so far as to turn Catholic and to proclaim his political intentions by passing the contribution plate in the church attended by the leading Irish politicians. The parishioners understood and commented, 'When I saw him going around with that plate, I knew which way he was headed!'

The Spanish colony on the extreme western edge of the district, though small, remained absolutely distinct, and hardly touched most of the elements in the locality closely enough to produce either conflict or contact. With their separate church, their own cafés, grocers, tailors, and barbers, the only institution that brought them into contact with others was the school. Relations with their Irish neighbors were far from cordial. These were currently described in what had plainly become a conventional phrase, 'The Irishman fears the Spaniard's knife; the Spaniard fears the Irishman's fist.' Active conflict existed on the waterfront, where the Irish had waged a losing fight to hold their own.

The Irish considered the Spanish dirty as well as dangerous, regarding them, even more than the Italians, as 'foreigners' and lumping together all Spanish-speaking people of various complexions — 'Cubians,' Filipinos, Mexicans — as 'niggers.' The Spanish either disliked the Irish for being unfriendly, having 'bad morals,' or 'thinking the world is theirs,' or, more generally, they ignored them completely. Some who were questioned directly said they had never lived or worked among them, when actually there were Irish families in the immediate vicinity of their homes. Although the Spanish had occupied the same blocks for two decades, there had been no *rapprochement*. There was some intermingling on the part of the children. Spanish children were found in 1930 in one solidly Spanish-speaking street play group and in four mixed groups where they were in the minority.

The Italians had practically no contact with the Spanish because they lived at the opposite end of the district. Those few who had had any contact with them were much more ready to say a good word for them, however, than were the Irish. On the whole, the Spanish kept very strictly to themselves, the women never going out except to church and the men associating closely within their own group. They knew other Spanish people in upper Manhattan and Brooklyn rather than non-Spanish in the locality. They maintained an attitude of extreme suspicion toward all others. Whenever the interviewer who canvassed the district knocked, he was greeted from behind the closed door by the same question, 'Who is there? Do you speak Spanish?' Although most had been in America for more than ten years, few of those interviewed could speak English. They had remained entirely isolated from the life of other elements in the community.

The only two ethnic groups in the locality which had really shown social amalgamation had been the Irish and Germans. It may have been the advent of the Italians, alien to both, which brought the Germans and Irish together and made relations between them seem closer than they actually had been. But even when discounted for this attitude, the evidence of such *rapprochement* was strong. Irish and Germans alike, in describing the old neighborhood of the early days of the century, offered the statement that the two groups always got along well together — lived together, 'shared' the neighborhood, attended each other's church picnics in spite of differences of religion, and formed a harmonious community. Intermarriage between Irish and Germans was said to have been general, and those few German families who still remained in the neighborhood bore out this generalization. Among the eighteen German families interviewed, all stated that marriage between Germans and Irish was usual and two had Irish wives. Half of these, however, did not approve of such intermarriage, insisting 'like should stick to like, otherwise there's always trouble.' Although intermarriage with Protestants was strongly opposed among those Irish who remained, difference in religion appeared not to have been an insuperable barrier to the marriage of German boys with Irish girls a generation before.

The contrast between the close relationship among the earlier groups in the locality and the distance among the later groups clearly reflected the fundamental change in the character of the neighborhood. Thirty or more years before, when the neighborhood was a community with many of the characteristics of a small town, its assimilative powers were good. Whoever came into the community was, in due time, incorporated into it. In the community of the post-War period, no such assimilative powers remained. It had become merely an area, no longer a community.

2.   THE CODE OF THE STREET

In the absence of a unified social neighborhood and in the presence of divergent groups, such social standards as were determined by public opinion were largely the product of the street and were enforced upon those who lived their lives publicly. Within the several ethnic groups certain standards of conduct received more or less social sanction and influenced to varying degrees those who lived more or less closely within their respective groups. Where blocks were solidly inhabited by members of one or another of these groups, their social attitudes became, at least partially, incorporated into the street code. Otherwise, the social pressures of community opinion operated chiefly through the street and on those who lived much of their lives upon it.

The children who played on the street were under strong pressure to follow the social codes of their blocks. They learned to snarl and threaten almost as soon and as naturally as they learned to talk, and their toughness was a recognized means of protection. A local social worker had no success in trying to persuade a small Italian girl that it was unnecessary, while beating up the little boy next door with her fists, to pour a stream of filthy language at him. The child insisted, and her companions agreed, that her victory was not complete until she had 'told him something.' However vigorously the schools might struggle, the local children had to talk with the accent of the gutter and with a profane vocabulary which rigidly followed a local code. Whereas in some neighborhoods boys swore, here they merely 'spoke that way.' The stranger could be identified by his use of a phrase which might be equally descriptive and obscene, but was not the one accepted for the particular situation. Those who in their youth had moved away to a more refined neighborhood and then returned reported the difficulty of their readjustment when they got back. What they had taken for granted when they were here had become unfamiliar to them through their residence elsewhere, and they were accused of being 'sissies' and of 'talking funny' when they behaved in the manner approved in their suburban residence. Though the teacher at school urged the children to 'talk classy,' they necessarily expressed themselves with the accent, intonation, and vocabulary of the street.

It was in the street, too, that children learned to be not only protective but predatory, to grab whatever they could find. In this district, a minimum regard for property rights was the code throughout these years. If a house was vacant, it was fair game — especially since the junkman would pay for old lead pipe. Anything left for the moment unattached might become the property of the 'finder.' It was a regular pastime for the local boys to organize impromptu foraging parties which tramped the neighborhood and its vicinity to 'find' things. 'Finding' was in no sense a euphemism for 'stealing.' The rules on which the world was run were definite and known to everyone. If one had something and valued it, it must be watched and nailed down, or else it would become fair game, convertible without notice into some more enterprising individual's private possession. It was only when the nails were a bit loose that any ethical question was involved.

Sports were universal, both in the forms common elsewhere and in forms which were specially adapted to the physical conditions of the locality, but fair play and sportsmanship had no place in the street code. The most general forms of sport were the street ball games adapted to the physical conditions of crowded streets and breakable windows. The district abounded in block teams, ranging in age from eleven or twelve to twenty or more, who played the ubiquitous game of punchball — a sort of baseball played with a soft ball, using the arm as a bat and adapting the rules to provide for scores made on opponents' errors rather than by taking advantage of traffic conditions; or stickball — the same game substituting a broom handle for the arm and usually played in the evening on factory-lined streets where space was greater. These games revealed the height of adaptation to physical environment, for they took account in their rules of such physical conditions as stoops behind which balls could become lodged and traffic lanes which must be avoided. The players developed an almost unconscious reaction to passing vehicles, stepping out of the way to let vehicles pass and falling back into the game again, hardly sensing an interruption.

These games were no exception to the general neighborhood assumption that everyone was out for what he could get. Games were played less to play than to win, and the means by which this was accomplished were secondary. The merits of a case were irrelevant in the settlement of disputed points. If a member of one team owned the ball, the fact that he could and would break up the game by taking the ball home was a guaranty that decisions would go in his favor, unless there was some balancing power on the other side. When a match game was to be played, neutral territory was usually chosen because neither team wanted to expose itself on the other team's territory to the attacks of supporting cohorts which the latter might muster. In these circumstances there was no room for such conceptions as fair play or uncompulsory honesty.

Characteristic of street conduct was that of the local block teams which had put up a small pool for their game. When one of the teams saw that the game was going against it, it absconded with the pool, leaving the game unfinished and the opposing team out of pocket. In one of the championship matches between a local team and an East Side team, the decision of the umpire was regarded as unfair and a battle very nearly ensued. The following year this same team went out to play in Brooklyn in the finals of another tournament, and this time things reached such a pass that knives and guns were drawn and bottles were thrown. It was the boast of the street on which the home team lived that the Brooklyn team would not dare to come down there to play back the match.

Along with the necessity of being foul-mouthed, tough, and playing to win, boys were under social pressure to hate school and all forms of school activity. Out of 134 boys in street groups who answered a questionnaire under conditions where the interviewer appeared to be a 'teacher' and the boys would be likely to say that they liked school to make a good impression, 52 per cent checked school among the things which they liked, as against 75 per cent who checked church, and 17 per cent gratuitously wrote 'no' opposite school, although they had not been asked to indicate their dislikes. Pressure from other boys was sometimes so strong as to warp an actual desire and liking for school into the general pattern of rebellious hatred. Girls, by contrast, could safely like school, and often played school on the stoops.

The rigor with which these street codes were enforced on the individual by the group varied from block to block. On the Irish blocks, it was not necessary to be quite so profane or to hate school intensely. Street fashions changed with years. It became less part of the code to be physically tough, but no less the code to be foul-mouthed. On the whole, the essentials of the local street pattern as it applied to children remained in 1930 what it had been ten years before.

As children got older, some differentiation in codes resulted from differences in education, and particular groups had their particular standards. But the hangovers of early training were so strong, and the number who had been educated to the point, usually college, where an important difference in standard would begin to arise was so small, that there was a general pattern for young men and girls as well as for children.

Except at mealtimes and when they were asleep, young men spent practically all their leisure moments in public and in company. It was as unheard of that boys should do chores around the house, other than running errands, as that girls should not, and they almost never spent their leisure time at home if they could possibly help it. They were, consequently, constantly exposed to the strong pressure of public opinion.

They were expected to outgrow their early inclination toward extreme toughness, but they still must avoid signs of refinement or culture. It was all right to be educated, but not to act in speech, manner, or etiquette as if education had made any difference. They were expected, too, to be more sophisticatedly smutty than when they were younger.

Upon young men who hung around the neighborhood, the strongest pressure was never to do anything without getting something out of it — the adult version of the children's playing to win; never to earn the taunt of being a 'sucker.' One young man was laughed at and scoffed from all sides because he had charged a young drunken couple of Villagers, newly married on Christmas Day, only two dollars for a fifty-cent tree, though the young man in his tipsiness had been ready to pay more. 'What the hell's the matter with you?' 'Why, in the name of Christ, didn't you take more?' 'If he could afford to get drunk, he could afford to pay you. You at least know how to spend your money,' stormed his friends. 'I'll never let myself in for a razzing like that again,' the boy concluded ruefully. 'I tried to explain that I wanted to give the fellow a break because it was Christmas and he was just married, but it was no use. This is the last time I make that kind of a mistake.'

Yet, in spite of the fear of being a sucker, certain forms of excessive expenditure were approved. It was not only permissible but essential to spend liberally when one 'went out' for an evening. The same young man who would scorn a Villager who spent more than was necessary on liquor for a party would delight in throwing money away — if he had it to throw — on a show, a night club, or a speakeasy, because in doing so he was, in his own eyes, not buying entertainment at sucker prices, but furnishing his own entertainment in the act of spending. Expenditure for clothes, too, was reckless from the point of view of budgeting, though care was taken to get good quality for the price. For the younger generation of local Italians, especially, clothes were the chief mark of Americanization as they conceived it. Neatness and fastidiousness were marked throughout the group; the question of clothes was a matter of real importance and interest, and the latest in style was achieved at the ready sacrifice of many other things which required cash. Young men lounged around corner ice-cream parlors in the height of fashion, unemployed and penniless, but the knot of their ties, the press of their pants, and the faultlessness of their taste, matters of glory.

Gambling was accepted as a suitable use of funds and was a fundamental part of the local social code. In some form or other it was to be found throughout the district, from the six-year-olds who played for pellets of putty, through those who played cards for match-boxes, then pennies, then higher stakes, to the older ones who shot craps for pools running sometimes into hundreds of dollars. The police rarely interfered with either card games or craps except when called by righteous Villagers to remove games of chance from the stoops of remodeled houses. Those players who feared interruption had a ready device for turning a money game into one which appeared to be a form of sidewalk baseball with the ball score serving as a code for the financial score.

Even in athletics, money counted quite as much as the game. It was the regular thing to put up bets on every game, whether it was a scratch game between two block teams or the finals of a city-wide tournament, the winning team receiving the pot. The amount put up varied all the way from five cents per player to fifty dollars. It was striking evidence of the readiness to put up money in a gamble, but not to spend it directly for recreation, that when one of the local centers attempted to run an interblock punchball contest, a sufficient number of teams were not willing to pay the very small entrance fee to make possible the purchase of a trophy and other minor expenses of running off the tournament. These same teams were ready to put up much larger sums on the chance of their team's winning these sums back, along with a corresponding amount put up by the opposing team.

Neighborhood boys were under as much pressure to chase women as to gamble, play to win, and keep from being a sucker. The characteristic Italian 'tom-cat' attitude had become a sufficiently strong part of the neighborhood code for young men of other nationalities to be expected to join the same chase. To the young men of the neighborhood, the city constituted one great hunting ground — a jungle in which the game was women; and anyone whose taste ran in different directions had difficulty maintaining his local reputation if he did not take part in the chase. He must be a 'fairy,' under physical disability, or at least 'queer in the head.' Among the Italians this attitude was taken for granted and tacitly assumed by the elders, but among the non-Latin groups of the locality it was not so universally the expected thing.

Since girls of their own class were not available to the local young men as they were to the Villagers, they had to be content with local professionals, or semi-professionals, or else to search elsewhere in the city. Few girls of the type who would be 'accommodating' in return for a meal and an evening's entertainment were known locally to local boys, though a few hung around some of the drugstores and lunch wagons. Such girls were known locally to East Side boys, while boys from here went to the East Side or the Bronx. Girls who guarded their reputations closely in their own neighborhood were known to boys from other communities.

Hunting a woman thus usually meant exploring the city. If the catch was a good-looking one, there was prestige to be derived from parading her around the neighborhood. The supreme neighborhood ideal was pretty well represented by a son of one of the local bootleggers. In a sporty car — 'the girls always look at your car, not at you' — he would venture forth to see what he could pick up. When he had captured the appropriate blonde, he would reappear, call a greeting to the boys in the ice-cream parlor, step ostentatiously into a drugstore, and then whirl triumphantly away. Few, if any, of the other boys could compete with him, but all tried to come as near as their means permitted.

Because they were less on the streets, girls were less subject to neighborhood pressure, but because their activities were more confined to the locality, they were at the same time forced to live more completely under the neighborhood's eye. As youngsters, their experience varied according to whether they lived on an Irish block where they learned to fight and play and hold their own with the boys, on some of the solidly Italian blocks where they held their own with their tongues even more than their fists and matched the boys for profanity, or on some of the mixed blocks where they played separately and had a somewhat gentler code of their own.

When they reached adolescence, the main problem became that of watching their step and protecting their reputation against the gossip of neighboring women and of local young men. At the age of twelve or thirteen, it was customary for girls who were not restrained at home to migrate to the park and engage in horse play with the boys, but only those who were more careless of their reputations stayed around the park as they grew older. Others sat upon the stoops of their houses, but many were not permitted even to do this — certainly not late in the evening. Some, who were not prohibited from going out, found their recreation in walking about the neighborhood. On any warm evening some girls would dress themselves up, frequently in evening dress, and parade down the street in pairs. Often they were not out for a pick-up and would repel advances, but were simply on display.

Girls whose families were more liberal than the common run were especially resentful of the perpetual gossip to which they were subjected, whether for the hours at which they came home at night, the boys they went with, the clothes they wore, or anything else that they said or did. Their desire to move to another community was a wish to escape this sort of pressure. Boys were none too generous in their judgment of local girls, and to escape a 'doggy' reputation the latter had to avoid being alone with boys, or, at least, to be careful to preserve a proper distance.

The Italian girls in 1930 still asserted proudly that they did not 'neck,' and managed to make gossip of other girls who did. The girl who was known to neck could not count on her reputation being safe in the hands of local boys. Necking, in fact, had not become part of the local code, except among the local Jews, who took their pattern of behavior from other Jewish districts such as the Bronx rather than from the locality. It was more general among the Irish, but still much less general than in the Bronx or in an American suburban community. It was also not the code for these girls to discuss sex as a social problem, or birth control, in the 'advanced' manner accepted in the Bronx, and they regarded an attempt on the part of a boy to start such a discussion as a personal insult.

The Jewish girls of the neighborhood were in a particularly

awkward position. Their code was that of the Jewish neighborhoods in the Bronx or Brooklyn, not of the Italian district of the
Village. But they lived under the unfriendly eyes of the local
neighborhood, and too far away from the Bronx and Brooklyn to
profit by the kind of informal activity which was open to the
Jewish girls in those sections of town.

Adults were less subject to the pressure of public opinion than
were the children or the boys who hung around outside the
corner store. This was especially true of the men. Women were
chiefly subjected to neighborhood comment on the score of their
houses — either because they were bad housekeepers or because
their housekeeping was too fancy — and for the way they kept
their children. The old-timers told of resisting the installation
of running water in each flat in the place of a common tap in the
yard on the score that anyone who was too lazy to lug her water
upstairs was no good. Such extreme pressure had been relaxed,
but individual housewives were still known on the block on the
basis of their housekeeping, and were the object of gossip if they
had an extra fine 'living-room suite' or other special pieces of
furniture. There was so much pressure on the mothers from
health centers, schools, and other social agencies to make them
alter their methods of child care that the whole subject of child
rearing was a moot one and women did not have to conform to a
rigid neighborhood code in this respect.

Time had made some change in the street code as far as the
young people were concerned, but much less than was the case
during these years in the American community at large. The
fact that there were many Italian girls who went out and even
some who necked was evidence of a departure from the rigorous
condition of the past. The presence of even a few Italian college
boys who resisted the pressure to chase women was further evidence of change. Among the Irish, too, there had been changes.
Those who were in their mid-twenties in 1930 agreed that 'these
kids know all about sex and do nothing but talk about it nowadays.
Why, we would never have thought of discussing the subject at
their age.'

The standard of behavior as here described applied simply and
directly to those in the community who lived their lives conspicuously. Those who did not play on the street, hang around

on the street corners, sit on the stoops, or stroll down the avenue were not subject to its pressures. There were many families scattered through the neighborhood who considered themselves superior to the people among whom they lived and either did not expose themselves to the pressure of public opinion or ignored it. Others, especially boys, who did not like the code of their own block, sought out more congenial groups on other blocks and conformed to their codes. Still others, especially some of the Italian women and girls, were so much more strongly under family control that other pressures were unimportant to them.

The aspects of this behavior pattern which came out of experience on local streets were its predatory, irresponsible, unsocial elements — the guarded distrust with which the local people regarded the world. Such positive social standards as existed, once the old neighborhood unity had been broken in the early years of the century, were the product of the behavior patterns and social controls brought in by the several ethnic groups. As the social organization of these groups was relaxed and their social patterns dislocated by American experience, they ceased to impose social attitudes and standards of behavior on their members, and the law of the jungle which dominated the street became for many the only guide which remained.

VI. THE ITALIAN COMMUNITY

1. SOCIAL ORGANIZATION

THE Italians of Greenwich Village, largest of local ethnic groups, experienced in the post-War years a fundamental shift in the social organization of their community and a rapid disruption and dislocation of their social standards under the impact of the American environment. Virtually no part of American culture except the acquisitive drive was incorporated into their social code, and the only major institution which became an integral part of their life — namely, the Tammany brand of politics as developed by the Irish — was less the product of American tradition than the creation of an earlier immigrant group. The social history of this group is not only the story of half of the people of this locality, but a fairly representative sample of the process through which the mass of city-dwelling 'new' immigrants were passing during the years when their children were growing to maturity.

The beginnings of the Italian community of Greenwich Village dated back into the 1880's, though the rapid development of the area into an Italian district was a matter of the twentieth century. Before 1900, when the South Italians began to come in, it was made up chiefly of North Italians who came both as an overflow from the East Side and directly from the ship to the immigrant hotels which were opened in the West Side district.

The earliest group of Italian settlers had come from Genoa with the first wave of Italian immigrants, most of whom had gone on to California. Before the mass movement from the South and Sicily had got under way, they had established themselves in a position from which they could look down with scorn upon the 'low' Italians, could take pains neither to know nor to be classed with them, and could dominate the affairs of the Italian community from a lofty distance.

Compared with the later multitudes who moved in and out of the district, the Genoese were few. Yet up to 1930, their small group furnished nearly all of the prominent men whom the district had produced. The families which had owned the two original immigrant hotels had retained the major positions of prominence. One had supplied the community with a banker, movie-palace operator, prominent politician, and fight promoter; the other furnished another movie proprietor, a member of the bench, and important investors in local real estate. From the same group of original Genoese were drawn the leading real estate operators, politicians, priest, undertaker, and older business and professional men.

The position of this group rested primarily on their longer opportunity to become acclimated and on their somewhat superior education, but it was greatly enhanced by their rather fortuitous acquisition of considerable wealth. In the 'great bull market,' few stocks soared more spectacularly than the securities of the Bank of Italy — venture of A. P. Giannini whose family had come from Genoa to California at the same time that the Genoese of Greenwich Village were establishing themselves. In spite of their traditional reluctance to invest in other than real property, the local Genoese invested heavily in Giannini stock, in sufficient amounts to make it worth while for Giannini's representative to hold a meeting in the local church when Giannini was waging a proxy fight for control of his company. The fortunes which were made overnight gave prestige to the group, at least until these fortunes were again lost.

On the heels of the Genoese, other North Italians from the Piedmont and Tuscany had come in, but it was not until after 1900 when the South Italians began to swarm into the district that the area had become thoroughly Italianized. The North Italians, both Genoese and Piedmontese, had moved in amongst the Germans and French, the Irish and Negroes in the eastern part of the district. In contrast to the North Italians who had come in family by family, the southerners arrived *en masse*. Town by town they occupied individual houses; here, as in other parts of the city, people from the same province gravitated in the same block.

The mass movement of South Italians and Sicilians into this district in the fifteen years before the War resembled the corresponding movement into the country as a whole. In contrast to the first settlers, a large proportion of whom had established their homes and families here, the newer wave of immigrants were largely migratory, pausing in the area for a few years and then returning with their gains to their native village. The turnover of population between 1910 and 1914 was estimated at 75 per cent by one of the doctors who took care of the members of fifty or more fraternal lodges and had reason to keep a fairly close record of overturn. Many of those who remained to make up the Italian community of the post-War years had come with the intention of a temporary stay, and had remained through the accident of the War, because their gains had not met their expectations, or because they had put off the day of return so long that their children, established in the American community, could not be uprooted.

Some few of the South Italians early obtained a position in the community. One or two of the very earliest had come in with the Genoese, and their children, raised in the district, had become the local doctors, pharmacists, political leaders, teachers, and lodge presidents. Others, educated on the other side, had established their professional practice or their business among their compatriots here. They had been particularly active in small business and in the organization of fraternal lodges.

Except for those few South Italians who had antedated the mass migration of their people, and such of the northerners as had continued to dribble into the district of later years, half a generation or more separated the Genoese from the people of the south. During the post-War period, most of the old Genoese settlers died, and their children, locally born and raised, reached a generous middle age. These in turn were raising their children out of the area in Staten Island, Jersey, Brooklyn, and the Bronx, while the children of the more successful were having their weddings described in the fashionable papers of exclusive Westchester County. The southerners, on the other hand, were reaching and passing middle age, their older children were growing to maturity, marrying, and moving out, while their younger children continued to make up the ranks of the local schools.

As the number of Italians multiplied, the community took shape. To the Italian mission church which had been located in the area since 1859, a special Italian-language parish was added in 1892. In the manner common to the ghettos of every nationality whose distinctive habits constitute distinctive needs, Italian stores were set up to sell products appropriate to the Italian taste. Macaroni, olive oil and cheese, fish, pork, and live poultry — these, along with such distinctive vegetables as red peppers, broccoli, and squash blossoms, all began to appear on sidewalk stalls, in stores, and on the inevitable pushcarts.

Social organizations were formed on the basis of the part of Italy from which people had come. Village and provincial groups from both North and South Italy organized mutual benefit societies for mutual aid in case of sickness and death and for carrying on their social life. The number of these societies was legion, and even their names were often not known outside of their own membership. In 1930, nobody could be found who knew the names of all the societies which had survived, and a newspaper editor who was attempting to compile a city-wide list reported that when his list was completed, it would be unique. Upwards of seventy-five were said to have drawn their membership from the local district. One doctor, who in 1930 was 'lodge doctor' for twenty-five different societies, had 'had' as many as fifty societies at one time or another, all from South Italy, as the North Italians never would use him because he was a southerner. Fifty per cent of the local Italian men in 1910 were estimated to have held membership in town or provincial societies. A few of the more prosperous of these societies had had their own clubrooms, but most had held their meetings in the various public halls.

Informal social relations, as well as formal organization, were almost wholly restricted to people from the same town or province. Difference in dialect made it easier to communicate with *paesani* than with other Italians. Although this community differed from other Italian areas of first settlement in the city in that it contained a larger number of provincial groups within a smaller radius — the local schools had children from nearly every province in contrast to the East Side where solidly Neapolitan and solidly Sicilian schools served adjacent territories — houses and, usually, blocks were homogeneous. In fact, it was only the experience of being in a foreign land which made many of the immigrants feel themselves to be Italians at all rather than citizens of the particular town or province.

This lower West Side Italian community, organized into provincial groups and equipped with its own church and stores, numbered some fifty thousand people in 1910. Of these, about half lay within the area covered by this study. The community, however, had never been large and self-contained, for it had always been flanked by industry and by better-class residences; its members could fall out of the community by walking a few blocks. It had constituted an island rather than a continent — in contrast to the East Side or East Harlem. Though many of the older Italian women virtually never left their own blocks, or went farther from their homes than to market and to church, the men and the young people saw other types of people and other ways of life within ten minutes' walk from their doors.

The outbreak of the War reversed the process through which this community had been built up. New immigration virtually ceased and many Italian citizens returned to join the Italian army. The reversal of the balance of immigration which transformed the national excess of 198,000 Italian immigrants over emigrants in 1914 to a deficit of 65,000 in 1915 took its toll from this section. In spite of the additions of large numbers between 1910 and 1914, the foreign-born Italian population of the district decreased between 1910 and 1920 by 3000. This decrease reflected primarily the cessation of immigration and the return of single men, while the families who had become established in the area stayed on. School enrollment continued to increase and the wholesale exodus which was to decimate the community had not yet set in.

At the close of the War, the Italian community was occupying the eastern half of the Village; most of its members had had at least ten years in which to become acclimated to their new homes; its ranks were being rapidly enlarged by natural increase, though, after the quota law of 1921, no longer by fresh arrivals from overseas; its wants were supplied by stores purveying characteristic wares; it was still organized on the basis of Old World lines into mutual benefit associations and fraternal lodges; it had gained stability as the turnover of population decreased. But it had been subjected to the disruptive influences of the War period; it had been aroused to Italian national consciousness by the War spirit and had, at the same time, been exposed to the War-time pressure for community activity and American patriotism.

In the years that followed, this Italian community disintegrated rapidly. Its social structure was broken, partly through the loss of members in the migration to outlying boroughs, partly through the impact of American institutions, and partly because the old provincial alignment ceased to be relevant and newly developed interests cut across old lines. Organization on the basis of Old World backgrounds gave way either to disorganization or to the reorientation of local Italian life in terms of American interests and, especially, American politics.

Many of the institutions which served the Italian community lost their vitality. Most of the stores which supplied the Italian population in 1930 were relics of the period of community building, many having served the area for upwards of twenty years. Though stores had gone out, new ones had not come in. A few had shifted their location slightly, usually moving a block or two farther to the west in the direction of the population drift. Street and subway construction had forced pushcarts to move. But, on the whole, the same storekeepers as before the War, located at the same places, continued to offer the same favorite Italian wares.

As the provincial ties became weaker, the provincial mutual benefit societies dwindled and many died. When the stream of immigration stopped, both the constant supply of new members and the close connection with home villages were cut off. By 1930, all informants agreed that these societies had almost ceased to constitute an important element in the social organization of the community. One informed estimate placed the loss in membership at one half to two thirds, reducing the proportion of local men who belonged from perhaps 50 per cent before the War to possibly 30 per cent in 1920, and 10 to 15 per cent in 1930. Such membership as remained was dispersed throughout the city. Headquarters and meeting places moved uptown or to Brooklyn and only a handful continued to center locally. The 1930 membership of a lodge which had been one of the most vigorous of the local societies showed what had happened to these organizations as centers for local social life. The meeting place of this society had been moved to Twenty-third Street and a quarter of the membership lived in Brooklyn. Only 18 per cent resided on the lower West Side. The rest were scattered as far as California — 11 per cent elsewhere on Manhattan, 16 per cent in the Bronx, 23 per cent in the suburbs, and 7 per cent in other parts of the United States. Members thus scattered retained their connection with their organization for protective rather than for social reasons.

The provincial societies made no appeal to the younger generation raised in the community, or to those foreign-born who had transferred their center of interest to America. In contrast to the ethnic organizations of some other groups in America whose educational and cultural programs have attracted and held at least part of the younger generation within the bonds of ethnic consciousness, the provincial emphasis of these organizations tended to represent to the young Italo-American the worst aspect of his heritage and to be associated with the 'backwardness' of his parents. Some few young people retained membership in their fathers' lodges because they hoped to gain either political backing or, if they were professional men, clients, but they complained that they had never been able to count on either the professional or political support of fellow members.

Yet, though time destroyed provincial cohesion and subordinated provincial difference, it did not eliminate provincial jealousies altogether. These lines remained to divide the Italian community when they had ceased to give it a basis for social organization.

As people moved in and out, blocks no longer were so solidly of one or another province, but not all lost their provincial identity. Among thirty-four blocks in the district inhabited by Italians, seven were almost entirely North Italian, five exclusively South Italian, one Sicilian, and the remaining twenty-one were provincially mixed. Individual houses frequently remained provincial. In explaining how he happened to know so many different kinds of people, one man was able to enumerate the houses where he had lived successively as Neapolitan, Sicilian, Piedmontese, Basilicatan, and Genoese. Most of the older people still associated primarily with their provincial group, no doubt because similarity of dialect made it easier to communicate with people from the same province. As one person put it, 'It is not that we cannot understand one another, but we feel more at ease in a language which is thoroughly familiar.'

The younger generation, too, moved largely, though less exclusively, in provincial groups. When several second generation young men were being selected to interview a body of Italians in the community, the boy who was choosing the group made his selection on the basis of the part of the country from which each boy's people came, saying that this would be the way to get a representative body of interviews, since each one would be sure to know the people from the same part of the country as his parents. Out of 144 persons of both generations who were directly questioned, 10 expressed an unwillingness to marry, or have a member of his or her family marry, someone from a different province. At a local mental hygiene clinic, the psychiatrist reported having to deal with cases where even American-born girls objected to marriage with men from another province. A stranger from the same province was regarded with much less suspicion than one from another province. A Neapolitan interviewer found that she had considerable difficulty getting good interviews from North Italians, but could hardly tear herself away from Neapolitans. On one occasion, a Neapolitan woman from whom she inquired the direction to a priest's residence burst into a flood of questions — Why did she want the priest? Was somebody sick? Was somebody dying? — followed by the tale of her own woes. The girl's comment was, 'That would not have happened if she had not been from my province.'

Certain elements in the American situation helped to keep provincial differences alive, in spite of time, distance, and the irrelevance of these differences to American affairs. The North Italians were at pains to maintain the distinction between themselves and the southerners, not alone on traditional grounds, but because they felt more Americanized and therefore superior. They had found adaptation to American customs somewhat easier, both because of longer residence, and because, on the

points at which the clash between the Italian and American
cultures was most acute, they had traditionally been less insistent
than the southerners. They could meet the problem of freedom
of girls in America, since they had not been so strict at home as
had the South Italians and the Sicilians. A larger proportion
came from cities and were literate and thus had an advantage in
making the transition into an American urban situation.

Whenever a North Italian thought that a question implied
criticism of something which was not American, he took pains,
often gratuitously, to insist that the particular thing was done by
the South Italians and to turn the question into a criticism of the
latter. A Genoese undertaker, when asked about funeral customs,
denied the existence of any distinctive Italian practices and insisted that differences among funerals depended entirely on
money. 'It is only the South Italians who go in for processions
and elaborate funerals. That is the way they always act — trying
to seem more important than they are. The North Italians are
much more like the Americans in being ready to stand on their
own merit.'

Where home attitudes had been thus reinforced by American
circumstances, it was not surprising to find the expression 'low'
and 'high' Italian, which in Italian merely referred to geographical
areas used to denote differences in quality and social status. While
provincial consciousness remained strongest at the two extremes
— Piedmontese and Sicilian — even violent insistence on differences was not limited to them. Among the 144 who were asked
directly whether they thought that people from different provinces were becoming more friendly, most agreed that provincial
distinctions were of decreasing importance. Though there were a
few who said, 'No. They never will be friends. They are enemies,'
96 per cent found that, according to their observations, unfriend-
liness was disappearing. Eighty-seven per cent reported that they
had friends and acquaintances among people from other provinces.

To the younger generation, provincial differences had ceased to
be of major importance in determining their associates — except
through accident of residence or family friends — or their points
of view, but they still produced a strong automatic reaction — a
readiness to hurl the stock phrase about the person from the other
part of Italy if a quarrel should arise.

With the growth of Fascism and its emphasis on Italian nationality, it looked for a time as if the local community would become organized on a national rather than a provincial basis. The Sons of Italy, a fraternal order of Italians in America, was active in the locality during the War and was brought into prominence locally at the time of Mussolini's rise to power. But it came into bad repute when Fascist activities in America were revealed and a Fascist representative who had set up headquarters locally was expelled, and it lost strength when part of the membership seceded on the ground that the whole organization was becoming too much concerned with Fascism. By 1930, the Sons of Italy were of slight local importance and no other Italian organization had any local standing.

As essentially Italian organizations dwindled, local politics, or, to a slight extent, local social agencies, furnished the basis for new groupings. Those who left their Italian lodges and joined political clubs looked upon the benefit society leaders as 'those little people.' Political aims had so largely superseded fraternal interests by 1930 that people frequently insisted, 'there are no such things as non-political Italian clubs or societies.'[1] One social club felt obliged to protest its non-political character by stating on its entertainment program, 'This club has no other purpose than to provide pleasant hours for its members.'

A few attempts to salvage what remained of the mutual benefit societies by uniting the small-town groups into provincial or regional units showed some signs of achieving success by virtue of their political purpose. As the president of one of the united groups put it, 'We are not satisfied with what we have been getting from Tammany. We want not only jobs but patronage. We want a number of commissioners and judges *and what goes with them.*' Even the Sons of Italy had begun to shift its emphasis from the Italian to the American political scene, with both parties to the split over Fascism laying stress on American political activity. One part, in fact, was considering changing its name to 'Americans, Sons of Italy,' and acknowledged that its purpose now was to educate Italians in American political methods in order to make possible their political participation.

The single flourishing organization within the local Italian com-

[1] Cf. Chapter IX, Politics.

munity in 1930 was an Italian business and professional men's society which was exclusively Italian — it was rumored that a prominent Jewish clothing merchant had not been admitted even though he sent the club five hundred coat hangers — and which was known both in the locality and by Italian organizations outside the locality as an essentially political club, though it insisted that it was purely social. Its officer acknowledged, however, that it would be its policy to support an Italian political candidate. Most of the political organizations in which the Italians took part were not the outgrowth of provincial or other Italian societies, but were newly formed under individual political leaders.

Where affiliation with one or another of the social agencies became a basis for association, the social realignment which was involved was more extreme. In this situation, not only did New World interests supplant those of the Old, but they centered around the associations and interests of women and children — members of the community who had no place in the old structure which involved only men. Such new groupings had not become numerically very important by 1930, for the membership of Italian lodges was probably still greater than that of the mothers' clubs at the centers which their children attended. A large part of the community, moreover, belonged to no formal organization whatever, and informal associations were most likely to involve the men and to follow traditional rather than newly developed lines. Even a slight trend toward making women's groups important, however, was significant because it fundamentally altered the structure of the Italian community and reversed the roles of its members.

The effect of time and of the American environment did more to disrupt the Italian community than to reorganize it. By 1930 the community had ceased to acknowledge any leadership. To all questions about local leaders, those consulted replied with a negative answer. When pressed with individual names there was always some good reason for not regarding the individual mentioned as a leader — 'He would have nothing to do with people of the locality,' 'We know too much about him to respect him,' 'He takes no interest and will not contribute anything to the neighborhood.' The only person for whom everyone was ready to say a good word was one of the old Genoese leaders who had died. With his passing the community felt that it had no one to look to.

Those who had risen in the community during its thirty or more years of development had gone their several ways. The various positions in relation to the community which they occupied in 1930 revealed much about the social forces which had been at work. Most of the old Genoese families had moved away, and among those who remained the sons were very much less highly regarded than the parents had been. A few of the earliest South Italians and their sons had been distinctly 'neighborhood' leaders in the period of community building — active in organizing lodges of such American fraternal orders as the Moose as well as in the Italian societies, 'hail-fellow-well-met' with everybody, whether Italian or non-Italian, and ready to support all types of community ventures.

With the disappearance of the social neighborhood, their position had gone. The one who remained most prominent in 1930 had made his way into politics and had become one of the outstanding Italian politicians to whom people came from all over the city for help in getting jobs. A second, who had held the presidency of several lodges, had moved out of the locality and had concentrated his interest on American fraternal societies and politics; another continued as lodge doctor for a number of societies whose membership was widely scattered, but the lodges now furnished only his income and not the basis for his social life. Still another of these early South Italian leaders, also a doctor, sat in his new and empty office in an up-to-date apartment building talking wistfully about the good old days when there was always something going on at the lodge hall and you just had to step out of an evening to find your friends. All sighed for the days when the benefit society ball — 'there was no finer entertainment in New York City' — was the great annual event and 'every single member of the committee was dressed like George Washington.' Those who remained active in lodges and societies had mostly moved to Brooklyn or other types of communities.

The professional people, both those who had come into the community already trained and those who grew up in it, differed in their adjustment to changing conditions, but agreed in having little to do with the neighborhood.

There were the aggressively American young doctors with conspicuously up-to-date offices who wanted an American practice and only remained to serve their compatriots until they could get firmly enough established to leave them behind.

There were well-known and prosperous doctors who at one time had served the locality, but who, in 1930, were specialists with offices on lower Fifth Avenue and a city-wide American clientèle. One of these was an ardent supporter of all efforts to promote Italian culture and an active member of the Italian Historical Society and the exclusive Italy-America Society. His interest, however, was in the culture of Italy, not its people; his associations were with cultivated people, both Italians and Americans, all over the city and he had nothing to do with the local community.

Quite another type was represented by a younger doctor who had been one of the organizers of the Association of Italian Physicians. American-born and American-trained, his friends as well as his clientèle were largely American, but he had joined in forming the Association of Italian Physicians in order to secure status for the Italian doctor in New York. He had little or no patience with the Italian-trained older man who had wanted to use the society for cultural purposes, to maintain the Italian language and Italian interests. For him, and others of his type, the only reason for acting in an Italian group was to remove the handicap under which Italian doctors had to practice and to break down the attitude of the American community — 'He may be good even though he is Italian.'

Some of the successful, whose business relations were entirely with Americans, belonged to the upper 'four hundred' of the Italian metropolitan community, and though their social life was led completely within an Italian circle they had no contacts with the local community, even with its professional members. Others, who were not numbered with the city-wide Italian upper crust, moved within a small circle of well-to-do Italian friends, largely but not exclusively drawn from the professional and business people of the locality. Some of these who had made a lot of money were generous in their donations to local institutions such as the Italian church and even to non-Italian agencies working with Italians, but they had no social dealings with the community beyond their own group and were constantly on the defensive for

fear of being approached for money. A third type of the prosperous and successful Italian was represented by the business men
who had moved out into a definitely American neighborhood,
would have no social relations with Italians except with those
few whose prestige in the American community was high, would
contribute nothing to the support of local activities — 'they are
always trying to get us to contribute to the Church or a society
because we are Italians' — and were emphatic in their opposition
to all forms of Italian-American solidarity.

At the opposite extreme were those who remained completely
immersed in their Italian point of view, doctors who withdrew
from the Association of Italian Physicians because it used the
English language — 'They call themselves "Italian Physicians"
but it seemed as if they wanted to forget everything Italian when
they gave up the language' — and who were determined to shield
themselves and their families from the contamination of the
American scene. These had little to do with the local Italian
community, partly because it was low-class and partly because
they feared that if they let their children play in the neighborhood, even with Italian children, they would pick up 'those
foreign ways.' They sent them to private church schools, confined their own associations to other like-minded Italian professionals, and undertook to maintain a solidly Italian culture spot
in spite of the rest of the community.

Some few of the old professional men managed to retain a
practice after their clientèle had moved away by exploiting their
common ethnic origin and keeping their people as nearly as possible in the old traditional mould. One of the latter type continued to treat hundreds of patients, mostly older Italian-born
women but an appreciable number of the younger Italian-
American women, in his bare, grimy office, where stacks of papers
adorned desk and floor, the mantelpiece served as a medicine
cabinet for the few necessary bottles, an enema bag hung from
the hatrack along with his overcoat, and one tilting chair was the
only equipment. According to his estimate, 95 per cent of those
who filled his waiting room every afternoon came from a distance.
In his role of 'the old, Italian family doctor' he escaped the fate
that overtook many of those who had had a practice and a professional standing when the community was at its height, but

who had been left waiting year by year in increasingly empty offices.

Among the younger generation which was beginning a professional or business career in 1930, only those few who had political ambitions showed any interest in the local community, any desire to occupy a position of local leadership or any feeling of responsibility toward the group among whom they had been brought up. 'We educated Italians are too few in all the city to get anywhere through leadership of our people. We have no choice but to fight our way up individually.' The hard-working wife of a struggling attorney insisted that it was all right for people who had made money to lead and help the Italians, but a person who was poor and had to make his own way could not afford to jeopardize his position and his earning power by identifying himself with the Italian group.

The failure of the local Italian community to develop local leadership reflected a combination of factors — class distinction in Italy which produced a wide gap between the cultivated Italians with background and money and the immigrant mass; the fact that those who achieved business or professional success looked rather toward the avenues into American life which money opened to them than to prestige among their own people; and the fact that their success came in terms of money rather than of fame, and hence did not attract a following.

The jealousy with which Italians regarded everyone among them who became prominent was proverbial in 1930. 'Look how the Jews stick together and where they are — but the Italian, he is always jealous.' 'If the Italians stuck like the Jews,' observed one of the Italian politicians, 'they would have half the city government by now.' Failure to support each other, distrust of their own, quarrels over club officers that were sure to break up Italian clubs — these were the stock comments that a mention of Italian group life was sure to produce.

Most of the conscious pressures to which the Italian community was subjected had sought to break up its solidarity and transform its members as individuals from Italians into Americans. It has never been part of the American code to treat its ethnic minorities, in any official or positive way, as groups rather than as individuals. The assumption that all persons may become 'Americans' simply by setting foot on American soil and going through the legal form of naturalization has had its counterpart in the policy of the public school to treat all children as nearly alike as possible without regard to the ethnic background from which they have come. Only when the War revealed the fact that hyphenism had survived this process of laissez-faire individualism, and that the country was made up, not of a mass of 'Americans,' but of a number of undigested lumps of different nationalities, was official cognizance taken of ethnic differences. The Immigration Act of 1921 gave legal status to this consciousness of difference as far as the exclusion of future immigrants was concerned, and the publicity for Nordic superiority which accompanied the passage of this act greatly increased public awareness of nationality differences. But the awakened consciousness extended only to external, not to internal, policy; while immigrants at Ellis Island were rigidly scrutinized for their national origin, public schools and other agencies continued to ignore ethnic differences and to make individual 'Americans' out of the children of foreign origin who came under their sway.

In this respect, most of the schools and agencies of this district, as well, of course, as the indirect influences of movies, radio, and press, worked in the same direction. One of the local agencies gave instruction in the Italian language and put on Italian plays. In another, the director treated the patrons as part of the Italian community of the city by securing publicity in the Italian press for affairs at the center. The local branch of the public library kept a large collection of Italian books. But the local schools were indifferent to the loyalties and customs of the Italian group and did not consider it necessary to be familiar with the ethnic background of the children in order to prepare them for their role in American life. Health agencies accused patients of 'trusting only their own' in following their own doctors in preference to those of the outside agencies. The few constructive local efforts to deal with the Italians as a group were made in the face of American public opinion and the pressure of those supplying the funds. When an Italian woman — selected for her administrative skill rather than because she was Italian — was put in charge of one of the local agencies, a principal sponsor of the agency threatened to withdraw her support. A health center which used a corps of

Italian girls as assistants and interpreters in its work of health education had to justify itself to its patrons for spending money in this way.

Unconsciously many agencies bewildered the Italians with whom they came in contact. 'My people understand two things, kindness and force,' explained an observant Italian woman. 'The rational, temperate attitude of the Americans does not move them.' 'You must reckon with the intense loyalty of the Italian,' a prominent Italian advised a group of local social workers, 'and remember that he expects loyalty, not reason or justice, in return, and is very quick to suspect that by the latter treatment you are letting him down.'

To a considerable extent, the conscious and unconscious efforts to make individuals lose their identity with their own group had been successful and the solidarity of the Italian group had been undermined. Those who had gone to college had little good to say of the neighborhood and its associations, and of Italians and their ways; they repudiated the suggestion that they were potential leaders of their own people. Only occasionally did they show any other attitude. One college boy came under the influence of an Italian high-school teacher who had made it his program to develop pride of race among his Italian pupils; a girl of wealthy family joined the 'Junior League' of a fashionable Italian American society; a young lawyer hoped to secure clients by retaining some of his Italian associations and another hoped to achieve prestige by becoming a political leader, but regretted that the district where his chances for success were best was largely Italian and hoped to avoid Italianism as much as possible. In part it was the 'low-class' character of this district which these college people had repudiated; in part it was the process of having their conduct measured by Old World standards to which they objected. But their wish to avoid being identified as Italians entered in. Their desire to move to a better neighborhood usually included a preference for a non-Italian community.

But the sense of being Italian was very far from having been destroyed. The second generation as well as the first had retained a sufficiently strong 'consciousness of kind' to make Italian boys bet on an Italian prize-fighter even when their best judgment told them that he was the weaker combatant; to make Italians overcome their age-long prejudice against investment in stocks when an Italian enterprise was involved; to make an appreciable change in the balance of votes when an Italian candidate appeared on the ballot; to make an Italian college student remark that he always felt uncomfortable when an Italian recited badly in class; to make an Italian girl whose associates had been largely non-Italian wonder why it was that she felt more at home and got on better with Italian people; or to make ten per cent of the persons directly questioned state that they would object to marriage on the part of a member of their family with anyone who was not an Italian.

In a large measure, consciousness of being Italian was a defense reaction against the attitude of others — against being treated as a 'Wop' — rather than a positive manifestation of group solidarity. There were plenty of situations which brought to the Italian a consciousness of his nationality. So long as his life was led strictly within his own community, he might escape such consciousness. The women who lived out their lives between their tenement kitchen, their church, and the market were aware of their nationality only indirectly, through the experiences of the children or the men. But those men and young people who went out of the neighborhood to work were not allowed to forget.

The Post-War drive for 'Americanization' took the concrete form of bringing every possible pressure to bear upon aliens to become American citizens, often to the point of excluding aliens from jobs or at least giving preference to citizens. Among the industries of the locality, many of the managers or owners interviewed asserted, quite gratuitously, that their employees were all citizens. In a number of cases there was good reason to doubt the truth of this assertion, a fact which only emphasized more strongly the presumption in favor of citizens as against alien workers. The three building-trade unions which local Italians were most likely to want to join — tile-setters, masons and bricklayers, and carpenters — all required at least first citizenship papers for membership. The fear of deportation which was awakened during and after the War persisted through the following years and increased with the depression when the drive to rid the country of 'reds' and alien criminals was supplemented by the expulsion of unemployed as 'public charges.' In view of their treatment under the quota immigration law and the tendency to assume them to be gangsters, the Italians were left in no doubt of the fact that they had been classed among the 'undesirables' and were in the country on sufferance. The fact that a large part of the community became engaged in some form of extra-legal activity, chiefly bootlegging, made the threat of deportation still more real and exposed the timorous to exploitation by 'protective associations' which purported to have inside information that the person was to be deported and offered to protect him from deportation — at a price. In 1920, 60 per cent of the foreign-born men and 76 per cent of the women in the Italian section of the district [1] were unnaturalized. In spite of these pressures, 47 per cent of the men and 64 per cent of the women remained aliens in 1930. The necessity of learning to read English was the reason given by the older and the illiterate for not securing the advantages of citizenship. Those who had not become citizens by 1930 had apparently largely abandoned the effort, for little demand for citizenship classes was reported, though English classes continued.

The younger generation had not the opportunity to forget its ethnic origin if it would. The alien tongue spoken in their homes remained as a constant reminder. Though as children they might, perhaps, have played with children of other nationalities with only slight consciousness of difference, as they reached maturity they became aware of parental pressure to marry within the group. They stood a good chance of being rejected by employment agencies — and if they had not had such an experience personally, their friends probably had. Practically all of the young people interviewed could volunteer stories of discrimination which they or friends or relatives had experienced. Ten per cent of the younger people questioned admitted that they would hide their Italian nationality if it turned out to be a handicap to them in getting ahead. In contrast to the intense nationalism which immigrant groups of other nationalities brought with them, especially those with experience of oppression such as Irish, Polish, or Slovak, the Italians had their Italian consciousness thrust upon them by the conditions of their American life.

At the same time, the new Italian nationalism of the post-War

[1] *U.S. Census, 1930.* Citizenship by nationality not available.

years contributed something to the self-respect of the Italian group in America — just how much it was virtually impossible to discover. To one young Italian American who was opposed to Fascism it appeared nevertheless that, 'it is worth something to have made two million Italians in America hold up their heads.' The subject of Italian Fascism was still too dangerous a subject to be freely discussed in 1930, and its influence was consequently impossible to gauge. There were some who regarded it as the most disruptive of influences, holding that it had torn the Italian community apart. It was noteworthy, however, that nearly half of the persons asked to name the two greatest Italians mentioned Mussolini — 59 as against 30 who mentioned Columbus, 23 Dante, 23 Garibaldi, 19 Marconi, and 18 the Pope. European political attitudes carried over sufficiently to make half of the older and a sixth of the younger persons who were questioned object to intermarriage with the French — several more than objected to marriage with the Irish, the other Catholic group included in the question. The self-consciousness of the Italian group in this community clearly survived the breakup of its social organization.

2. THE DISTORTION OF ITS CULTURE

When the Italians arrived in the community, they brought with them not only their Old World associations but their inherited culture. Like that of the many other immigrants who have made America their home, this Old World culture was severely modified by New World experience. At the same time, it modified the life of the community into which it came.

The fate which the culture of each immigrant group has met in its new home has depended partly upon the extent to which the central features of its life could survive transplanting and partly upon the social situation into which it was transferred. For the Italian group of this community, conditions were almost equally unfavorable to the maintenance of much in Italian culture, and to the adoption by the Italian immigrants of the traditional pattern of the American community. The result was that during these years the disintegration of the old pattern was rapid and violent, while the confusion in the American situation gave little opportunity for the successful acquisition of new standards. The Italian community in 1930 was almost wholly lacking in cultural coherence.

A culture is in a position to be transplanted and to survive in a different environment if it is self-conscious and articulate and if it has organized institutions integral with it. Especially is it able to survive when severed from its roots if it has been strengthened by persecution — a fact amply attested by the experience of the Jews, Armenians, or Poles. It is weak if its distinctive features rest in any important measure upon relation to any particular place, if its organized institutions are not fundamental to it and if it has not been on the defensive.

Of the cultures brought into America by various immigrant groups, none has been in a weaker position for survival than that of the Italians. Never the object of persecution, it has not had the fortifying experience of fighting for survival. Its articulate expression has been confined to the cultivated minority, which has been almost entirely unrepresented among the body of immigrants and which, when present, has been separated by a wide social gulf from the illiterate peasantry. Its folk culture has been poor in articulate content — in the folktales, dances, and the wealth of strong group customs characteristic of the Slavic peasantries. It has lacked even a common language for the many who have known only a local dialect. No important institutions have been integral with it, for the Church has never played the central role among Italians that it has among such others as Irish or Poles, and nothing comparable to the Slavish Sokol or the German Turnverein has furnished a center for cultural and political activity. Place associations, which cannot be transported, have been important to it.

The family has always been the central institution of Italian culture. This has, in one way, made their culture easier to transplant than those which depend upon more complex institutions. Embedded in the intimacy of family relations, the most fundamental Italian attitudes have been beyond the reach of many influences that have affected external relations and practices.

At the same time, their culture pattern has been peculiarly vulnerable, for any weakening of its foundations has undermined the fundamental basis of social organization. Were the family less central, it could continue to function socially, though the culture pattern were disrupted. Were the culture less tied up with the institution of the family, its destruction or modification would be less socially disorganizing in its effect. But whatever tended to place the Italian tradition in disrepute or to draw the members of the group, either first or second generation, away from it, struck directly at the institution of the Italian family, while the American influences which loosened the bonds of that family produced a collapse of the whole inherited code of behavior. In contrast to the American who could retain many of his institutions — the community, for instance, or certain codes of honesty, fair play, and decency — though his family might be destroyed, or could lose many of his traditional values and still retain his family, the tradition of the Italian made his family and his culture inseparable. Any agencies which sought to amalgamate this group with the American community thus had the choice of accepting its Italianness and dealing with it in family groups or of attempting to deal with a group of individuals who were not only traditionless but socially disorganized as well. In this community, the line of development has followed the latter course.

The culture which the Italian peasant brought with him to America was closely rooted in the soil, and centered in the family which was patriarchal in form and integral with the land. It rested on oral tradition rather than literacy. It accorded a place of dignity to manual skill and fine craftsmanship. It took for granted the Catholic faith, but accepted religious indifference as well as piety. It contained a body of superstitions revolving about the 'evil eye' and the use of occult powers. It contained no element of community participation or social organization beyond the family group. Although this pattern had been substantially modified before emigration among some emigrants, especially those who had lived in cities in Italy and some of those from the north who were more literate, most of those who came to America brought with them this pattern intact.

In 1930, it could still be found in Greenwich Village. A middle-aged woman from the South who was described by the young local Italian man who interviewed her as 'a type prevalent in the neighborhood among the older Italians' and 'the stubborn kind whose opinions you cannot budge,' gave her views in no uncertain terms. According to this woman, every girl should marry, the man to be determined by the parents' choice with particular reference to the reputation of his family, his health, and his having steady work. A girl's qualifications as a wife consisted in the reputation of her family, her skill at housework, and her ability to bear many children. Prior to her marriage she should not be permitted to go out unchaperoned even with other girls or to entertain a man at her house. The husband should have complete authority in the home and on no account should there be divorce or even separation. Parental authority must be complete. Children must obey their parents absolutely all their lives, be guided by them even after marriage, bring home to their parents all their pay if they were at work, and be always prepared to sacrifice their own interests or ambition in order to promote the welfare of the family group. A boy should be allowed a little spending money, while a girl should have none at all.

She desired no education for her children, except that they should learn a trade; a son should follow the trade of his father. It was preferable for a girl to work in a factory rather than in an office, presumably because of the necessary association with men in an office and the fact that a dress factory would call for a suitable type of manual skill. She was a devout Catholic, celebrating all Holy Days and appropriate saints' days, attending confession regularly, and sending her children to parochial school. She had retained such superstitious practices as protecting a baby with charms against the evil eye because 'it is always best to be sure of everything' and insisting that a pregnant woman eat whatever her fancy dictated lest failure to do so should disfigure the child. She thought that America was not a good place to live or to raise children because there was 'no respect for family or parents' and the atmosphere was 'too free and instructive.' Her ambitions for her children were that the boys should be good workers and respect their parents and the girls good housewives. The outstanding change in the life of the local Italian community which she had observed was the loss of respect on the part of children. She deplored this as 'un-Italian,' and hoped for a return of filial love and respect. Children and a comfortable home she considered more essential to a good life than money, friends, prestige, leisure, education, or congenial work. She retained her provincial prejudices as well as her Italianness unshaken. She was opposed to intermarriage by Italians, not only with non-Italians, but also with someone from a different province. She herself did not associate with people from other parts of Italy because she 'did not like them,' and she not only did not think that the people of different provinces had become more friendly, but doubted that they ever would. She hoped to return to Italy to live.

Of all the elements in this traditional pattern, none has been in more fundamental conflict with the new environment than the patriarchal family. It has been under fire from practically every American institution with which it has come in contact, for, with the exception of the family welfare agencies, American institutions have normally been designed to deal with people as individuals rather than in family or other groups. Democracy, community participation, public school education, have all rested on individualistic assumptions. Recreational agencies such as settlement houses dealt with their members in individual terms, and Protestant churches have still further stressed the ultimate separateness of the individual. Activities of all types have been characteristically planned for and carried on by the several age groups rather than by young and old acting together. In the community in which this Italian population thus found itself, there was little or nothing to reinforce and everything to undermine the unity of the family group.

American pressures penetrated below its external unity and gave its internal structure a severe wrench. Whatever operated to individualize the women and the children upset their subordination to the group as a whole and to the man who was its dominant head. As this occurred, the most fundamental of all traditional Italian relationships was destroyed. The breakdown of Italian culture can, thus, be traced in the changing position of Italian women and girls.

In many communities, immigrant women have hardly felt the direct impact of American institutions, since they have largely led their lives within the confines of their own homes. In this community, however, social agencies, and especially health agencies, undertook to reach these women in their homes and to modify their lives. Where such modifications involved only minor matters of housekeeping technique, they did not necessarily influence

the family structure. But where they gave to the women independence and a sense of importance, especially where they took
them out of the home, organized them into classes or clubs, and
offered them recreation, or where they forced the mothers to take
responsibility for decisions about the children without deferring
to the head of the house, they pried these women loose from their
positions within their family units.

Health agencies and recreation and church groups, during the
years under review, all joined in taking the married women out of
the home and building up a taste for club activities. The principal
health center, starting first with baby, prenatal and children's
clinics, added classes for mothers which began to take on the aspect of clubs so completely that a group of younger women, ignoring the fact that they were dealing with a health agency, asked to
have a club which could simply run dances. In connection with
the kindergartens at several centers, mothers' groups all developed
into social clubs which shifted their interests from the problems
of their children that had first brought them together to affairs of
their own. Children, in fact, were brought along and set to play
in the corner or allowed to sleep in their mothers' laps while the
club meeting was going on. When in 1930 one center organized a
new women's club — which, significantly enough, called itself a
'women's club' and not a 'mothers' club' as the others had — the
membership mounted rapidly. Inside of a few months it numbered
200 and at the end of six months it claimed 400 members. There
was pressure during these years to turn Italian wives and mothers
into American clubwomen.

The proportion of women who had joined clubs by 1930 was
somewhat difficult to estimate, as membership was not drawn
from a limited area and there was considerable duplication. Certainly, the great mass of Italian women, especially the older ones,
belonged to no organizations. Nevertheless, several hundred
women were enrolled and the men were beginning to mutter,
'Oh, Italian women will join anything.' One of the Catholic
churches introduced a mothers' club like those organized at the
Protestant churches and independent social agencies, because the
priest saw that the women wanted that kind of activity. The
younger women predominated among the various club memberships, but one center had two clubs, English-speaking and Italian-

speaking, and another reported that a large proportion of its clubwomen spoke only Italian.

In their organizations, the women quickly developed all the attitudes and sense of importance of clubwomen. They spent a great deal of time over problems of organization, appointing committees, and planning activities. They had the requisite number of quarrels among people who were trying to run things. On one occasion an effort to hold a joint meeting of several clubs was very nearly broken up over the question of whether a woman who was a member of two clubs should walk to the meeting with one club or the other.

The development of these clubs was opposed in the home by the more conservative men. As one husband expressed it, when a worker from the center at which the club met called to find out why his wife had not been attending, 'I won't have her go because they learn her things there.' This attitude, however, was absent in a sufficient number of cases to permit the enrollment of the clubs to rise rapidly. One center, in fact, reported that some husbands were actually co-operating with their wives by taking care of the children in order to enable them to attend club meetings.

Though it was not possible to make a scientific appraisal of the effect of such activity upon the women, there was no doubt that it had very importantly altered the relation of the women to their families and their homes, primarily by giving them the idea of living for themselves rather than exclusively for the family group of which they were a part. In fact, the organizer of one club whose purpose had been to give them this sense feared that the change in point of view might carry them too far. She acknowledged that she was shocked to see how selfish her group of women had become and commented, 'If I really thought that this was the result of my work I should feel very much distressed.'

At the same time that the American environment gave Italian women a life outside of their families, it removed the traditional basis for their prestige. In a patriarchal family, child-bearing was a woman's principal source of distinction, for the economic usefulness of children in an agricultural society, reinforced by the teaching of the Church, made a large family proverbially a blessing — 'It is better to be rich in flesh than rich in goods.' In the local community, pressure toward family limitation was very strong.

Virtually every agency dealing with this group tacitly assumed, if it did not directly express, the position that large families were evidences of irresponsibility and foreignness and that the basis for the size of a family should be the economic capacity of the parents to support their children. When a questionnaire including a question as to how many children they wanted was submitted to a girls' club at a settlement, the girls' worker reported that she found the girls not taking the questions seriously, but putting down that they wanted six children. She upbraided them for their levity, and the questionnaires as finally filled out all gave the desired number as two. Among a sample of twenty-two young married women who patronized a baby clinic, the number of children which they stated they desired ranged from one to three. The young girls consistently assumed that to have a large family was 'low-class,' or else they insisted that they were not going to wear themselves out looking after a 'bunch of kids' as their mothers had.

The fact that this group was located in the heart of an extremely urban district, where all the disadvantages and few of the advantages of large families obtained, furnished a strong economic influence toward family limitation. The school added its pressure by its stress on standard of living. In the words of one local young man, 'They made us feel at school as if we were being actually unpatriotic — almost traitors — if we did not achieve a high standard of living.' In these families, whose earnings were low, a high standard of living was incompatible with a large family, and it became almost heresy among the younger people to maintain the traditional 'rich in flesh' attitude.

The burden of carrying out a changed attitude toward family limitation fell, in the older generation, entirely upon the women. The evidence from doctors and individuals consistently agreed that the older men would take no precautions. The women, moreover, were under pressure from their husbands, their tradition, and their Church not to practice birth control. The clinics, in spite of the fact that their health education pointed directly toward infrequent pregnancies, had nevertheless been scrupulous in withholding the necessary information out of regard for the fact that the community was Catholic and they were unwilling to jeopardize their position by antagonizing the Church. In two cases there was some slight departure from this general local clinic practice. The result was that those women who sought to use contraceptives were driven to acquire them secretly through the Italian midwives. As the spread of clinical services and the increased hospitalization of confinement cases cut down the latter's practice, a number turned to the bootlegging at enormous prices of types of contraceptives out of favor with the medical profession. They thus achieved a double income from high initial fees and from the patient's later visits to remedy the effects of the device used.

These midwives also performed abortions, and one at least was known to maintain a sort of private hospital where abortions were performed and where girls who had got into trouble were sometimes secreted until after the birth of their child. According to one of the reputable midwives, 'That woman is perfectly brazen. When she gets caught, she just lets the police wagon call for her, rides up to the station, pays her fine, and goes back to her work.' A very popular old Italian doctor who had practiced for years in the neighborhood revealed the situation as he saw it in the course of giving advice to a woman medical student. 'If you are planning to practice in this kind of community, go in for obstetrics. Even though the birth rate is going down, there will be plenty of work because the midwives often do a bad job in performing an abortion and a doctor has to be called in. It is much easier to collect a high fee when there is obviously a crisis than in chronic cases or where the effect of the treatment cannot immediately be seen.' There was some slight evidence that abortion was more common than the use of contraceptives — a nurse's statement that Italian women were too lazy to take precautions, but waited until they were pregnant and then begged the nurses to tell them what to do about it; the report at a clinic that women who had been pregnant would turn up at that clinic a few weeks later with a knowing grin and shrug of the shoulders.

Among the younger generation, the traditional idea that the more children a family had the better had been very generally abandoned. Three quarters of the younger people directly questioned gave a negative answer to the question, 'Do you favor large families?' That they disagreed over what constituted a 'small' or a 'large' family was immaterial for the purpose under discussion. Among the boys interviewed, the use of contraceptives was known and taken for granted; among the girls, somewhat less so. The attitude of the Church on the subject was not found to be of great importance to the younger Italians interviewed. There were, of course, some young people in the community, chiefly girls, who took their attitude from the instruction of the Church, but, at least among the boys, disregard of the Church on this point was widespread.

By setting up the small family as the standard, and at the same time placing legal and social obstacles in the way of securing birth-control information, the American situation was doubly destructive of the integrity of the Italian women, first by undermining their status in the family group and attacking the tenets of their Church, and second, by forcing them to resort to subterfuge and to be exposed to physical danger and exploitation in the process. The result was a state of conflict in the older generation and, among the younger generation, very frequent abandonment of the traditional attitude, and with it much that was essential to the structure of the family. Though the loss of personal integrity which this situation produced was very far from universal and did not involve the many women who were scarcely touched by these pressures, it made the conflict and breakdown at this point peculiarly disorganizing — more especially as the woman had always been the stabilizing element in Italian life and as the influences of the American community were certainly not likely to give any added stability to the men. An Italian social worker who knew her people well realized the serious implications of this development. 'It is important to talk about the boy as the future citizen and to develop a program of "boys' work" and to help him,' she agreed, 'but what about his companion and the mother of his children who has been overlooked? We cannot afford to let these girls grow up without any focus to their lives.'

It was around the position and activity of the girls who were growing up that the clash between the tradition of rural Italy and the dynamics of modern America really centered. Traditionally, a girl's marriageability depended upon her chastity, and fear that she might lose her virginity before marriage led parents to establish the strictest sort of surveillance from the time of adolescence. Supervision, in fact, was increased at adolescence beyond that accorded to young children. When a group of seventh- and eighth-grade girls was required to go to a more distant school by the closing of upper grades in a smaller building, the mothers objected that the girls were too old to be walking such a distance, and they sent their girls to the near-by parochial school instead. Traditionally, contact between the sexes from adolescence to marriage was assumed to be solely with a view to marriage. No outside play contacts were favored and work contacts were restricted to the necessary minimum. All contacts must theoretically be made under the supervision of parents or relatives, and no man might enter the girl's home unless serious in his intention to seek her hand. All intimate acquaintance began with marriage, or, among the more lenient, with betrothal. All physical contact was regarded as defiling and was completely taboo.

There were still some girls in 1930 who actually never left the house unaccompanied by a member of the family from adolescence until marriage and who accepted the candidate of their parents' choice as a husband. But every American institution and every influence with which she came in contact tended to dislodge the girl from this position and to transfer responsibility from parents to the girl herself. The school, the neighborhood, the example of everything which she read and saw, and the opportunities resulting from the necessity of going out to work all combined to make her seek the 'freedom' which American girls enjoyed in place of the restrictions which were normal in her parents' eyes.

Her traditional position fitted a rural and small-town situation where marriage was a matter of families rather than of individuals, where the houses containing marriageable men were all known and the problem of each family was simply to choose among them in an effort to better their social position and landed holdings. In a strange land among strange people, the parents could not know those who were eligible for their daughter's hand. In an industrial civilization, where each marriage meant a new household rather than the carrying on of an inherited farm, marriage tended to be more an individual and less a family matter. Under these circumstances, it became extremely difficult for the parents to find suitable husbands for their daughters and for the daughters to accept as a matter of course the husbands provided for them.

This situation inevitably bred conflict and strain. The negative parts were held on to when the positive could no longer be supplied. The prohibitions on girls' going out, and particularly on their associating with men, lasted when the parents no longer had the power to find a husband which had made it unnecessary for a girl to do her own hunting. 'Our parents think you can just sit home and wait for a man to come asking for your hand — like a small town in Italy. They don't realize that here a girl has got to get out and do something about it.'

The situation which resulted was curious and anomalous. In the stricter families, and even in those families which had departed appreciably from the pattern and had acquired some understanding of and tolerance for American ways, it remained the rule that a girl could bring no man to the house unless he was to marry her. Even in the families where this rule had been set aside, girls still complained, 'Whenever I bring a boy to the house, my father starts propositioning him.' Prohibitions against going out with men alone, and, usually, even in groups, were equally rigorous. In fact, every effort was made to prevent contacts between men and girls, thereby making it most difficult for a girl to find herself a man. At the same time, she was expected to find such a man, since her parents were not in a position to do the hunting, and it was taken for granted that she would walk in some day with a man whom she never was supposed to have had the opportunity to meet and to announce, 'This is the man I am going to marry.' Such a method of finding a mate placed great reliance indeed upon the traditional matchmaker — Fate.

By 1930, the local community contained Italian families ranging all the way from those where the girl continued to occupy her traditional position to those where none of the traditional controls had been retained. All evidence agreed that girls were on the whole less strictly supervised and accorded more liberty than they had been in the past. Efforts to discover how far a change in this respect had permeated the community and what factors in the family situation went along with the modification of the traditional attitudes, brought out conflicting and inconclusive evidence. The one point upon which testimony was united, however, was that the relations between girls and their parents were very frequently characterized by subterfuge, defiance, or resentment — precarious foundations for the maintenance of stable family relationships.

The evidence of those who had come in contact with Italian girls in the neighborhood varied according to the group with which they had been dealing. At one center, the girls' worker declared that so far as her experience was concerned, the idea that Italian girls were strictly kept was a myth. She had never had any difficulty in getting them to come to athletic clubs and there had always been enough to make her teams. On the other hand, one of the Italian priests found it difficult to fill his girls' clubs because either the parents would not let the girls out even to the church or else the girls were engaged to be married. Another worker was engaged in a special effort to overcome parental objections, running her girls' clubs as nearly in accordance with the attitudes of the mothers as was possible.

In an effort to get some idea of how representative of the community in 1930 these several experiences of different individuals might be, a sample was made of some forty-five girls, picked up at random on the stoops of houses, the steps of the church, the street or the park as they sat or strolled on a summer evening. This sample did little more than to refute all the generalizations which had been made by persons familiar with one aspect of the situation.

Neither this sample nor the scattered evidence from other sources showed differences in the position of the girl to be consistently associated with differences in economic position, the part of Italy from whence they had come, length of time the family had been in America — none had American-born parents — or with education. In a single family, even, one woman could be found bringing her girls up with a great deal of liberty, while her sister, living on the same block, never let her daughters out unless the little brother went along too. It seemed as if the personal adjustment which each individual had made was the only determining factor, although some blocks were more nearly in the old pattern, and the girl who went out there was the butt of more gossip than on some of the other blocks where a larger proportion were lenient.

Even though this sample was biased by the obvious omission of those girls who were not allowed out at all, it included girls who were held almost completely within the old mould. Representative of the apathetic type which had met the situation with inertia was the poorly dressed, fifteen-year-old daughter of a laborer who lived in the worst type of dingy house on a run-down, crowded block. Forced by law to attend continuation school in spite of the objections of her parents who wanted to send her to work in a dress factory, she was required to come immediately home, spent most of her time helping with the housework, and was only allowed to bring a chair down and sit in front of the door between supper and eight o'clock in the evening. She used to play basketball at the church until she was twelve, but then her mother told her she was 'too big to be jumping around.' When some of the boys from the block passed with a greeting, the girl remarked, 'My mother would kill me if she saw me speaking to them.'

More ambitious but equally conservative was an alert, attractively dressed girl of about twenty who was picked up on the steps of the church while she was waiting for her companion to come out from confession. Church was the only place where she was allowed to go. She had no friends, 'What is the use if you can't go anywhere? It is easier not to be friendly than to have to tell the girls you can't go with them.' She worked as stenographer in a large plant which provided clubs and various recreational facilities, but these she could never use but must always return instantly after work. She hoped to get engaged soon, but when asked how her parents expected her to find a man to marry, she laughed and said she supposed they relied on Fate. To illustrate, she told the story of her sister's marriage. One evening, they had smelt smoke and had gone into another flat hunting for its source. They found two boys playing the piano. One asked the sister to dance. She had never danced and drew back shyly, but the boy, laughingly telling her how easy it was, whisked her off to dance. At the end of the dance, he declared, 'This is the girl that I am going to marry' and went off to announce the fact to his parents. They came to see the girl's parents and the match was found to be satisfactory to both. The girl was then engaged, 'and what a swell time she had then.' This girl hoped that Fate would treat her as kindly as it had her sister. For her part, she would not defy her parents' commands in order to aid it, except that if she found a man who she thought was to her taste, she might tell her mother that she was going to church and go out with him instead to find out.

Even families who had set aside tradition to the point of entertaining professional ambitions for their daughters might be rigorous in supervision. There was a high-school senior who was planning to go to college and be a teacher and whose family was sufficiently well off to give her music lessons and to take her on trips as far as Washington, D.C. She was not allowed to go walking or to a show with other girls, and she had never danced. She was interested in joining an Italian-language class at the neighborhood settlement and thought she would be allowed to because the family had had dealings with the settlement and 'knew what nice ladies the people there were,' but when she found that the class met in the evening, she knew that she could never get permission to stay out as late as nine-thirty or ten. She hastened apprehensively away from the interviewer to join her aunt from whom she had become temporarily separated while strolling in the park.

The socially élite of the metropolitan Italian community included people as eager to bring their daughters up in the old ways as the poor and 'backward' laborer. The daughter of a prosperous and cultivated business man had been sent back to Italy for part of her schooling and was attending a Catholic college in the suburbs. She had made few contacts through college, however, for her friends were carefully selected by her parents from among the children of their friends. She belonged to a select Italian cultural society and her mother took immense pride in the fact that her daughter spoke Italian beautifully.

Many of the girls interviewed expressed interest in attending dances at the local settlement house, but reported that they could not do so because they were not allowed to go out to dance. Some had never danced; others only at dances given by their fathers' benefit societies.

At the opposite extreme were those who were entirely unrestricted because their parents did not pay any attention to them at all. A group of this type was found in the park one evening.

Certainly, they could go anywhere they chose. There was sometimes a battle if they went out before they finished helping with the dishes. Nobody at home cared what they did or where they went. According to their own interpretation, it was not that their parents trusted their judgment, but that they were indifferent to them or had long ago given up trying to control their children. This type appeared to be relatively infrequent, however, since few examples of it were found and it would, by its nature, have been in evidence.

Much more general than complete parental indifference were situations in which efforts at varying degrees of supervision and restriction were met by subterfuge on the part of the girls. In probably a majority of the families, though it was not possible to establish the proportion with any certainty, the old controls were first eluded and then worn away by evasion and deception. 'What mother doesn't know won't hurt her,' was the standard comment of the girl who would tell her parents that she was earning less than she was and pocket the difference; who met boys around the corner if she was allowed out for a walk; who sneaked out to a dance and got home without being caught; or who went to a movie outside of the neighborhood and 'happened' to find a boy friend sitting in the next seat.

Once the rigidity of restriction had been relaxed, the way was open for activities not at all within the family's code. The first step — being allowed to go down and sit on the stoop in front of the house — did not offer much opening, but to be allowed to go out for an evening stroll with another girl gave an enormous loophole. Groups of girls started out in one direction and then worked around the block so that they would meet their boy friends in a place where they would not be likely to be found. Neighborhood boys took it for granted that if they met a girl and walked with her, they would have to leave her a couple of blocks away from her door. One group of girls went night after night to a clubroom maintained by a group of boys to listen to a detective story over the radio — all as part of their 'walk.' A number of girls said they could slip away to a dance and get home without being caught, as they had done so before. Nearly everybody had a ready fund of stories of things that they had done in defiance of parental prescript, and the tales of how their older sisters got their men were well stocked with episodes involving deception.

Even those who were allowed to go out were required to be in at an early hour. This put them at a certain disadvantage in competition with the girls who were under fewer restrictions. Boys complained at having to deliver their companions home when the evening was still young. The girls complained that to be kept under these restrictions made it very difficult for them to find a man because boys went with girls of other nationalities, or Italian girls from other communities who were less strictly kept, while they had no chance even to go with the neighborhood boys, let alone to forage outside. Boys confirmed the grounds for these complaints with accounts of their discomfort when irate parents scolded them over the hour at which they brought girls home. Among girls who were subject to the fewest restrictions, the hour of home-coming was quite universally the sorest point, probably because it was the one on which evasion was most difficult. Girls who wanted to move to another neighborhood gave as their reason the desire to escape from the lash of local gossip, for even if their own parents were lenient, the tongues of the neighbors on the solidly Italian blocks certainly were not.

Not all, however, who did not submit to the old controls and yet were not ignored completely by their parents took to deception as the normal course. Some were allowed to go out if the parents knew exactly where they were. Others were allowed to go freely to the settlement house or the dances, but they still could not go out alone with a man. Still others could go with men specifically approved by their parents. A very occasional parent was actively sympathetic with the interests of her children, like the mother of a girl interested in athletics who never missed a match game if she could help it and, when questioned about her attitude, saw nothing out of the way in it.

What girls of nearly all types were struggling for, whether successfully or unsuccessfully, was the negative advantage of freedom from restraint rather than any of the positive opportunities or responsibilities which went with a different sort of position on the part of women. Where they had acquired any positive aim, it was the bourgeois-romantic ideal — *True Story Magazine's* version of 'love' and the *Ladies' Home Journal* style of a 'lovely home.'

Interviews could not be secured with a sufficient number of comparable families to establish whether the difference between the older and younger children in the same family was likely to be as great as the difference between all the children of different families. From fragmentary evidence it seemed that, although there were frequent indications of change within the same family, the difference among families still appeared somewhat greater.

Where there were several girls in a family, the older was apt to bear the brunt of the struggle. 'My sister's going to have a snap when she comes along,' commented many an older sister. 'Mother'll take my word for it and let her do the things that she's never let me do.' And from the younger ones, 'My older sister had it tough — always having to sneak off or make up some sort of lie as to where she was going. I guess mother has given up with me.' In one family the older girl could go no farther from home than to take her dog onto the roof, while at the same time her two younger sisters were allowed out freely for evening strolls in the neighborhood.

Other aspects of the traditional Italian family — masculine dominance, filial obedience, and the subordination of the interests of children to the welfare of the family group — were subject to modification, while those features such as the dowry which went with the more strictly agricultural society of which it was a part were dropped. The vital point, however, was the place of women.

At other points, less essential to Italian culture but nevertheless a part of it, American influences broke down inherited attitudes and institutions. Economic pressures swiftly and completely routed the work habits which had been brought in. Neither the spirit and the working conditions of American factories nor the drive of American business methods permitted the survival of the sense of craftsmanship and the high regard for manual skill which distinguished many Italian groups.[1] Except in a few determined families which made arrangements to apprentice their children — like one man who opened a barber shop of his own in order to keep his boys off the street by apprenticing them in his shop — the second generation grew up almost entirely free from the craftsman's point of view. In the effort to make use of the traditional skills or to sharpen them, one of the local settle-

[1] Cf. Odencrantz, *op. cit.*, p. 41.

ment houses opened a workshop in charge of an Italian master who undertook to train boys in woodcarving and stonecutting by the apprentice method. But even this organized attempt to preserve crafts and skills was faced with an economic set-up which had little place for such types of work. It was disheartening to those in charge of the shop to find scarcely any of their graduates who had been out any length of time still employed in the crafts to which they had been trained.

The Church, never so prominently a part of Italian as of other Catholic cultures, was nevertheless the one formal institution which the Italians brought with them. It had to struggle in this community against the tendency of the American-born to link it with the old culture from which they were breaking away. Its effort to maintain itself by out-Americaning the Americans is a story in itself.[1]

A very few families were drawn away from their Church completely and brought within the Protestant fold by the work of Protestant missions. These were introduced to the traditional American pattern in a somewhat more coherent form, but a form which took little or no account of the newer influences which were modifying the attitudes of the American community. For most who attended the Protestant missions without, however, turning Protestant, the influence of these centers did not go beyond that exerted by schools and non-sectarian agencies to disrupt the old attitudes without introducing a body of new ones.

One of the adjectives which the young 'Americanized' element was most ready to apply to the older generation was 'superstitious.' The type of superstition most at variance with the institutions of the American community was that which substituted the practice of magic for scientific medicine. In view of the statement from all sides that these superstitions had been dropped by an increasing proportion of people in the neighborhood, efforts were made to discover how far witchcraft had survived and charms were still used. It was very difficult to get people to talk about witches and fortune-tellers, and their very hesitancy revealed the fear which they felt for the power of the witch or *strega*. One woman acknowledged that her daughter had gone to a *strega* to secure a powder to put on her pay envelope so that

[1] Cf. Chapter X.

her pay would not be cut, while others had sought love potions. Doctors and health centers still complained of the patronage of witches, although one doctor reported that for some time he had not seen a case of mumps with the black marks which the witch made behind the ears.

The use of charms to keep off the evil eye was more readily acknowledged than belief in witches. That the use of these charms was on the wane was perhaps indicated by the number offered for sale in the local pawnshops. The nurses reported that it had become very much less usual to find babies with charms tied around their necks. Yet, 27 out of 144 questioned — and these questions reached primarily the more rather than the less Americanized — considered it advisable to protect babies with charms. Among a group of five young men, four of whom were professionals, all acknowledged that they had carried at one time or another, or still did carry, a charm of some sort. An Italian woman observed to an interviewer that she supposed that a lot of the people whom she interviewed were 'making horns' at her with their hands behind their backs all the time she was talking, to ward off any evil influence which she might be bringing.

Some who ceased to use horns, fishes, or red string as charms against the evil eye substituted religious medals to secure the protection of God and the aid of the Saints. The most general form of this was the habitual carrying of the picture of Saint Christopher by all who had cars or were in the habit of driving. In some cases there seemed to be an important distinction between the use of charms and religious medals, but in others they were regarded as essentially the same — either potent or evidences of superstition. Some of the younger generation who dropped away from the Church altogether classed all religious observances with the rest of their parents' traditional beliefs as 'superstitions.'

Certain practices which were considered superstitious or which were part of an older medical tradition came into conflict with the health practices prescribed by the agencies in the locality. The use of herbs was sufficient to support stores purveying them and to afford an opportunity for an enterprising dealer of doubtful reputation to make a business of Indian herb remedies. Superstitions connected with pregnancy were fairly general. Among the same 144 persons interrogated, 48 were of the belief that the child would be disfigured if a pregnant woman was denied any kind of food which she craved. 'You're like a pregnant woman' was the taunt thrown in the face of anyone, man or woman, who indulged his own whims. The cruder beliefs, as, for instance, that venereal diseases could be cured by intercourse with a virgin, had been discarded by 1930. Since health standards were among the American attitudes most vigorously forced to the attention of the immigrants and were among the things most easily recognized by them as 'American,' the pressure to discard superstitious beliefs and practices was strong. Their interrelation with religion and the basic insecurity of the immigrant group which made every possible aid seem important, however, tended to permit the survival of these beliefs.

Customs which were not in conflict with local conditions survived, while the more basic social attitudes did not. Spaghetti remained the staple in the diet, and the social worker who valued her relation with her client was well advised not to try to stop her from 'wasting' money on good olive oil. Weddings continued to be celebrated in the customary manner, with the guests giving presents in money which were counted on to more than defray the expense of the affair. Customs which were attached to the land and those, such as swaddling, which were directly attacked by local agencies, did not survive.

Neither the absolute extent to which the Italian culture pattern was modified, nor the rate of change could be determined, for there was no adequate measuring stick by which to test the degree of modification. It was possible, however, to get some indication of the kinds of distortion resulting from the fact that traditional attitudes had broken down much more thoroughly and more generally at certain points than at others. The process of distortion was not confined to the post-War years, but had been going on ever since the group arrived in America. In these years, however, influences combined to hasten the shift, and other influences which had retarded it disappeared. It was only after the War that large numbers of children reached maturity; that the community shifted its orientation from Europe to America with the cessation of immigration and the decision of many to make their American residence permanent; that their lives were invaded by radio crooners and Villagers.

In an effort to determine where the pattern was crumbling fastest and where it was holding most firm, an interview schedule was drawn up and used by local Italians with 144 local residents. Younger residents were especially sought, since they were most involved in the shift. Ninety-three of the 144 cases were between 18 and 35 years of age and 51 were over 35. The sample was biased partly by accident and partly by design, in the direction of those who were more self-conscious and articulate, better educated and more Americanized than the mass of the community. For a study of the cultural disequilibrium which has been produced in the Italian community by contact with the American influences, these interviews reached the appropriate element, for unless future developments should thrust the immigrant group farther back into its ghetto, American influences can be expected to spread through those who have made the first contacts and adjustments.

The interview schedule which was used was so drawn as to give the person interviewed an opportunity to register his adherence to, or departure from, the traditional Italian pattern with respect to marriage and the family, work preferences, education, the Church, and some of the more general superstitions, and to indicate familiarity with the content of literate Italian culture. The authenticity of the pattern assumed was verified by submitting the schedule for criticism to two Italian high-school teachers, two American-born Italians of North and South Italian parentage respectively, and to the group of five local Italian young men who were to use it in the neighborhood. The latter's comments were reassuring. 'How do you know so much about the Italian people?' 'An Italian certainly had a hand in drawing this up.' When two older women, noted for their conservatism, gave exactly the answers expected of those who had retained their traditional views, there seemed every reason to think that the points selected were well calculated to test divergence. Many informal interviews furnished support to this conclusion in the form of generalized statements, of conformity to expected standards, or of comments on cases of divergence from those standards.

The results of these interviews were in no sense a measure of the absolute extent of disintegration. Because sixty per cent of those interviewed maintained a certain attitude, there was no reason to assume that sixty per cent of the community shared that attitude. But by comparing the questions with each other, it was possible to see where the process of modification was proceeding fastest and where more slowly. If ninety per cent of the answers repudiated one attitude and only forty per cent another, there was at least *prima-facie* evidence that the first was breaking down more rapidly than the second.

TABLE VIII. DIRECTION OF THE DISTORTION OF THE ITALIAN
CULTURE PATTERN

PROPORTION WHOSE ANSWERS DEPARTED FROM THE TRADITIONAL PATTERN [1]

	Over [2] 35 years	Under [3] 35 years
Family		
Does *not* believe that:		
Marriages should be arranged by parents	70%	99%
Large families are a blessing	48%	86%
Girls should not associate with men unless engaged	45%	83%
Husband's authority should be supreme	34%	64%
A child should sacrifice his personal ambition to welfare of family group	31%	54%
Divorce is never permissible	12%	61%
Children owe absolute obedience to parents	2%	15%
Church		
Person does not attend church	4%	16%
Person does not observe Holy Days of Obligation	33%	70%
Superstitions		
Does not believe in either 'evil eye' or superstition about pregnancy	40%	61%
Does not believe in 'evil eye' (though may about pregnancy)	70%	81%
Does not believe pregnancy superstition (though may believe in 'evil eye')	46%	69%
Italian Civilization		
Cannot dance Italian dances	58%	93%
Cannot name familiar Italian operas	15%	9%
Cannot name familiar Italian songs	8%	15%
Unable to speak Italian language [4]	57%	50%
Cannot name great Italian artist, scientist	3%	2%
Italian Neighborhood		
Italian neighborhood not preferred	49%	72%
American neighborhood preferred	9%	28%

[1] 144 questionnaires. Where question is not answered, the per cent of those answering has been taken.

[2] 51 cases.

[3] 93 cases.

[4] Knowledge of Italian vernacular, not dialect.

This inquiry showed that different aspects of the patriarchal family institution were breaking down at different rates,[1] those which had been bound up with land and family estate — i.e., the arrangement of marriage by parents and the giving of dowries — going the fastest. The younger people were nearly unanimous and over two thirds of the older agreed that the choice of a husband should fall to the girl rather than to her parents. The younger people had clearly dropped the idea that marriage involved a union of families and had adopted the bourgeois-romantic assumption that it united individuals, for they included only personal attributes among the qualifications of a good husband or wife, while a majority of the older group regarded the reputation of the girl or man's family as an important consideration. There was some slight indication that the man had become more completely individualized and distinguished from the family group than the girl in the fact that a few among the younger element included family reputation as a consideration in viewing a girl's qualifications, but none regarded it as relevant in the case of the man.

The central patriarchal assumption that large families are a blessing had broken down only less completely than the idea that marriage unites families rather than individuals. Again it was the younger group that had repudiated the assumption, but half of the older group joined in this view. The difference between the older men and women hinted that social influences weighed in this shift rather than the economic consideration that children were less likely to be economic assets under city conditions. Two thirds of the older women no longer favored large families as against less than one third of the older men. While both men and women in the younger group were very generally opposed to the large family system, the young men were slightly more tolerant of the institution than the young women. Although the younger people, and many of the older, had ceased to regard children as an economic asset, many still, in 1930, did not look upon them as heavy economic burdens. 'It doesn't cost anything to educate a child in New York City,' observed an ambitious young lawyer, 'and it doesn't hurt a child to have to work his way as I have had to work mine. I can certainly give my kids a better start and

[1] Cf. Table VIII, p. 193.

more advantages than my dad gave me.' 'My children have got to have the best there is,' commented the lawyer's companion, 'and I can't get the best for more than one or two.'

The positive drive toward a higher standard of living was a more potent influence in making a small family the ideal than the fear of being unable to support children. The girls, especially, longed for a nice home and escape from the 'dumps' in which they had been brought up. All evidence agreed in indicating that a home was the central interest in marriage for local girls of all types, and Italian girls were no exception. The homes of girls who had married and left the locality reflected care, effort, expenditure, and the influence of advertisements. 'She's forever fussing about the house and hasn't any time for me,' complained a young husband as his wife proudly displayed to the interviewer the lavender bathroom, the green kitchen, the pink bedroom, and the red-and-gold 'Spanish' runner on the living-room table. In describing her friends who had moved to the various outlying boroughs, a young married woman had nothing to say about their husbands, their children, or any of their activities — nothing except that each and all had such 'lovely homes.'

Personal appearance was also part of the higher standard of living. 'I wouldn't think of letting my appearance go after I married,' declared a carefully dressed young girl. She and her friends intended to continue to spend money on themselves after marriage. Nor did they expect to sacrifice their own pleasures in order to be like their mothers who didn't have a chance even to go to a show.

There were no indications that any idea of a 'career' attracted Italian girls as an alternative to complete absorption with child-rearing. One Italian woman lawyer was found who resented having to give the necessary time and attention to her child because of her professional interest, but the case appeared to be virtually unique.

All agreed that the only reason why a girl might work after marriage would be economic, in order to provide a better home. The alternative value which the young Italian had substituted for the traditional pride in many children was a high standard of material culture.

There were even some — more than a third of the younger

group and a tenth of the older — who were ready to apply the term 'successful' to a marriage where there were no children at all. Here was a striking confirmation of the extent to which the patriarchal ideal had broken down with respect to its chief purpose — the raising of children.

The younger group had discarded the principle that there should be no free association between boys and girls before marriage nearly as generally as they had the larger family ideal. Among the older group, too, this part of the traditional code was next in the frequency with which it had been dropped.

Masculine authority continued to be accepted by a larger proportion than held to the ideal of a large family, but it was challenged by two thirds of the younger and a third of the older groups. Again the women in both age groups were, quite naturally this time, more opposed to the traditional attitude than the men. Though professed views on this score may frequently not have accorded with practice — women refusing to acknowledge an authority which in practice they accepted, and men asserting a position which factually they could not maintain — there was little doubt that the head of the household would have to be alert in order to maintain his traditional position and exact unquestioning obedience from his wife.

Masculine authority was still strongly enough entrenched for social agencies to find it impracticable to go against it in working out their program for a family. One of the health centers introduced night visiting because it felt that its educational work with the mother was ineffective unless the husband's support was gained. Another agency reported cases of refusing to act at the request of the wife, even though its judgment concurred with hers, unless the husband were agreed. But the traditional authority had begun to be referred to as 'tyranny' by some of the younger members of the Italian community. A young married woman who complained that her husband ran around with other women was asked by a neighbor whether she wouldn't prefer a husband who ran around to one that came home and ordered her about as so many husbands did. She agreed that she would prefer her own ills to the ills which so many young women of her acquaintance had to face.

But though the individual rather than the family group had

become the center as far as marriage itself was concerned, and slightly less so in the drift away from the large family principle and in the challenge to masculine domination, over two thirds of the older and nearly half of the younger group maintained that a child would be expected to sacrifice his own ambition and advancement to the interests of the family group — interrupting his educational or his professional career to aid the family, for instance. For many of the families of the locality, the question was a purely academic one because family need was so great that the child could not choose but aid if called on to do so. Though there were many reports of heavy sacrifices by parents to give their children a chance at education, it continued to be taken for granted that the child had obligations to the family group. Among all the various types interviewed, no resentment was expressed by any child who had been forced by family circumstances to give up his own aims. Some expressed regret and disappointment, but never the feeling that life had cheated them or that their families were unjust in bringing them into the world under circumstances so unfavorable.

Parental authority was not called into question with anything like the frequency of other relationships. The older group was practically unanimous in expecting absolute obedience from children, at least to the age of about eighteen, and all except a seventh of the younger group agreed, frequently admitting that it was due up to marriage and even beyond. Among all the young Italians encountered in the course of the study, respect and obedience were taken for granted in principle, however little they might be observed in fact.

Though children were ashamed of their parents and though those parents failed in their responsibility to their children, the filial relation remained, and parental authority was entitled to recognition. The father who came home drunk, beat up the mother, was mean to the children, and was entitled to little or no respect as a human being, was still to be looked at by his children as a father and honored accordingly.

The two aspects of the traditional family least subject to question in the older group were its absolute permanency and its economic solidarity. The younger element agreed in placing the economic unity of the family group among the features unani-

mously retained, but it was far more ready to admit the dissolution of the family bonds. Only twelve per cent of the elders admitted divorce on any count, though some were willing to accept
a separation. Sixty-one per cent of the younger element, on the
other hand, expressed themselves as not wholly opposed to divorce.
The difference between younger and older was greater on this
score than on any other. This difference was doubly significant
in that tolerance of divorce by the younger people reflected the
weakening of the hold of the Catholic Church on the group questioned as well as the loosening of the family ties. The attitude on
the question of divorce was closely correlated with the attitude
of the individual toward the Church, but it did not follow the
latter exactly. Where the permanence of the marriage bond
was firmly maintained, the motive was not always religious
scruples, but frequently a conviction, independent of the Church's
teaching, that the family was too valuable an institution to break
on any account. The women, as might be expected, were less
willing to admit of divorce than the men, both because their lot
was more closely tied up with the family and because of their
greater adherence to the Church.

   In the matter of the economic solidarity of the group, the low
income level of the families in the locality readily accounted for
the unanimity of the entire 144 in agreeing that the earnings of a
working child should go toward the family's support, but contributing these earnings had a social as well as an economic sanction. The only question was whether all the earnings should be
so devoted or only a part turned in and the rest retained. The
latter arrangement was favored by half of the young persons, but
admitted by few of the older ones. Cases of family friction over
the disposition of the children's earnings were found, but on the
whole the principle of economic solidarity seemed to have been
so firmly grounded that money disagreements did not constitute
a major source of friction in the Italian home. In discussing the
question of whether or not a child should turn over his pay envelope unopened, several of the parents interviewed put the matter on purely practical grounds — it was cheaper for them to let
the child keep part of his pay and let him clothe and entertain
himself out of it than to take it from him and then pay out for
his expenses more than he earned. This attitude showed the be-

ginning of a realization that even working children might be liabilities rather than assets under the conditions of local life. Rarely was there any hint of an assumption that anything belonged to a child by right. One woman, in praising her child's school because it had school banking, explained how fortunate it had been for her, because when her last baby was born she had needed forty dollars for her hospital bill and the child had just that much money — saved over four years — in his school account.

Distortion of the central Italian cultural institution, the patriarchal family, thus involved the loss of its central drive — many children — and the partial individualization of its members, especially in the courtship and marriage relationship. Subordination, obedience, and responsibility of children to the group and, especially, their parents, continued, and was reinforced by economic necessity which remained the strongest binding force. The elements which tended to survive were those common to the patriarchal and the bourgeois-romantic family forms — male superiority, permanence, filial respect. Those who had departed from the traditional attitudes on the points most frequently discarded had almost as little in common with the Villagers who held by the independence of women and a highly individualized, experimental family form as had their more patriarchal elders.

The Church was a much less good test of the dislocation of Italian standards than the family, for there was already the greatest variety in attitudes when the group first came from Italy. The difference between the younger and older groups answering, however, indicated that a trend away from the Church was represented by this sample. Sixteen per cent of the younger did not attend church at all, as against four per cent of the elders. Seventy per cent of the younger were not faithful in their observance of Holy Days as against thirty-three per cent of the older. The testimony of the many persons interviewed, however, was so contradictory, when it came to the matter of church attitudes, that it was very difficult to establish what the situation really was. For the group directly questioned, the maintenance of some church connection appeared to be in the same category as the duty of filial obedience; a substantially larger proportion of both age groups was faithful in church observance than supported the institution of the large family.

One or another of the characteristic superstitions — fear of the evil eye and belief that a child would be disfigured prenatally if the mother were denied her whims — were retained by as large a proportion of the younger element as was the opposition to divorce and to masculine authority. In spite of the familiar attitude among the young people of the community that their parents were 'superstitious,' there was less difference between older and younger people in their attitude toward these superstitions than in any aspect of the family or the Church.

Though the group as a whole had abandoned Italian social attitudes on many points, it had retained a sense, at least, of Italian culture. Few, either old or young, were unable to name promptly Italian songs which they knew, Italian operas with which they were familiar, and great Italian artists or scientists who had made their mark on the world. The circulation of Italian books at the local public library branch, after falling off by fifty-seven per cent from 1920 to 1926, increased again by almost fifty per cent of the 1926 low figure between that year and 1930.

Only half of the younger, however, and an even smaller proportion of the older, could speak the Italian language, other than a local dialect. Folk culture, moreover, had not been imported. Scarcely any of the younger and less than half of the older knew how to dance such traditional Italian dances as the tarantella or the quadrille.

The group questioned was not interested in maintaining solidarity with its Italian compatriots, at least as far as living among them was concerned. Half of the older and nearly three quarters of the younger had no preference for an Italian neighborhood as a place to live. In fact, nine per cent of the older and twenty-eight per cent of the younger specified to the contrary — that they definitely preferred an American to an Italian locality.

When the various aspects of the pattern are put together and compared for their differential rates of change, distortion of the whole becomes apparent. Institutions difficult to maintain and at most direct variance with the environment, such as arranged marriages, were going fastest. Distinctive forms of amusement, as represented by Italian dances, were disappearing as far as the younger group was concerned. The husband's authority was being undermined while parental authority was maintained. The assumption that many children are a blessing was being dropped more generally than the attitude that the interests of the family group are paramount over the interests of the child. The lapse in church observance was not keeping pace with the spread of the idea of family limitation, but it was going farther than the acceptance of divorce. Indifference to living in an Italian neighborhood was slightly greater than the average of the divergences on specific points — perhaps a reflection of the corresponding desire to be free from community pressure to Italian conformity. Although some superstitions were being widely abandoned, others were persisting, and less difference appeared between young and old on this than on important points of conduct. The evil eye was surviving American pressures slightly more successfully than was the large family or the supervision of girls, as far as the younger element was concerned.

As between younger and older groups, important differences in rates of change appeared. Whereas the younger group quite naturally departed more generally from the tradition than did the older, it was moving relatively faster on some points than on others. This was especially true in respect to divorce, where the difference between the per cent of younger and of older approving of divorce was forty-nine per cent as against an average of twenty-five per cent by which the younger exceeded the older group in its divergence on the items listed under family, church, and superstitions. Large families, too, were disproportionately opposed by the younger group, as were restrictions on girls. The younger were also relatively more negligent in church attendance, though not in complete disregard of church observances. In respect to superstitions and to the obedience and submission of children, they were relatively closer to the older group than on the other points.

Among the older group, the men were stronger in their support of virtually everything relating to the traditional patriarchal family than the women. The latter remained relatively more religious than their husbands, doubtless because they started so in Italy. Among the younger ones, there was little difference between the sexes on any point except, quite naturally, the husband's authority, approval of divorce, and loyalty to the Church. While the younger men showed greater sympathy with masculine dominance than the young women, they were more ready to approve of divorce and to neglect their religious duties.

There was some noticeable difference between North and South Italians, but less than the familiar generalizations about them would lead one to expect. The southerners were more favorably disposed toward large families, were more ready to maintain the husband's authority, and took more account of family reputation in considering the qualifications of a husband or wife. On parental authority, divorce, and the supervision of girls, however, this sample showed no important difference between southerners and northerners. The former were slightly more faithful in matters of religion and more tenacious of superstitions about pregnancy, but no more in awe of the evil eye. If a large encugh sample of older people could have been questioned, important differences between North and South Italy might have been brought out. But this material indicated that those differences tended to be unimportant in the adaptation of the younger group which had been subjected to Americanizing influences.

VII. OTHER ETHNIC GROUPS

I. THE IRISH NEIGHBORHOOD

THE Irish of Greenwich Village were at a stage of cultural adaptation quite different from that of their Italian neighbors. A generation had passed since the Irish had been incorporated into the American community. Their problem in the post-War years was that of a group for whom the basis of their original adaptation, the self-contained, functioning neighborhood, was destroyed.

The Irish came into the Village at four distinct times during the hundred years before 1920, and all except the first group represented by these four times of arrival remained distinct up to 1930.

The first group of Irish came into Greenwich Village during its original boom, probably either as domestic servants or to work on the construction of the new suburb, in sufficient numbers to cause the erection of a Catholic church in 1829. By 1930, all record of these and of their descendants had disappeared; among fifty Irish persons interviewed, none had ever had any knowledge of a descendant of these first Irish settlers.

The second group came to America during the early famine years, settled first on the East Side or lower down on the West Side and, when they became more prosperous, or were married out of their immigrant boarding houses and set up for themselves, moved out of these Irish neighborhoods and up to the 'American Ward' which was considered more 'ritzy.' With their hay and seed stores, blacksmith shops or stables, they became substantial members of the community, bought their homes with the first money they made, and, where possible, trained their children to the professions 'so that they would have to depend on no one.' The children often lived on with their parents and some were still occupying their fathers' houses in 1930. These were the Irish who had 'owned' Greenwich Village, had given to one of its principal thoroughfares the nickname of 'County Clare Street,' had monopolized the principal saloons 'where only an Irishman was allowed in,' had belonged to Irish county clubs, and had been able to start a street fight any day by threatening to 'lick any Irishman on the block.' Up to the War, they still constituted the nucleus of the Irish community.

The third group of Irish in the Village moved into the neighborhood from farther south in the 1890's when the area near the waterfront was being built up to tenements. Some of these had been born in the city. Others had come in with the wave of Irish immigration in the 1870's. They were of a lower economic status than the 'old Irish.' They formed solid Irish blocks, made merry in block parties, organized social clubs, patronized Irish dance halls and raised large families. Their children intermarried among themselves and settled down on the streets 'where they had been brought up. The latter, like their fathers, held poorly paid jobs as janitors or watchmen or minor posts in the civil service.

The last group of Irish to come into the Village were those born in Ireland who came to the United States after 1890, came directly to the district when they first arrived, and worked principally as longshoremen or truck-drivers. When the longshore business was good, they and some of the others who prospered bought their houses. When their families of children married and moved away, some took in lodgers. Their friends were their neighbors. They knew the first group of 'old Irish' only by hearsay and had very low opinions of the American-born — the 'narrow backs' — who lived around them. Some of their children got into the city service, or into real estate and insurance, while others went to work on the docks or drove trucks like their fathers. A few went on to college and the girls became clerical workers.

In contrast to the Italian group whose social organization was based on Old World associations, the social structure of the Irish community, acclimatized through more than a generation of American residence, rested upon a distinctive adaptation to life in America — a structure which remained unchanged except in so far as the disintegration of the community broke it. This social structure rested primarily on three foundations, the Church, the political club, and the neighborhood which the Irish had made theirs in a way that the Italians never did. Irish county clubs, the partial equivalent of Italian mutual benefit societies (though never so generally inclusive because they lacked the mutual benefit features of the Italian societies), played no considerable role in the lives of the local Irish within the memory of any except the oldest inhabitants. Rather, associations based upon the length of time and the place of their American residence, their American interests and successes, gave to the Irish community in the twentieth century its social form.

The Catholic parishes had not been simply convenient geographical limits to the charge of a given pastor, but the social units within which much of the social life of the Irish was carried on. Some of the older Irish residents had heard their fathers tell of the days when 'this was a Know-Nothing ward. Do you know what a Know-Nothing was?' and the 'grand old man' of the community, great grand sachem of Tammany Hall, who died in 1932 at the age of 102, dated from the pre-Irish political period. But before the turn of the century the Irish were thoroughly entrenched politically. More even than the churches, the political clubs had furnished centers for the social life of the Irish of the locality. The older Irish waxed eloquent about the joys of club picnics, when wagons or trucks, piled high with beer barrels and people, set off for a Sunday outing, when block parties were staged by district captains, and the neighborhood turned out with bonfires and torchlight processions on election day.

A variety of social clubs, with or without a political tinge, had maintained clubrooms, sponsored ball teams, or held dances. Certain of the saloons had been famous as gathering places and hangouts and the saloonkeepers had ranked high in prestige and wealth. A neighborhood house had helped to focus neighborhood consciousness and civic interest and had brought together some women's clubs and some groups of young people. The life of the Irish group had been led within the bounds of the district, where everyone knew all the neighbors on the block and rarely found it necessary to go outside for entertainment or friends.

Up to the War, the Irish community with its several elements remained intact. Though the Irish retreated west before the Italian invasion, they retained a sense of possession, their neighborhood life, their social clubs, their parish rivalries, and their political preoccupation, and all turned out 'to celebrate the wedding of a carpenter's daughter to a saloonkeeper's son.' But the transformation of the Village in the post-War years broke up the Irish neighborhood and dispersed the several parts of the Irish population.

The old, substantial element, which had ignored the coming-in of the low-class Irish and even the Italians, could not ignore the Villagers, for the rise in real estate values which the latter brought induced some and forced others to sell their houses and to move to the suburbs or into apartments. A very few of the old survivors lived on with their children, married and unmarried, in the houses which they bought when first they came to Greenwich Village in the 1860's. One sat on his steps all day long and vowed that the 'riff-raff' would not drive him away, while his daughters wondered when they would be able to get a good price for the house. Another sat in the rear of the undertaking parlor where his sons carried on the family business and counted over the families that he used to know as they came back to him for burial. The son of a liveryman practiced medicine on the street where he grew up and 'listened to Jimmy Walker make his first speech off a soapbox,' depending for his practice on city cases and on such of the 'old-timers,' and their children whom he had brought into the world, as would come back from Brooklyn and Long Island to their old family doctor. The son of a blacksmith continued to conduct his real estate business in the Village in the manner which his father taught him, and, though he had moved to New Jersey in order to bring up his children in the country, he brought each child back to the local parish to be baptized. A Murphy declared that 'the Murphys have always lived in this neighborhood, so I guess this Murphy will die here.'

A few of this old group, who had never been prosperous and who lacked either the means or the inclination to move, stayed on, still holding down the watchmen jobs that their fathers had held before them or striving desperately to make the small business which they had inherited succeed, never acclimated to a very high standard of living and responding to rising rents by successive moves into more cramped quarters.

But most of this old group had become scattered, to sections of Brooklyn where the same names that were prominent in Village politics a generation before were outstanding in the post-War years, or to towns in New Jersey where 'you can see more of the sons of the old Greenwich Irish in a day than you can in the Village in a year.'

These 'old Irish' were very proud of the names which they and their fathers had built up for themselves; of the celebrities which their neighborhood had produced — the judges and other prominent city officials — and especially of the fact that they grew up with Jimmy Walker. They were long-winded in praise of the Irish — with the exception of one priest who felt that the Italians had pushed the Irish to where they were. They confessed that every Irishman thinks himself a king and tries to prove it. They all would have liked to see the Irish in possession of Greenwich Village again.

The second group, too, was dispersed during the post-War years, either moving voluntarily in the search for better quarters or pushed out of the neighborhood by demolition and remodeling. The more prosperous led the way, and the younger people nearly all left at the time of their marriage. Those who remained were apt to be the less capable — a shiftless, 'down-at-the-heel' lot, constantly looking for cheaper quarters and wondering how they could pay the next rent. While these were not so possessive about the Village as the 'old Irish,' they felt resentful that the old neighborhood in which they grew up had been destroyed. Forced to move from block to block as their houses had been remodeled, they felt like strangers and intruders in their new blocks among the Irish who had made those blocks theirs at an earlier time. Since there was no longer the kind of block spirit which used to incorporate newcomers into the group, they could not recapture the sense of 'belonging' which they had lost. Under the disintegrating forces of these years, this group seemed to have lost completely such coherence as it had possessed, and to have been left with only hazy reminiscences of the 'good old days.' Its members were not active in political clubs, though some of their fathers had belonged and they themselves depended on the political clubs for jobs; they had little or no contact with the 'old Irish' whose children looked upon them as 'riff-raff.'

The Irish-born, longshore group, many of whom were tied to the locality by the nature of their job, felt possessive about the neighborhood — 'here we have lived and here we will die' — and wistful about the 'good old times' when it was a 'horse to every man in New York and now you can shake your hat at them.' If they had not prospered, they might grow sentimental about the way 'heaven watches over the blessed Irish,' lament the green hills that they left behind, and hope 'to be buried in Irish soil.' But most were not very curious about returning although they grasped at all news of Ireland and followed with avid interest the Irish ball teams playing in the United States. Rather, they hung on, trying to make up for inadequate incomes by claiming the status which their jobs formerly gave them.

While most of the Village Irish had been moving out and little besides the dregs of the old community remained, a few had moved in from the blocks which had been more thoroughly demolished farther to the south. These were of two types, the sons of laborers who were taking a step up in the world, moving from 'poor neighborhoods,' and the sons of professionals who owned their own houses on the respectable blocks to the south. The former were enabled to live in the Village by the fact that they were in business. The latter were prosperous — several among them prominent in politics — and regarded the Irish of the Village as 'left-overs'; they considered the neighborhood inferior to the one that they were forced to leave — 'I never thought that I should have to move as far uptown as Sheridan Square' — and they rejoiced that up-to-date apartments had been erected so that 'their kind' would have suitable houses in which to live. They had no relations with the 'left-overs' except through the political clubs. Their number was few.

The fate of the Irish community during the post-War years was summed up by the Village ragman, 'The Irish with the rags have moved away.'

The exodus of so large a proportion of the younger and the more successful and the break-up of the homogeneous neighborhood destroyed much of the social coherence of the Irish group.

Little or nothing remained of the many social clubs that had been an integral part of the old Irish community. Three which had become extinct within the decade were recalled by 1930 residents as clubs of fairly long standing, some reputation and a semi-political as well as a social and athletic slant. Two others had been reduced to annual get-togethers, where prominent political leaders, now living all over the city, met in dress suits at expensive hotels to commemorate their humble origins on the lower East or West Side. Another had retained a clubroom in the vicinity for a small, select, and scattered membership, while still another had been revived with a political tinge after its lapse during the War and had gaily renewed its Thanksgiving Day costume parade. The coming of Prohibition had contributed to the decline of these social clubs by interfering with their characteristic forms of entertainment.

The independent social clubs which had come and gone with generations of young men, and which were very numerous in the early days, had almost entirely disappeared from among the Irish. Two women's clubs at the neighborhood house survived with what remained of their old membership, adding a few new members. No corresponding groups of younger Irish women had been organized in more recent years. Parish social clubs, still largely made up of the remnant of the old-timers, found it difficult to keep their organizations alive.

There was sufficient social activity among the Irish, however, for the leaders of two different organizations to use almost identical words to describe the situation. 'Women have so many "affairs" nowadays that it is hard to get them out to our meetings or to fit our activities into their programs.' The increase in the activities of women at the political clubs with the advent of women's suffrage accounted for the busy-ness of some. Besides the political clubs, there was the local court of the Catholic Daughters of America, whose one hundred and fifty members held monthly card parties in each other's houses and raised money for charity. One of the leaders considered the mortuary benefits as the chief inducement to membership in this organization. A near-by council of the Knights of Columbus drew membership from among both the older and younger men of the locality, while others belonged to the fraternal order of Foresters, and both the American Legion and the Veterans of Foreign Wars maintained local posts largely composed of Irish. It was impossible to estimate the proportion of the Irish community which was enrolled in these various organizations in comparison with those who belonged to parish, social, or other clubs in the old days, for the areas from which they drew their membership were not coextensive.

The principal contrast between the social organizations and activities of the Irish in 1930 and in 1920 or before lay in the fact that they had ceased to be so essentially local. To amount to anything, an affair had to be held in an uptown hotel. The chief participants, moreover, were those who could afford the banquets and balls at the Hotel Pennsylvania, or the excursions to Long Island for a shore dinner costing 'only $2.' The poor 'riff-raff' — the 'low Irish' who constituted a large portion of those who remained — could not afford these 'affairs' and lacked the cheap, neighborly activities of the early days. Only the frequent wakes, as one after another of the old inhabitants died, continued to bring rich and poor together periodically for nights of informal festivity. In spite of continued social activities, moreover, the sense of being a social unit had departed. Only among the very old was there any group feeling and this because they were living in a past which had ceased to be. The rest of the Irish talked of the time before the War when everybody knew everybody else and every street was like a large Irish family. In 1930, all that remained were shattered fragments of groups that used to exist but had long since lost their significant unity.

The post-War years thus brought a very different type of social experience to the Irish and to the Italians. The Italians, whose lives centered within their ethnic group, looked at the improved economic postion and better social status which their group had achieved and, except for the very conservative, answered 'yes' to the question, 'Are you glad of the changes in the Italian community in recent years?' But among the Irish who had centered their life around the neighborhood, no one interviewed failed to reminisce and lament. The effect of the disruption of the neighborhood upon the Irish was to make most of the younger move or intend to move, while most of the older were left wistfully living in the past.

Yet, socially shattered though it was, the Irish community still possessed its leaders in the persons of its priests and politicians. Only the old saloonkeepers had lost their prestige when Prohibition interrupted their business and brought to the fore the new type of bootlegger — chiefly Italian — who might merit envy by reason of his wealth, but could not attain to the position of leadership which the old saloonkeeper enjoyed.

No substantial evidence of any important weakening in Church loyalty among the Irish was found. The religious leaders thus retained much of their importance and their power, although the social dissolution of the neighborhood parish robbed them of one of the sorts of loyalty and interest upon which they had counted in the past.

Since many in the community had their eyes on City Hall quite as much as on heaven, those who had risen from the locality to occupy high city posts were the pride of the community. After all, Mayor Jimmy Walker himself was one of them. He came from the neighborhood, retained his house with its special lampposts in front, though he actually lived in a fashionable apartment on Park Avenue, maintained his membership in the local parish and was on intimate terms with its priest. His family and relatives were still in the neighborhood and the Irish all felt that he essentially 'belonged.' To be sure, it was to the neighborhood, rather than simply to the Irish group, that he belonged, but it was the old neighborhood, not the 'geographical expression' of recent years, which claimed him. To the Italians, he was not their leader, though he offered the use of his cellar to house the statue of a Saint honored in an annual three-day festival by a group of Sicilians, but repudiated officially by the Church, and though, too, the politically ambitious young Italians might curry the favor of the district leader who 'made' Jimmy Walker in the hope that he might possibly 'make' them. Emphatically he was not 'of' the neighborhood of the new Villagers — even the real estate promoters of the Village did not find it desirable to advertise Mayor Walker's residence. He belonged as a leader to the 'old Irish,' who watched him grow up, nodding their heads and declaring, 'That young one will go far,' and to those of all ages who proclaimed confidently, when his administration was under investigation, 'The bigots will never get anything on Jimmy. He is too smart for them.'

Others in high city positions who had come from the locality —

judges, sheriff, city budget director, corporation council of the city — were the men who had led the way which most Irish would like to follow. Even those who had moved had retained their contacts and sometimes their official residence in the old community and they could be counted on to honor an important neighborhood function with their presence and to express the appropriate amount of neighborhood sentiment and of fond reminiscence. Among those who remained more closely within the limits of the district, the district political leaders, judges, and state senators held first place. More than one of these was following in the footsteps of his father. Leadership had long remained in the same hands.

Although all types of Irish interviewed were not on equally familiar terms with these leading figures, all clearly recognized their prominence and referred the interviewers to the same people for information on the community — to the same judges, the same leaders, and the same priests — and pointed to the same great men of the neighborhood occupying the prominent positions in City Hall. In contrast to the Italians, who one and all refused to name any leaders and had something disparaging to say about each one whom the interviewer could mention, the unanimity of the Irish in this respect reflected the continuity and relative coherence of their social organization. While the Italian young men who were reaching manhood in 1930 had no one toward whom to look, the Irish had available to them a social structure into which they could fit and a leadership which they could and did follow.

They were under no pressure, moreover, to disassociate themselves from their ethnic group. Though most of them automatically gave 'American' as their nationality, many would immediately state their Irish origin as soon as the question was pressed. Even those who insisted, 'No, we are not Irish. We are Americans,' usually gave themselves away in the next breath by talking about the 'dances we Irish used to attend,' or the saloons where 'you couldn't walk in unless you were Irish.' In terms of the 'foreigners' — i.e., the Italians — they were American, but in their attitudes and assumptions they had never lost their elusive sense of 'Irishness,' and a second generation priest could say of his second and third generation parishioners, 'They seem to be mostly County Clare people.' The attitude was well phrased in a description of a local woman who 'could never understand why anyone would fight for Ireland, for a country that couldn't support its own people. Of course, she was Irish through and through — Irish in thought and Irish in action; but she didn't like to be told about it. That is the way it is.'

The younger Irish were eager to escape from the locality in an effort to improve their status, but it was the 'low-class' associations of their environment that they wished to avoid and they had no urge to lose identity with the Irish group as such. Why, indeed, should they, when their group held a privileged position in the city — when to be Irish was no handicap, but rather, in many circles, an asset? Held by no strong ethnic ties within the group and at the same time under little pressure to escape, moving within a recognized social structure and within organizations that were factually Irish, but not Irish in purpose, the Irish of the locality drifted out of the group or remained passively within it. Only with intermarriage was the current out of the group set up. Those who married outside of the group were sometimes the ambitious girls who were determined to marry 'college men,' and, more usually, those who 'would marry anyone' or who pragmatically concluded that 'Italians are nice if they are educated, and, besides, you can't always get your own kind.'

In a very few cases which were found, 'Irish' was identified with the 'low' Irish in which the neighborhood abounded, and individuals sought non-Irish contacts as a means of raising their status. In three instances, surprisingly parallel, an ambitious mother, pushing her children ahead, taught them to feel superior to the rest of the community — though the economic and social status of the parents was not superior; was more eager than many other Irish parents that her children should be educated; instructed the girls to be choosy about the boys with whom they went and to look for something more than an ordinary neighborhood boy; and, to complete the picture, sent them to a Protestant church. Whereas these cases may reflect the mere idiosyncrasies of individual parents, they suggested the possibility, at least, of seeking status by identification with the Protestant, American non-Irish community. For the mass of the Irish, however, this remained a possibility which did not enter their consciousness.

The Irish community gained social stability, moreover, by the fact that all elements among the Irish accepted the same social hierarchy. Economic and occupational position gave a recognized status within the Irish community as it did not among other elements in the population.

At the bottom of the economic and social scale were the janitors, watchmen, and scrubwomen, many of whom remained in the neighborhood because they could not afford to move. They occupied the worst quarters in the worst old tenements and the smaller ramshackle houses that had been evacuated by those who could pay even moderately low rents. Some squatted in one house after another which was either to be remodeled or demolished and in which landlords permitted tenants to remain rent free during the process of negotiation so that when the deal was closed the property could be turned over without waiting the time required by law for notice of eviction. Though equally poor, the longshoremen were a step up socially, along with the truck-drivers — the occupation which served as a catch-all during this period for those who could not or would not go into any other line. Longshoremen and, especially, the sons of longshoremen, whose trade went from bad to worse turned to truck-driving; teamsters, if they were young enough to learn to handle a motor instead of a horse, joined the same ranks; boys who could not make the grade to clerical positions or civil service jobs took to trucks rather than to factories. Automobile mechanics and some few building-trades workers were numbered socially in the same group. Though the line between them and the white-collar class was not sharp, the office workers, telephone operators, firemen, policemen, and others in city jobs tended to hold themselves superior to the truck-driving and artisan element. At the top of the social scale were the politicians, lawyers, real estate men, and a few doctors who had stayed in the locality because they could afford to remain, either in their own houses or in the new apartments.

These four principal economic classes — the 'down-and-outers,' the truck-drivers, longshoremen, and men with a trade, those with white-collar and city jobs, and the politicians, professional and business men made up the social ladder which the Irish recognized. All were consistently seeking to climb, or at least to maintain the position on the ladder which they held, and all accepted the same relative position of each occupation. All wished to see their children in civil service jobs — the more successful as a second choice to business or law, or, for the girls, teaching, the more realistic as a first choice. This recognized hierarchy gave to the Irish group, mere remnant though it was, a coherent social organization which the other ethnic groups lacked. And except for the longshoremen whose loss of economic position made it more difficult for them to retain their claim to status, this structure remained unchanged and was passed on from one generation to the next.

For the greatest of all contrasts between Irish and Italian in the community was the fact that, for the former, there was no important gulf between the generations. The Irish family, which had survived in America under more favorable initial conditions than the Italian was facing, had not been under the strain to which the Italian family was subjected in these years. The complaints of Irish parents about 'the way young people carry on these days' were no more than the eternal criticisms of youth by age. Irish children in Greenwich Village were born and reared in the world of their parents, and in that world they continued to live.

The culture pattern of the Irish-American world of Greenwich Village was not in process of disintegration and reconstruction as was that of the Italian, but had already been developed a generation or more before. As a pattern, it was distinctive — differing essentially from the remnant of old Americans, from the Italians, and from the Villagers. In these years it underwent no vital modification.

Basically, this pattern was Irish, though it had dropped off much that had been characteristic of it in Ireland and had added features peculiar to its American situation. In many ways the culture brought over by the Irish immigrants had been better suited for survival in America than that of the Italians. Made self-conscious by generations of persecution, centering around the strongly organized institution of the Catholic Church, brought over by an immigrant body representing a cross-section of the population rather than the lowest economic and social levels, and under no handicap because of an alien language, it had every important prerequisite for survival. To have a finer farm than

one's neighbor and to be blessed with many children, to be secure
of salvation and to be buried in Irish soil, to enjoy the delights of
dance and song, a good story and plenty of drink, and to look
forward to the day when the land of Erin would be free from the
English yoke — these were the values which the Irish immigrants
had known at home. Only those which were closely associated
with the land could not be transferred.

Strong attachment to the soil and the powerful place associations of Irish life gave way under generations of emigration to a
sentimental fondness with perhaps a lingering wish to go back
to die. In contrast to the Italians, who rarely talked about their
home town except among their townsmen, the Irish were ready
to launch into a rhapsody about their home — 'where you could
look out onto the River Shannon itself, and you standing in the
door of the house.' Since Irish attachment to the soil was a very
particular place attachment rather than a preference for a rural
way of life, it did not carry over into a desire to farm in America.
The Irish in Greenwich Village, like most of the Irish in the United
States, settled in the city even when other immigrants were going
onto the land, and in the completely urban adjustment which
they made, everything which had been an essential part of their
land relationships was left behind. Thus, the necessity for a girl
to bring a dowry with her to 'enter' a house, the responsibilities
placed upon the father and the brothers by this necessity, and the
relationships growing out of it had no place, even in a modified
form, in Irish-American life. But the loyalty to the kin group
came out and remained an integral part of the pattern.

The Irish family, in fact, constituted one of the foundations of
Irish-American life with which other aspects, especially politics,
were interwoven. It was traditionally large and united under the
authority of the father, with the children contributing their labor
to the support of all, internally quarrelsome but not divided, and
unfailingly loyal in its relations with the rest of the world. It
resembled the Italian family in being essentially patriarchal, but
it differed in according much more independence to its women.
The large proportion of single women who came out with every
wave of Irish emigration — it was the only large immigrant group
where the number of women exceeded the men — and the fact
that they went into domestic service, gave the Irish-American

family from the start a very different structure from that of the Italian.

Every part of the Irish pattern that had to do with its second principal institution, the Church, could be, and was, brought with the group and reinforced here. Serving as the center of their social organization, the source of their major social controls, and one of the avenues to power, the Church constituted both the frame within which the adaptation of the Irish group took place and the source from which most of the important attitudes and habits of the group were derived.

Apart from the family and the Church, no institutions were brought out from the old country. Those which became part of the Irish-American pattern were built up here. Traditional attitudes, however, came out a-plenty. There was enough hatred of England to draw the second and third generation of Irish in Greenwich Village closer to the Germans of the locality during the early part of the World War. There was the Irishman's traditional 'chip on the shoulder' and readiness to pick a fight which made their neighbors in 1930 characterize them as 'pugnacious.' There was no strong educational tradition — those who came out before 1900 had known little except the 'hedge schools' secretly kept by the priests — and Irish interest in education in America reflected the educational requirements of the jobs which gave status rather than intellectual interests such as those of the Jews. In 1930, the statement that Irish families were, of course, sending their children to high school was characteristically followed by the explanation that 'you have to have so much education to qualify for city jobs these days — the political leaders can't just fix it up for you at City Hall as they used to.' With an easygoing attitude toward work and the complete absence of any craft traditions or special skills, the Irish changed their jobs to get status, digging ditches or working as hod carriers until these occupations became 'foreigners' work,' and the Irish stepped out. The priest who thought that his people had been pushed up into the economic position which they occupied, and the local Irishman who explained that the Irish had never been good storekeepers because they would never put themselves out for their customers — 'and who am I to be waiting on the likes of you?' — were registering this work attitude.

A high material standard of living had never been part of the Irish tradition, although one part of the population was at great pains to live down the 'pig-in-the-parlor' reputation and to describe the element to which that epithet applied as 'shanty' or 'low' Irish. In this community, as in Ireland, Irish homes were bare and dull in contrast to the Italians.' The leader of an Irish girls' club remarked on how little interest the Irish girls showed in fixing up the clubroom, but the minute the Italian girls joined the group they couldn't wait to make curtains. Only very recently had the American pressure toward high living standards begun to 'take.'

Little of the folk culture of Ireland was brought out, for most of it was too closely attached to particular places. Irish dances and songs had dropped out of the experience of many — though a few of the school children in 1931 included 'dancing Irish dances and singing Irish songs' among the things done in their homes at Christmas. At the Irish dance halls in the city, it was the 'green Irish' who packed the floor where sets were danced while the second generation danced 'American' dances on the floor below. Folk customs, more than folk expression, came out and survived in such forms as traditional celebrations of weddings, christenings, and wakes.

The distinctive institution which the Irish built up in America was, of course, the city political system. First forged to fight their battle for status in America, Irish politics gradually invaded ward after ward until Tammany and its ways were entrenched through the city. On the triple foundation of the family, the Church, and the business of politics, the Irish of Greenwich Village created their local, Catholic, Tammany pattern and made it the dominant pattern of the community.

In the post-War years, this way of life was under less pressure toward disintegration than that of any other group represented in the local community. The Irish family, supported by the Church, and free from the disrupting gulf between generations which strained the Italian, continued to stand at the center. Half of the fifty who were directly questioned thought that the Irish families were sticking together as closely as before the War, while most of the rest observed less closeness with distant kin, but not within the immediate family unit. More than half were of the opinion that families were taking their entertainment together as much as ever and that working children were contributing as generally to the family's support. They agreed, however, that although the assumption of the authority of the head of the house was given lip service with the 'Go ask your father' formula, there was more likely to be a fifty-fifty distribution of authority in actual practice in most homes. Divorce continued to be almost universally condemned, primarily on religious grounds.

Loyalty to the Church, too, and the maintenance of church observance stood essentially unmodified. All the basic assumptions and habits bound up with the Church — attending Mass, going to confession, having the children make communion, observing Holy Days of Obligation and days of fast and accepting the tenets of the faith — continued to be taken for granted, although the centering of social life about the church declined. All the older persons questioned were unanimous in opposing intermarriage with Protestants, 'unless there was nothing else around' — as compared with the Italians, where only half of the older generation questioned objected to such intermarriage — and both old and young were even more emphatically opposed to letting children be brought up as Protestants. Some of the poorer complained of the cost of parochial schools and were sending their children to public school, where they didn't have always to be buying tickets for this affair and that and where they had the advantage of free lunches. But the relative increase in parochial school attendance, the statement of one of the priests that there had been no change in the proportion of his confirmation class which was drawn from public schools, and the assumption by three quarters of those interviewed that children would automatically go to parochial school, all indicated that the Church's authority on this point had not weakened.

It did not occur to the local Irish, old or young, to question the political system, though political clubs had become less the center of social life. The same occupational preferences — civil service, teaching, or law — were characteristic of young as of old. Weddings and christenings continued to be celebrated with the traditional gusto, and wakes were still held. In most essentials, the Irish-American pattern of behavior remained unmodified, though the social organization of the community was undermined.

But at two vital points the pattern was under pressure from much the same sources as the Italian — in respect to the practice of birth control and in setting a high standard of living above other considerations. From the point of view of the institution of the family, and even more from that of the authority of the Church, the question of birth control became the live issue of these years. It was the opinion of many of the older people consulted that birth control was being practiced by the younger members of their families and of their neighbors' families. Most of them heartily deplored the condition. Even the older people admitted the difficulty of raising a large number of children under contemporary conditions, while a few complained bitterly, 'The priests can talk all they want — they never had to raise a family on $12 a week.' They asserted, however, that the Irish would be the last to give up their principles in the face either of economic pressure or the American belief in small families, 'and then it won't matter because there won't be anyone to carry on anyway.'

The young married persons interviewed all reflected a conflict on the question. All were agreed that a small family — usually two — was the ideal, and that parents should not have more children than they could afford to bring up, and several talked about not having children for a while until they had saved money. They mentioned their friends who had been married some little time and had no children. But when it came directly to the question of practicing birth control, they either became apologetically embarrassed, observed, 'Of course, the Church tells you that you ought to go on having children, but...' or would not commit themselves. Although they were unanimous in maintaining church observance and in taking parochial school education for granted, their attitude toward the Church became less respectful when the question of family limitation was at stake. Whereas ten years before the question was scarcely considered — young women in their mid-twenties stated that they were ignorant of sex matters up to the time of their marriage — the subject was a vital problem by 1930. It had become a matter of serious concern to the priests.

As with the younger Italians, the pressure toward family limitation was the result of a new concern for a higher standard of living. At this point, the influence of the developments in the American community during these years was directly reflected in the way in which the young Irish people one and all were moving to sections where they could get better apartments, the girls continued to work after marriage to improve their standard of living — 'just to have a few more things' — and the one criterion was the 'lovely home.'

Although the Irish-American community retained its institutions intact, it faced the problem of reconciling with its traditional values the American drive toward material comfort.

2. MINOR GROUPS

Jews

The situation of the Jewish group corresponded neither to that of the Italian nor to that of the Irish. Its stage of adaptation was similar to that of the Italian, for it was a 'new' immigrant group which had come into the area at the same time, but it was too small and scattered to impose its standards on any part of the community. At the same time its greater distinctiveness protected its social organization from the disintegrating influences which affected other local groups.

The Jews of Greenwich Village had not come in as a group, but had entered the community as isolated individuals at different times when they saw opportunities for setting up stores. Their number was never large, probably no more than two hundred families at any one time. The Hebrew school to which nearly every family that was part of the group sent its boys was attended between 1925 and 1930 by the children of ninety-two families. There were not enough families in the neighborhood in 1930 to support a Kosher market, though one such had existed some years before. In fact, the number of Jews was so few that it was often difficult to get together at the synagogue the ten observing men who must be present before the prayers could be said, and local Jewish boys reported having their street games interrupted when they were haled into the synagogue, handkerchiefs tied over their heads, to help make up the quorum.

They did not live together in a physically compact community, but were scattered from one end of the Village to the other, mostly

above or near their stores. Among the ninety-two families represented by the Hebrew school children, only seventeen lived in
houses which contained any other family on the list. One house
had contained five of these families, but not all at the same time.
The block where the largest number of these families lived had at
one time contained six of them. In most cases there was only one
Jewish family on a block.

Though small and scattered, the Jewish group was the most
cohesive and self-conscious of any in the community. It constituted a distinct element in the economic life of the locality, for
the Jews were practically all local storekeepers. At school, the
few Jewish children in each class were consistently outstanding,
reflecting in school the parental pressure for education which
many of the Italian and Irish homes lacked. Most of the college
students from the locality were Jewish, and they thus acquired a
prestige and, if they retained neighborhood contacts, a certain
local influence out of proportion to their numbers.

The local Jewish community did not include all the Jews in
the locality. The nucleus was the body of resident shopkeepers,
mostly in the clothing business, who served the local people rather
than the Villagers. Those with local business who did not reside
in the neighborhood had never been part of the group. The more
recently arrived Jewish stores serving the Villagers — the drugstores, laundries, and cleaning and tailoring establishments which
occupied stores on the ground floor of the new apartment buildings — did not bring additions to the local Jewish group, for they
were operated by people from the Bronx and elsewhere who
usually retained their residence and at least their associations
outside. Still less were the Jews among the Villagers in any way
identified with the local group, for they, characteristically, had
severed their strictly Jewish connections and would have had no
interest in local Jewish life even if the gulf between Villagers and
local people had not kept them apart. Among the resident storekeepers, a few without children might escape identification with
the group by not being drawn into the affairs centering around
the Hebrew school. But those Jewish families among the local
population who reared their children in the locality were a clearly
defined social unit.

Group solidarity was easy to maintain because of the similarity of their economic status. All were storekeepers. For this reason and this only did they live in the neighborhood. There was a wide discrepancy in income between the man who kept a newsstand and the one who owned a big, famous clothing store, patronized by East Siders as well as by people from the local community, but as independent enterprisers, all the Jews had a similar outlook and similar interests. The essential democracy of the synagogue, moreover, leveled out distinctions of wealth. Though a certain few habitually outbid the others at the synagogue for the privilege of carrying the Torah, one of the lesser members of the congregation might be able to correct these in the way in which they read the prayers. The social gulf between rich and poor in the group was less even than among the Italians, and much less than among the Irish.

Their organized life centered around the synagogue, with its sisterhood and Hebrew school. Though virtually none were as assiduous in synagogue attendance as the Talmud prescribes, or as were some at least of the Jews of the East Side ghetto, practically all were members of or interested in the work of the congregation. While the membership of the sisterhood at any one time included only a part of the Jewish women of the neighborhood, most had belonged at one time or another, and even if they allowed their membership to lapse from time to time they joined again. The women, in fact, had been the mainstay of the congregation because the long hours made participation by the men difficult and the women had assumed responsibility for supporting the Hebrew school. Attendance at Hebrew school was very nearly universal. The one or two boys in the neighborhood who did not attend were known for this fact. Since Hebrew school was attended daily from an early age until, at the age of thirteen, the boy was confirmed, the Jewish boys who lived scattered on widely separated blocks became well acquainted with each other and formed a definite group. While some were members of their local block groups, much of their association was at the school. Both within the Hebrew school and outside, Jewish children's clubs had from time to time been formed, short-lived to be sure, but indicative of their self-consciousness as a group. With very few exceptions, the older Jewish boys and girls of the area associated primarily or exclusively with Jews, hanging out at the house of

one or another member of the group or at a Jewish store, holding
Jewish parties, and going out to Jewish homes in Brooklyn or
the Bronx for such recreation as they sought beyond their own
immediate circle. The childhood associations with Italians or,
occasionally, Irish were dropped off, and with age the group
became more and more exclusive — until they married Jews and
moved to a Jewish neighborhood. Since most of the Jewish young
people attended college and were headed for the professions,
superior education and a wider horizon separated them from the
Italian and Irish neighborhood elements, though not from those
among the Italians who also attended college. These latter, however, were isolated individuals rather than a group as the Jews
were.

Throughout the post-War years, the Jewish group retained its
social organization unaltered. Although the strictness with which
Jewish practices were observed was relaxed, the social cohesion
of the group remained unchanged.

The cultural traditions of the Jewish group were both more at
variance with those of the rest of the community and better
equipped by experience to exist in an alien setting. Jewish culture
has had the immense advantage for survival of being a city culture, rooted in no place. The interrelation of religious and racial
bonds, the sense of exclusiveness and superiority, and the fact
that, even more than the Irish, Jewish immigrants have been a
cross-section of the Jewish population and have included the
leaders, all have made it peculiarly strong in its New York environment.

In this community, however, the Jews were not able to give
their stamp to the neighborhood as they could to so many other
parts of Manhattan because they were so isolated and scattered.
Such of their institutions and attitudes as could survive were,
thus, those which did not depend upon being part of a large, observing Jewish community. The fact that Jewish practices differed so extensively from those of the Gentile community, moreover, made it much harder to retain them in the course of daily
life than it was for groups whose rhythm was only slightly different
from the majority. It was much more difficult to keep a Kosher
house in a community where there was no Kosher butcher than
to stick to fish on Friday. It was easier to attend early Mass on

Holy Days before going to work than to keep the Sabbath when to do so meant to close one's store on Saturday while the other stores around did their principal business on that day. As a result, the strictness of Jewish observance had been somewhat relaxed.

While there had still been a Kosher butcher in the neighborhood, the local families had kept Kosher houses. When it became necessary to go over to the East Side for their meat, the women did so — but occasionally it was too far to go and it was necessary to shop in the vicinity. In one family the children remembered that when non-Kosher food was first occasionally brought into the house, they were not supposed to notice it. 'If we said it didn't look like Kosher meat, we got smacked.' By 1930, this same family was frequently eating non-Kosher food, it no longer had separate pots and dishes for 'meat' meals and 'milk' meals, and it was not always particular about not serving milk products with meat. But it still used a separate set of dishes for Passover; whenever it was convenient, the woman made a trip to the East Side for Kosher meat; and she vowed, in spite of the pleas of her children, that 'no one is ever going to bring pork into this house.' Instead of invoking the Laws in her defense, however, she sometimes gave herself away by finding it necessary to argue, 'After all, pigs are dirty animals. Look what they eat.' Most of the families in the neighborhood still kept the dietary laws better than the one here described and maintained nominally Kosher houses. But an important member of the congregation was seen eating a ham sandwich in a local cafeteria, and it was the opinion of one of the younger generation that 'there is not a Jewish boy in the neighborhood who has not tasted pork — though they're pretty self-conscious about it when they do.'

Similarly, in the keeping of the Sabbath, regular synagogue attendance had ceased to be general; activities prohibited on that day, such as handling money or riding, were practically universal out of business necessity; and although there were some families where cooking was still not done on Saturday, there were others where it was. Even those who had become relatively lax in their observances, however, were apt to light the Friday night candles with the customary blessing.

But the fact that the difficulties of observing the dietary laws and keeping the Sabbath had seriously modified the habits of the local Jews did not mean that they had become any less Jewish in fundamental practices and attitudes. Whereas failure to keep strictly to the detail of the dietary laws or to observe the Sabbath was not a cause of comment in the local Jewish community, failure to have a son Bar Mitzvah — confirmed — definitely was. Ceremonies accompanying birth, marriage, and death — circumcision, having the eldest son redeemed, the orthodox marriage ceremony, the funeral customs, and the observance of the year's mourning and the anniversary of the death — all were taken for granted. Though a few among the younger generation might employ a doctor instead of the traditional 'mohel' for circumcision and might possibly have a civil marriage, most took these traditional practices as a matter of course. In spite of laxness in weekly synagogue attendance, the High Holidays saw virtually all in their places of worship, with their stores closed and a fast maintained for the Day of Atonement. The feast of Passover at least, and usually one or more of the other holidays, were celebrated in practically every home.

In their social attitudes, even more than in their religious practices, the local Jews maintained their major traditions. In spite of the gulf between the foreign-born and American generations, the Jewish family as an institution remained intact. Jewish solidarity extended beyond the immediate face-to-face relations to include contributions to Palestine and to Jewish charities. Membership in some sort of Jewish organization — the Brotherhood or Sisterhood of the Congregation, Young Judea, the Y.M.H.A., a Jewish burial lodge, membership which did not necessarily involve social activity, but represented an expression of solidarity — was general, while membership in non-Jewish organizations, except for occasional members of the political clubs, was rare. Intermarriage with Gentiles was vigorously opposed. The intellectual tradition was strongly maintained and it was taken for granted that the Jewish boys in the neighborhood would be trained for a profession. The traditional musical education was also generally, though less universally, the rule. With the insistence on education and willingness to sacrifice for it, however, went the attitude that a boy should make his own way and should prove himself a 'mensch' by earning at least part of his living while studying. The most well-to-do took pride in the fact that their boys did not have to work while the struggling were forced to do so. But those who, by the time their children were in college or professional school, had obtained a competence which enabled them to pay their sons' way were likely to force them to go to work while attending school, for 'Wasn't that the way every great man got his start? And look at the other Jewish boys in the neighborhood — hadn't they all done it that way?'

With the immense advantages of having inherited an urban culture, with social and religious attitudes which, though variant in detail, were fundamentally similar to those of the Protestant American community, and with a traditional tendency toward introspection which fitted them to meet conditions of social disorganization, even so scattered a minority as the Jews of this neighborhood faced fewer fundamental problems of adaptation than the other groups in the community.

Spanish

The small Spanish settlement on the waterfront was the most separate of the ethnic groups in the community and the least touched by contacts outside of the group. Its distinctive social organization resulted from the fact that it was a waterfront settlement, largely made up of a floating population of seamen and those who kept the boarding houses, poolrooms, speakeasies, and *cantinos* that they patronized, with families who worked ashore in the minority. It had always lived compactly within a radius of a few blocks, although Spanish did not constitute the sole inhabitants of those blocks, and although a few of its members were scattered through adjacent streets.

A small group of Spanish, chiefly men, was already in the locality before 1910, according to the evidence of the census which showed 100 Spanish men, 18 women, and 20 persons of Spanish parentage in that year. Of the 52 persons interviewed in 1930, three had been there since before 1910. The bulk, however, came during the following decade in the boom times of shipping during or just after the War. The largest number of those interviewed had come between 1915 and 1920. By 1920, the census recorded 416 Spanish-born individuals, 113 of them women, within the immediate settlement. A Spanish church had been founded in the vicinity in 1902.

The group was a homogeneous one, both in background and status. Practically all its members came from the same part of Spain — the northwestern section and especially the province of Coruña. Most were of peasant background, although a quarter of those interviewed had come from the city. As seamen, dock workers, or factory and other manual labor, they occupied in common a low occupational and income status. They thus constituted a group within which there were almost as few social distinctions as among the local Jews. Even the barrier between the 'respectable,' serious families and the 'devil-may-care' type of seamen was slight. In the boarding houses, the seamen were very much one of the family, coming back to the same house whenever their ship was in port and even being on friendly and intimate terms with the daughters of the family. The parents interviewed complained that it was hard to bring children up in America — they got so wild; but none suggested that the kind of people who were to be found on the waterfront might not be the best influences for the children, and all but three of the 52 interviewed stated positively that they considered the neighborhood a good one in which to live.

The isolation of the group from the rest of the community was practically complete. A shopping trip of six blocks to the 'Main Street' of the Village was almost as much of a journey as to go uptown to the central shopping district.

The principal social organizations of the group to which most people belonged were the Church and the mutual benefit societies. The Church in Spain has traditionally been of greater importance to the women than to the men. That difference was carried into this community, where the devoutness of the women was general, but more than half of the men interviewed did not attend church at all. For the women, the local Spanish church was the only thing which took them out of their homes. For the men, the *centros* of the mutual benefit societies and the informal hangouts were of greater social importance. Even the Church, however, brought little social life to the women, for the only church societies in 1930 were for the men. Evidence of a weakening of the Church's hold in this group appeared in the fact that only two of those questioned were sending, or wished to send, their children to parochial school. Although the practice might have been different if there had been a definitely Spanish parochial school, the failure to follow the Church on this point was noteworthy.

The mutual benefit societies were situated in the locality, but drew membership from all over the city. In contrast to the Italian group, where such societies had become feeble by 1930, the Spanish societies continued to flourish, although intersociety rivalry for membership had threatened to destroy them. At the regular dances attended by Spanish-speaking people from all over the city, the program was always divided between distinctively Spanish numbers and ordinary American dances. These Spanish societies thus contributed more to the preservation of Spanish customs as well as to Spanish solidarity than the Italian societies ever had. Both the culture and the solidarity were primarily bound up with the Spanish language, for the Church and the societies included Spanish-speaking people from South and Central America as well as from Spain, and on the question of intermarriage, only two of those questioned extended their objection to marriage outside their own group to include Spanish-speaking *mestizos*.

In addition to their Church and their societies, the Spanish of this colony had a great many hangouts. Book stores, tailor shops, and barber shops were the chief of these, but restaurants, poolrooms, and even grocery stores served the same role. This was a natural role in a community where the Spanish-speaking men were three times as numerous as the women. The barber shops, especially, were more hangouts than hair-cutting establishments, while the tailor shops were a combination of hangouts and markets for stolen goods. The restaurants, of course, had their regular clientèle, as did the speakeasies. All of these catered to the permanent element in the neighborhood, while the poolrooms and *cantinas* along the waterfront were patronized by the floating population of seamen. They were all completely Spanish, and it never occurred to the Irish or 'Polaks' on the same blocks to go into them. They were centers for the distribution of news about the metropolitan Spanish community as well as of the local group. For the adult Spaniards, the world within which they existed was, more than that of any of the other local groups, the world of their own ethnic group. They had no provision, however, for raising their children within the social structure of that group. The latter had few of their own number with whom to play. Though most of the boys in 1930 belonged to their own Spanish gang, a number were members of mixed groups on the mixed blocks where they lived.

The Spanish group experienced little change in the post-War years. It varied in size as boatloads of seamen came and went, and it lost in numbers during the depression of 1921 when its members were still sufficiently close to the home country to go easily back. Only in 1930 was it forcibly broken up as the tenements in which the more stable Spanish families resided were demolished to make way for railroad tracks. In 1930, there were not enough Spanish left to make the census give them a separate classification. The same social organization, however, remained characteristic of the group in spite of its loss of members.

The Spanish culture which it had brought in remained intact. The fifty-two local Spanish residents directly interrogated expressed great unanimity in their attitudes. In respect to the traditional structure of the family, and most especially the relations between men and women, there had apparently been little change. The completely subordinate position of the women, the fact that their only sphere of activity was the home, and their subjection to the authority of the men was very generally accepted. Only seventeen per cent questioned the wife's duty of absolute obedience. In insisting on chaperonage of girls, the assumption was almost as strong. Two thirds would not permit a girl to go out even with her fiancé, while eighty per cent objected to her going out with a boy friend.

The fact that the children in the Spanish group had hardly begun to reach the age at which the strain between generations becomes most acute meant that the Spanish had not yet been subjected to the kind of pressure from their American-born children which the Italians were facing. Furthermore, there were so few girls in the Spanish colony that they were in great demand as soon as they reached a marriageable age and were matched off before they had occasion to strike for independence. It was noticeable, however, that out of the four girls under twenty who were encountered while canvassing the Spanish group, two were opposed to letting a girl go out with any man except her fiancé. The Spanish women in the locality who were interviewed were all found to be living within the bounds traditionally prescribed for them, confined to their home, knowing no one outside of relatives and immediate neighbors, knowing no English and having no desire to learn. No outside agencies had touched these Spanish women in the way that they had reached the Italian women to upset their traditional status and traditional attitudes.

Attitudes toward the Church remained unmodified; distinctive customs, such as the rigid observance of mourning for different prescribed periods, were almost universally retained; Spanish foods were eaten exclusively.

As far as the women were concerned, the American community might almost as well not exist. For the men, this was almost equally true, so distinctively and exclusively Spanish were all their activities and attitudes. It was only with the second generation that any outside contacts or evidence of adaptation began.

Germans

Virtually all that remained of the once flourishing German settlement was a scattered group of shopkeepers who lived above their stores and frequently owned the property where they lived and worked. Among the nineteen of these families who were interviewed, there was great similarity of status and unanimity of attitude.

Like the Irish, and preceding them in possession, the Germans had identified themselves closely with the 'neighborhood,' and had become thoroughly amalgamated with the old Yankee 'Ninth Ward' element and with the more substantial of the Irish.

The coming of the Italians had pushed many out, and the War had upset their old position. Their long residence in the locality did not protect them during the War from the experience to which Germans everywhere in the United States, especially on the eastern seaboard, were subjected. In 1930, it was still untactful to mention the War to the local Germans even for the purpose of dating an event. After the War, nearly all of them that remained, and especially their children, drifted away to areas where they could own their homes and would not be exposed to contact with the 'low-class' Italians. Such as stayed on owned property and either had businesses or were too old to move and continued to live in the houses they owned. A very few who had married Irish or Italians remained as part of the Irish or Italian community.

Of those found in 1930, nearly all had been born in the United States, frequently in the local community. Those born abroad, or elsewhere in the city, had settled in the neighborhood before 1900. They were all old acquaintances and met at church, but did not visit much with each other. Most had lost contact with practically everything German except the Church. Out of the nineteen interviewed, only four read German newspapers, belonged to German societies other than the Church (an undertaker belonged to nineteen German societies for business reasons), had taught their children the German language or felt that the German group stuck together. Those who belonged to German societies were also members of the Masons or Elks, while those without German group affiliations had no corresponding American associations, but were largely isolated individuals.

More than the former local residents of other nationalities, the Germans who had moved away retained connection with the neighborhood. All the residents interviewed reported that friends dropped in once or twice a year for sentiment's sake. Enough came back to keep the Lutheran church going. Though the church was poorly attended except on special occasions, people returned for marriages and christenings, and those who had moved away supplied the Sunday School teachers and many of the active members of the church societies. But as the older generation died out, the ranks at church grew thinner, for the younger people's associations were, of course, in their new communities.

The Germans in 1930 mixed with their neighbors in business, for they conducted typical neighborhood stores where a friendly relation was maintained between merchants and customers. They had some informal dealings with the Irish, but they had little or no use for the Villagers and were determined that their children should not be contaminated by the 'vulgar and profane language and the foreign notions' of the Italians.

Some of their social attitudes had been retained, while others had been dropped. Their attitude toward work survived — the central place of industry and thrift in their culture which made them fit so well into the American situation when they first came — and the oldest continued to work and to exact long hours from their children. They continued to cherish their craft tradition and their respect for the independent business man, but they recognized that, practically, these types of activity had become out of date in the American economy. Although six of them had their own sons working in their business with them, only one considered that the desirable career for a boy was to own his own store, for they saw that there was little or no future in that sort of business. Similarly, they observed that machine production had made their old skills no longer valuable. They mourned for their old values which changing times had destroyed.

In part their idea of the family and the conduct of its members had survived and in part it had not. Their own families were small — only two had more than three children and they considered families of one to three the desirable size. Nearly all approved of divorce and birth control — not even the five Catholics among the Germans interviewed opposed these two institutions — and few wanted to maintain the absolute authority of the man in the home. But they were opposed to married women working outside of the home and were strong in demanding absolute obedience of their children. Though they frequently gave their grown children a key and let them pay board instead of turning all their earnings into the family coffer, they were unanimous that the freedom accorded to the modern girl was excessive, and insisted that grown children living under the parental roof should render strict account of their whereabouts. There were six who were unwilling that a girl should go out with a man to whom she was not engaged. As in the case of the Irish, there was no clash between the older and the younger generation.

This remnant hung on in the neighborhood, isolated, wistful, aware of the changing economy which called for small families and different economic attitudes, and devoted to the essentials of their solid, bourgeois family pattern.

Old American

The remnant of old Americans who preferred to term themselves residents of the Ninth Ward rather than of Greenwich Village attempted to maintain the old American pattern unmodified through the years of change. Such few as remained contrived to feel proprietary toward the Village and resentful of everything that had transformed it during the past generation; they turned out *en masse* and almost alone to any demonstration of neighborhood sentiment; they supplied members to the district school board and gave support, such as it was, to the Protestant churches. Their values were clear — the Protestant church, the public school, an honestly cast vote, a reputable family, a respect for property and its acquisition, and the friendly relations of a simple neighborhood. From these values they had not swerved in the face of either immigrant or Villager.

By 1930, they recognized that the alien culture of the Catholic group had become that of the community, and they saw the Protestant churches not only losing membership, but ceasing to constitute the social centers which they had in earlier years. When these Ninth Ward Americans could no longer see the neighbors' families all starting off to church on Sunday morning, they closed the front blinds to shut out the sight of the swarming Irish and Italian children, and the Villager girls with cigarettes in their fingers. Both sets of invaders were equally offensive to them. They bemoaned the degeneration and disruption of the old neighborhood; if they had enough money they sent their children away to private schools. Their children who had moved out to the suburbs or uptown urged them to move, but because they owned their homes and had held on to them until the peak of the real estate boom was past, because they were loath to give up the convenience of the location or because they could not bear to leave even the ruins of the neighborhood in which they had felt at home, they hung on, counting the old ones drop off, and prepared to remain until they died.

VIII. VILLAGERS

1. ART AND SEX AS AVENUES OF ESCAPE

DURING these years, the Village acted as a magnet which
drew to it a wide variety of people with one quality in
common, their repudiation of the social standards of the
communities in which they had been reared. Here gathered in
these years a whole range of individuals who had abandoned their
home pattern in protest against its hollowness or its dominance,
and had set out to make for themselves individually civilized lives
according to their own conceptions. They had found the traditional Anglo-Protestant values inapplicable and the money drive
offensive. In the Village, some sought to discover other positive
values upon which to reconstruct a social system in America;
many carried on those activities, especially artistic, which had
little or no place in a civilization dominated either by the remains
of the Calvinist ethic or by the purely acquisitive impulse; an increasing proportion simply sought escape, and brought with them
little except negative values, throwing over more or less completely whatever smacked of 'Puritanism' or 'Babbittry'; the
more serious sought some compromise which would enable them to
avoid the features which they did not like, but to retain those
which they consciously or unconsciously cherished.

The Village was not the only place where those who repudiated
their traditions took refuge during these years. Although it was
the most notorious of such places, its counterpart could be found
in Chicago, San Francisco, and other large cities, and elsewhere in
New York. Its notoriety did not make it unique, but only made it

an advantageous point from which to observe the disintegration of old American culture in the post-War years in an acute, and, therefore, clearly visible form.

The Villager population, in 1930 and the years preceding it, included at one end of the scale those who cherished old American values, but found them so lost or submerged in the bourgeois world that they took refuge from the pressures of that world and sought the opportunity to re-create the old values in their own lives. At the other extreme were those who threw over altogether both the American and the bourgeois patterns and sought complete freedom, defiance, or escape in flight to Greenwich Village. In between these two elements was the great mass of Village residents whose repudiation of their background was only partial and who consequently presented various conflict situations where that which they had retained interfered with that which they had cast aside. The first of these groups was the one which discovered the Village in its early, unsung days. The second gave it its reputation. The third made up by 1930 the largest element in its Villager population. Though these groups were not completely separated from each other, and lines between them were not hard and clear, they presented essentially distinct forms of adaptation and associated in groups which roughly followed these lines. All, however, shared certain basic common qualities which distinguished them both from their neighbors in that other social world and from their home communities — namely, a disregard for money values and for prestige based on either income or conspicuous expenditure, an awareness of some sort of cultural values, and tolerance of unconventional conduct even when their own habits were more constrained.

Unconventionality, especially in the matter of sex, was taken for granted, and attitudes ranged from tolerance of experimentation to approval rather than from condemnation to tolerance. The sober superintendents of 'respectable' apartment houses made no bones about enumerating 'girls and their fellers' among the occupants of their houses when trying to rent an apartment to a middle-aged lady. Villagers of conventional tastes were distinctly on the defensive in explaining to the interviewer that 'all the people in Greenwich Village aren't the kind that you expect to find. There are plenty of ordinary respectable people like us.' No one felt called upon to be on the defensive about the opposite type of conduct.

All types of Villagers were intensely individualistic in both their social relations and their point of view. Their social contacts were confined to more or less purposeful relations with those who had common interests. Independent of virtually all institutions and scorning the joining habit, taking full advantage of both the selectiveness and the anonymity which the city offered, they avoided the usual casual contacts with family, neighbors, or members of the same economic or social class and the relations growing out of institutional connections. Instead, they maintained individual ties with friends scattered all over the city. If they had professional or artistic interests, these were apt to furnish a basis for their social life. The pursuit of an avocation or common tastes in recreation brought others together.

It was not always easy or possible to make connections with those of common interests. In the early days of the Village, when numbers were few and most Villagers had common interests in art or social reform, it had been possible for newcomers to find their way, chiefly via eating-houses, into congenial company. As more people and more different types came in, newcomers could no longer count on falling in with congenial company. Yet at each stage in the Village's history some one group was identified with the locality and offered easy contacts to newcomers. In 1930, it was the pseudo-bohemians and especially the Lesbians, into whose group it was easily possible for strangers to find their way.

To trace the modification of traditional American behavior patterns during these years by means of any sort of statistical sample of Villagers would be impossible, because the essence of their effort at adjustment was its extreme individualism. Whereas among the other elements in the community it was usually possible to reconstruct the essentials of their social attitudes from a knowledge of certain parts, many of the Villagers had gone so far in their repudiation that their values followed no pattern. In the case of the young people in whom the Village abounded, moreover, there was no way of predicting their future, and their Village life was difficult to analyze without a knowledge of whether they would return to their small home communities, settle down to a bourgeois existence in the suburbs, make some successful form of city adaptation, or drift from bar to bar for the rest of their lives. As this community, like other city neighborhoods, furnished a refuge for many persons who were psychologically mal-adapted, a heavy overlay of psychological problems frequently obscured the sociological implications of the position and attitudes of many Villagers.

It was possible, however, to block out the main types of adaptation and repudiation and to describe the groups which fell within those types. The members of the groups did not remain constant, but the types endured, represented by some old and some new individuals from year to year. Succeeding groups with their different sorts of reactions in turn imparted their reputation to the Village as its dominant element, at least in the eyes of the outside world. In 1930, all these groups were still present, the earlier represented either by remnants of the personnel which had constituted the original groups or by newcomers of the same type as those who had left. The same range of types found in 1930, moreover, had been present in the years before, differing only in their relative numerical strength and in some of the specific attitudes which characterized them.

As the backflow to the Village increased, however, the relative prominence of different types changed. The first group of Villagers had been made up of individuals of exceptional independence, who had faced social problems with earnestness and had sought positive solutions. When the community had come to contain a large proportion of persons of ordinary caliber whose position reflected the social situations from which they had come more than the personal quality of the individuals, the negative desire to escape took the place of any positive quest, and social earnestness gave way to a drifting attitude. At the same time, the actual expression of repudiation became more extreme as the conduct which had constituted social defiance at one time became commonplace a few years later. The disappearance of smoking as an issue, the spread of drinking, and the passing on from free love to homosexuality were only the more obvious of the manifestations which were successively adopted to mark the outposts of revolt.

Art, sex, and a disdain for the pursuit of wealth were the key points by which it was possible to test the nature and the degree of departure from the old American tradition.

Interest in money-making for its own sake and in the world of business was rare among all types of Villagers. Though those who refused to compromise with the materialistic world even to the point of earning a living were a small minority, even a sample of distinctly conservative Villager men showed sixteen per cent never looking at the financial section of the newspaper, in contrast to a corresponding group of townspeople in similar occupations where only two per cent failed to follow the financial news.[1]

Neither in the old American culture pattern nor in that dominated by bourgeois values had either artist or writer an integral place. Although it was the part of cultivation to know the works of classical writers, it was not in the genteel tradition to be an artist or a writer by profession, particularly either a struggling or an experimental one who was not a success on the money-making front and who did not accept the dictates of respectable taste. Except for the circumstances which produced the Concord group in the years before the Civil War, artist and writer had found the American environment thoroughly uncongenial and, in the absence of social status or a critical audience, they had either been driven, like Henry James, to seek expatriation or to retire into themselves like Emily Dickinson. Those who made much of art were, by the mere fact of this emphasis, registering a repudiation of traditional attitudes. In addition, the Village artists departed conspicuously from those forms of art expression which were acceptable to the American community. The attack on the genteel tradition, led by the genuine artists, became a secondary symbol of the scorn in which the staid world was held, and those whose art registered their social attitude rather than their talent felt compelled to violate all the established rules of versification, punctuation, or composition.

Art, moreover, served a purpose which no other form of repudiation filled in that it offered positive as well as negative values, not simply the discarding of an empty or unacceptable social pattern, but a way of life in itself. And upon this fact rested its relation to the many groups in the Village, none of whom possessed any coherent alternative to the social pattern which they more or less vigorously despised. It was to art as a way of life that all turned, either

[1] Moshier L. M. A Comparison of the Reading Interests of a Selected Group of Adults in New York City, and Similar Group in a Town in New York State. MS. Thesis, Columbia University, 1931.

as a means of satisfying themselves or of giving themselves status in a society in which art was the one recognized form of divergence. Hence, practically all groups in one way or another, even though they had no artistic capacities themselves, attempted to justify themselves to themselves and to society in some artistic or literary terms or longed to be able to do so.

In throwing over traditional attitudes toward sex, the Villagers were, again, attacking simultaneously Puritanism and bourgeois morality. Their attitudes toward sex were the product of a combination of trends — the attack on Puritanism which gave the *American Mercury* its vogue, the growing equality between men and women of which the success of the suffrage movement was only one manifestation, and the 'arrival' of Freud and psychoanalysis to bring sex into the center of the stage. They ranged from those engaged in a serious and genuine effort to discover a basis for a freer relationship to those for whom sex was merely a symbol and who turned to promiscuity or homosexuality to express the completeness of their defiance. The former struggled against the odds of economic and personal insecurity and the strain of city living to find a basis for personal independence. The latter used Freud to rationalize as all-important what was much nearer sheer lust than the experience with whose ramifications the psychologist dealt. In between were many who were honest in their desire to cast off the shackles of Puritanism, who might or might not lean on Freud for support, and who used the equality of the sexes as a useful concept to justify the new conduct of girls. Characteristically the latter found themselves in a conflict situation, for they had often not changed their attitudes as completely as they thought, and in spite of lip service to freedom and equality, they retained many of their bourgeois values.

The setting for all these changes was furnished, somewhat fortuitously, by Prohibition, and drink became not only an avenue of escape but a symbol of defiance. However irrelevantly, sobriety went overboard along with 'virtue' and 'success.'

The artists as a group — painters and literary people especially — were the first to make the Village a refuge from the social controls of Main Street, and to establish the positive features of its challenge. A proper treatment of their role would call for a literary and artistic history of post-War America, for a large proportion of the writers and artists of these years resided at one time or another or had their associations in the Village. Since this is a social rather than a literary study, however, this tempting field must be passed over for a limited consideration of the social place of these artists and writers in the Village.

In the early years the stream of artists and writers who were identified with the Village included such real talent as that of Edna St. Vincent Millay or Theodore Dreiser. The fact that almost any paragraph written or spoken about the Village sounds like a textbook on modern American literature is ample testimony. These early Village residents, moreover, either originated or actively promoted pioneer efforts in such varied fields as free verse, the Little Theater movement, interior decoration, radical periodical literature. In the early days, too, this group was poor and lived impecuniously, informally, and often co-operatively. According to all testimony, many of its members constituted a fairly close group, eating together, criticizing each other's work, and, though intensely individualistic, feeling a common bond holding them together against the world.

In the post-War years, the old group of artists gradually broke up and drifted away, leaving behind them the echo of their renown and the oft-repeated question, 'Is the Village still the literary capital of America? What has become of those who gave it its fame? Has the artist colony of the Village been supplied with new blood as the years have gone by?'

As the Village became better known and more generally sought as a place of residence, it lost the cheap rents which made it particularly attractive to artists and writers. At the same time, many of those who had struggled in the Village in poverty and fraternity had become famous and sufficiently prosperous to live elsewhere with greater comfort and independence. Thus, those with the money to stay could also afford to leave and those without money could not afford to remain. Some few who became successful retained their studios at high rents either because they liked the locality or because they found a Village address an asset, while some who showed little signs of achieving success found cheap quarters in out-of-the-way places and stayed on, dependent on the encouragement of others in the same position.

For those who had chosen to depart when they had had the opportunity either to go or to stay, many reasons for leaving the Village were given both by those who were left behind and by those who went. Charges that the artists had left because they had 'gone bourgeois' were met with the statement that it was the Village which had gone bourgeois. The upshot of the testimony seemed to indicate that the breakup of the old artist colony had involved a gradual process of dispersion, each leaving for a personal reason when he had become bored or at odds with the group or indifferent to it. Although some moved together to places which were or became new centers, there was no group movement of artists out of the Village — no transfer of the Village to another place.

The exodus of the old group did not check the flow of new young writers and artists into the Village. These continued to come, to find themselves cheap quarters, to congregate in little groups and to struggle along with varying degrees of effectiveness and talent. It was still possible in 1930 to have the man on the next stool at a drugstore lunch counter explain that he had just come to live in the Village and was looking for 'the artists' and try to sell you a portrait sketch which he had made while you were eating. A local newspaper editor, playing up the artistic side of the Village, was able to arrange with a druggist to use his window for the display of the works of Village artists, a different painter usually each week. The newcomers were both befriended and exploited by older artists, newspapermen, printers, tea-shop and speakeasy proprietors. Most especially they were made self-conscious, as 'Village poets' or 'Village painters.'

Time only could tell whether those new groups would turn out to contain as distinguished talent as the earlier groups had. Certainly their position in the community was very different from that which their predecessors had occupied, for they had become so submerged by the various other groups as to be almost inconspicuous. The truck-drivers' cafeteria, where budding authors sat late into the night over their five-cent cups of coffee, was known to fewer of the Villagers than the corresponding places had been ten years before. But, as one of the older group expressed it, 'Who knows that the youngsters who argue the relative merits of James Joyce and Virginia Woolf over their coffee or gin have not as many geniuses among them as we had in our day?' Circumstances were against the production of the sort of talent in 1930 that had risen to fame around 1920, for the literary developments that had been inaugurated in the earlier years had petered out into a sort of formless and self-centered futilitarianism.

The survival of an artist element in the Village was brought to light when an open-air art market was set up in Washington Square in 1932. The use of the Square for the market was in itself an evidence that the locality had retained its reputation. Of the 275 artists enrolled for the exhibit, approximately a quarter were from the Village and its immediate environs. These included old-timers who had hung on with slight success, and a few repatriates who had returned from the Rive Gauche, as well as youngsters recently drawn to the Village; people who led very isolated lives and others who professed to value the Village because there were always people who would talk over one's work, look at it, and criticize it. By no means all of the Village artists had come out to exhibit, for the successful had no need and some with a growing reputation feared to acknowledge their poverty. Those from other parts of the city reported that they found midtown living both cheaper and less distracting than the Village — that the Village was fine for talk, but not so good for uninterrupted work. The ones who most nearly resembled the serious, struggling group of the Village's early days were now coming from the lower East Side where the infiltration of artists seeking really cheap rents echoed the beginnings of the Village twenty years before.

The influence of those who achieved artistic and literary fame did not depart when they left their Village haunts. Recalled as a glorious memory by those who had shared with them the early Village and mourned by those who came in later years seeking their equivalent, they cast the shadow of their fame over the community. Whatever savored of artistic expression or of community life in later years suffered from the sense of not being equal to the good old days, and the romanticized pattern of those days determined the form of new efforts at group activity and perpetuated the type of celebrity-featuring tea rooms, the 'poetry evenings,' and the 'Village' myth. When those who had moved away came back to the city, they sometimes gravitated back to their old haunts, where each occasional presence gave a new lease of life to the places which they patronized.

While they left the Village lying in the shadow of a faded splendor, these former Villagers gathered on Cape Cod, in Connecticut, the Hudson Valley, and Paris, in communities which might almost be regarded as suburbs of the Village. Although these areas were not consciously colonized, and emphatically denied being offshoots of the Village, the process of drift sometimes almost reproduced groups and situations which had existed in the Village. In one such country community, the nucleus of a few Village friends who bought near-by tracts of land quite accidentally started to give the place a reputation. Among the ex-Villagers attracted there was one who went into the real estate business. The community grew until there were enough families to organize a progressive school which in turn became an attraction and a center of the community. A visit to this community in 1930 disclosed several different generations of literary and artistic ex-Villagers and many of the attitudes which had characterized successive groups in the Village.

It is perhaps unnecessary to follow through the ramifications of the Village's artist life, to include the suckers and the pseudos — the neurotic Park Avenue ladies who paid fabulous sums to have their verse of dubious quality printed 'uniquely' by an erratic Village patron of poets; the millionaire playboy who, via the Village, squandered his fortune on minor versions of the arts; the fantastically mad parties; the arty and exotic publications; the power of the word 'creative' to enhance the crudest production and the most irrelevant conduct — all the barnacles which tended to cling to the ark of 'art' and the grandly futile gestures which were made in its name. These are less germane to a study of social change than is the place which the pursuit of art occupied among the variety of groups who were seeking some form of social readjustment.

In contrast to the Babbitt-ridden communities from which they had escaped, virtually every group in the Village at any time was definitely art-conscious. The professional, conventional people looked upon the genuine arts with respect and discrimination, entertained a hearty contempt for the pseudos, and were quite likely to pursue some form of artistic expression themselves as an avocation. The bohemians and those whose repudiation was complete, claimed efforts toward creative expression as their *raison d'être,* quite regardless of the success of those efforts, while those who had partially discarded their traditions were more than likely to yearn toward the arts, perhaps maintaining some form of expression as an avocation, and in some cases, hoping to abandon their bread-and-butter jobs in favor of an artist's life if they should ever become sufficiently proficient to do so. The social adjustments of the artist, in their turn, varied through the whole range of Village groups, with some concentration at the more experimental end of the scale.

The group which first sought social readjustment in the Village and which numbered some of the serious artists and writers among its members was genuine in its effort to discover new values and far from wishing to abandon all parts of the code of behavior in which it had grown up. Rather, its members sought to carry forward what they regarded as vital in the American tradition and to maintain, in the face of disrupting influences, the cultural values which they had inherited. What they repudiated primarily was the money drive, the 'Babbittry,' the purely acquisitive values which had come to dominate the American scene.

This group, which remained well represented in the area in 1930, was made up chiefly of professional people, social workers, and teachers, drawn largely from cultivated families of old American stock who had occupied comfortable middle-class or professional positions in widely scattered communities. Single women, living alone or in groups of two or three, predominated over either families or single men. Some had made their first acquaintance with the neighborhood by way of residence at the local settlement house; others had been among the first occupants of remodeled stables. They had come to the Village in search of a place where they could live inexpensively, conveniently, and with taste. These people had always considered themselves the 'real' Villagers, regarding the Village very much as theirs and resenting equally its reputation for bohemianism and the building of expensive, respectable apartments.

In the early days, members of this group had joined together in an attempt to provide congenial forms of social life at low cost. Some had formed eating-clubs where food was combined with good talk; some had been members of the famous Liberal Club, had made up or patronized the group of playwrights which grew into the Provincetown Players and the players who evolved into the Theatre Guild. But their social life had always been without formal social organization and by 1930 it had lost even these informal efforts to supply a touch of friendly neighborliness in the midst of the harsh impersonality of city life. An attempt to revive the spirit of the Liberal Club, and of the Civic Club which had championed free speech during the War, awakened the old community interest of a few; but though they joined, they rarely attended and soon dropped their support. They were not gregarious, their contacts were chiefly with professional associates or individual friends, and their formal membership, if any, was in professional societies. By 1930, they no longer needed an organized opportunity to meet new people as did younger groups in the community. The eating-places which they frequented did not serve as clubs and had not developed into 'pick-up joints' like other types of local eating-places. Except for those who sent their children to one of the progressive schools, no local institutions entered into their social life.

Some still liked to believe, however, that the neighborly spirit which they had possessed among themselves when they had been a small group living in the midst of the slums had not disappeared. One such, who had been one of the very first to discover the Village, asserted in 1930 that the external changes had never fundamentally altered the small neighborhood which was the Village. Others, however, declared that this representative must be blind or preoccupied with her own affairs not to realize that the old, simple community had disappeared. A few had become defensive about 'their Village' and responded to questioning with assertions about 'those bohemians.' More characteristically, however, they continued to live their own preoccupied lives, mingling with professional associates and friends from all parts of the city, retaining in their consciousness those characteristics of the neighborhood which they valued, exploring such new tearooms of their own type as were opened, patronizing and watching the coming and going of bookshops, but being nearly as unconcerned with the cabarets and dives, the advent of stenographers and brokers, as with the cafés where the Italian men hung out or the cigar-store gossip of the Irish boys on the corner.

The elements in the American tradition which the members of

this group cherished included a taste for the way of life and the standards of conduct which went with its simpler, less industrialized, more rural stage. City life was rarely congenial to them. Many maintained camps or cottages in the country to which they escaped over the week-ends. Others joined the Appalachian Mountain Club and spent Sundays on long tramps. They relished the charm of old, brick houses and greatly preferred their made-over interiors with high-ceilinged rooms and fireplaces to better-equipped apartments in buildings served by liveried doormen. They preferred the Village to other parts of the city because its buildings were low, its streets 'quaintly' violated the checker-board principle, and the green of Washington Square lent a sense of space. Some liked to praise the Village for its Old World or colonial atmosphere. With slight variation on account of income level, they exerted every effort to make their apartments into homes rather than dormitories, with antique furniture, etchings, perhaps some old European brass, and many books. The tea-rooms which they patronized were in the same decorous taste as their homes, with a fire burning on the hearth and excellent and inexpensive food tastily served on well-worn wooden tables set with peasant pottery or English ware.

Their leisure was quietly spent in 'cultural' pursuits, in reading, conversation, or in trips to the country. They rarely played cards; they attended the theater frequently, but condemned the movies as cheap. Few by 1930 had come to the point of recognizing in the movies a contemporary art form in which varying quality was to be critically distinguished. If they had a radio, they listened to the Philharmonic concerts and perhaps to political speeches, but not many of this group felt it necessary to own a radio. Their reading included the classics and the more serious of modern works. Their magazine reading was confined to the quality journals. They prided themselves on taste, simple living, and wholesomeness. They considered it their duty to vote and frequently supported the Socialist candidate, especially after the Socialist Party acquired a new respectability under the lead of Norman Thomas.

With all the conventionality of their own behavior, however, members of this group were intensely individualistic and conscientiously tolerant of the conduct of others. Eminently sincere themselves, they respected sincerity even where it led to forms of behavior which they found unpalatable. On most questions of conduct they were unwilling to be dogmatic, taking the position that the individual was in a position to judge what was right and wrong for himself. Though they had mostly dropped away from the Church, they had retained the assumptions of individual conduct guided by individual conscience which was fundamental to the Protestant faiths. Again in the best tradition of the old American community, they possessed a strong social consciousness and sense of social responsibility which frequently expressed itself in interest in reform. Many who worked for social betterment or educational advance were pioneers in fields of technique, yet the concepts of the society which they sought to rebuild were essentially those which retained the values of early American life. Though the genteel tradition no longer dominated their literary horizon, it continued to tinge their taste.

The distinction of this group lay in the fact that the social values which it sought to preserve had come to rest on taste rather than on social pressure. Enforcement by community pressure of forms of behavior which they regarded as the mere empty shell rather than the essential spirit of American institutions, they repudiated as readily as the money drive. They had as little sympathy for Mrs. Grundy's social pressure as for the race to keep up with the Joneses. But they confidently hoped that the good judgment and taste of individuals would lead them into lines which would include a preference for antique furniture and Anglo-Saxon decency.

Some had gone over to the 'psychological' camp of those who accepted a complete breakdown of social patterns and sought to build on the basis of the individual as a psychological entity. For those who taught in the progressive schools or shared the views of the more advanced social workers, this emphasis on the psychological individual was easily grafted onto their traditional acceptance of the individual as an independent moral entity. But the tastes and points of view which they hoped the individuals would freely develop, and the cultural values which they, perhaps unconsciously, supported, were largely those which had come down from the past rather than those imaginatively conceived for the future.

As the years went on, these people became somewhat wistful.

They regretted the passing of the old, genuine, informal Village. They regretted the coming of apartment houses which spelled the Babbittry which they repudiated. They regretted the bohemian reputation and the bohemian practices which surrounded them. They regretted the multitude of speakeasies and the emphasis on drink. Except for the Church, they had repudiated no major traditional institution. They continued to respect the institution of the family and, though tolerant of individuals who broke through its bonds, nevertheless deplored the abandonment of traditional forms of marriage and family life. They resented the commercializing of politics and were ready to join movements to restore political activity to its original purity. In so far as they looked at the economic system, it was with the eyes of the reformer rather than of the revolutionary. This group, in its social consciousness, its earnestness, and at the same time its tolerance, dated from the pre-War period. Its point of view and its social adaptation had not been set under the fire of Fascism, Communism, or the revolt of youth in the post-War years. Throughout these years it retained its liberalism, its personal earnestness, its tolerance. It remained in the locality, meeting the problem of increased rents from its rising salaries or by moving to parts of the district which were less completely reclaimed, letting itself be neither drawn into nor driven out by any succeeding element.

Closely resembling this old professional group in background, attitudes, and manner of living, but unrelated to it through social contact, was a body of young professional and business people who had come in in increasing numbers to be close to their work in the near-by laboratories, the adjacent university, or the downtown area. Economic reasons primarily had brought them into the city and convenience and the availability of suitable apartments had led them into the local community. These were drawn largely from the same old American background as the older professional group, and, like them, had little or no desire to throw overboard entirely the values of their home communities. They ate at the same kind of well-appointed tea rooms and took their entertainment, in so far as limited finances permitted, in much the same ways, with theaters, reading, and parties. Perhaps they were a shade more inclined toward 'Babbittry,' a bit less cultivated, and a little more likely to patronize a speakeasy, go to the movies, or read the *Saturday Evening Post*. Because they had reached maturity during the post-War years, they were less universally possessed of a social consciousness. Their interest in the neighborhood and their conception of the Village as an interrelated community were non-existent. On the whole, however, they were not in revolt, and would have liked to mould their lives fairly close to the pattern in which they had grown up.

These younger people, though similar in taste and point of view to the older professional group, rarely had any contact with the latter, for in the community no means of making such contacts were open to them. Even among themselves there was little social organization or opportunity for contact. Apart from an occasional encounter with someone in the same house, most of their connections were made through work, and their friends were scattered through the city. A real need of providing an organized means for making social contacts was revealed by the response of this group to the organization of a young people's society by one of the Protestant churches. In view of the fact that the Church had been more consistently dropped than any other institution among all the Villager groups, the readiness to join church activities was an indication of how little of its background this particular group had cast off.

Some members of this group — how representative of the whole body it was difficult to ascertain — felt their position a difficult and anomalous one. They desired to live according to the standards of their homes and to found homes of their own which would carry on those same standards. But their income was low and there was slight possibility, in the community in which they found themselves, of securing either the physical surroundings which they deemed necessary for the maintenance of inherited standards or the social position which they felt they should achieve.

Although some of them mingled with people who came to the Village because of its unconventional reputation and patronized the speakeasies and entertained at Village parties, the majority were only a little less disgusted with the Village's reputation and what passed as Village life than the older, conventional group. In their own communities they might lean in the direction of the Babbitts. Here in the city, the absence of social pressures had freed them from the necessity of conforming to the Babbitt mould, but it had not given them the opportunity to carry with them the rest of their social inheritance which they desired to retain. They had brought the values and ambitions of an economically freer society, where their fathers had been able to count on rising to positions of independence and prominence, into a situation in which they found themselves parts of closely organized, gigantic economic units with little chance at independence or much more than a meager economic competence. In their own way, too, this group yearned for the traditional values for which they saw little opportunity in their own future. Their attempt at a solution was likely to be a move to the suburbs, with the accompanying discomfort of commuting, as soon as they started to raise children.

At the extreme opposite end of the scale from those professional groups who sought to perpetuate in taste their cherished social values were the out-and-out bohemians whose repudiation of the values and the controls of organized society was complete. These discarded money values to the point of making little or no provision for self-support and tossed all trace of moral earnestness and other aspects of old American culture into the scrap-heap as well. The influence of this group was out of all proportion to its actual numbers. It had come in originally, as 'bohemias' are prone to do,[1] in the trail of the Village's early artist colony, and had then become a distinct group in itself. In spite of the reputation which the bohemians' publicly led lives gave to the Village, not more than a small group at any one time would truly have answered to this description — would really have fallen within the category of those who deliberately disregarded the standards and the drives which governed the ordinary world, either on grounds of philosophy, preoccupation with art, or laziness.

Certain houses, owned by a landlord whose reputation for befriending bohemians was known from coast to coast, housed most of these, although some were scattered in the garrets of unremodeled houses. In these apartments, no one was put out for failure to pay the rent, but was simply moved to smaller quarters or put in with another occupant. The landlord even went so far as to help out his tenants with money or food when they were badly off, or lent them typewriters. He recognized that many were shiftless and took advantage of him, that others lived from drink to

[1] Parry, A. *Garrets and Pretenders*, New York, 1933, *passim*.

drink, while others were really struggling and devoting themselves to artistic or literary pursuits. This group drifted in and out, but some members stayed on for years. The type and its habits remained constant from the earliest days of the Village until 1930, though the proportion whose artistic pretensions were real appeared to have dropped, and the homosexual types became somewhat more prominent.

The influence of the genuine bohemians extended beyond the confines of the houses where they lived and the eating-places where they met, for their reputation lured many young people who were not really bohemian in their philosophy and temperament, but eager to 'see life' by living in what they considered the bohemian manner. In the course of the decade, more and more of the Village population came to consist of young single people holding ordinary jobs, coming from ordinary backgrounds. Some of these had come with the deliberate intent of following the bohemian path. Many had come to live in the Village simply because it was convenient or offered the right type of apartment, but even these found themselves exposed to the contagion of bohemianism. Other people who did not live in the Village, but resided with their families in other parts of the metropolitan area, were also drawn there for social life. The hangouts which went in most heavily for 'bohemian atmosphere' were centers for people from Brooklyn or the Bronx.

The pseudo-bohemians developed two closely related social institutions, the hangout and the studio party. Since their daytime occupations were the minimum compromise with economic necessity, their night activities were the focus of their life. Formal societies constituted to them part of the pattern which they repudiated. At the same time their insecurity and the directions of their escape produced a gregariousness of habit which led them to gather nightly in some studio apartment or public meeting place. To capitalize this gregariousness, a succession of gathering places were opened, some serving sandwiches and furnishing informal entertainment, others, more imposing in name but not in practice, calling themselves studio salons or clubs. They offered unlimited opportunities for contacts to those who sought to join this type of group. A description of one of these hangouts in 1930 would have been equally applicable to its series of predecessors.

'Jo's' was located in the basement of a tenement building. In the low, narrow room, cheap, brightly colored tables, rickety chairs, a few booths and an old piano were crowded as tight as they could be jammed. Liquor was not served, but it was assumed that the patrons would bring it, and order sandwiches and ginger ale. The place was usually crowded and always informal. Girls making a first visit to the place could be sure that the men beside whom they found themselves seated would assume that they were a party for the evening and night. If the girls were first at a table, they were sure to be joined. From time to time someone started to play the piano and people danced in the crowded aisles between the tables with whatever strangers they happened to be sitting beside. The proprietor stood by the door, greeting everybody, eyeing all newcomers and making announcements. Many of those present were young girls and boys with pale faces and circled eyes who drank heavily. The rest were a few middle-aged men who had obviously come for relaxation and to pick up a girl, and a number of older people, some with an artistic or literary past, who were known as habitués. A young Chinese communist came to pick up someone who could help him translate and criticize his work. Certain familiar figures who were always known to be trying to borrow money were cold-shouldered by everyone. A couple of young girls from the South who obviously came from substantial homes and a cultivated background, were regularly present and conspicuous, dancing together and constantly drunk.

These people had two preoccupations — sex and drink. In the early years of the decade, free love and promiscuity had been a sufficient subject for talk and entertainment in most groups. By 1930, promiscuity was tame and homosexuality had become the expected thing. One girl who came nightly was the joke of the place because she was trying so hard to be a Lesbian, but when she got drunk she forgot and let the men dance with her. A favorite entertainer was a 'pansy' whose best stunt was a take-off on being a 'pansy.' To lend a touch of intellectuality and to give people a sense of activity, the proprietor set aside two nights each week for discussion or performance by regular patrons. These evenings, however, did not interrup the group's major preoccupation, for the subjects chosen for discussion were such things as 'the social position of a gigolo' and 'what is sex appeal?' On the latter subject, the views of the Lesbians present were especially called for.

Studio parties followed the style of Jo's with only slightly greater privacy, while the clubs and salons were distinguished only by the fact that they charged admission, more regularly had a program, and laid somewhat less stress upon drink. Their literary and artistic pretensions resembled Jo's 'intellectual' evenings, with the subjects for lectures and discussions also featuring sex. The 'poetry' which was read or hung about the walls was in a similar vein. Their clientèle varied more widely and contained a larger proportion who lived elsewhere in the city and who sought rather to gain an evening's excitement in the midst of a more or less conventional life than to abandon such a life altogether.

For this group sex in its most irresponsible form was a means of escape either from the type of life in which they had grown up or from some inadequacy in themselves. In the absence of clinical data, it was not possible to determine how many of the group were running away from personality problems and family situations and how many from the emptiness of inherited social codes. Neither was it possible to determine the extent to which repudiation was a mere episode or a permanent attitude. A little fragmentary and inconclusive evidence suggested that, for a substantial number, this type of escape was more than a temporary phase. For those who lived elsewhere in the city and simply came down for their entertainment, it may well have had little permanent importance. But for those who came from a distance to live in the Village, a more serious break may well have been involved. The testimony of the doctor whose office was located most conveniently to the center of such activity bore vigorous witness to the number of girls whose health was permanently impaired. For individuals who for any long period of time remained part of this group, the possibility of returning to the home communities, once they had so thoroughly repudiated the values of these communities, was certainly reduced. The older persons who had become long-time habitués testified by their persons to this potentiality. On the other hand, the proprietor of one of the less extreme of the hangouts reported many former patrons who had settled down to bourgeois lives.

Of all the groups in the Village, this one had the widest influence on the rest of the country, for it helped to popularize the 'wild party' from one end of the land to the other; it was the purely negative set of values which this group developed that set its stamp upon America during these years. 'It's well to remember that the Village isn't unique,' observed one of the interviewers who was working on this study. 'If that necking party I went to in Brooklyn last night had been in the Village, I'd have taken it for "typical" — but there it was, as wild as you please, and right in the most substantial part of respectable Brooklyn.'

Between the professional group which, while repudiating bourgeois values, definitely retained its appreciation of old American culture and those who repudiated that culture altogether, were various groups, mostly but not all made up of younger people, who attempted to make some combination between what they wished to retain and what they sought to discard. They ranged all the way from completely unsophisticated youngsters who knew enough to 'hate their jobs, of course,' and wanted to 'see life,' but could feel satisfactorily devilish as soon as a little gin began to flow and noise to mount, to those who attempted, seriously and thoughtfully, to solve the problems of their personal lives with as much emancipation as possible from the pressure of social standards.

These groups were all less scornful of the money drive than both the more conservative and the more bohemian, for they were apt to feel the force of economic pressure more acutely. Most looked to art as the positive alternative to those standards of their home communities with which they had little sympathy. All were preoccupied to some degree with the problem of sex, giving lip service, at least, to the principle of sex equality, ready to use 'Puritan' as a term of reproach, and equipped with at least a second-hand version of Freud.

Among all these groups, social organization was either informal or non-existent, and opportunities to make contacts locally varied with an individual's readiness to resort to speakeasy pick-ups. When the number of Villagers had been smaller, there had been much greater informality in tea-rooms and contacts were more possible there. In some tea-rooms, even in 1930, the proprietor acted as host and introduced guests to each other, and in a few small places it was not unusual to enter into conversation with someone at a neighboring table. One girl reported that when she first came to live in the Village, she had difficulty making acquaintances until one evening she invited all the guests in the small tea-room where she had had supper to come to her house for a party. But most contacts for all these groups were made through work or through friends. Once an individual had acquired a nucleus of friends, however, he had little difficulty in enlarging his acquaintance because parties in individual apartments were habitually informal and those invited were expected to bring along as many of their friends as they chose. As among the more extreme group, informal studio parties constituted the chief form of social life and took the place of more formally organized gatherings.

Attempts at formal organization consistently ran aground on the fact, complained of by one club sponsor, that 'you can't get people interested in anything except themselves.' An effort to revive something on the pattern of the old Liberal Club of pre-War fame was the only formal society which existed in 1930, and even this club was a struggling affair. Its lectures and teas for literary lights were attended by a number of local and non-local people, but the daily use of the club was confined almost exclusively to the more ill-adjusted, and it became a pick-up joint for those whose technique was to preface their seductions with chapter and verse from Freud. Although to the stenographers and salesmen who did not belong and craved contact with artists and intellectuals, this club looked most attractive, those who actually made up the membership relied upon professional contacts and informal social life at each other's homes to meet their social needs.

The conduct of these groups varied widely, but it involved conflicts and inconsistencies arising out of the effort to hold some attitudes and to break through others. The types of conflict situations in which they found themselves reflected the problems of adjustment faced by many, here and elsewhere, during these years of social breakup.

Characteristic of a growing proportion of Village residents was a group of girls with fair to good stenographic or secretarial positions and men in moderately paid office jobs with large corporations, banks, or brokers. Their reason for residence in the Village was principally convenience and the type of apartment available, but often also a slight desire for freedom and adventure. Some considered it a distinct advantage to be able to give a Greenwich Village address to new acquaintances, while others found it a great nuisance. Members of this group found themselves often in an *impasse* because they had retained too much of the traditional conception of the relation between men and women to take advantage of the changed positions into which they had put themselves. The girls were self-supporting and independent, and, though not preoccupied with sex, were not inhibited from such experiences as might occasionally 'grow out of an evening.' Yet they counted on balancing their budgets by being taken out by men two or three times a week. The men would admit, if pressed, that if a married woman wanted to work she should, but, for their own part, they felt that they must not marry until they could support their wives. The girls who wished to marry and were prepared to go on supporting themselves were prevented by the attitude and the low earnings of the men. These young people represented a group which valiantly kept its head above water, but saw little chance of achieving either the status or the security which it wished to combine with its city freedom.

Somewhat more experimental than these, but at the same time not free from conventional attitudes which got in their way, were groups of young people who thought they had repudiated certain standards, but found that they had not fully done so and could not be comfortable when not living up to them. Typical of this sort of conflict was a couple who despised bourgeois standards, to whom the worst of all crimes was to be boring, and whose conscious ideal was to live vividly and intensely with cultivation, ardor, and creative expression. But though the man scorned his prosaic job, he was too much bound by the convention of what a man should do not to care whether he made a masculine success or not. The girl, though she had been attracted by his sensitiveness and artistic leanings, found herself resenting his lack of success and nagging him into an added sense of inferiority. In less than a year their marriage had broken down.

In most groups, pressure toward sex experimentation was strong. There was difference of opinion as to the most desirable sorts and quantity of sex experience, but there was general intolerance of any who were disinclined toward experimentation, and a virgin was the object of expressed contempt. Although their vocabulary on the subject contrasted radically with that of the Italian young men of the neighborhood, the conduct of many Villagers differed much less. They differed from their local neighbors chiefly in expecting the girl to be the one taking the necessary precautions, in assuming that they would not become infected, while the Italians took venereal disease as a matter of course, and in having enough medical friends to make it easier for them to see that the necessary abortion was performed in case their contraceptive measures had been ineffective.

In those groups where the women tried to achieve a genuinely emancipated status, difficulty often arose out of the fact that the men gave only lip service to the principle of equality and took advantage of the girls' seriousness to exploit them. The changed attitudes toward sex were much more of a wrench for the girls than for the men, for the latter could fit the facts of freedom and experimentation in sex relations into the tradition of the double standard which they might have officially abandoned, but which remained an essential part of their attitude. The girls, on the other hand, had the whole weight of their tradition against them, and could not go in for 'experimentation' as lightly as could the men. The result was that when the girls talked about sex equality they really meant it, while the men often did not. The very girls whom men persuaded to sleep with them by a learned discourse later became objects of their contempt, and their conversation when no women were present would have done credit to any similar bourgeois group.

The status of the 'emancipated' woman, whose living as well as her thinking was unconventional, but who remained serious and self-respecting and had not taken to sex and gin as an avenue of escape, was thus very insecure. Uncertain of respect, whatever her choice, she had to battle her lonely way without the assurance of social support. Upon her fell the whole brunt of an uncertain position in a shifting culture, for she embodied in herself much of the break with tradition. Upon her vitality and the capacity to effect an individual solution rested much of the success or failure of her adaptation. Where her economic position was also precarious, the strain was acute. Without sufficient vigor and toughness and enough economic security to keep afloat, she was in danger of drifting into a state of instability from which little but good luck could extricate her.

Typical of those whose individual adjustment bade fair to be unsuccessful was a young woman who had come to the city to escape from the smugness of her home community and to study music. Eager, adventurous, and intense, she threw herself into the city with vigor and courage. In the course of a year and a half much of her resilience had been destroyed. She had lived successively with a man who befriended her when her funds ran out before she found a job, with a musician whom she supported out of her slender secretary's salary which was barely enough to enable her to have a room with a piano, and, when he dropped her, with an aggressive, middle-aged man who boasted of the number of women whom he had possessed. In each case, her own emotion was intense and genuine, she believed that the relationship was reciprocal, and, though hurt by being thrown over by each lover in turn, she accepted this on the simple assumption that their love for her had passed. Yet these men and their friends talked caustically and contemptuously about her, and she found herself without the respect of the group with whom she moved and worn down with the strain of her genuine effort to make an adjustment. Although a girl of exceptional vigor and vitality, her precarious economic position, and the very genuineness which made her unprotected emotionally, left her isolated and insecure. To return to her home was the last solution which seemed to her possible. It appeared that only the accident of happening to fall in with some man who would not exploit her would give her a chance of gaining emotional, economic, and social stability. The story of this girl could be repeated countless times from the records of the Village, varying in each case according to her luck, her economic security, and her emotional stability.

At least for such of these girls as remained in the locality, marriage was no solution, for the married couples with similar backgrounds and attitudes were under a similar strain. The families who sent their children to the local progressive schools, and more who had no children, attempted to carry into their married lives the principles of individual development and a disregard for such traditional standards as they intellectually condemned. Here again, inconsistency placed them under a strain which fell primarily on the women. In these families, the idea that the man should furnish the full support of the family had been discarded and the wife contributed as a matter of course to the support of the home. Subordination of the interests or personality of either to the other or to the interest of the family as a whole had also been scrapped in favor of the assumption that each was to retain the full measure of his or her individuality. If a man's creative work was incompatible with his contributing even a pro-rata share to the joint household, the household rather than the work should suffer. In these families, however, the idea of the home as a unit and as a center was not abandoned. In fact, the standard for the home which these couples struggled to achieve was usually set by the comfortable and attractive surroundings among which they had grown up.

The effort to maintain such homes under city conditions placed a heavy burden on the family budget and especially on the capacity of the women. Often forced to do a large part of the housework because they could not afford maid service, while at the same time they went out to work and carried the supervision and care of the children besides, these women did not find it easy to impart to the home the serenity and sense of security which they felt it should possess. In embracing the newer educational and psychological doctrines, they expanded their concept of the responsibilities which they owed to their children, but were thereby still further pressed in time and money to provide the opportunities, guidance, and care which they thought essential. They usually felt unable to take advantage of public facilities and had to pay for recreation which, in a country community, would have been provided by nature. Added to all this was the necessity of making a harmonious group out of intensely individualistic and self-expressive instead of disciplined and subordinated individuals. Saddled thus with heavy economic burdens, with constant calls for activity, with the personality problems of themselves, their husbands, and their children, they constantly faced the final insecurity of their whole marriage state. Because of the assumption that marriage was an arrangement terminable at will rather than a permanent union, they could rely on neither moral nor legal backing to help them hold their husbands, nor — and here was the crucial point of uncertainty in the whole situation — could they be quite sure that their husbands really preferred their type of independent companion to the women who made a business of love and home and for whom they might any day be deserted. It was not surprising that one of the experimental schools found evidence of more or less strain in the homes of half of its children.

Nor was there any evidence to indicate that the problems of this group had moved any nearer to solution as the years passed. In fact, the evidence of those young married people who had most recently come to the Village suggested that the battle had in some cases been given up. Among these were found many women, some with professional training and experience, who were not working because their husbands did not want them to, who could not have children because their husbands' earnings were too small, who scraped along on a closely figured budget — answering the interviewer's question, 'If your income were reduced, where would you cut down?' with a panicky look and 'I don't see how I could cut anywhere' — who deplored their position and hoped for a 'break.' These had accepted economic limitations, the surrender of their professional interests and often loneliness and boredom in preference to the psychological obstacles to the other type of solution.

For those who could not accept the social pattern into which they had been born, the constructive alternative to escape into art or drink was social reorganization. The pre-War Village had been a center for radical thought — not, to be sure, the fighting Marxism of the East Side ghetto, but nevertheless, the literary proletarianism of the *Masses*, the vigor of the suffrage drive, and the challenge of I. W. W., anarchists, and socialists. In the decade of the twenties, few had the heart or the faith to predicate their conduct and their thought on the assumption of a new social order. The negativeness of all the forms of protest except the artistic, and the pursuit of art for its own sake rather than its use as a social tool, reflected the eclipse of the revolutionary spirit.

In the defection of some members, the failure to enlist new blood, and above all in the psychological reaction to the War, lay at least a partial explanation of the Village's loss of vigor as a radical center. The first break in the ranks had been made by the War itself when some of the better-known Village socialists went patriot in 1917. But vigor enough remained to organize the Civic Club as one of the few places in the city where free discussion could be carried on in spite of the Espionage Act. It was the close of the War rather than the War itself which took the wind out of the radical sails, as post-War disillusionment replaced the faith and zeal which had propelled both radical and patriot in the crisis years. The 'tired radical' of these post-War years was as familiar a figure as the 'younger generation' which kicked over the traces in scorn at the failure of their elders.

In communities where a body of conservative people had retained their pre-War attitudes, there might be something to fall back upon, but in the Village, where those pre-War codes had already been repudiated, there was no heart left in the drive for any form of social action. In the field of literary and artistic expression and of social freedom, much of the fight had been won. There was no zest in battling for free verse and free love as social issues when these bade fair to become commonplace. The social radicals who had survived the wartime defection found the radical ranks split and their parlor radicalism reduced to an amateurish pastime by the realities of the Russian Revolution. They faced the choice of placing themselves under discipline as active party members — a bitter pill for any Village individualist to swallow! — of contributing to various of the national organizations which were striking at specific social evils, or of taking the side lines as observers. A few chose the first course, many responded to appeals for funds by various organizations, but most chose the third line.

As a radical center, the Village ceased to function, in spite of the feeble survival of the Civic Club and the presence of radically minded individuals, including members and officers of liberal, socialist, anarchist, and communist organizations, and in spite of the fact that a local Tammany judge's epithet for women with low heels was 'socialist' and the priest was quick to dub any Village activity he could not identify as 'communist.' A considerable measure of social and political radicalism was taken for granted in most Village circles, but, as one of the old radicals who, in 1930, still had the confidence to try to 'start something,' said, 'It does not seem as if it was possible to get people together to do anything nowadays. They used to be all for action, but now they cannot be made to care.' Even in thought, very few were prepared to push their way through to any revolutionary philosophy.

Thus the Villagers, virtually without social institutions, scornful of bourgeois values, seeking escape through sex, rationalizing their conduct with the aid of Freud and of art, and in despair of social reconstruction, developed an individualism as irresponsible and as extreme as that of the local Italians who were out for themselves. Through their actions, they made the Village a symbol of defiance to whatever the established social order might be. It mattered little that most who lived in the Village did not share in the extremer forms of its reputation or that the rest of the country adopted many of the habits which had been unique in the Village at an earlier time. Greenwich Village remained always the place where one could go farther than in other communities, and as such it acted as a social leaven for the rest of the country. Its manners and attitudes, its art forms and its gin parties, became familiar from coast to coast. Herein lay its entirely uncalculable social influence, an influence which grew as it drew less exceptional and adventurous residents than it had in its early days.

But in its own social life the Village offered no solution to the cultural problems which drove people to the area. Escape it offered but not solution. It accelerated the breaking of old forms, but it contributed no new ones to take their place. In the face of cultural disintegration, it either fostered escape or erected the individual as a psychological entity into an end in himself.

PART III
INSTITUTIONS

IX. POLITICS

1. IN THE TAMMANY MANNER

THE ordinary community functions, as carried on in this locality, tended to preserve the distinctions among local groups and to confirm differences among their standards rather than to weld the community into a functioning whole. Political activity was strongly individualizing, except as it intensified the group rivalry of the major ethnic groups. Schools with diverse aims moulded the children of the several groups in different directions. Even the Catholic Church played a different role among different groups. Health agencies secured the acceptance of common standards, but other social agencies did not.

The political process through which this community functioned lay outside of the American tradition, though not outside of the factual experience of American cities. Attitudes involved in the principles of democracy, those which prescribed the role and responsibilities of citizens and envisaged a politically organized community in action, were not part of the political experience of the local people, except as they learned of them in books. For the Villagers, political activity retained its traditional American meaning, however indifferently or cynically it might be regarded. But the politics which the local people knew had little or nothing to do with democracy, with the responsibilities of citizenship, and with the government of the community. It was, rather, a business organization, grafted upon the governmental structure, operating for itself, and only incidentally performing the functions of government. Much political activity, in fact, was devoted to the negation of governmental actions — to setting aside the rules established by governmental authority and impeding their even-handed execution. The district was, in short, part of New York's Tammany system. In this it was not unique. But the thoroughness with which the political system was taken for granted, and the fact that the Italians became adapted to it more than to any other institution in the locality, made it central to the life of the community.

Those who were concerned with the expression of community sentiment and with the use of governmental agencies to secure benefits for the community — police protection, fire protection, clean streets, adequate recreational facilities, health service, housing inspection, good schools — operated outside of the local political institutions. Neither the social agencies who aimed to 'better' the community by governmental or other means nor those engaged in real estate operations belonged to local political bodies or functioned through them.

The social agencies acted as self-appointed spokesmen for their clients and demanded in the name of the community those things whose lack they felt in the course of their work. The real estate operators, in their turn, were primarily concerned with the interests of their high-rent tenants and invoked governmental action to close places giving the district a bad reputation, and to make the neighborhood more quiet.

But the groups with civic interests had a negligible influence in the selection of persons to public office. Their achievements were secured through lobbying, not at the polls and their voices sank into silence on election day. Their numbers were few and they were without a following to enhance the weight of their single votes; they were not politically cohesive and did not thus throw their weight in a single direction; and they did not have the opportunity to select a representative who would carry out their civic desires, since these desires were of no moment to the candidate of either party.

The local political institutions through which governmental personnel was selected had all the characteristics of business organizations. Political jobs were to be *had*, not *done*; the prime consideration was what the office-holder got out of the office. 'She ought to be able to make a good thing out of it,' was the normal comment of a local Irish woman to an outsider's remark,

'The new girl just appointed to your office is able and will do a good job.' Phrases about serving the public meant no more to the politician than to the business man.

Political leaders had two types of wares with which to enter the market-place and bargain with the voters for support — jobs and favors. In spite of civil service restrictions, practically all jobs were locally assumed to be obtainable only by political influence. Appointive jobs had their well-known prices, while elective positions depended upon the willingness of those in political power to place a candidate upon the ticket. For those who could not be supplied with jobs, the politicians offered a variety of services, summed up under the general term favors, which usually took the form of exempting the favored individual from the application of laws to which the body of the citizenry was subjected. The quashing of complaints against violators of police regulations, especially traffic rules, and the securing of preferential rates of taxation on real estate were among the most common.

By the complexity of relationships whereby the active members of the political organization were the chosen representatives of the public in the carrying on of governmental functions and at the same time were the ones who set aside those functions in favor of certain of the people who elected them to office, the paradoxical situation arose in which the public gave its support most heartily to those who performed the functions of their office least — to those who were most ready to set those functions aside.

Since the economic philosophy with which the community was most familiar was that of directly sought self-interest for immediate personal profits, it was in no way surprising to find the voter regarding his relationship to the political machine as a business relationship in which it was clearly bad business to waste his principal asset, his vote. Correspondingly, the person who was in politics as a business and did not make his profit from it showed as much evidence of incapacity as did the business man whose company was in the red.

For the purpose of conducting the business of politics, the Democratic organization of New York City maintained a series of clubs, one in each of the assembly districts into which the city was divided. Since Greenwich Village comprised parts of four of these assembly districts, four such Democratic clubs were involved.

The club form of organization dated from the days when Tammany Hall was a mutual benefit, fraternal order rather than a political machine. It was so integral with the system that the name club had been virtually pre-empted by the political organizations. The political clubs were thoroughly personal affairs, not simply the party headquarters for the first or second district. Though officially they might carry an appropriate Indian or Jeffersonian name, they were habitually known as the clubs of one or another of the leaders who maintained a personal following which did his behest and received favors in return. A leader's power was threatened only by the rise of a rival leader who might stage a palace revolution if the first became too arrogant or was unable to furnish the favors necessary to keep his following in line. With a mixture of domination and generosity the local political chiefs maintained their districts, feathering their own nests and those of their family and friends and 'making a good thing' out of the processes of government, using the clubs as their instruments and passing them on to their sons when they retired from the scene.

From the time when the Irish first took possession of the area, Greenwich Village had been a Democratic stronghold. One of the local leaders liked to point to his district as the cradle of New York Democracy, and the powerful Tammany clubs were, next to the churches and schools, among the oldest institutions. Three of them had been in existence and under the same leadership — or in the same family — for over forty years. Their leaders belonged to the 'old Irish' group and psychologically, if not actually, to the period of its dominance. One club, organized in 1890, 'belonged' in 1930 to the son of its founder; in another, the old man was still in evidence, but his son frequently took his father's place at the club; in the third, the leader boasted that he had been in that club for forty-two years and knew everybody in the neighborhood who might come in asking for a favor. The first two of these districts were and had been for over a generation solidly Democratic districts, so that the district leaders had never had to reckon with serious party opposition. In the other, the Democratic organization which had been a strong minority acquired majority control during the 1920's.

The nucleus of each club was made up of families whose connection with the organization dated from the last decade or two of the nineteenth century and whose community attitude dated from the same period. In the old days the clubs had been centers of neighborhood sociability. Outings, picnics, block parties brought the young and old of the neighborhood out in full force. With the breaking-up of the neighborhood, the departure of the old families, and the disappearance of the small-town atmosphere, the clubs continued to play their old social role for only a small group of old-timers and their families. It was this small group, too, which carried most of the clubs' activities. At the principal club in 1932, 229 out of the 291 committee positions were held by 60 active individuals or persons with the same family name (in-laws with different names were not identified). The nucleus of 25 most active members, some of whom belonged to the same families, occupied 111 committee positions.

For the rank and file of the several thousand members, the club was simply a means of securing jobs or favors. For the active members it was an office-holders' organization. Those who hung around the club in the evening had jobs in City Hall, ranging from city marshal to elevator operator, at which they might — or might not — be found during the day. The leader and the members of his family were receiving $45,000 among them in city pay checks. The woman co-leader was known in the neighborhood as 'that woman with the swell job.' As one person put it, 'She's fairly sitting in the lap of the mayor.' The leaders of the other clubs in the district occupied the positions of sheriff and comptroller of the budget and their henchmen and active club members similarly drew their salaries from the city.

As job-getting institutions and job-holders' clubs the political clubs operated by means of a circulatory relationship between votes, favors, and jobs. The leaders in the clubs dispensed favors in order to retain support in the form of votes. They needed this support in order to get their own jobs, and they needed these jobs in turn to dispense the favors which gave them the votes which enabled them to retain their jobs. The circle of jobs and favors, combined with a certain amount of entertainment and social life on the side for some, with power for the very few who dispensed the favors, and hard work for those industrious henchmen who 'worked 365 days in the year,' was broken only momentarily when periodically, at the primaries and on election day, the balance of power was tested at the polls. The key to this circulatory structure was, of course, the vote.

The vote was more nearly the expression of a customer's satisfaction or dissatisfaction with the services which had been rendered by those in power than the voicing of a citizen's will. The state of the political market at any time determined the balance of prices between votes and political services. To one of the local leaders who had been dispensing favors for over forty years, 'it sometimes does not seem that one vote a year is worth all the work that is done.' Yet the dispensing of favors went on, for the leader was always under direct pressure to keep his people sufficiently satisfied to make them keep him in office.

The people of Greenwich Village were well aware that the business of politics in New York City might be an extremely lucrative one — how lucrative the investigations of the Seabury Committee well revealed. In the words of a young man who was starting to work his way into the machine, 'If you know how to play the game right, you can make a mint of money.' A group of three local young men, two in college and one in a Wall Street investment house, came to the conclusion that if they had ten thousand dollars to invest they would put it into politics, for 'money spent in the right way in politics is surer to bring in a good return than anywhere else.' In playing for such stakes, even the strongest club leader had to work constantly to maintain his position. In these stoutly Democratic districts there was little danger from the Republican opposition. But there was always the threat within the Democratic Party that some rival aspirant to leadership might 'take the district away' from the local leader.

In the three Irish clubs in the Village, no serious challenge to existing leadership had been offered, but the leader of the local Italian district, and too arrogant leaders in other districts of the city, fell from power during these years, and served as a warning to any leader disposed to neglect the upkeep of his political fences. The ever-present danger of defection by a dissatisfied ethnic minority was here avoided by a series of political devices — gerrymandering the districts, sponsoring an Italian Republican club which helped to divert the Italian membership, and judiciously dispensing jobs and favors. Two leading Italian politicians were sure that these policies would continue to be successful and that the local Irish leader would never suffer the fate of the neighboring Irish leader who was put out by his Italian constituents. 'He has "made" enough Italians politically — judges even — to show them that their best interests lie in following him.' 'I know my political home,' declared one of the strongest potential Italian leaders, 'and I know my leader. And there I stay.' In one district, however, serious revolt was beginning to threaten from Irish quarters. The basis of this revolt was instructively simple — a rival leader opened his own club and promised his followers that $45,000 worth of jobs held by the old leader's family would be distributed, and the section of the district where he lived would get its share. On the sole issue of the distribution of the spoils, the rival published a newspaper, maintained two clubrooms, and was beginning to look like a real menace to the old leader's hold.

The local people were also aware that the political system was closely interrelated with the criminal element and the underworld and took this fact for granted in the same way that they assumed politics to be a business proposition. They did not hesitate to discuss the fact that one of the leaders had told his men to 'lay off' collecting protection from the little storekeepers and to concentrate their efforts where there was real money. Nobody was surprised to find the name of the well-known 'shake-down' man, whose gang had been making life miserable for the local merchants, featured in a full page 'ad' in the political club's program book. When a large street sign supporting the local leader appeared in front of the principal gambling joint of the Village and the principal bootlegger hung out a corresponding sign, the local reaction was simply that gambler and bootlegger, of course, had to do something in return for what they got. The well-known gamblers and petty gangsters serving as election captains, or the local judge who went bail for one of the neighborhood gangs of young criminals, were just parts of the game. A club of thugs and hoodlums which called itself a 'Democratic club' was said to have 'added "Democratic" to its name for protection, I suppose.' The neighborhood chuckled a little when an independent political club hung out a sign in support of someone who had challenged the regular leader and within a few days hauled the sign down and substituted one in support of the regular boss. They accepted the rumor that the independent had been reminded of how the disloyalty of a certain politician had been rewarded with death.

The community took it for granted that the politicians derived a direct income from the illegal liquor traffic, in addition to their indirect returns from the bootleggers who supported political clubs with their contributions and sent supplies to the clubs and to individual judges and politicians. The 'higher-up' in the liquor traffic was presumed to be a major politician — 'maybe a senator or somebody.' The politicians were said to exempt speakeasies from the protection toll levied on common businesses because 'they get the profits from the speakeasies and don't want to cut those profits down.' One young man summed up in a description of an East Side place where he had worked what appeared to him, and to the other young men present, as a natural course of events. The place was run as a dance hall where girls were secured for the white-slave traffic until its proprietor was shot by rival white-slavers. Then it became a dope-running and a gambling joint, but there was some trouble, so the police got after it, 'and now the politicians are in it, so, of course, it is a speakeasy.' The bootleggers were known to be among the most privileged members of the community in their ability to disregard ordinary police regulations. One young bootlegger was noted for running by red lights and driving against the traffic on one-way streets just to show off, because he knew that he could get away with it in the district where he knew the leader. People turned to the bootleggers when they needed pull to get them out of trouble. They knew that the liquor-dealers' power was not confined to their own district — witness the three automobile thieves whose release from a New Jersey jail had been secured by a local bootlegger the very night that they were captured red-handed, and who had never been brought to trial.

The tie-up between politics and the law-breaking element was openly acknowledged on both sides. The 'programs' of the clubs' annual banquets — large books half an inch thick — furnished a yearly record. These books, which ostensibly contained 'advertisements,' were 'shake-downs' by which the clubs levied toll on those who were under obligation to them. While many bootleggers or strong-arm men printed only first names or initials in the program books of the political clubs, these were widely recognizable, and others printed their names in full. More conspicuously still, the official ballot contained the names of people whose illegal activity was well known in the locality. On one ballot, the thirteen men and two women sponsored by the regular organization for party committee members were submitted to a local citizen for identification. Seven of the men, according to the opinion in this informant's circle, were of the sort that belonged in jail. That the remaining six were somewhat less notorious among this particular group was no evidence that their record was any more savory. The report that came back on the seven identified was:

1. Proprietor of gambling joint — bookie, numbers man, straight gambling, election bets. Place raided the previous year only after numerous complaints and after proper warning. Raid fixed and prisoners released.
2. Speakeasy proprietor at same address as (1) and friend and confidant of (1). Arrested once for breaking a college boy's arm in his speakeasy when the boy, under the influence of drink, became noisy. Furnishes a spare room to which girls may be brought by one or more men when they have been picked up and made unconscious by drink. Never raided.
3. Does nothing for a living. Lives at same address as (1) and (2) in apartment formerly used for gambling. Used to run numbers and bookie for (1).
4. Proprietor of largest gambling establishment in Village. Complete equipment of cards, dice, roulette, and other gambling devices. Big numbers man. Made one of principal bootleggers quit the numbers game. Tried horses until (1) objected. In primary election put up large street banner for district leader. Arrested several times, but never brought to trial. Knocked a policeman down stairs of his house once. Both were drunk. Policeman later apologized under fear of being dismissed.
5. Brother and partner of (4).
6. Suspected of having had something to do with a speakeasy shooting. Was missing for about a year after that event.
7. Cab-driver; pimp. Lived with one of local prostitutes. Arrested in a fight between cabbies and college boys. Released at once. Allowed in station house to pummel one of the boys.

There was no evidence of any change in the relations between politics and the underworld during these years, except for the special situation brought by the liquor traffic, or in the community attitude toward this relation.

The jobs-and-favors political system was more strongly entrenched in 1930 than it had been in 1920 and it had become interwoven with all aspects of the community's life. While other institutions of the locality — with the exception of the health agencies — had to struggle to hold their own, the political clubs grew and their power was extended in several directions. The hopes of reformers that the Tammany system might be on the wane were flatly contradicted by the evidence of this district. Tammany captured new territory, it assimilated a new group of voters — the women — its methods penetrated the rival party organization, that of the Republicans, and its principles became part of the culture of the Italian-American group.

In the section newly built up with apartments, the former home-owning, civic-minded Republicans were supplanted by mobile apartment dwellers who had little or no political interest and were, on the whole, content to leave political activity to the Irish Tammany element. Though the apartment-house population came out to vote in presidential years, it had little interest in those local contests with which the politicians were chiefly concerned. Whereas in the Irish part of the Village, registration for the purely local elections of 1923 and 1927 was 80 per cent of that for the presidential years 1924 and 1928, in the apartment section it was only 71 per cent as great. Moreover, by the fortuitous combination of a natural swing toward the national and state Democratic candidates on the part of the liberal elements, and the equally fortuitous presence of a large proportion of traditionally Democratic Southerners among the Villagers, Democratic power in the district was reinforced more or less accidentally.

With the extension of suffrage to women, a new element in the population was brought within the orbit of the political system. Although registered women voters in the Tammany-controlled Irish districts were much less numerous than the men, they had increased proportionately. Their number was approximately 43 per cent of the number of men in 1920 and approximately 63 per cent in 1930. Not only were the women voting but they were seeking favors and jobs and working the clubs in the same manner as the men. One leader observed that 'women are becoming more

and more interested in joining the club because they are beginning to realize it is necessary if they want to get anything done for
them in the way of favors.'

But though the women had become a part of the club system as
far as the circle of jobs, favors, and votes was concerned, they had
not, by 1930, become a fully integral part of the club's membership; they did not take part in the inner councils and share in
planning the major strategy; the men were clear that 'this is,
after all, a man's club. The women are members of the district
Tammany organization rather than of the club itself'; and one of
the oldest and most prominent women leaders could point proudly
to how 'good' the leader was to the women — 'he *invites* us in on
all the meetings.' At the same time, there were women co-leaders
in each district, women election captains for most of the election
precincts, and women's committees paralleling those of the men
even where, in such cases as the law committees, they occupied
only an ornamental position. While it was the men who used the
clubhouse as a place to hang around, it was the women who
organized and engineered its principal social affairs. Such
part of the system as they were privileged to share, they
accepted without question and without in any way modifying
its form.

The Republican organization of the district was reduced during
these years to little more than an adjunct to Tammany. As the old
type of home-owning Republican who scorned Tammany and the
system which it represented moved to the suburbs, taking his Re-
publicanism with him, a weakened Republican organization was
left on Manhattan. At the same time a new factor entered the
situation, the Prohibition Amendment. By the coincidence of the
accession of the Republicans to power in Washington simultaneously with the enactment of the Eighteenth Amendment, the
administration of this law became a Republican function and continued so throughout the decade as the Republican Party remained in control of the federal machine. The Volstead Act gave a
new lease of life to Republican activity in the city, for of all the
laws on the statute books there was none which the people of the
city, and most especially the people of this district, were more
eager to have set aside. The control of federal favors also made it
possible for the Republicans to adjust the income taxes of their

friends — and enemies — as the Democrats could the locally assessed property taxes.

An examination of the local Republican clubs in 1930 showed the source of their support. In the former, old-style Republican stronghold, a Republican club, organized during the decade, numbered in 1930 some 75 members who had paid their dues and more than double that number enrolled. Though less than one sixth as large as the Democratic club in the same district, this club had, nevertheless, grown. The program of the annual dinner and ball — the chief general way by which the clubs raised money for support — contained a revealing list of contributors of 'advertising space.' In the club's large program book fifteen per cent of the space was taken by persons identified as proprietors of speakeasies or of other business known to sell liquor; twenty-two per cent by what appeared to be speakeasies but could not be verified; eighteen per cent by bail-bondsmen or lawyers having some connection with the administration of the federal courts, and ten per cent by various types of politicians. Of the remaining thirty-five per cent of the space, half appeared to be taken by legitimate business men, while the rest may well have included among the unidentified names, individuals falling into the first categories. The annual book of the other much larger Republican club in the area showed a similar array, sixteen per cent of the space supplied by known speakeasies and twenty-nine per cent by what appeared to be bootleggers. The indications were strong that the existence and operation of these Republican organizations were bound up with the enforcement of the Eighteenth Amendment.

As independent organizations or as rivals to the Democratic machine, the Republican political clubs had no standing in the locality. As appendages to the Democratic organizations, following the same system, and resting their strength largely on their ability to set aside Prohibition enforcement, these clubs grew during the decade. This was especially true of the Republican club which contained Italians from the solidly Italian district.

This club was Republican in scarcely anything but name; located almost next door to the Democratic club it played hand in hand with this organization. As a prominent member of the Democratic club put it, 'We are like one big family.' On the occasion of a death in the family of the Republican leader, the members of the Democratic club stated that 'we had a funeral the other day.' The Republican leader's version was, 'We are enemies of the Democratic club from six to six on election day only. For the other 364 days in the year we are the best of friends.' The voting figures and the statements of members of both clubs belied the assertion that, even on election day, the two clubs were on any but the best of terms. Each did favors for the other, sending applicants 'down the street.' The Republican leader had, on occasion, attempted to dissuade the Republican committee from running a rival candidate against the local Democrat. The clubs exchanged courtesies by taking pages in each other's program books. As a sign of the close relationship between the two, a leading Italian Democrat printed the same full-page picture of himself in both Democratic and Republican program books, in the section of the book devoted to officers and principal members in each case. A standard local joke made a Republican leader, asked by his own party members to resign, say to them, 'Sorry, boys, it can't be done. I'd like to resign, but the Democratic boss won't let me.' Out of this excellent team work there had thus been built a common Republican and Democratic system, each organization making accessible to the other those favors and those jobs which it controlled and both using identical political methods.

The process by which the Italians learned the business of politics and were brought within the Tammany fold represented an even more vital extension of Tammany methods and control. While direct efforts at Americanization sought to teach the Italians the principles of democratic government, the activity of the local political leaders and the example of their Irish neighbors instructed them in the practice of politics. The former efforts at instruction had, at best, meager results; the latter example they quickly learned to follow, and with increasing vigor they put into practice the methods which they learned.

By 1930, the Italians generally accepted the assumption that politics was a form of business. One storekeeper, who paid protection to gangsters, stated that he preferred to pay gangsters rather than to pay the police because the former were more efficient as protectors. Upon further inquiry it turned out that he assumed that the police had to be paid as a matter of course — not as a matter of graft. A prominent Italian, singing the praises of the local political leader, could say nothing more laudatory than 'He is as good as gold. He never promises a favor unless he can grant it.' In discussing his efforts to get together an incipient political club, an Italian young man aptly summed up the young Italians' attitude toward politics — as well as toward all other activity in the locality — 'When they saw that it was for themselves, they joined right away and didn't mind the high fee a bit.'

Before 1920, the local Irish politicians were apparently already concerned with the political part which the Italians might play. In the redistricting of 1917, they had seized the opportunity to carve out from their old district the body of Italians who had been invading it in increasing numbers for twenty years. The neighboring East Side district was already solidly Italian, and though leadership still rested in Irish hands, it was plain that the Italian element would ultimately dominate there. As early as 1915, the Democratic organization had put up an Italian assemblyman from that district. Rather than risk the loss to the Italians of the lower West Side district, or the necessity of granting them too much in order to keep them satisfied, the controlling group drew a new boundary through the West Side in an irregular line which roughly coincided with the boundary between Irish and Italian settlements. In spite of the fact that a strip of industrial blocks separated West Side from East Side, the West Side Italians were annexed to the East Side Italian district instead of to the West Side Irish district to which they were in close physical proximity. By throwing the West Side Italians to the East Side in this fashion, the two strong Lower West Side Irish districts were 'saved' to Irish Tammany control.

This put the West Side Italians in an awkward position. Their numbers were comparatively small in relation to the total of the new district to which they were added and they could hope for little attention, since the substantial East Side element could make so much stronger demands. Some of their members had already become enrolled in the West Side Democratic organization and a Republican organization under Italian leadership had been formed on the West Side. To withdraw from these organizations and enter the East Side club was to exchange a position which was beginning to show signs of possible advantage for one of clear inferiority. The political organization of the local Italians was thus confused by a complicating geographical situation.

The first of the local Italians to enter the field of politics had been the oldest of the second generation Italian residents, sons of the original Italian settlers who arrived in the 1880's and 1890's. These were the ones who grew up in the community when it was still a neighborhood and who had had contact in their youth with their Irish neighbors. More recently some of the younger Italians — especially those entering the legal profession — were attracted to the political organizations, and the many Italians who acquired real estate became interested in political contacts in order to secure lower taxes and other advantages to property-holders which the clubs were in a position to render. Except for those of the first generation whose personal interest called for political protection or favor, it was the second generation which showed most interest in American politics, while their fathers remained preoccupied with Italian national affairs.

Various conditions favored the entrance of the Italians into politics during these years. A larger proportion of the Italian community was in a position to take part in politics, for more of the foreign-born of voting age were naturalized in 1930 than in 1920, and the American-born adults of Italian extraction formed an increasingly large proportion of the Italian population. The increase of city jobs attracted the Italians, especially the younger members, just as it did the younger Irish, and the example of Irish neighbors with positions in City Hall proved a political stimulus to the Italians. The extension of the illicit liquor industry through the community made political protection vastly more necessary. Finally, with their lengthened stay in America and with the experience of the prejudices and difficulties which they encountered, the desire to improve their status as Italians grew. Although this desire produced little formal group organization, it made for solidarity and activity in the political field more than in any other, because advantages so clearly went to those in favor, and politics was one of the few areas in which numbers rather than wealth or prestige counted.

Most important of all to the ambitious Italian of this neighborhood, however, was the attractiveness of political activity as a potential road to wealth. The bootlegger knew that the politician was getting his rake-off from the liquor traffic without the risks which attended the bootlegger or speakeasy-keeper himself. The person engaged in an ordinary trade or occupation saw the impossibility of making earnings which in any way compared with those which came either to the politicians or to the promoters of illegitimate business. To the economically ambitious — and these would include virtually all of the Italians — politics thus offered an extremely attractive field for activity.

The Italians eager to engage in the business of politics had the choice of three courses. They could penetrate the existing Democratic clubs, gaining through the force of their numbers an influence and a share of the spoils; they could organize Republican clubs through which they could secure such advantages as were at the disposal of the Republican organization and such bargains as they, as Republicans, could strike with the stronger Democratic machine; or, thirdly, they could organize separate Italian clubs either Republican or Democratic, and could strike political bargains with the existing organizations. All three of these courses were followed in this community.

In the district whose principal membership was on the East Side, the Italians captured the Democratic leadership in 1930. The Irish leader of the district was accused of giving jobs to Irish applicants when his district was almost wholly Italian, was deserted by his followers in favor of an Italian rival, and found himself ousted not only from the party leadership of the district, but from the lucrative posts which he and his family held in City Hall. In the purely West Side district which had been freed from the bulk of its Italian population by the redistricting of 1917, many joined the Democratic club. By 1930, they constituted more than one third of the club's enrolled membership, but furnished only ten per cent of the active nucleus. Although this active ten per cent included two judges, there were those among the ambitious Italians in this section who felt that the Democratic club was not the most direct road to political advancement. Some, consequently, found their way into the Republican organization.

The Italian Republican club occupied a peculiar status, not only in being virtually a protégé of the Democratic organization, but in drawing its membership from two assembly districts instead of being the club of a single district. The reason for the anomalous position of this club appeared to have been bound up with the question of Irish leadership in the adjacent Italian district. For many years it had been known that sooner or later the Irish leader would lose the district. That he held his position until 1930 may, perhaps, be traceable to the activities of the West Side Irish Democratic leader in encouraging the enrollment of politically active Italians from both districts in a Republican organization. By drawing them into a Republican club which he could control, he helped to keep them from swamping the Irishman's club and depriving him of his leadership.

More characteristic of Italian political tactics than either the penetration of the Democratic clubs or the growth of the Republican organizations was the setting-up of independent clubs, usually ostensibly social, under the leadership of a man with political ambitions. The leader of such a club would gather a body of voters around him and then talk business with the regular organization — striking as good a bargain as he could drive and demanding as good a job as the votes at his disposal could purchase. These clubs were highly unstable organizations, depending almost entirely upon their leader, who used them for his own ends. If the leader was successful in securing the job that he wanted, he was likely to drop the club, since he had no further need of it. If he was not successful, his followers were likely to fall away.

An independent Italian club in the western part of the strongly Italian district had such a history. Formed because the Italians could get nothing from the Irish leader, it accumulated in less than a year some five hundred members, all but twelve of whom were Italians, mostly of American birth. The leader of this club insisted that his efforts and not those of the Italian East Side leader threw out the Irishman on the East Side, but for all his efforts he got from the victorious Italian neither jobs for himself and his followers nor favors. 'That's the way they always cut your throats. We are very important when they want us behind them, but when they don't need us we are not good enough for them.' This club was forced to close its doors for lack of funds, but its leader, embittered but not discouraged, declared that as soon as he could get money again he would be back in the game to challenge the East Side Italian's monopoly and to get favors and jobs for himself and his West Side group. This club frankly acknowledged its political character.

Another, likewise a single-leader club, tried to claim a purely social character, but its leader readily complained that at the regular Democratic club 'Italians can't get favors. If we can go up to the Democratic boss together, we may be able to get favors sooner. We are not trying to go over anybody's head. All we aim to do is to get favors and city jobs from the regular organization by standing together. You always get kicked down if you try to go over the leader's head.' This Association attempted to induce the leading Italian member of the regular Irish Democratic club to become its sponsor, but he refused to be allied with such an organization of 'ambitious little people.'

The most flourishing independent Italian club in 1930 was the Italian business men's society, whose membership gave it a prestige that the other independent organizations lacked. Since it was not openly political, however, it was not possible to discover what tactics it employed, outside of supporting Italian candidates, to accomplish its aim — according to its secretary, 'to remove the inhibitions against the Italians.'

As all the independent Italian organizations in this district were a rather new development, their capacity to survive and their strength had not been demonstrated by 1930. Their significance lay in the fact that they represented a political method that was coming into widespread use. Up to 1930, it had been principally employed by the older element among the second generation Italians, but there were a few signs that the younger members were beginning to devise similar tactics. One of the independent political associations had maintained a junior branch in the form of a Boys' Association which won considerable note and notoriety as punchball champions. Although the independent social clubs of young people in their early twenties were essentially nonpolitical, the politicians encouraged them with conspicuous advertisements in their program books.

A striking reflection of the way the political game looked to the younger generation came from one of the ablest young local Italians who, though not yet of voting age, had already gathered a small group of his contemporaries into a club. There was no mystery about his intent. 'Am I politically ambitious? I hope to

CHART IX

DEMOCRATIC REGISTRATION*

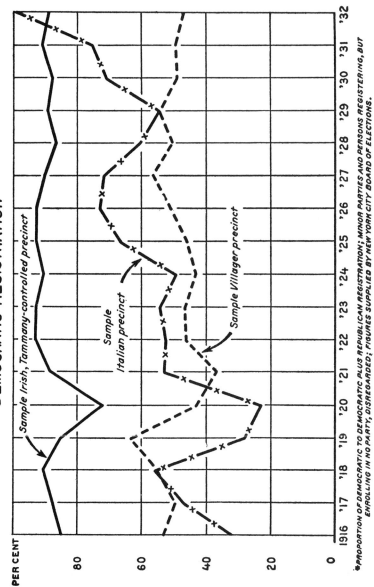

PER CENT

Sample Irish, Tammany-controlled precinct

Sample
Italian precinct

Sample Villager precinct

*PROPORTION OF DEMOCRATIC TO DEMOCRATIC PLUS REPUBLICAN REGISTRATION; MINOR PARTIES AND PERSONS REGISTERING, BUT
ENROLLING IN NO PARTY, DISREGARDED; FIGURES SUPPLIED BY NEW YORK CITY BOARD OF ELECTIONS.

tell the world!' He regarded himself as the champion of the younger generation against the older politicians in control — 'They will have to listen to us because we are the youth and they depend on us to carry on.' He was convinced that the road to power did not lie in joining the regular club where everything went to the old crowd — 'We'll never get anything there until we are gray-haired' — but in getting into a position to bargain with the club. As between numbers and money he concluded that the latter gave a stronger bargaining position, so he set his club dues at twice the amount of the dues of any other local club and built up a carefully selected membership from among the property-owning families of the neighborhood. As his version of the best road to the judgeship toward which he aspired, this venture in political organization was a revealing indication of separatist tactics in the hands of the younger generation.

Whichever road the Italians chose, they took on the technique, the assumptions, and the manner of the Tammany Irish until they became indistinguishable from them. They knew just what they wanted from politics and were frank in their statement, 'We want the judgeships and commissionerships *and what goes with them.*' They completely accepted politics as a form of business activity and learned to regard it wholly in terms of self-advancement.

They learned, too, the function of the party, the lesson of party loyalty, and the essential wisdom of casting in their lot with the group in control.

In 1920, the party complexion of the Italian element was not firmly established and party regularity had clearly not become one of the group's political assumptions. Between 1916 and 1921, party enrollment in the Italian district had fluctuated widely. From thirty per cent Democratic in 1920, it jumped to fifty-one per cent Democratic in 1921. In a representative election precinct the proportion of registered voters enrolled in the Democratic column varied quite irregularly from year to year.[1] Voting was even more irregular. From 1916 to 1924, the proportion of voters in this precinct who failed to vote a straight ticket but split their ballots ranged from seven per cent to fifty-one per cent and averaged twenty-seven per cent.[2] In the same years, the average proportion of split ballots in a representative Irish precinct was eight

[1] Cf. Chart V, p. 284.   [2] Cf. Charts VI, VII, p. 286.

per cent. Each time that there were Italian candidates on both tickets, in 1920, 1921, 1923, and 1924, the Italian precinct was carried on the same election day by an Italian Democrat and an Italian Republican. In the absence of an Italian on the ballot in 1922, the precinct voted overwhelmingly for the straight Democratic ticket, but in the next year the split developed again. In the second half of the decade the situation changed. Although Italians ran on opposite sides and always polled more votes than the rest of their tickets, the proportion of split votes in the same Italian precinct after 1925 never exceeded thirteen per cent and averaged eight per cent from 1926 to 1932.[1]

The net result of these years of political experience was to establish firmly the habit of voting for a ticket rather than for a series of individuals. And more and more that ticket was Democratic. Democratic registration mounted steadily. In 1925, 1926, 1927, and 1928, the whole ticket carried the sample Italian precinct by an increasing margin, the lowest candidates receiving sixty-nine per cent of the votes in 1928. But Italian loyalty survived to break out in no uncertain form when the Italian La Guardia ran for mayor on the Republican ticket in 1929. In this precinct the victory of La Guardia was overwhelming, in spite of the fact that fifty-five per cent of the precinct was registered as Democratic. More remarkable than his poll, however, was the fate of the rest of the ticket. For the first time since 1919, in a district which had become regularly Democratic and was so registered even in 1929, the entire Republican ticket received a majority of the votes. In the following year, the entire vote snapped back into the Democratic column. In the larger predominantly Italian section of the Village, La Guardia polled fifty-five per cent of the votes where Hoover had polled only twenty-seven per cent the year before. By 1929, Italian loyalty to a major Italian candidate was undiminished, but a vote could be reversed more easily than a ballot could be split. Thus had the local Italians learned to conduct themselves politically in these years of adaptation.

While the Italians were learning the political business and the Irish continued to regard it as one of the cornerstones of their social and economic organization, the Villagers were becoming more and more remote from political or governmental activity. Most of the

[1] Cf. Chart VI.

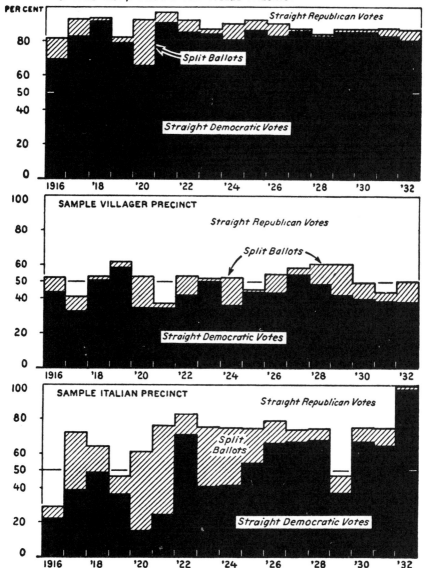

CHART-VI

PARTY REGULARITY NUMBER I

PROPORTION OF STRAIGHT DEMOCRATIC, STRAIGHT REPUBLICAN AND SPLIT BALLOTS,*1916-1932△

SAMPLE IRISH,TAMMANY-CONTROLLED PRECINCT

PER CENT

Straight Republican Votes

Split Ballots

Straight Democratic Votes

80

60
50
40

20

0

1916   '18   '20   '22   '24   '26   '28   '30   '32

SAMPLE VILLAGER PRECINCT

Straight Republican Votes

Split Ballots

Straight Democratic Votes

100

80

60
50
40

20

0

1916   '18   '20   '22   '24   '26   '28   '30   '32

SAMPLE ITALIAN PRECINCT

Straight Republican Votes

Split Ballots

Straight Democratic Votes

100

80

60
50
40

20

0

1916   '18   '20   '22   '24   '26   '28   '30   '32

*DIFFERENCE BETWEEN PER CENT OF VOTE RECEIVED BY PERSON ON TICKET RECEIVING GREATEST AND ONE RECEIVING SMALLEST PROPORTION OF VOTES.
△ VOTES PUBLISHED AFTER EACH ELECTION IN CITY RECORD; ADJUSTMENTS MADE FOR CHANGES IN BOUNDARIES OF PRECINCTS

CHART—VII

PARTY REGULARITY NUMBER 2

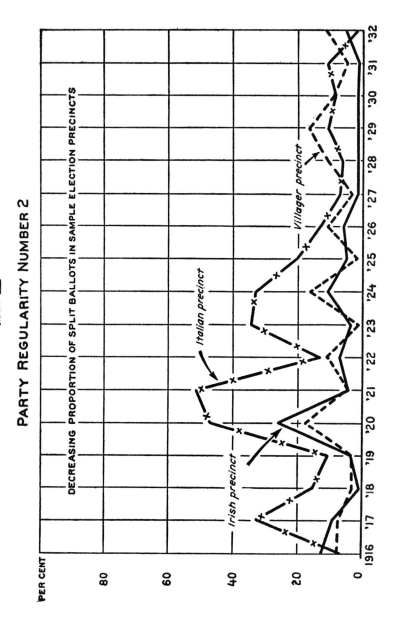

DECREASING PROPORTION OF SPLIT BALLOTS IN SAMPLE ELECTION PRECINCTS

Villager precinct

Italian precinct

Irish precinct

PER CENT

80

60

40

20

0

1916 '17 '18 '19 '20 '21 '22 '23 '24 '25 '26 '27 '28 '29 '30 '31 '32

Villagers were unaware of local political activity or were cynically aware of it but did not participate in it, while a few were in active protest against it. There was a remnant of those to whom political activity was a civic duty and who conscientiously cast their annual vote with the idea that they were performing the function for which the vote was ostensibly introduced. But almost the only active political interest among the Villagers in these years was to be found in the Socialist Party.

On occasions this group was capable of appearing in fairly strong force. The vote for La Follette in the 1924 campaign amounted to fourteen per cent of the votes cast in the assembly district occupied by the Villagers, while Norman Thomas, the Socialist candidate for mayor in 1929, polled fifteen per cent of the vote. These Socialist votes, however, exaggerated the amount of consistent party interest, for the Socialist enrollment in this same district never exceeded three and a half per cent of the total enrollment in all parties, and the Socialist vote in other years fluctuated between one and a half and six per cent. On the other hand, the body of inactive Socialist sentiment was probably even in excess of the maximum votes cast, for it included those who were opposed to the existing political and economic system, but were too cynical or too lazy to register a protest vote against it at the polls.

Among a few of the local politicians there was an impression, not borne out by registration and voting data, that the Villagers were all Socialists and constituted a menace to the political hold of the regular organization. But most of the leaders looked with scorn or indifference upon the Socialist element, concluding that if they took care of the regular vote they could be sure that enough Villagers would stay away from the polls to leave their hold secure. They were not even seriously concerned over the annual efforts of the Socialists to prevent the voting of floaters from the usual hotel and boarding-house addresses, and they relied on their own strong-arm methods to prevent any undue interference with multiple voting or the other practices on which they relied to pile up their comfortable majorities. They had no fear, moreover, that the Socialist Party would begin to draw its members from the ranks of the local people. Even in the face of depression the Socialist local in the Village continued to have an almost exclusively 'white-collar' membership. An occasional Jewish peddler who had come over from the East Side might have been a Socialist there, but was likely to conclude that his peddler's license was better protected if he remained safely Democratic here.

Their respective political attitudes thus left Villagers and local people poles asunder. It was inconceivable to most Villagers that the political system could be taken for granted by their neighbors. Most of the local people were equally uncomprehending of either the civic or the revolutionary attitudes of the Villagers. Only indifference was recognized by both.

Yet for all the preoccupation with the business of politics on the part of the local people and the indifference of the Villagers, the community got governed more or less effectively, not through direct action on a local basis, but as part of the whole metropolitan community. A great and increasing number of things which were done in this community were done by properly constituted public authorities in the performance of their public duties. The increase in governmental activity, here as elsewhere, was chiefly along lines of public programs for social welfare — the taking over by public authorities of functions formerly assumed to be either unimportant or properly the sphere of the individual. In addition to teaching the three R's, the schools became what amounted to welfare agencies. In addition to maintaining peace and order, the police department established a Crime Prevention Bureau manned by social workers to undertake a constructive program.

But while governmental activity was extended, the economic and political philosophy current in the community retained the assumptions of individual rather than social responsibility. The newer governmental services were at variance with the underlying social philosophy which presumed that they should not exist, and in 1930 these services were still not taken for granted, but had some of the elements of privileges or favors. The effect of the new activities was thus to augment the power of the political clubs by increasing the range of grantable favors and services. The political leaders were called upon to assist people in getting compensation, pensions, or relief to which the applicants were technically entitled by right.

The community, moreover, acquired a considerable volume of

service from the political clubs themselves. Tammany has been described as the greatest social work institution in New York City and the city's principal employment agency. The clubs of this district amply fulfilled this description. Several times during each week the leader or one of the principal members of the club 'saw people' — sometimes to the number of fifty or more in an evening. The number of those seeking aid from the club varied from year to year in accordance with the needs of the times. In 1930, the depression was beginning to send swarms of people to the club, just as it was crowding other social welfare agencies. The line waiting at the club to see the leader often extended down onto the sidewalk, and people waited two hours or more while those ahead were taken care of.

No possible measure of the volume of community service performed by the clubs was available, for no record was ever kept. A list of the types of service was all that any club leader could ever produce. Principal among the services were those of job-finding — not only in public but in private employment as well; but in addition the leaders dispensed actual money for rent and supplies. Each club had a legal committee made up of the club members who were lawyers and who constituted a legal-aid service for those who applied. Since a vote was a vote whether cast by a club member or not, the clubs' services were not confined to members, although members received preferential treatment. From one club, two or three hundred children were annually sent to the country in summer. All these services were rendered in the manner in which they had always been rendered — with the utmost familiarity and informality. There was no co-operation with welfare and other agencies offering similar services. Up to 1930 the community agencies had never been able to find out which children the political leader had sent to the country in order to avoid duplication with their list of children sent out on vacation.

The leaders prided themselves on knowing their districts, knowing their people, and being sure who was worthy and who was not. They scorned the formality and red tape of the properly constituted welfare agencies. The price of a few who got help from the club even though they were not politically worthy was a cheap price to pay for the good will which came from a direct, sympathetic response. In fact, it was of the essence of the services that these clubs rendered that they should be rendered personally. Much of the politician's strength lay in the fact that while other social relationships were becoming increasingly complex and impersonal, he continued to cut through the web of a system, across regularly established lines, and bridge social distances with a face-to-face personal contact.

Quite naturally, the community was full of complaints of the way in which it was served politically, but criticism was always directed against the failure to secure jobs and favors rather than the failure to carry out the direct forms of governmental activity. Among those who belonged in the district dominated by the East Side, the complaint was, 'The West Side cannot get anything — everything goes to the East Side.' In the solidly Irish Tammany districts it was, 'These districts are too easy for Tammany to keep. It doesn't bother to take care of the West Side.' The Italians complained, 'All the favors go to the Irish.' The young people declared, 'Everything at the club goes to the older people.' And from a wide assortment of individuals came the complaint, 'You can't get anything from the club unless you know somebody there.' In a system built upon favors, everyone, of course, looked for those favors to come in his direction, while the clubs, presumably, did no more than was necessary to keep their followers in line.

Yet in a real sense the political clubs served the community better and more to the community's satisfaction than did the regular welfare agencies because the political club was trusted and respected where the welfare agency often was not. The basis upon which the political club functioned was perfectly clear and easily comprehended. The politicians were in it for what they got out of it; what they could get out of it depended on what they could give; on this basis they gave. Their aid was, therefore, sought and accepted without hesitation — except the hesitation which arose from doubt that they would be able or willing to give the aid requested. But because the idea of community service was completely foreign to most of the people of the neighborhood and because their experience gave them no reasonable explanation of the presence of social agencies, they frequently suspected the social workers of ulterior motives. In these cases, the latter's services were less readily accepted than those of the political clubs whose ulterior motives were well known and fully acknowledged.

The political organizations thus performed a very definite function in this community. To be sure, they hindered rather than advanced the ordinary governmental processes. They did little to make the community a civic whole. In the long run, they exploited those whom they appeared to serve, for the cost of their maintenance fell on the taxpayers who were chiefly the landowners and who passed the burden on to the people in the form of high rents. They not only allowed the predatory elements in the community to survive but assisted them.

But they were, withal, a product of the inequalities and hardships in the life of this sample American urban community, and they gained much of their vitality by mitigating the lot of those born or thrown by circumstances into the small end of the economic and social scale. For those whose position was, for some reason or other, unenviable, they secured some measure of the benefits which regularly constituted society had denied to them. They offered, moreover, the one type of collective action which the community understood. They provided, for people who did not have the habit or the foresight for co-operation, a mutual relationship which was only one step removed from unco-operative individualism, but which carried with it some of the benefits of co-operation. The political institutions were the major social institutions best able to survive and to grow, because they knew how to capitalize self-interest.

X. RELIGION

OF ALL the institutions operating in the area, none has suffered more from the disintegration of traditional American culture than have the Protestant churches. From standing at the very center of the old American community, these churches have been reduced to the merest remnants of their former selves, serving, at the highest estimate, some five per cent of the population and actually vital to a very much smaller proportion. The loss in position which these churches experienced antedated the period of this study and by 1920 they were already feeble. Their development during the post-War years represented a variety of efforts to discover some means of survival in a community to which they were no longer directly relevant.

By contrast, the Catholic churches were among the strongest institutions of the locality, comprising among their members the great mass of the population and influencing their way of life. With the exception of the remnant of 'Ninth Warders,' some Germans, and, of course, the Jews, the local people were nearly all members of the Catholic Church. The few Catholic individuals among the Villagers were numerically insignificant and did not participate in the social life of the local churches. Again the division among institutions coincided with the major social divisions in the community.

During these years, religion, especially in the Protestant faiths, was on the defensive against the attacks, or supposed attacks, of science. Although conflict between science and religion did not become a direct issue in this community, it was an underlying basis for the churchlessness of the Villagers and it made the churches less central to the life of the community than they had been a generation before.

Between the Catholic and Protestant institutions of the community there was the usual measure of distrust. Tradition, at least, had it that in the old days of the friendly neighborhood Protestant and Catholic groups had associated on free and friendly terms, even attending the social affairs at each other's churches. This mutual relationship disappeared with the change in the population of the community and the personnel of the clergy, and with the extension of the activity of Protestant missions. The Protestant organizations regarded the Catholic as unco-operative, while the Catholics looked upon the Protestants as intruders and menaces. Neither thought that the other quite played the game. The Protestants complained that though the priests let their children attend Protestant centers, they saw to it that they were confirmed in the Catholic Church. The Catholic priest's retort to an offer of co-operation from the minister in charge of a mission was quite final — 'The only way you can co-operate is to close your doors.'

Much of the conflict grew out of the essentially different character of the Catholic and Protestant churches which made each unaware of the basic assumptions of the other. The minister of the mission went to the priest in good faith, assuming that any church was simply a social organization, erected to assist in the carrying on of religious functions, but unnecessary, in the last analysis, to the religious experience of the individual whose salvation rested in his own hands. The priest replied on the assumption that the Church was identical with the religious experience of the individual, that the sacraments which it administered were the key to salvation, that it was universal and divine, and that to leave the Church was to repudiate God, heaven, and the whole spiritual realm. There was little evidence that either side recognized the essential difference between an institution identified with God himself, and one which acknowledged itself to be merely God's self-appointed lieutenant, organized for the better service of God, but not essential to that service.

1. PROTESTANT EFFORTS AT SURVIVAL

The Protestant churches were a carry-over from an earlier time. They antedated the break-up of the old, middle-class residential community of small brick houses filled with artisans, shopkeepers, and professional men. They were family churches with all that the term implied. Some were born *in situ*, others had already experienced community changes before they were established in this locality and had entered Greenwich Village in order to follow their parishioners from communities farther to the south. None had been distinctly a poor man's church in origin or in any but a missionary sense thereafter.

There were eight Protestant churches located within the bounds of the Village. In the immediate vicinity, but not within the exact limits, were seven others, two of the mission type and two in the fashionable Fifth Avenue section. In addition, the local church buildings were used by several non-local groups, such as the Waldensians and the Latvian Baptists, which were too small and scattered to maintain churches of their own and which found the location of the Village churches convenient. The youngest of the Protestant churches in the immediate locality celebrated its seventy-fifth anniversary in 1930. Three had passed the hundred mark by that date. All had had continuous histories as parishes within the locality since the time of their founding. In contrast to other communities where the history of population shift is often revealed in changed ownership or occupancy of church buildings, these churches were, with the exception of one which had changed hands in 1855, in the hands of their original congregations. Four owed their survival to amalgamation with other congregations.

Denominationally, the Protestant churches within the locality included two Episcopal, two Presbyterian, two Baptist, one Methodist, and one Lutheran. Of the adjacent churches one was Episcopal, two Presbyterian, one Methodist, one Reformed, one Christian Science, and one non-sectarian. Differences among the churches did not rest upon difference in denomination. With the exception of the Christian Science church, all denominations had been represented locally since the early or middle of the nineteenth century. Membership had not fallen much more or less rapidly in the churches of one denomination than in those of another, except that the Episcopal churches showed a somewhat smaller decline than others.

Socially no denomination held a position superior to any other, though the Episcopal and Presbyterian denominations were the ones represented by churches in the more fashionable area of lower Fifth Avenue. Their activities were similar, except that the

Episcopal group was not engaged directly in missionary activity within the locality. By reason of their essential similarity, therefore, denominational lines can be disregarded and these Protestant churches can be treated as a group.

Prior to 1920, community changes had reduced the Protestant churches to a minor position, as the Catholic immigrant populations had supplanted the old Americans from whom their congregations were drawn. Already before 1900 the impact of the Catholic element had been felt. Thereafter membership in the Protestant churches declined. Consolidation of two parishes outside of the Village with two of the Village churches around 1910 brought in as many new members as had been lost by the Village churches in the first decade of the century, but there was a substantial falling-off in total membership during the War. In 1929, the combined membership of the eight Protestant churches was fifty-eight per cent of what it had been in 1900. Sunday School membership had suffered very much more severely. In 1929, it was only twenty-nine per cent of what it had been in 1900. From 1920 to 1930, it had declined forty-five per cent.

Percentage Change in Membership in Protestant Churches

	Adult Membership	Sunday School Enrollment
1900–1910	+ 3 per cent	− 30 per cent
1910–1920	− 15	− 25
1920–1930	− 34	− 45

For the Protestant churches, the post-War decade may thus be regarded as one in which these institutions, already having lost much of their original function and membership, were subjected to the increased effects of the forces in the community which had caused their earlier decline and to the influences at large in the religious field. Weakened by the break-up of the culture of which they were a part no less than by the loss of members by migration, their problem in these years was largely the problem of justifying a continued existence and making adaptations in the interests of survival.

At the close of the decade, one church merged with another. In two churches, attendance at ordinary Sunday morning services in 1930 was less than twenty-five. One church burned and was rebuilt locally in spite of the fact that only half of the total church membership of four hundred lived in the locality, attendance at Sunday services in the secular building where they were held during the construction of the church numbered a mere handful, and mid-week prayer meeting was conducted for a half-dozen elderly ladies. Not all the Protestant churches had fallen to so low a point of attendance and membership by 1930. No one, however, boasted a membership list of over six hundred and fifty in 1920 and in 1930 of over five hundred.[1] The largest congregation observed at Sunday worship in any of these churches was one hundred. At most of the services observed in 1930 there were less than fifty. One church after another had at some time contemplated closing its doors; none was supported by current collections from its own membership.

The pressing problem in all the Protestant churches was their decline in membership. Although their collective loss of one third in total church membership was no greater in proportion than the decrease in the total population, it represented a sharp decline relative to the local Protestant group, for the population loss was primarily in the Catholic sections and the newcomers moving into the district had come from Protestant background. A very large proportion of the membership of these Protestant churches, moreover, was non-resident, retaining its membership and attending services irregularly after moving uptown, to Brooklyn, the Bronx, or New Jersey. In six out of the eight churches, the ministers' estimates of the proportion of their membership living outside the Village in 1930 ranged from fifty per cent in three churches, and sixty-five per cent in another, to 'nearly all' in the case of two more. Only two Protestant ministers reported that a majority of their congregations resided locally. Most of the ministers, however, were optimistic about the future of their church membership, pointing hopefully to slight additions in 1929 and 1930 and insisting that the bottom of the decline had been reached and passed. Though they shook their heads over the 'godlessness' of the apartment-house population, they still regarded the indifferent Protestantism of the latter as more favorable to church mem-

[1] Cf. Douglass, H. P. *One Thousand City Churches*, New York, 1926, pp. 327, 365. This study showed church membership to be under 500 in 55.5 per cent of all the city churches studied, but small membership characterized 83.5 per cent of the 'unadapted' churches and only 26.2 per cent of the 'socially adapted' churches. The average number of members per church in cities of over 100,000 was 327.

bership than the Catholicism of those who were being driven out.

With respect to their Sunday Schools, however, they could hardly be so sanguine. Sunday School membership in 1929 was only a little more than half what it had been in 1920. In the churches whose membership was largely non-local, the children of people who kept their connection with Village churches for old times' sake made their Sunday School connections, if any, in their new neighborhood. Such new church membership as came from Villagers was made up of unattached adults. Two churches in 1930 reported that almost their entire membership was made up of detached individuals rather than families, while others were increasingly assuming that aspect.

Yet, with the drop in membership and in attendance, the annual expenditures of each church rose during these years. The increase between 1920 and 1929 in the aggregate expenditures of the five churches whose figures could be compared was twenty per cent. The expenditure per enrolled church member in these five churches nearly doubled, from $34.70 in 1920 to $64 in 1929.[1] The proportion of the annual budget furnished by the contributions of the congregation amounted in 1929 to from seven per cent in the church with the largest budget to fifty per cent in the church with the smallest. Income from property owned by the churches or from endowments raised at earlier and more flourishing periods of the churches' history were, throughout this period, the chief source of support for local Protestant activity.

Several of the churches made efforts to stimulate attendance by adapting their Sunday programs or by resorting to advertising. Two churches instituted Sunday evening feature programs especially designed to interest the people of the locality. Lectures by distinguished speakers on such live subjects as 'Socialism,' 'Why Girls are Lost in New York,' or programs of Negro spirituals, were offered by these churches to attract the local intelligentsia or student group.

Attempts to stimulate attendance through advertising had negligible results. Several of the churches joined in putting on an extensive but admittedly ineffectual advertising campaign, using newspapers, posters, window cards, and bulletin boards. Individ-

[1] Table IX, Appendix F, p. 467; cf. Douglass, *op. cit.*, p. 206. Average expenditure per member in sample covered by Douglass study, $18.17.

ually they advertised their weekly services in the newspapers, one minister regularly publishing his notice in four papers. The ministers, however, did not consider newspaper advertising particularly effective. Two churches distributed handbills. One had, in 1930, a mailing list of four hundred for its weekly bulletins; another sent out mimeographed letters. Printed or mimeographed programs were distributed at the services. Sermons and other events were announced on large bulletin boards outside the church. One church hung out a large printed cloth sign to attract 'the man in the street.' But church attendance continued to fall and remained at so low a point as to make survival problematic.

The measures taken by each of these churches in their efforts to survive showed a wide variety of response to a common problem. The church which succeeded in retaining the largest membership, both of adults and children, pursued a policy of intensifying its work with its reduced membership. Amply supplied with funds by the parent church of which it was a chapel, under the leadership of a pastor who identified himself heart and soul with his congregation, this church made every effort to permeate the lives of its members. The minister kept in intimate touch with the children who attended church school twice a week; the older boys and girls were made to feel that the church was their home, some of the older boys even having keys to the parsonage; and the Sunday attendance at the various services amounted to more than a third of the nominally enrolled members of the parish, a very large proportion in view of the fact that nearly fifty per cent of the nominal membership was non-resident. In describing his parish in 1930, the minister reported that there had been little decline in the size of the active nucleus of church members, but that it had become increasingly hard to hold those who could not be reached by an intensive program.

The group which made up this congregation was one of the most stable in the community, a factor which facilitated the church's efforts. They were old Americans and second and third generation families of German, Scandinavian, and North Irish extraction, drawn from the lower middle income group, fairly homogeneous in background and tradition, and located in the part of the Village which had undergone the least physical change. Neighborly friendliness combined with a strong spiritual emphasis and moral influence could still hold the interests of both old and young in this group.

Two of the churches whose parishes were invaded by the Italians turned to a missionary program among their new neighbors. One, a well-to-do parish, financed this work from its own funds. The other merged with a fashionable Fifth Avenue parish and was administered as its chapel. As first organized, their Italian mission work took the form chiefly of a welfare program carried on from the churches by an English-speaking minister and his staff. One of these missions had just moved in 1920 into new quarters which would house its kindergarten, playground, gym, and clubs, and was preparing for an enlarged institutional program. Both these churches, and two others just outside the district, fundamentally altered their approach during the years under review, turning away from extensive institutional programs to intensive work with a limited and shrinking clientèle. The change came partly because they placed their Italian work in the hands of Italian ministers who, as recent converts to Protestantism, had a more evangelical and less institutional approach, and partly because they found that their extensive program was not actually bringing their traditionally Catholic neighbors within the Protestant fold. The ministers who took over the Italian work of these churches in 1929 found an Italian church membership of twenty-five in one and sixty-four in the other.

While these two churches were virtually forced by their location to meet community changes with missionary activity, a more favorably situated church attempted to draw to the neighborhood a type of respectable family that would make up part of a dignified congregation. In the midst of the real estate boom, the church undertook to remodel a group of adjacent houses, adding to the church income and hoping to add to the church congregation from the occupants of the apartments thus erected. If the reported figures of church memberships may be taken as a measure, this church was the most successful in the Protestant group, for instead of the steady decline in membership from 1920 to 1930 which characterized the group of churches as a whole, the low point in membership was reached by this church in 1923, with a fairly steady rise in the years which followed. The location of this church in the heart of the reconstructed section may have been principally responsible for its more solid position. Prior to the remodeling of the 1920's, its decline had been similar to that of the rest of the Protestant churches in the neighborhood.

Two other churches, one within the district and another in its outskirts, joined this church in the effort to secure a congregation of Villagers. These made direct appeals to the unattached young people that were coming in, both students in the near-by university and young business people. Both stressed their young people's service, each maintained a 'church house' where young people resided or congregated, and planned social and educational activities especially for that group. In the case of the large, metropolitan congregation outside of the district, a 1930 membership of two hundred in the young people's society, largely drawn from the neighborhood, testified to some success with this program. In the other church, efforts to bring in the floating, unattached Villagers were less successful, a large proportion of those who attended the young people's services belonging to old church families who had moved away. This church distributed publicity in the near-by apartment houses, but without bringing any but the most occasional addition to its congregation. It succeeded, however, in maintaining, after 1924, a constant or slightly increasing figure of official church membership. The principal officers and active members of the church, however, were scattered all over the city and did not represent a local membership.

The reaction of the other local Protestant churches was essentially a passive one. They went on with the same type of service, the same kind of sermons, the same church societies, primarily for spiritual and missionary interests, with a minimum of institutional activity and with little regard for changes in the neighborhood or in the times. One of these churches in particular maintained a traditionally evangelical program, continued to lend its support to foreign missions, and made no attempt to go outside of the remnant of its old constituency to reach any of the new inhabitants of the community. It also lost more and more of its already small membership during these years. Its decline was less spectacular than that of some of the other churches, but no less steady. As far as the evidence of the membership record goes — and it is a notoriously unsatisfactory measure because of the difference among churches in what they report as 'members' and the habit of having periodic check-ups of church lists with the wholesale dropping of names which should actually have been dropped gradually — there was little to indicate that the positive measures taken by some parishes to regain membership were appreciably more effective than the passive attitude of the latter churches.

While the local Protestant churches were struggling against un- favorable neighborhood conditions, they were also subjected to the influences which affected the Protestant churches at large. During the twentieth century, ideas as to the function which the Church should perform underwent important changes. To the old preoccupation with salvation was added in some quarters, and substituted in others, a definite social purpose. The modernist element rediscovered the Bible for its 'social gospel' — its direct social teaching and the social implications of the life of Christ. By 1920, this emphasis had become characteristic of one of the leading theological seminaries in New York which was supplying ministers and parish workers to several of the Village and neigh- boring churches. Under this influence, churches, especially in metropolitan centers and suburban communities, developed 'in- stitutional' programs — i.e., provided a great variety of social services similar to those of the secular welfare agencies. In some cases a church's social program was carried to the point not only of obscuring the church's traditional religious purpose, but of supplanting much of the customary religious activity, virtually transforming some churches into social welfare centers.

By their very existence, the churches of Greenwich Village had to react to the wave of institutional programs, if only to repudiate them passively. By 1920, four out of the eight churches within the locality and three of the seven near-by had undertaken a series of welfare activities. The two which were located in or near the Italian district had, in fact, been among the pioneer churches to introduce institutional features. As early as 1885, the pastor of one of these churches had insisted that his church should remain to minister to its new neighbors instead of following its prosperous congregation uptown. He conducted a nation-wide campaign to raise funds, started a wood yard to provide work for unemployed men, sponsored lodging houses for men, sent mothers and children to the country during the summer, constructed an ice-water fountain outside the church, instituted the first kindergarten in

New York, organized sewing classes, and supplied coal and milk at low cost to the poor families of the neighborhood. These initial activities of the 1880's were expanded during the following decade to include a children's home, a day nursery, and a dispensary. The other church had started as a mission Sunday School, was housing a kindergarten and a library and operating an ice-water fountain early in the twentieth century, and by 1910 had established a day nursery, a sewing school, and club activities. Three other churches in similar situations, one within and two to the south of the district, developed similar activities in the years before 1920, and at the close of the War the churches on lower Fifth Avenue adopted institutional programs.

During the post-War years, the 'social gospel' spent itself as a motivating force. In its place psychological interests and pre-occupation with the personal adjustment of the individual entered the Protestant churches just as they entered the field of education to produce the progressive education movement and the field of social work to stimulate the psychiatric approach. In 1920, the spokesmen of liberal Protestantism were pointing out that 'with the rise... of the conception that salvation is a matter of the here and now as well as of eternity and that the individual does not live his life in a social vacuum, but if saved at all must be saved in social relationships, more attention has been given to the teachings of the Bible as to social relationships.'[1] In 1929, the same group, while still considering it to be the major task of the Church to grapple with the bewildering and complicated problems of modern life, insisted that 'creative living must be the goal.... What are the issues and the problems particularly baffling to the individual in his struggle for adjustment with which the Church is capable of helping?'[2] With this shift in emphasis from social reform to individual development, the case work rather than the institutional approach found approval. Intensive, personal work with a strongly spiritual emphasis took the place of extensive social programs.

The local Protestant churches reflected that shift. The social

[1] Gillen, J. L. 'New Developments in Religious Education,' *Religious Education*, (1920), p. 103.
[2] Artman, J. M., and Jacobs, J. A. 'Basic Factors in Program-Making for a Local Church,' *ibid.* (1929), p. 955.

programs of those churches which had earlier and most strongly endorsed such programs were greatly weakened. Though the most institutional of these churches continued to operate its neighborhood house, though at three of the churches a series of men trained for institutional work by the most liberal of the theological schools in the city conducted energetic social programs for the Italian young people, children, and mothers, and also for the girls living in local residence clubs, this work was everywhere diminishing in volume, though not in cost. There were many ready explanations for the shift to a more strictly religious program. 'When anybody could just come in to use our facilities,' explained one minister, 'we could not exercise any personal influence over them. Now, no one may use our gym who does not come to Sunday School.' The church worker at another church complained that 'The Catholic children didn't respect our property. They were rowdy and destructive and interfered with our own children. So we had to cut them out.' 'They told me that you could not interest young people in religion in this sort of neighborhood,' proclaimed another worker triumphantly, 'but I have found that they come to that sort of meeting just as readily as to any other.'

The reaction of the mission churches paralleled that of other Protestant missions operating among immigrant populations. In membership the local ones had become smaller than the average of sixty to seventy estimated for all the Protestant home mission centers in 1930.[1] They had discovered that the number of members possibly available to them was strictly limited. The church worker who had been longest engaged in Protestant work among the Italians recognized the fact, which the latest student of home missions has brought out,[2] that a community in flux through constant immigration is more favorable to the activity of such church centers than is one which has acquired a more established social structure. According to this worker, it had become increasingly difficult to bring new members into the church or even to get them to take part in church activities because all the families of potential members had formed their institutional connections during their ten or twenty years in the community. They could not be pried away from the Catholic Church if their religious connections were

[1] Abel, T. *Protestant Home Missions to Catholic Immigrants.* New York, 1932, p. 35.
[2] *Ibid., passim.*

there nor attracted by institutional activities if they had become affiliated with one or another of the local settlements. The church and its workers had become known to the community, had lost the mystery of novelty, and could be discounted and ignored. Losses through families who left the neighborhood, therefore, became net losses to the church, since it was almost impossible to bring in new members. In these circumstances there was no choice but to concentrate on the few who remained from their earlier membership or to close the doors. In shifting the emphasis to their personal influence on the individuals under their charge, the ministers and church workers of the locality — not only in the missions but in other churches as well — were responding both to local conditions and to the trend in the liberal wing of the Protestant churches during these years.

2. IRISH CATHOLIC CONSERVATISM

The Catholic Church was faced with no such difficulties in retaining its membership or such doubts as to its proper function as were the Protestant churches. Secure in its long-time view, its divine character, and the superiority of the spiritual sphere to which it belonged over the temporal one in which lay issues were fought out, the Church retained its historical point of view and took the problems of this period and this community in its stride.

As in other aspects of community life, not only the major division between Villagers and local people but ethnic differences distinguished the churches. The group of three Irish Catholic churches, though distinct from each other, were fundamentally similar in their basic characteristics and in the adjustment which they made to the social changes in the post-War decade. Distinct from them were the two Italian churches, again differing between themselves but with common characteristics which distinguished them even more clearly from the Irish churches than from each other. And, finally, there were three small foreign-language churches, Lithuanian, Spanish, and French, on the borders of the district, drawing from the neighborhood and showing certain common dissimilarities to both Irish and Italian.

The several Catholic parishes had been organized as the

Catholic community had grown, the oldest in 1829, the most recent, the Lithuanian parish, established in 1909. In contrast to the Protestant churches whose memberships were less than five hundred and whose Sunday attendance was usually less than a hundred, the Irish and Italian Catholic parishes numbered several thousands each, with Sunday attendance at Mass in 1930 ranging from fifteen hundred to three thousand.

The local Catholic parishes varied very substantially within the latitude provided by the church organization, according to which each parish unit is self-supporting with respect to its own clergy, church fabric, school, and, largely, its poor, and each priest has very considerable autonomy. Of the three types of Catholic churches, the Irish responded the least to the pressure of external circumstances, the Italian churches definitely shaped themselves to the American environment, while the other foreign-language churches barely held their own, as the ethnic groups which they served became depleted.

The different policies adopted by the two principal groups of Catholic churches reflected the dual role which the Catholic Church has always played. The Irish churches exemplified the tenacity with which the Church has clung through the ages, not only to its essential tenets but to most of its external forms. The Italian churches revealed its equally characteristic practice of assimilating to itself the external manifestations of social change and even the most alien *mores*, whether they be pagan rituals or the materialism of the machine age.

The Irish churches largely ignored the trends and changes of the time and, with a firm sense of their age-old foundation and the assumption that the essentials of human character are unchangeable, stood firm, shaping as far as possible their people to their mould. For the Irish churches, the measure of their weakness or their strength was thus the success or failure with which they kept their following within the pattern which they had drawn and maintained. For the Italian churches, by contrast, their measure of success or failure was the success with which they caught the key to the changing spirit of their people and so adjusted themselves to it as to pass with them through a process of change.

During the post-War years the Irish Catholic Church was subjected to two influences which made its work more difficult and which altered in a measure its relation to its members and its position in the community. These two influences were the growth of what the Church termed worldliness — the increasing number and variety of temporal interests and worldly possessions which its people acquired; and, secondly, the disintegration of the old, close Irish neighborhood. The first of these influences tended to impair the spiritual hold of the Church over its members. The second modified its former social role. But the two influences, affecting two different sides of the Church's activity, were not unrelated. In the old, close Irish community in which the church was a social as well as a spiritual center, social and spiritual functions reinforced each other. Church societies made it easier or more imperative to perform religious duties, since the members performed those duties together, as at the monthly communion breakfasts of the Holy Name Society or the Children of Mary. The satisfaction which the leading parishioners derived from running a church affair and the fact that these affairs were the principal occasions for social enjoyment during the year cemented the parish more closely than ever into an observing religious unit.

The older generation of Irish had been very close to their Church. The loyalty which had been bred through long years of persecution in Ireland had been, if anything, strengthened rather than weakened by the migration to the United States, for to the loyalty which had been built up in adversity was added the possibility of developing a powerful institution on American soil, free from the hounding to which it had been subjected in Ireland. To one of the local priests it appeared that the second generation Irish — the older, American-born generation — was the strongest element in the Irish Catholic Church, stronger even than their Irish-born parents and very much stronger than their children. It was these who had given vigor to the Greenwich Village Irish churches.

In the years after the War other interests competed with the religious for the attention of the Irish Catholics of the locality. The larger world outside of the local people's immediate experience was no longer simply the Catholic world, both that of the Church on earth and the spiritual world to come. At the same time the disintegration of the neighborhood and the development of other bases for social groupings than the religious one shook the exclusive social position of the Church. In these years it no longer furnished the center of the social life of the Irish community.

The changes in the Irish parishes which both priests and laymen noted all revolved around the loss of social unity. Changes which involved the Church's direct hold on the individual through his sense of sin and concern for his immortal soul were hinted at, but could in no way be appraised. The priests of the community were plainly troubled by what they regarded as increasing worldliness, but the evidence cited as pointing toward a decline in religious feeling was always the disappearance of the old, close social parish. Although technically the social life of the parish did not matter so long as people performed their religious duties, the religious societies were actually the pulse of the old parish. In the language of one of the church bulletins, 'Each of these organizations is an artery through which is flowing the life-blood of the Church to ever-widening regions.'[1] The decline of these societies and of other social activities was an indication of a weakening pulse. Most of the usual church societies for men, married women, girls, boys and children continued to exist in each parish, had monthly communions, and occasional social affairs which were sometimes well attended. In at least one case, some of the former members of the parish even came back to the Holy Name Society meetings. But the energetic president of the most active of these societies complained that the men 'lacked spirit'; a former active member of the Children of Mary considered that her society had become 'less progressive'; and all agreed that church societies were not what they used to be.

The priests' feeling of uncertainty about their flocks arose partly from the fact that they could no longer keep such close track of their parishioners as formerly. Although technically every Catholic was supposed to attend the church of the parish in which he resided, the people of this community did not attend the same church Sunday after Sunday. Churches were too near together and parish lines not strictly observed. 'Parish loyalty,' which used to make the children of one parish 'root' against the boxing champion from the neighboring parish, had seriously flagged. As one priest put it, 'Here people go where their fancy takes them.' Some were led by 'fancy' from church to church, de-

[1] St. Francis Xavier Church, *Bulletin*, April, 1932, p. 13.

pending upon the weather or their state of mind. Others habitually attended churches at a distance from their own parishes because they preferred the priests or regarded the parish as socially superior. The increasing tendency of people to select their own church made the priests decidedly uneasy because they could not know whether or not their charges were failing in their religious obligations. 'Last Sunday there were 2300 people at Mass in my church,' observed one of the priests. 'Next Sunday there may be as many, but they will be different people, and who knows where last Sunday's crowd will be?' In an effort to counteract this tendency, one, at least, of the priests made a determined effort to know everyone in his parish and to notice everyone who came to his church. 'You see, I have the Holy Hour; I take all the special services; I teach all the children's classes; I go to all the funerals and wakes; I answer most of the sick calls, and every Sunday I speak to all the people after all four of the Masses.'

On the whole, the technique of the local Irish churches — that of the close neighborhood parish — was not adapted to the mobile, impersonal metropolitan conditions which became increasingly characteristic of this community. In these circumstances the priests passively accepted the futility of the old technique — 'this is not an age for societies'; 'fairs and bazaars and such social affairs are things of the past' — or made a pass at retaining as much of the old parish quality as could be kept by the energetic efforts of the priests in their personal contacts with their parish and its affairs.

Apart from these personal efforts, the priests of the Irish churches did not resort to any other means to stimulate religious zeal. With one voice they asked the rhetorical question, 'What can we do? It is not the Church's fault if people do not come. If God's word, which has held people through the ages, does not hold them now, we have no power to strengthen it.' However great their distress over their parish problems, they unanimously refused to stoop to the kind of institutional program favored by the Protestants. To introduce purely extraneous activities into the Church in the hope of drawing people into and holding them within its walls seemed to them an utter waste of energy. 'Why should I spend my time taking boy scouts on hikes? And where have the Protestants got with all their clubs and basketball teams anyway?' The one device to which the Irish churches resorted was in line with the old social idea of the parish — namely, an effort to raise the parish's social prestige.

In this community one parish had always stood markedly above the others in social position. As the oldest parish and Catholic church of the community, it had the dignity of age on its side. It had, moreover, the status which came from possession of a permanent rectorship — that is, from the fact that its priest might not be shifted at the will of his superiors, but could serve out his life in an ever more closely cemented relationship with his own parish. The class of people residing within the boundaries of this parish had always been superior in economic and social status to the longshoremen and truck-drivers of the other two parishes. This parish consequently set the social pattern for the local Irish churches. The great social event in each parish had long been its annual card party and dance, formerly held in the very plain church hall or the auditorium of the local school. As the neighborhood began to break up, the leading parish started to hold these affairs at uptown hotels, each year more pretentious, instead of locally. The climax came in the midst of the depression in 1932, when this church held a card party at the newest and most expensive hotel in the city. Hard on its heels, the neighboring poorer parish held its affair for the first time at an uptown hotel instead of in the auditorium of the local school. The increased elaborateness of the churches' social affairs helped to retain for them the character of outstanding social events, but only the full resources of the city could keep these functions in a position of prominence, and could attract those former members of the parish who had become prosperous and had moved away. Though these uptown affairs were partly designed to raise money by holding the notice and the support of the wealthy potential donors, they were not purely money-making affairs, for their cost was such as to make them comparatively poor devices for raising funds. Their primary service was to add prestige to the individual parish and to the Church, in a materialistic, disrupted metropolitan community.

Money-raising was an important aspect of church activity, because the Catholic churches were necessarily self-supporting and could not depend on endowments and past accumulations as did the local Protestant churches. While some of the church funds came from annual social affairs, some from former parishioners who retained a loyalty to their old parish, some from card parties organized by the Ladies of Charity, or other church societies, and some for candles and special Masses, most came through direct appeals from the pulpit. One church made a practice of printing a contribution list after such special collections as those at Easter or for the support of the parish school. So much emphais was laid on collections that the Irish churches all had the reputation of being places where money was continually asked for, often to the impatience of the parishioners. One woman reported that she had stopped going to the local church and was attending a Franciscan Mission church uptown because she was so tired of hearing appeals for money, and criticism of the priests on this count was almost universal. But in spite of constant complaints, funds to maintain these churches, to support four or five priests in each, to maintain parochial schools, and to care for their poor continued to be contributed with apparently no serious diminution. An analysis of the Easter contribution lists of one church showed the kind of support which this church received and something of the type of parishioners upon which it relied. In this parish approximately seventy per cent of the Easter donation was given by persons who were sufficiently identified with the parish to hand in their names along with their contributions. More than half of the adults contributed one dollar or less to this special collection. The large donations of ten dollars, twenty-five dollars, or even more, came chiefly from people with high political connections. In spite of the decline in parish societies, the support given to the Irish churches indicated that they still remained close to their parishes and to the community.[1]

[1] *Easter Contribution in Most Prosperous Irish Parish*
(from printed contribution lists)

	1922	1925	1932
Number of listed contributors:			
Adult	} 715	870	546
Children		395	201
Size of adult contributions:			
$10 or over	3 per cent	5 per cent	4 per cent
$5.00–$9.95	13	17	17
$1.05–$4.95	30	21	29
$1.00 or less	54	57	52
Total contributions listed..............	$1742 (est.)	$2552 (est.)	$1510
Total collection......................	2500	3600	2176

3. ITALIAN CATHOLIC ADAPTATION

The Italian churches owed their position and their development during these years to the fact that their people were passing through a process of adaptation. The problems growing out of increased worldliness and neighborhood disorganization which they shared with the Irish churches were overshadowed by those created by the process of Americanization.

The Italian Church was faced with the necessity of dissociating itself from what the younger Italian element regarded as the 'backwardness' of the Old World and of assuming an integral position in the new life of the Italian-American community. Several factors combined to make this a difficult achievement — the Church's position in Italy, the lack of prestige enjoyed by foreign priests in a Church dominated by the Irish, shortage of funds both because of the poverty of new immigrants and because the Italians had not the habit of giving, and, above all, the tendency of the younger generation to regard their Church as 'foreign' or 'superstitious.' In contrast to the Irish Church, which commanded the loyalty of the Irish patriot by virtue of his patriotism as well as his devotion, the Italian Church was for many who came to America either a symbol of oppression or, along with other aspects of the state, an object of indifference. So widespread was the religious indifference of the Italians that the pastor of a local Protestant mission could insist that he was neither proselytizing nor opposing the Catholic Church, since he was approaching only that half of the Italian group which was Catholic in name only. While the poorest Irish church could count on generous support, the richest Italian parish might be handicapped for funds, for the Italians, thrifty in the handling of their funds and used to a system of state aid to the Church, were notoriously bad givers.

In its effort to make and hold a place for itself in the changing Italian community, the Italian Church pursued three principal courses. It abandoned those characteristic Italian religious practices which marked it in the eyes of the younger generation as 'foreign,' while at the same time it retained enough of the atmosphere of a characteristically Italian church to make the older generation feel that it belonged to them; it sought to attain prestige and to give evidence of being able to meet an American situation in American terms by the construction of an imposing church building conspicuously 'up-to-date' in its fittings; and it adopted the institutional programs which the Irish churches scorned, in an effort to bring members within the fold and to compete with the social agencies and the Protestant missions of the locality.

Of the two Italian churches, one was established in 1859 as the first Italian mission in the city. Originally it had occupied the basement while the Irish congregation heard Mass in the main part of the church. In time the main membership of the parish became Italian, served by Italian priests, while the parish retained its geographical organization. The other was always a purely Italian parish, founded in 1892 when the Italian community was still young, made up wholly of Italian members and organized on a language basis without regard to the boundaries of geographical parishes. In 1920, the Italian language parish was still very poorly housed in a church which had been abandoned by the Negroes at the time of their migration out of the district. Probably because of its better quarters, the other church had a slightly higher social status, but lost this superiority when the former acquired a new building. In 1930, neither parish was recognized as socially superior to the other, but one was held in higher regard by the conservative Italians, the other by the more Americanized element.

Though both these churches had been entirely Italian for twenty to thirty years, neither had been characterized by the strongly Italian features which marked the Italian churches of the upper and lower East Side. Neither of these churches sponsored the feasts so typical of Little Italy. The only feast which was celebrated during these years was sponsored by a Sicilian society and was not recognized by the Church. The prominence of the North Italians in the community was partly responsible for the absence of feasts, for they were at pains to point out that it was the South Italians 'who go in for that sort of thing.' But there were many people in the neighborhood who cherished these traditional celebrations. On the occasion of the biggest Italian feast in the city — that of our Lady of Mount Carmel in East Harlem — troops of barefoot women and some men annually walked the long seven miles over the hard pavement during the night and stood packed for hours on the sidewalk outside the church door in order to attend this feast. It was the efforts of the priests rather than the attitudes of the people which primarily determined the policies of these churches. The priest who had been longest in the community, a North Italian himself, never allowed feasts. The one who presided over the other church during most of the post-War decade was emphatic in his insistence that the feasts had lost all religious significance and had simply become business affairs. He refused to permit his church to celebrate them. Although the absence of feasts might have cost the allegiance of some of the older people, it helped to keep the younger element from regarding their churches as un-American.

Since the Italians brought with them many practices regarded by their American children as superstitious, such as the use of charms, the Italian priests had to strive to prevent the practices of the Church from being classed with these other practices and disregarded as evidence of Old World superstitions. For this reason the same priest who was so opposed to feasts refrained from urging his people to offer candles even though these constituted a chief source of his very inadequate income. If he did so, it would, he feared, be wrongly interpreted, for 'people are very likely to misinterpret.'

Yet, though these churches did not follow in the footsteps of the churches of the East Side Little Italy in promoting feasts, in encouraging the use of candles and the offering of wax images, they still did not become the exact counterpart of the Irish churches or lose their Italian flavor. Informality during Mass was strongly reminiscent of the comings and goings in the churches in Italy and was in sharp contrast to the strictness with which the Irish priests maintained silence and order. Observance of such customs as that of having the whole congregation at midnight Mass on Christmas Eve file to the front of the church and kiss the statue of the Christ Child was characteristically Italian and its counterpart was not to be found in the Irish churches. Whether these distinguishing features were conscious concessions to the older people or unconscious carry-overs by the Italian priests was not determined.

The Italian Church, however, went beyond the mere avoidance of the most conspicuous marks of foreignness in demonstrating its 'progressive' and 'American' character. In spite of the moving away of a large proportion of his parish, and in spite of the poverty of the district, the Italian priest carried out what he regarded as his 'disposition' to build a fine, large church and school. Occupying a conspicuous corner, standing above neighboring houses and tenements in its Renaissance dignity, and ringing out over the neighborhood every evening its fine chimes, this new church was the pride of the priest and of its people. In showing visitors over the edifice, however, it was not the architectural beauty of its style to which the priest called attention, but the extensive equipment and the immaculateness of the school, the roof playground, the gymnasium, the boys' and girls' clubrooms, the stage for dramatic affairs, the hall for dances and wedding receptions, and, most important of all, the tiled showers equipped with the latest and finest American plumbing. By its modernity in thoroughly materialistic American terms, this church sought to identify itself with the American scene.

Loss of population and social disruption did not prevent the Italian churches from expanding their activities as well as their plant. Both churches adopted institutional programs similar to those found in Protestant churches. In addition to the religious societies for both sexes and all ages — societies which continued to flourish in these churches while they were maintained only with difficulty in Irish churches — both Italian churches had clubs for boys and girls which were primarily social and not purely religious. They had athletic teams and clubs which held dances; one church had a flourishing dramatic society, another a flourishing mothers' club. In addition to their recreational activities both maintained day nurseries and kindergartens, and one took care of public school children with play groups in the afternoon. The difference in policy between Irish and Italian churches might have been partly the result of a difference in the age composition of their parishes, since the proportion of children and young people was greater among the Italians, but this seemed an insufficient explanation in view of the very different attitude on the part of the priests.

In contrast to the Irish, the Italian priests regarded these activities as suitably placed in the church and looked upon their administration as a proper responsibility for a priest. One priest, when he could not raise sufficient money to hire a basketball coach, coached the girls in the gymnasium and conducted the boys' club himself. He complained of having to do this, but only because his pastoral burdens were heavy, not because he regarded such activities as unsuitable for him. In fact, he expressed his regret that he was too busy with parish duties to do as much with the clubs as he would have liked to do.

A very principal concern of the Italian priests was clearly the social welfare and not simply the spiritual condition of their parishioners. In commenting on the absence of decorations in the church itself, one priest stated that he did not approve of spending money for statues when it was needed for 'the poor of the parish, the clubs, the schools, and the things necessary to keep the children, who have such poor home conditions and live in a bad district, on the good path and give them some enjoyment.' He was very much concerned with the children on the street. Although unwilling to spend money on the decorations of the church, he expressed real regret that the rooms where the young people met were so bare, as he would have liked to make them attractive so that the children would be drawn into them and off the streets. The other priest was equally concerned with his social clubs and was especially proud of the clubrooms which he had provided in his new church. His one complaint was that of recent years the multiplicity of dances given by private social clubs competed with his and made it impossible for his girls and boys always to attend the church dances.

In both Italian parishes the priests were anxious that their churches should be central to all phases of their members' lives. When one priest found that the women of his parish were attending a neighborhood club which met at one of the Protestant centers, he established a mothers' club in his own church, 'not because I objected to their going to the other club, but because when I saw that they wanted such a club, I knew that I should give it to them. For whatever the people of my parish want, they should be able to find it in this church.' Though some doubts were cast on the first part of his statement by the fact that he brought pressure upon the members of his parish to leave the other club, the second part reflected the attitude running through all his views of the church's activities. This attitude was summed up in the legend over the door of the gymnasium and meeting rooms describing the place as the church's 'settlement.' At the other church, the priest responded in the same vein to the comment that apparently his church was doing much more than saving souls, 'Everything is in this church and that is as it should be.'

In their aim to make the Church mean everything to its members, the Italian priests sought to achieve a position somewhat similar to that occupied by the Irish churches a generation or half a generation before. The difference lay in the fact that the Irish churches constituted the center of their people's lives when the community was simple and compact and when rival interests had not pushed the religious interest into second place, whereas the Italian churches could not achieve the same result by the use of the same tactics. Confronted as they were with a community much more scattered socially and much more diverse in its interests, only a diversified program and an appeal to these other interests could, in the decade 1920–30, give the Italian Church a status that in any degree approached that which the Irish Church had formerly held.

The Italian churches thus strove to place themselves in such a position that the process of Americanization would bring the Italian people to them rather than draw them away. It was very difficult to gauge the success with which these programs had held their people. As in the case of the Irish churches, decrease or increase in the intensity of religious feeling could not be measured. The attitude of the Italian priests, however, was noticeably different from that of the Irish priests in that the former did not think that their losses in any way exceeded the population decline, nor did they regard their young people as increasingly irreligious. They were worried, to be sure, about the social customs of the country with which their young people were falling in line and they were especially concerned with the problem of lawlessness, but they pointed out that their young people were attending Mass and declared that there was no evidence that the Church's hold was weakening. Neither did they claim that it was growing. The difference in the starting-point from which the two sets of priests measured the trend in their respective churches may well account for the difference in attitude, for while the Irish priests started with the standard of extreme devotion to the Church and absorption in it which characterized the last generation of Irish in this community, the Italian priests started with an assumption of prevalent indifference.

Among the laity, experience and opinion varied widely. Those who were close to the Church were sure that everybody else was also. Those who had drifted away were sure that everybody was drifting away too. There appeared to have been a slight trend toward parochial school attendance, but it could not be established that this trend arose from any growing religious loyalty rather than from such extraneous factors as the discontinuance of certain grades in some of the public schools, the feeling that parochial school was more 'select' or the up-to-dateness of the new Italian parochial school which appealed strongly to the parents.

The best evidence of the support which the Italian churches received was the raising of money for the erection of the large and costly new church edifice. Though built partly with borrowed funds, the actual contributions ran into many thousands, and generous donors told with pride of the banquet of prominent Italians at which each table vied with the others in the effort to make the largest contribution. Expensive memorial windows installed by local donors were added evidence of generous support. Though the regular Sunday contributions were much smaller in the Italian than in the Irish churches — the priests of the former refused to show up inequalities in donations by printing contribution lists and had the reputation of making many fewer requests for money than did their Irish colleagues — and though the sums contributed to the Catholic charities by these parishes were very small,[1] it was no mean achievement for a poor Italian parish to provide such a new church for itself.

Unquestionably the Italian Church had by 1930 achieved a position of prestige in the Italian community. In contrast to the Irish, the Italian churches did not need to bolster up their prestige by going outside of the community for their affairs. Even more significantly, the Irish parishes were not regarded among the Italians as socially superior to the Italian. Whereas it is not unusual to find in immigrant communities that foreign-language churches are looked down upon by the more Americanized who

[1] Contribution of the three Irish parishes to the Catholic charities averaged $8195 per parish in 1920 and $6832 in 1930. The two Italian parishes averaged contributions of $1941 in 1920 and $1525 in 1930 — From *Annual Reports of Catholic Charities*, 1920, 1930.

seek to improve their own social status by attending the Irish or American churches, here diligent inquiry revealed no Italian, even among members of the dominant Irish parish, who would acknowledge that there was a social advantage in attending an Irish church.

The adaptation made by the Italian churches was set into relief by comparison with the other foreign-language churches in the environs. The Lithuanian and Spanish churches were perhaps hardly comparable to the Italian because they represented so much smaller communities. They had, however, been confronted with the same problems of adjusting themselves to the process of Americanization through which their groups were passing during approximately the same period. Neither of these churches made any of the adaptations which the Italian churches made. Both conducted their affairs 'just as they are done in the old country.' Neither made any effort to be 'up to date,' or made a bid for the younger generation by adopting any forms of activity which would appeal to them. As a result these churches were identified with the old culture of the parents in a way which Italian churches had avoided. The little French church maintained by a refugee order of nuns had never had a close relation to the community.

As agencies for social control, the religious institutions of this community functioned with varying degrees of effectiveness. While the Protestant churches determined the conduct of only a very small part of the local population, and while the Villagers were practically free from all social influences emanating from any church, the Irish Church continued to act as a strong source of social control for its members. And, though the Italian Church had less control over its followers, by building up its status in the community it was developing a position from which it might exercise an enlarged influence in the future.

XI. EDUCATION

THE American community has traditionally had great faith in its schools and in the efficacy of education. It has relied upon its schools to provide the intelligent and responsible citizenry essential to a functioning democracy; to serve as the melting pot which would eliminate significant differences and make the words of the Declaration of Independence real; to be bearers of tradition and impart to each new generation the standards of the community. The ample provision of school facilities has been the mark of a progressive community; a high compulsory school age the sign of an enlightened state.

In Greenwich Village, much of the faith in education was present, but the schools fell somewhat short of fulfilling the high role assigned to them. In the first place, there was not one school system which imparted to all the children of the locality the same standards, but rather three distinct educational systems, each with its distinct aims and standards and its distinct clientèle. Public schools, parochial schools, and private schools with experimental programs worked by three different methods toward three different goals. One only, the public, was primarily concerned with the problem of citizenship. The standards and traditions which the public and the parochial schools passed on to their pupils were essentially different — the old American tradition on the one hand and that of the Universal Church on the other; while the progressive schools were scarcely, if at all, concerned with traditional standards. None of the schools imparted the values actually recognized in the local community. Since the clientèle of the separate school systems corresponded, by and large, to the three principal groups in the neighborhood — Italians, Irish, and Villagers respectively — the schools did not bring these elements together and serve as a melting pot.

With one exception, no schools brought local people and

Villagers together, for such of the Villagers as had children avoided the public schools and maintained private institutions for the education of their children. Neither did the schools bring the ethnic groups together, for the Italians mostly sent their children to the public schools while nearly all the Irish attended parochial schools. In the few cases where Irish and Italian children were not trained in different systems, they attended different schools. Up to 1930, one of the elementary public schools was almost exclusively Irish. Throughout the period, one of the parochial schools contained only Italians. The only two schools which brought together children from the different major groups were one parochial school, predominantly Irish, but a quarter of whose membership in 1930 was Italian, and one small public school which, after 1928, harbored an experimental unit which attracted some of the Villagers and brought together their children with those of the local people.

1. THE SCHOOL POPULATION

Numerically, approximately two thirds of the children of the locality were in public and one third in parochial schools. While the decline in population brought a tremendous decrease in attendance at both these types of school, the public system suffered more heavily than the parochial so that a larger proportion of the children were attending parochial schools as compared to public in 1930 than in 1920. The private schools alone grew and had, in 1930, more applicants than they could accommodate. But in relation to the whole school population this private school element constituted a numerically insignificant group, at the very highest estimate no more than four per cent of the total school enrollment.

Both public and parochial schools of the locality dated back to the early days of the Village and recorded in the dates of their several establishment steps in the community's growth. The earliest was already in existence before the Village's initial boom. Three others in the upper part of the district dated from the years when the Village was becoming an integral part of the city, two built in 1844 and one in 1850. One in the eastern section had been founded in 1887, and five years later a private welfare agency had opened a school four blocks away because it considered the school facilities of that region inadequate. Enlargement of two schools in 1905 and the building of a third in 1906 were insufficient to meet the Italian invasion. A large new school, erected in 1912, was accommodating 2700 boys on double shifts in 1920. The parochial schools came into existence when their respective parishes became sufficiently prosperous to maintain them, the oldest in 1855 and the newest, after the completion of the new Italian church, in 1930.

In 1920, the local school facilities were inadequate to house the school population except under conditions of overcrowding. By 1930, two public schools had been closed and a third remained in operation only because it was selected for an experimental demonstration; grades had been discontinued in three others; the first year of high school had been added and housed in one school, and there was sufficient unused space in one building for an entire floor to be given over to an annex of the continuation school and in another for the city relief agency to be housed. Though the parochial schools in 1930 were inadequately equipped in certain respects, they were not suffering from lack of classroom space. Physically, the community changed from being inadequately to being amply supplied with school space.

The total number of children in the grades [1] fell from 8297 in 1920 to 4761 in 1930, a decline of 42.5 per cent. This drop and the fact that the schools were adjusting to a declining population during these years definitely conditioned the way in which they functioned. Such impetus for expansion and innovation as came from the headquarters of the city school system was directed toward the schools of the outlying district where new equipment and new techniques were tried out on the growing, in preference to the declining, schools. When overcrowding in the local buildings had ceased to be a problem — shortly after 1920 — this district no longer commanded the immediate attention of the Board of Education, except as an area in which economies could be achieved by consolidation. Little new blood was drawn into the teaching force, for the schools became overstaffed as their numbers dropped and vacancies were readily filled from the existing ranks. Half or more of the teaching force in 1930 in each of the principal public schools had been in the same school in 1920.

These conditions were true of both public and parochial schools.

[1] Including handicapped and ungraded classes. Cf. Table X, Appendix F, p. 467.

When the sister in charge of one parochial school was sent into the district in 1928, she was told that she was going to a dying school community in which her school would not long survive. A number of circumstances, however, kept the numbers in the parochial schools from falling so rapidly. They profited from the consolidation and the closing of upper grades in the public schools — in addition to two public schools which were closed altogether, three lost their upper grades during these years — for children from discontinued school or grades went into the near-by parochial rather than to the more distant public school. In one case suspicion was freely expressed, but not substantiated, that the closing of the seventh and eighth grades in a public school was really a move to strengthen the parochial schools, since the school to which the girls were supposed to go was a considerable distance away and even the vigorous protests of parents received scant attention from the Board of Education. The ranks of the parochial schools were still further enlarged when a three-grade private welfare school, partially supported from public funds, closed in 1930 in accordance with the general program of the city-wide agency which maintained it, for again the parochial was nearer at hand than the public school. The newness of the up-to-date school at the Italian church, gave it a distinct competitive advantage and it was beginning to draw children away from the public school as it gathered momentum.

The parochial schools, however, faced certain handicaps as compared with the public schools, for their support came from their local parishes, not from city-wide taxes administered throughout the system regardless of the contributions from a particular district. Dependence on local support limited the schools of the poorer parishes — a limitation which became very apparent in one of the parishes whose members were largely longshoremen. Although the local parochial schools charged no tuition as did the schools of more prosperous parishes, they were constantly having to seek funds in addition to those which came from the collections at the church. Some of the poorer families sent their children to public school so that they would not be under pressure to buy tickets for affairs or for raffles or to purchase the equipment which the public schools either supplied or did not call for. There was no evidence that the proportionate increase in parochial school attendance reflected any change in the neighborhood's attitude toward either type of school, nor anything to confirm the assertion of one of the public school principals that the priests had increased their pressure for parochial school attendance.

The grade school population of 1930 was not only 42.5 per cent smaller than that of 1920, but it was very different in age composition. In 1920, the bulk of the school population was in the primary grades, with a sharp falling off after the fifth grade. In 1930, the number enrolled in the upper grades was as great as in the lower.[1] In accordance with the school law of 1921, a child could no longer leave school and go to work at fourteen unless he had finished the eighth grade. He could leave at fifteen if he had completed the sixth grade. In any case, he had to attend school full time until the age of sixteen if he was not employed and part time up to seventeen if he was employed. The widespread desire for white-collar jobs and the advantage of a high-school education in securing such jobs brought a definite pressure toward longer school attendance. Both school officials and the people of the community were ready with the generalization that high-school attendance was much more common in 1930 than it had been ten years before. Those, particularly the Italians, who had gone through high school or college regarded the extension of education as one of the most important developments in these years.

It was not possible to determine just how far the longer period of schooling was the result of the desire for more education, the absence of the extreme pressure on children to go to work as the families became better off, the increasing difficulty of finding jobs, or merely the effect of the legal requirement. There was definite indication of a tendency, however, to remain in school beyond the legal limit. The discharge records of the boys' public school showed that, in 1924, forty per cent of those leaving school had stopped when they reached the age limit without completing their grades. In 1928, the proportion leaving without completing the grade was 32 per cent; in 1930, 25 per cent. In these same years, the proportion of those completing grade 8B who went to work immediately dropped from 16 to 7 per cent, while those who stayed on to complete 9B increased from 62 to 87 per cent. The close of 9B found 51 per cent in 1924 and 59 per cent in 1930, registering

[1] Cf. Chart VIII, p. 324.

the intention of going on to senior high school.[1] Up to this point, the records were sufficiently reliable and complete to allow the conclusion that a decreasing proportion of the boys were dropping out of school the minute they reached the legal age limit. The attempt to trace these boys to the senior high schools, however, indicated that many did not reach the schools designated on their discharge cards and when they did go on to senior high school, they frequently stayed a short time only.

The records of the girls' school were less complete and showed little trend. The proportion leaving at the age limit without completing their grades varied from year to year, but remained around 30 per cent from 1920 through 1930. The proportion going to work after 8B, also, fluctuated between 30 and 40 per cent, but showed no trend. Since records of most of the parochial schools did not show anything about the destination of those who were discharged or who graduated, it was not possible to discover whether the parochial students differed from those of the public schools in the age of leaving and the tendency to go on to high school or to work.

Attendance at continuation school, which was required after 1921 of all who went to work before the age of seventeen, was however, wholly a matter of law rather than desire. The continuation school remained the object of acute antagonism and disrespect throughout the community. The antagonism arose partly from the fact that the children who had left school to go to work were, by and large, the ones who were least interested in school and therefore least interested in continuing, while the short period of instruction each week made for a disjointed program. According to reports universally current among parents and children, it was very easy to cut continuation school, and it was generally assumed that many did cut. Efforts to check these statements at the school were met with the report that continuation school attendance was not especially irregular, but the statement from the school, which could not be checked by examination of actual attendance records, did not eliminate the prevalent impression that continuation school could be disregarded. Moreover, although employers were legally required to let children stay away from work for the necessary four hours a week, many reports indicated that boys and girls had frequently been under pressure from their employers not

[1] Cf. Table XI, Appendix F, p. 468.

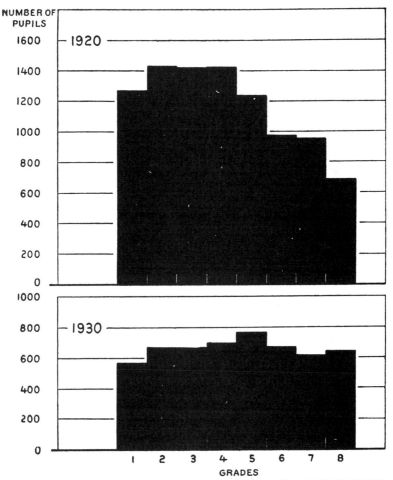

CHART-VIII

DISTRIBUTION OF PUBLIC SCHOOL PUPILS*BY GRADES
1920 AND 1930 △

*TOTAL PUPILS IN SCHOOLS SERVING THE DISTRICT, INCLUDING THOSE PUPILS RESIDING OUTSIDE OF DISTRICT.
△ NEW YORK CITY BOARD OF EDUCATION, MONTHLY SCHOOL REPORTS

to go to school and children who were below school age even lost their jobs if they attempted to obey the law. One woman insisted, 'It is not fair to the poor mothers who need their children's earnings that they should have to go to school and be unable to have a job.' Although the school insisted that in most cases of this sort the children had lied about their ages, the prevalent impression that continuation school stood in the way of holding a job added to the unpopularity of that school.

The net result of the trend toward longer school attendance was to increase the proportion of the population between the ages of sixteen and twenty which was attending school from 10.6 per cent in 1920 to 28.1 per cent in 1930. The bulk of the attendance was of those sixteen and seventeen years old, of whom 52.5 per cent were in school in 1930 as against 13.7 per cent of those from eighteen to twenty.

Those who went on to senior high school became a somewhat distinctive element in the community. The street-corner groups of older boys were usually composed of either high-school or non-high-school boys, rarely of a mixture of the two.

College was attended by most of the local Jewish boys and by some of the Jewish girls. In this group, college attendance, for the boys at least, was taken for granted. Those of the Italians who looked upon college as a desired goal included the very small cultivated element, a group of families eager to 'better themselves' and who set a high store on the professions, a few who had come under the influence of settlements or missions, and an occasional isolated individual or family. As nearly as could be discovered, not more than a couple of dozen Italian boys and girls from the district were in college in 1930, scattered among a number of colleges, public and private, religious and secular, in the city and out of town. A small group of Irish, chiefly those in professions, were sending their children to the Catholic colleges primarily.

The three types of schools in the district did not mould the youth of the locality to a common pattern, for their aims and many of their methods differed essentially.

2. PUBLIC, PAROCHIAL, AND PROGRESSIVE SCHOOLS

The public schools derived their *raison d'être* from a political democracy's need of a literate and intelligent electorate. They were concerned with the character of the citizenry which they turned out. In the words of the superintendent of New York City's schools, 'I call on all supervisors and teachers to hold before themselves, as the ultimate purpose of their school work, the development of the moral character of their children, with all that this implies, so that no matter what the conditions of the environment may be, the schools will do their utmost to develop in their pupils good conduct, high ideals, respect for law and order, wholesome sentiments toward the State, the home, the Church, and their fellow men, and the courage and steadfastness of purpose to carry out their ideals and to resist temptation.'[1] Public schools, the superintendent urged, must develop habits of regularity, cleanliness, good posture, correct speech, good manners, attention, promptness, neatness, order, accuracy, effort, and perseverance. 'If the schools do not inculcate habits of attacking work promptly and cheerfully, of putting forth sustained effort in the solution of problems, of persistency in the face of difficulties, children will form habits of laziness, indifference, lack of effort, and lack of concentration of attention.'[2]

The parochial schools, as an integral part of the Catholic Church, had a definitely religious goal, the spiritual salvation of the child. For them, religion was the core of all their instruction, permeating the school work, not alone in the form of specific religious teaching, but in the religious emphasis given to the teaching of other subjects, and in the fact that the members of religious orders who taught in the school were living examples of the religious life. The view that this life is a preparation for the next underlay the attitudes which the sisters instilled into the children directly or indirectly; it made the perspective of the parochial schools always and inevitably a long-range view, with temporal considerations subordinated to spiritual. The subject matter and the standards of conduct taught by these schools rested upon religious sanctions and not simply on the concept of the social good.

In sharpest contrast, the progressive or experimental schools focused upon the personality of the individual child as the end and

[1] New York City, Board of Education, *Twenty-Seventh Annual Report of the Superintendent of Schools*, 1924–25, p. 57.

[2] *Ibid.*, p. 61.

aim of their endeavor, little concerned with citizenship and still less with salvation. These schools regarded school life as a vital experience in itself. 'Living is a series of presents and not a continuous preparation for the future.' They were not interested in developing respect for authority, and most of the habits listed by the superintendent of public schools — deference, good manners, neatness, promptness — were not regarded as virtues by the progressive schools. Fair play was virtually the only moral quality which was stressed, and even this rested upon enlightened self-interest rather than on moral sanction. Eager to develop the capacity for independent thinking, they looked upon experience — never authority — as the only effective teacher, and liked to delay the teaching of reading so that the children would not become dependent on the authority of the printed page. Accepting neither the existing standards of the community nor any supernatural sanctions, they sought to develop individuals who could build their own standards in terms of their individual needs. In so far as possible, the environment was adjusted to the child rather than the child to the community.

Headed, thus, in three different directions, the three types of school could hardly be expected to impart to the younger generation a common outlook or a common tradition.

The different schools were under certain common pressures to modify the content and the method of instruction during these years. Developments in psychology and in teaching devices adapted to the child's psychological equipment, pressure to enlarge the cultural content of the curriculum and to strengthen the instruction in citizenship, and changes in the needs of industry and in the character of the home all bore upon the several school systems. Each responded to these pressures in the manner dictated by its own aims and standards.

The stated principles underlying the curriculum of the public schools made this group particularly susceptible to such pressures. 'Since modern life is extremely complex and modern education should enable the pupil to participate in life both when he is a child and when he is an adult, the curriculum should be... built which has large social adult values, appeals to the interests of children, is suited to their growth wants, and at the same time is sufficiently differentiated to meet the needs of pupils of varying levels of ability.'[1] It should provide for developing morals and health; familiarizing the pupils with the ideas which underlie the civilization in which they live and the social usages of that civilization; acquainting them with the treasures and masterpieces of the past. The subject matter and instruction should be so organized as to coincide with the psychological development of the children; the school is 'a place where children come to educate themselves and one another with the help of a good teacher'[2] to provide for their emotional as well as their intellectual needs and to furnish a satisfactory apportionment of time and subject, continuity and growth, and allowance for individual differences. These principles were applied to the curriculum revision planned by the Board of Education for the whole city public school system, but the head of each school had a great deal of leeway as to the way in which his individual school adopted the general changes.

The use of psychological tests to classify students into homogeneous groups on the basis of intelligence became an accepted principle. The superintendent of schools in 1925 declared that 'classification of pupils according to their ability is a fundamental element of sound school administration.... I lay it down as a principle that such classification, when possible, should be found in all schools.'[3] Rapid advance classes for the particularly able, and ungraded classes for those unable to keep up with any graded work, supplemented at the extremes the sectioning of ordinary grades.

The public schools of the locality all used psychological tests, but by 1930 the two largest schools placed less reliance on the results of these tests than they had ten years before. They all complained that their schools were too small to permit of as careful classification of students on the basis of capacity as they might desire. The two junior high schools established rapid advance classes which covered the junior high course in two years and 13 per cent of the students were enrolled in such classes in 1930 as against 1.6 per cent in 1920. Ungraded classes were provided only in the two largest schools, while the other schools felt their lack.

[1] New York City, Board of Education, *Twenty-Eighth Annual Report of the Superintendent of Schools*, 1925–26, pp. 73, 74, quoting N.E.A. Research Bulletin, 1925, 'Keeping Pace with the Advancing Curriculum.'

[2] *Ibid.*, p. 75.   [3] *Ibid.*, p. 67.

The school program was modified to meet the needs of the slow student in one girls' school where home-making and sewing were provided for the older girls and the academic subjects were adapted.

Pressure to adopt newer teaching methods in place of the old-fashioned drill resulted in a considerable use of the project method in two of the schools and a little visual education in three. None of the public schools, however (except the one containing the privately aided experimental unit), made any radical alterations in classroom practices or training technique. During the first six weeks of each school year, the front blackboard in the lower-grade classrooms of one school was devoted to the instructions, 'Eyes front. Hands in lap. Heads straight.'

Throughout the city, the public school curriculum was enlarged during these years to include more cultural material. Instruction in music and art added exercise in appreciation to the memory training which had been the chief content of the work before. The schools of this district modified their music instruction to conform to this new program, and two of the local schools made a specialty of their music work. The added stress on oral English and correct speech which was general throughout the city system was reflected in the local schools. At the same time, art and dramatic work at local recreation centers further augmented the children's cultural experience.

During and following the War, community pressure called for greater specific stress on the teaching of citizenship, and the Board of Education added civics to the history work from the fifth grade up and furnished a syllabus for citizenship instruction with programs adapted to each grade. The local schools followed the rest of the system in extending the amount of time given to citizenship training and to acquainting the pupils with their city. The local elementary schools found the subject a difficult one for their children. One attempted, under the heading of 'citizenship,' to develop loyalty, first, to the class; second, to the community; and, third, to the family. Another considered instruction in ethics and courtesy to be the most effective civic training it could give. All the elementary schools and one of the junior high schools avoided all discussion of the actual conditions in the city with which the children were familiar, while the other junior high school encouraged newspaper reading and maintained a current events club.

Pressure to adapt the school curriculum in such a way as to provide direct training for industry or business found a response in both of the local junior high schools. The boys' school gave an important place to shopwork when, around 1920, the Gary school system was in high favor and certain people in the New York system wished to demonstrate that some of the advantages of the system could be achieved without adopting the Gary plan in its entirety. Throughout these years, instruction in manual trades remained a prominent part of this school's curriculum. In the girls' school, the introduction of 'industrial' work — largely sewing and cooking — was designed to meet the needs of the older girls who lacked academic interest and keen intellectual equipment, rather than to prepare them for vocational activity. The need for vocational guidance was seriously felt in these schools, but up to 1930, no way to secure it had been developed, except for the brief period during which a vocational counselor had been on hand at one school.

The greatest extension of public school activity during the post-War period, however, did not come in response to demands of psychology, citizenship, or industry, but rather from the changed role and concept of the home. 'Home-making' was made a part of the city school curriculum — or rather the old work in domestic science was dignified by a new name. 'The great changes in the home life of today,' said the Board of Education in its 'home-making syllabus' (1925), 'together with the advanced standards of trade work, necessitated the incorporation of this subject into the schools.'

Many of the functions formerly located in the home were taken over by the schools, and the schools extended the social services which they performed until, by 1930, they constituted welfare agencies as well as places for academic instruction. All the local public schools reached the younger children through kindergartens. Two served school lunches and others felt the need of this service. All except one taught thrift through school banking. In the largest girls' school home-making occupied an important place in the curriculum. Etiquette and manners were stressed in all schools.

The schools during these years became public health agencies. The time allotted by the Board of Education to health instruction was increased from ten minutes a week in 1916 to four hours a week in 1929. The citizenship instruction provided for the earliest grades was primarily health instruction. Beginning in 1920, school health week was instituted for the city, and thereafter became an annual event at which time a special drive was made to discover physical defects. Health programs stressing such practices as sleeping with open windows and teeth-brushing were pushed in all the schools. School nurses and doctors were on duty, and, with one school in particular, a local public health center cooperated most vigorously, setting up a dental clinic in the school, conducting posture classes, giving audiometer tests for defective hearing, and sending nurses to follow up such physical defects as were reported by the school. The schools were under pressure to join in such campaigns as anti-litter and fly-swatting drives, and the local schools reported that they had responded to these pressures.

They also undertook a certain amount of direct welfare work, such as providing shoes for children who could not come to school because they lacked them. Although the visiting-teacher movement, which started during the beginning of the decade, never gained a real foothold in the New York City school system during these years — there were only twenty visiting teachers for the entire school system during 1930, and these were chiefly assistants to the truant officer rather than a combination teacher and social worker — one of the schools in this district had the advantage of having one of the best of the city visiting teachers to serve it. Increased provision was made in the city system for the most seriously handicapped pupils through the establishment of fresh air, cardiac, crippled, and sight-conservation classes. The first three of these special types were furnished in the locality.

So extensively had the public schools taken over social service and home functions by 1930 that the principals and teachers of some of the local schools were inclined to complain of the added burden and the confusion which these new school activities had brought. One principal resolutely refused to have any more of these functions in his school than he could help. School banking and school luncheons he had effectively kept out until 1930, even though there was considerable pressure from the local social agencies to make him serve school lunches, as the social workers declared that the children needed them. This principal felt that the school, by extending its services, was pauperizing the population, undermining their self-dependence and violating American principles of self-reliance, — 'they will be having us eat for them next.' In another school the principal declared: 'If they would only let us alone and let us teach. We are hard-working and conscientious, even though what we do may not always be wise, but what with all this pressure to bring everything into the school — health, community, civics, etc. — we have no time for our regular business. People behave as if there were no other agency in the community than the school through which anything could be done. Do you know, I think if it were possible the parents would be glad to have the teachers have maternity leave so that they could have their children for them!'

All the local schools, moreover, complained that, although they were under pressure to add so much variety to their school programs, they still were primarily held responsible for teaching the three R's. In spite of the school superintendent's statement that character-building was the greatest aim of the school, the teachers agreed that 'you would never know it,' for whenever the Board of Education sent down any tests, they were sure to be based on reading, spelling, and arithmetic. While some, at least, of the members of the Board of Education voiced the educational theory that children should be taught to think independently, they acknowledged that, in point of fact, the tests which they administered called for information rather than analysis and children were taught to accept the *status quo*.

The parochial schools felt under less need to respond to these pressures to modify the content and method of their instruction, for they had behind them a long educational tradition, and they were less concerned with, and even directly opposed to, some of the influences calling for curriculum modification. Individual parochial schools had in some respects even more latitude than the public schools and the local parochial schools showed considerable variety. They were under the direction of the religious order which supplied the teaching force, and the standards and tests of the particular order had to be met by each school. In addition a certain amount of unity was provided by newly developed diocesan tests applied throughout the archdiocese of New York.

The parochial schools felt less impelled to respond to the 'discoveries' of psychology than did the public schools, for they were not convinced that interest in psychology was more than a momentary phenomenon or that the psychologists had added anything important to the knowledge of human nature which the Catholic Church has enjoyed for hundreds of years. None of the parochial schools of the Village used intelligence tests to classify their students, and the principals of these schools either regarded the tests as unreliable guides or else objected to them as 'branding' the children. One principal only was interested in intelligence tests, but was deterred from using them by lack of funds. No parochial school had either rapid advance or ungraded classes. The latter were, perhaps, somewhat less necessary to the parochial than to the public schools because the parochial schools could discharge the pupils who could not keep up with the work, while the public schools had to take all who came.

The parochial schools maintained the attitude that it was unnecessary for them to respond to every new educational development, for many of these would turn out to be merely passing fads. Although the priest in charge of the Manhattan parochial schools expressed a desire to see the old singsong method of recitation supplanted and to add art, music, sewing, and physical training to the curriculum of his schools, there was little sign that new teaching techniques had been substituted for the type of drill which had been customary in the past. Nor had the curriculum of the local schools been enlarged to include cultural subjects, such as drawing and music or vocational work. The only exception was the Italian parochial school which introduced a post-graduate commercial course in an effort to hold some of its girls.

The parochial schools followed the public schools in stressing citizenship training. The local schools all felt that the problem for them was an easy one because their whole system laid so much stress on authority that parochial school children did not have so much difficulty as public school children in understanding respect and obedience to law. They were, if anything, less interested than the public schools in relating civics instruction to the community experience of the children, discouraging the children from bringing in material from their own observation, and, in one case at least, even from reading the newspapers. Perhaps they had been warned by the experience of the one local parochial school that started to encourage the bringing-in of outside material until the sisters found themselves deluged with all the neighborhood scandal, including details of murders.

Most especially, the parochial schools were less inclined than the public schools to take over functions performed in the home. Whereas failure to adopt the other changes which were modifying the public schools was due to the negative attitude that they were not necessary in the school curriculum, reluctance to having the school take over home functions rested upon the positive intent to preserve the family in its traditional role. Thus, the parochial schools were loath to extend school instruction below the first grade, believing that until the age of five the child belonged at the mother's knee, and that no matter what the condition of the home might be, it was a better place for the young child than any place outside. Two of the parishes maintained day nurseries, but only because of necessity, and the Catholic Charities which had charge of them insisted that these nurseries provide only for the physical care of the child and do nothing that bordered on a nursery school job. Similarly, though the public schools introduced home-making, the parochial schools continued to regard it as an art which the home should teach. Nor did they take on the kind of social welfare programs that the public schools developed. They were poorly equipped with play space, and, though they deplored the play conditions of their children, they rarely regarded the supervision of children's play as the responsibility of the school. None of the parochial schools served lunches. The one extension of parochial school function was in respect to health.

But though the parochial schools were in a position to disregard some of the major pressures to which the public schools were responding, they nevertheless took the academic standards of the public schools as their guide. The parochial schools made a positive effort during these years to eradicate from the community the idea that 'all the parochial schools teach is religion and form.' Although the regents' examinations were optional, they were given to parochial students in addition to the examinations set by the archdiocese and by the religious orders. A syllabus for parochial school instruction was worked out in considerable detail, paralleling as closely as possible the syllabus for the corresponding subject in public school. While the parochial schools did not feel the need of modifying their work importantly in order to do their job, they did feel the need of those modifications which would improve their status in the community.

The progressive schools were, in and of themselves, the product of some of the forces which modified the other schools — the psychological interest, the discrediting of old teaching techniques, changes in society and in the home. Their highly individualized instruction was designed to meet the psychological needs of the individual student. Traditional methods of teaching were almost completely reversed. Hand work in place of head work, learning by doing, the greatest possible informality and realism, and the effort to draw the subject matter and the pattern of conduct out of the child rather than imposing values on him, all were diametrically opposed to the ways of both public and parochial schools. How sharply they were opposed became very apparent in one of the public schools whose lower grades were made into an experimental unit. The old-line principal of the school was in despair because she could not enforce discipline in the rest of the school while the experimental grades were violating her rules at every point, and she showed no sign of understanding the fundamental tenets upon which this unit within her own school was built up. Citizenship was not taught by these schools either in the sense of the principles of democracy which the public schools underlined or respect for law and authority which the parochial schools instilled. In terms of acquaintance with the concrete functioning of the city — its ferries and markets, its subways and its bridges — the progressive schools offered the most realistic instruction of the three.

In their attitude toward the cultural content of the curriculum, these schools again differed from public and parochial schools. While the public schools were stressing acquaintance with the masterpieces of the past and were providing lessons in the appreciation of music and art, the progressive schools objected to having the children exposed to adult art forms, lest they become imitative and not creative in their own work.

The progressive schools responded most to the changing position of the home. Recognizing the shortcomings of a city apartment as a place in which to bring up a family, assuming that the mothers had other interests outside of their families, and believing — in direct conflict with the Catholic opinion — that the mothers' knee was emphatically not the best place for many children all of the time, it took over many of the home functions. Progressive schools extended schooling into the lowest age groups, making nursery schools part of their system. They served lunch, had the younger children take naps, planned and supervised recreation, handled the behavior problems of the children, visited the homes and, where possible, extended their influence into the home to make it conform to the standards set by the school.

From the point of view of the community in which these three school systems operated, their diversity served to accentuate the differences among social groups. Paradoxically, the school system whose aim was most directly to prepare for community participation — the public schools — succeeded the least because of the conflict situations which it engendered. The difficulties which the latter schools faced arose chiefly because the political democracy which they pictured to their pupils had little relevance to this sort of urban situation, and because the method which their democratic principles prescribed led them to ignore some of the most significant factors in the experience of those whom they taught.

One of the major tenets of the old American tradition has been the essential equality of all individuals. Upon that assumption it has been the policy of the public school, well exemplified by the schools of this district, to disregard differences in background whether those differences arose from an economic or an ethnic source. In pursuance of this policy, schools treated the children as isolated units in the classroom rather than as parts of family or culture groups, applying a single method and expecting similar reactions from all. Studies of New York City schools, however, have amply demonstrated that differences in economic status, social conditions, and ethnic composition of a neighborhood are reflected in the progress in the neighborhood school.[1]

In this district, disregard of the social background of the pupils militated against the school's success in conveying to Italian children the ideas to which it was devoted. The initial impact of the

[1] Maller, J. B. 'Economic and Social Correlatives of School Progress in New York City,' *Teachers College Record*, XXXIV (1933), p. 667.

school upon the children often was very confusing to them. When these children first came to school, they had already learned in their homes certain habits and attitudes, and they had been punished for failure to conform to certain standards of conduct. But the school's disregard for any home training which differed in its assumptions from that of the school frequently resulted in the children being treated as though they were personally misbehaving when actually they were conducting themselves as they had been taught. The effect of having to bear the burden of blame for cultural differences between home and school often set the children vigorously against the school.

Among the boys of the district, it had always been very much the code to hate school. Although there is nothing unique in boys' antagonism to school, the intensity with which the local boys hated school was conspicuous. The largest boys' school of the district had a reputation for being one of the roughest schools in the city. In 1920, part of its roughness was due to the fact that it was very crowded, and testimony agreed that in terms of noise and violence conditions had improved in this school by 1930. But there was no clear evidence that the intensity of the battle between pupils and teachers had appreciably diminished. The same group of teachers remained, employing the same methods, often including physical violence to keep in order during school hours an unruly and resentful group of boys.[1] Yet, except for one teacher who felt that foreign languages presented some difficulty, the teachers and principals who were interviewed insisted that they had no particular problems of teaching method to meet.

In the girls' public school, conditions were very much more favorable to effective instruction. The home training and neighborhood experience of the Italian girls produced fewer attitudes that were unpalatable to the teachers than was the case with the boys, and many of the things which the girls' school taught were things which the girls wanted to learn — such as manners and etiquette — or were especially designed for their needs — such as sewing.

There was little in the public school program to command the interest and respect of the local boys and to overcome their opposition or their indifference. The picture of the world which the schools called up seemed to the local children to be eminently un-

[1] Cf. Appendix E.

real. The principles of a political democracy and the detail of the
theoretical structure of city, state, and national government which
they learned in civics class had little in common with day-by-day
experience in the community. Descriptions of the duties of policemen of various ranks were not supplemented by a discussion of the
necessity for 'knowing somebody at the political club' to get a
police job. In a community which was riddled with law-breaking
of one sort or another, all problems involving such familiar occur-
rences were studiously avoided by some teachers, ignored by
others, and only rarely brought into discussion by one or two.

In private affairs as well as public, in the basis for personal conduct as well as in respect to matters of graft and the liquor traffic,
the attitudes which the school took for granted often seemed to
these children to belong better in a fairy story than in their own
experience. The teachers of the public schools assumed as their
standard of values and mainsprings of conduct those virtues
traditional to the old American pattern — to 'polite and pure-
minded society.' [1] To children whose survival depended upon a
kind of ruthless self-protection, the teacher's stress on courtesy,
honesty, and fair play set her precepts apart from the real and
present experience of the child.

The literary material to which the child was exposed often
lacked reality also. While children drew the bulk of their experience from movie attendance, the subjects and the attitudes
contained in the movies were ignored by the schools. The same
was true of language and speech. All the schools of the locality reported that they laid special stress on the teaching of English —
'the teachers almost break themselves trying to make the children
talk right' — because of the importance of having the children
from foreign homes learn the English language. But the language
which they taught was not that which had vitality for the children
— the accent of the street, the diction of the movies, and the
vocabulary of the tabloid press. To talk in the manner prescribed
at school was to act the part of a 'sissy' or to 'put on airs.' A
striking evidence of the divergence of school instruction from experience was presented by a group of themes on the subject 'An
Adventure' written by the seventh grade at the boys' school.

[1] New York City Board of Education, *Twenty-Eighth Annual Report of the Superintendent of Schools*, 1925–26, p. 74.

Among thirty-two themes there was only one which described any adventures which might have happened to the writer. They were literary in flavor, describing such adventures as finding treasures buried in the woods, and giving no hint of the manifold experiences of a city child.

The school experience of these children had no continuity with their cultural past or with that of their families. Most of the public schools found dealings with parents difficult, and several kept these dealings down to a minimum. 'We have enough trouble with the children; we certainly cannot take on the parents too.' To the principals and teachers of most of the schools, the parents of the Italian children either were unenlightened nuisances who came to complain, or were people who lacked integrity and a capacity to understand the purpose of the school. The teachers pointed to the parents who insisted upon having their children receive free lunches and then appeared well dressed when they called for them at school. They complained of their excitability and the difficulty of communicating with them. They regarded their ignorance of English as not only a handicap, but as a cause for blame. An individual teacher here, or an occasional parent there, bridged the gulf between home and school. In at least one school the principal made it her policy to support the authority of the parents in relation to their children by taking the part of the parents whenever a quarrel between parents and children was brought to school. But on the whole the children under the instruction and the discipline of parents on the one hand and teachers on the other were subjected to the authority of two groups of people who were largely ignorant of each other, lacked understanding, and were often antagonistic.

The teachers in the lower grades complained that the Italian children seemed to have nothing in their background upon which the schools could draw. If the children read *Pinocchio*, learned to sing *Santa Lucia*, or danced the tarantella, it was because these books, songs, and dances were part of the general school program, taught to school children of different backgrounds indiscriminately. Efforts to ascertain how much traditional folk knowledge the children of the locality possessed tended to confirm the experience of the schools. When groups of children were asked to sing, the Italian songs which they knew were either current popular

Italian songs which they had heard on the family's phonograph or those which they had learned in school and which they mingled interchangeably with songs of other origins. Out of a group of some thirty children who were asked whether any could dance the tarantella, the only two who could do so had learned it in school.

In the absence of co-operation with the home and the use of materials traditional to the children, there resulted a wide gap between the cultural background of the parents and the cultural content which the children were acquiring in school. For these children, the content of the school curriculum thus became peculiarly thin, lacking in the resonance which it would have had in an old American community where it rested upon the assumptions and the store of literary knowledge common to the home and the community.

The public schools were very much preoccupied with the problem of character education. According to the statement of the superintendent of schools in the City of New York, if the school had only one aim it would be that of character-building. In their efforts at character-building, the schools stressed those virtues which were predominant in the old American pattern, with honesty as a fetish. But the children of this community, for whom honesty in and of itself had no particular importance, often looked upon conduct which the school regarded as virtuous as merely stupid.

The kind of 'character' which the public school teachers factually welcomed among their students was the kind which made their job of instruction easy — that is, a docile receptivity. The Italian girls were universally commended as pupils because they were so well-mannered and so easy to handle, and because, according to one of the teachers who had taught in a Jewish school, they were not so grasping as Jewish children, and, according to the school nurse, they were acquiescent and did not retort, like the Irish, 'That is my own business; I will do what I please about it.' Yet the principals and teachers who were opposed to the extension of the welfare services of the school objected to these services because they broke down the kind of self-reliant individualism which, according to the old American tradition, the schools were trying theoretically to build up. It was hard to see how this attitude accorded with their praise of docility. On the other hand, the kind of self-reliant individualism which the community knew was the kind which prescribed taking advantage of every possible opportunity and getting all there was to be had out of the services of the schools or any other agency.

The net effect of public school education in this community was often to produce a dichotomy in the individual child between those experiences which were tied up with school and those which he lived outside. If an Italian public school child tried to make a coherent whole out of his home, his community, and his school experiences, he could only find himself trying to make order out of a set of contradictions.

Evidence of the failure of the local public schools to perform their assumed function was plentiful. An examination of the high-school records of the girls and boys who went up from the local schools to high schools showed the great bulk of them to have been unable to carry high-school work successfully. Boys reported, 'We were all automatically put back in languages when we reached high school.' Although the records in the high schools were too incomplete to be susceptible of careful analysis and tabulation, an examination of such records as were available in the schools to which most of the local boys and girls went showed a very large proportion of conspicuously low records among the boys and only a slightly higher record among the girls. The girls who did really well were those who attended trade school. Those who resentfully attended continuation school were regarded by the school as peculiarly hopeless educational material.

Failure on the part of local public schools to do an effective educational job with their Italian pupils did not apparently represent a unique condition, but one which was characteristic of similar schools in similar districts. A study in 1930 of all the schools in the city showed a consistently low rating in the schools in Italian districts, with the schools of this locality rating above many schools in other Italian sections.[1] Informal reports supported the statistical evidence of this study, indicating that the kind of battle between students and teachers which occurred in the boys' public schools of this district was familiar in similar schools in other parts of the city.

[1] Maller, *op. cit., passim*; comparable data for schools of this district furnished by Dr. Maller.

The parochial schools set up much less of a conflict situation with home and community, since the underlying point of view of the school was shared by parents whose religious convictions made them send their children to parochial school. Respect for the religious habit of the sisters and brothers prevented the kind of disrespect and conflict with teachers which characterized the public schools. The parochial school instruction, moreover, had less unreality to the children than much of the public school instruction, for it conflicted less with their experience. The children in the parochial school could learn in their geography lesson, without confusion, that 'the world is a place which God has given us for our home,' but only the most credulous public school child of the district could learn that the police were impartial guardians of the peace.

In sending their children to the private progressive schools, the Villagers acted consistently with their own repudiation of long-accepted values. The private experimental schools acknowledged that there was no fixed culture pattern to which they were fitting their pupils and encouraged 'selective conformity' on the basis of individual judgment. They set individual psychology above social standards, building their school curriculum around the individual child. In detail, as well as in general policy, they ignored or departed from established custom. Whereas the public schools laid great stress on the appearance of the children, their neatness and their shoe-shine, and emphasized manners and courtesy, the experimental schools dressed their children in overalls, laid little or no stress on manners, and encouraged spontaneity and expression at the expense of order.

The Villagers were very active in supporting experimental education, both in the private school which had been a pioneer in the field and in the attempt to demonstrate that it was possible to use the progressive technique in public as well as private schools. But the system of education which these schools represented did not recommend itself to the local population. The private school, originally designed for children who were attending public school, had received little support from the type of clientèle which it sought. Between 1920 and 1930, it acquired a sufficiently favorable reputation among intellectuals not only to fill its ranks from those living in the locality, but to make people move into the district in order to send their children to this school. But, though it maintained scholarships for children from lower income levels, it had virtually no applications from children of non-professional families.

The failure of progressive education to appeal to the local population was even more apparent in the progressive unit in the public school. Like the private progressive school, this experimental unit actually drew into the locality a number of families who came in order to send their children there. But it did not have the same appeal for the parents of the local public school children. These parents, with their orthodox ideas of school, objected to many things, such as overalls and lack of school discipline, and especially to the fact that in the progressive unit the teaching of reading was postponed until the second year. Although some of the parents acknowledged that their children were very wise about the city and knew about a lot of practical things, they still felt that because they could not read at the end of the first year, as the older brothers and sisters had been able to do, the school was not doing its job. Emphasis on various forms of group activity in the school, moreover, did not seem important to the local parents. As an intelligent Italian mother in the Parent-Teachers' Association viewed it, 'The program of that school is suited to the children of well-to-do homes, not to our children. We send our children to school for what we cannot give them ourselves, grammar and drill. The Fifth Avenue children learn to speak well in their homes. We do not send our children to school for group activity; they get plenty of that in the street. But the Fifth Avenue children are lonely. I can see how group experience is an important form of education to them.' Although the other mothers who were consulted were not so analytical in their objection to the progressive unit as was this woman, they shared the feeling that somehow the school was not quite what it should be for their children.

The lack of support which this experiment received from the local parents was very apparent when the experimental unit was disbanded by the Board of Education. Lack of sympathy on the part of the principal, the district superintendent, and the Board of Education led to a critical appraisal by the Board of Education, which came to the conclusion that the experiment was not successful because the children could not pass the same tests, especially reading tests, in the first and second grades that the children in the ordinary school could. When the announcement was made that the experimental unit was to be discontinued, some two hundred parents gathered in a protest meeting to express their enthusiasm for the experiment and to offer to raise funds for continuing it as a privately supported unit within the public school. At this and subsequent meetings which were held before the Board of Education finally ruled that even with private support the experimental unit could not go on in the public schools, parents from among the local people were conspicuously absent. The entire body of enthusiastic support came from the Villagers. Once again, difference in attitude and assumptions drew a sharp line between Villagers and local people even within the one organization where the two groups were most closely linked.

The two schools which penetrated most into the homes of the local people were both maintained by welfare agencies. A kindergarten and primary school at one center, partly supported by public education funds, required home visiting of all its teachers. A nursery school at Greenwich House made parental education in child training and care a part of its program. The latter school represented an effort to adapt to a lower income group the nursery school idea, which developed with the growth of progressive education during these years and was largely confined to children of professional classes. By 1930, this school included not only the children of local people, but of Villagers as well, although three other nursery schools had been established in the locality by the sponsors of progressive education — in connection with the progressive school, as a co-operative venture of a group of parents for their own children, and in connection with a training school for nursery school teachers.

Some adult education was provided by the public schools, chiefly in teaching the English language to foreigners. The evening language classes at one of the public schools counted an enrollment of from 300 to 500 in different seasons. Though these classes continued to be made up predominantly of men, the proportion of women increased from approximately 12 per cent in the first half of the decade to approximately 22 per cent in the second half, and, in addition, classes for women were held from time to time under private auspices. The ordinary elementary school subjects were offered in public evening classes, but the demand was small and the classes were periodically discontinued. Sewing and dressmaking were also offered irregularly.

Training in various of the arts was available to young and old of all groups in the locality. The private art schools which came and went in local studios bore little relation to the life of the community, but the art program of Greenwich House brought instruction in music and crafts within the reach of the local people. This work, an outgrowth of the settlement's original leisure-time program, had already assumed educational proportions by 1920, and was expanded during the decade. In a workshop, for which a new building was constructed in this period, boys received full-time apprenticeship training in cabinet-making, woodcarving, and stonecutting from an Italian master craftsman. The pottery classes filled orders for vases and other pieces to decorate some of the wealthy uptown and suburban homes. The work of the music school, also housed in larger quarters during these years, attracted the attention and praise of leading musicians. As the work of these departments reached new professional heights, it acquired a city-wide reputation and clientèle. The music school drew more and more from outside of the neighborhood, the majority of the boys in the workshop were non-local, and, though the neighborhood children continued to come to the pottery workroom, their benches were occupied during school hours by non-local adults who were becoming skilled potters for a profession or an avocation. As these activities occupied an increasingly prominent place in the work of the House, Greenwich House grew from a neighborhood settlement into one of the independent centers of music and craft education in the city.

The educational institutions of this community, varied and extensive as they were, thus made certain adaptations and responses to the general trends of these years and, to some extent, to the specific conditions of the local community. Their difficulties arose in part from the fact that their educational philosophy changed at a different rate from their specific practices, so that some resisted the socialization which they were actually carrying out, while others expressed their approval of new methods which, in fact, they did not employ. The schools did not, moreover, serve as an organizing force in this culturally disorganized community, since they had not undertaken to think their way through to new cultural patterns or to orient their programs in such a direction.

XII. RECREATION

DURING the post-War years, recreation came to be increasingly regarded as an important function for which a community should provide. In Greenwich Village the inadequacy of recreational facilities ranked next to bad housing in the minds of those who were interested in the social welfare of the district.

Formal interest in recreation was not new, for settlements, Protestant missions, such widespread organizations as the Boy Scouts, and some of the Catholic churches had included in their welfare programs some provision for the leisure time of young people. Several of these organizations, in fact, dropped much of their emphasis on recreation during these years in favor of greater stress on religion in the case of the missions and on health and education in the case of the settlements. What was new at this time was the role attributed to recreation. Instead of being just one more part of a general welfare program, it came to be looked on by the family welfare agencies as essential to a proper adjustment of the individual and by others as a safeguard against juvenile delinquency. Family budgets provided by relief agencies in 1930 included provisions for recreation which would, a decade or more before, have been regarded as a rank waste of money. The Crime Prevention Bureau, newly organized as a division of the police department, laid great stress upon proper recreation as a way to eliminate juvenile delinquency.

1. ORGANIZED SERVICES

Formal provision for recreation in this community started before 1900 as part of the institutional programs of the Protestant churches. It received a boom in the first decade of the twentieth century with the growth of the settlement movement, which brought three settlements and two Protestant neighborhood houses into this area and two boys' clubs into the vicinity. The burst of 'community' activity during the War was reflected in the enlargement of the recreational plant of the various centers. Between 1915 and 1920, five new gymnasiums were constructed with the funds of private welfare organizations and a public gymnasium was built. After 1920, one Catholic and one Protestant church built gymnasiums and clubrooms, and a public park was transformed into a playing field. Since the population was decreasing steadily, the community became progressively well supplied with equipment in proportion to those who were in a position to use it.

The recreational services of the welfare agencies were directed primarily to boys in their teens. Two were confined to boys, while in others boys predominated. There was a decided trend, however, toward extending to girls some of the facilities and activities formerly reserved largely — if not exclusively — for boys. One of the institutions, originally a boys' club, was turning its building over to girls once a week in 1930. In another the head worker became particularly interested in a recreational program for girls, and, while continuing her boys' work, directed special effort toward them.

The boys who patronized recreational centers were of a more or less distinctive type, known from the point of view of the centers themselves as 'better boys' and to the toughs on the street as the 'sissy' type. Although one institution made a special effort to reach the delinquent type, and others professed a similar desire, actually the boys with more clearly defined interests and more refined standards of behavior were to be found at the recreational centers, while the rougher type remained outside. There was some variation between centers — a somewhat rougher element being attracted by boxing, for instance, to one center as against those who were content with basketball at another; but the type of activity offered and the attitudes of the recreation workers combined to attract the less rough and the more organizable boys.

With recreation centers constantly seeking to enlarge their membership, and with their programs attractive only to a limited group, all the agencies found their turnover very large.[1] Each reported a small constant nucleus of select individuals who consti-

---

[1] No precise study of turnover could be made because records kept by recreational agencies rarely showed date or reason for leaving.

tuted *the* group which more or less possessed the center, while a large floating element came and went. In some instances the possessive attitude of the small nucleus kept others out. Boys in street groups stated as their reason for not going to the nearest recreational center, 'The crowd there acts as though it owned the place. We don't want to go.' As congestion decreased, centers drew less from their immediate environment and more from more distant blocks. This, in turn, meant that only the more energetic or those with more interest would attend, for the apathetic were almost always to be found close to home.

Yet even the boys who made up the possessive nucleus were often more concerned with what they could get out of their centers than with any feeling cf responsibility toward them. The complaint that the boys were lacking in loyalty to the center and in respect for its property was general. Recreation workers were distressed by the frequent attitude that those who attended centers were doing the center a favor rather than making use of a privilege or advantage. Since each agency measured its success in its ability to hold members, it was an easy step for the members to threaten to 'leave the house' or actually to walk out if things did not suit them. The workers at each center looked back wistfully to an earlier generation of members who were more interested, loyal, and cooperative than those of more recent years, but there was no way of knowing whether their memory of the past was more than the product of a rosy imagination.

Each of the recreational agencies stressed character development and training for leadership as the heart of its program. None, however, had been successful in the latter effort. One or two of the boys trained in the centers had returned to the staffs of their houses. But when, in 1930, every center in the neighborhood was canvassed for potential leaders for local boys' clubs, the answer from each and all was the same, 'We have no boys who have been associated with our center who could take positions of responsibility and leadership.' This testimony was not confined to any one type of agency. Independent settlement houses, Protestant missions, Catholic churches, and independent boys' clubs had all had the same experience and had come to the same conclusions about the leadership capacity and ability to take responsibility on the part of their members.

Boys predominated at the recreational centers partly because they were the 'problems' from the point of view of preventing delinquency and partly because neither Italian nor Irish girls were the 'type interested in activities' which could be found, for instance, in Jewish neighborhoods. The restrictions to which Italian girls were subjected, combined with the failure of the ordinary programs of athletics to attract the older girls, limited the number at recreation centers, until 1930, to a few dozen.

In their girls' program the agencies ran counter to the standards of the community, for they aimed to develop a type of self-reliant, athletic girl who was quite different from the type which found favor in the district. They sought, too, to interest girls in activity in place of an exclusive preoccupation with themselves and with their main problem of acquiring the best available man. Some of the Irish and a few of the Italian girls found athletics an absorbing interest, but the athletic type hardly became popular in the neighborhood among either girls or boys during these years. Most of the girls were interested in going to dances and in learning to do those things which would give them the necessary better manners and greater poise that might mean the chance at a better match. Instruction in etiquette, bridge, tap dancing were among the activities which appealed as aids toward this end.

Striking evidence of the fundamental persistence of this attitude was offered by a group of girls, who had been long associated with the center and were selected by the recreation worker as representative of those with whom the center felt it had been most successful. This group of girls was extremely scornful of the 'low' type who had no interest except men. They had learned to want something better than the other girls and to work for it. On being pressed, however, the difference between these girls and those whom they scorned turned out to be simply that they were aiming higher — they were not going to take any man who came along, but were going to hold off until they were, perhaps, twenty-two or twenty-three, on the chance of making a better match, and possibly even getting a college man.

It was only when one center, in 1930, developed a special program to meet the interests of the girls and the objections of the parents that the first considerable group of Italian girls from the more conservative families were brought out for recreational activity.

The leader of this center first undertook to make the girls' parents approve of the center and feel confidence in it. She opened a sewing class which, at the end of the year, held a fashion show where the girls paraded in clothes of their own making before the admiring eyes of their mothers. She kept very careful track of attendance and always reported absences to the home in order to assure the mothers that the girls were not using the center as an excuse to go out unchaperoned. Then she sought to develop a program which would hold the girls. On a questionnaire asking them what they wanted to be, she received the reply that two thirds wanted to be movie actresses — on the presumption that actresses had the best chance to meet and marry a millionaire. Nothing daunted, the supervisor took up the challenge, asking them to consider the movie actresses that they knew: 'Were they awkward and sloppy? Did they have messy hair and bad teeth? Did they have harsh voices?' If the girls wanted to become movie actresses, the center would try to make them into good ones, but that would mean joining the gym classes and the singing class, taking care of their hair and teeth, making use of the shower baths, and so on through all the activities of the center. The girls were soon hard at work on a varied program. The extension of recreational activity in connection with the Catholic churches also brought out some from conservative homes who were permitted to go to the churches because their conservative families were also religious.

The recreation centers with a definitely 'welfare' purpose differed among themselves in their approach to their problems. One group believed in offering a series of activities which would appeal to the interests of individuals. The other directed its efforts toward social groups, taking these groups as it found them and seeking to lead their activity. The former attitude was the more usual among the centers of this locality.

The types of activity which they offered were designed to be educational — pottery, sewing, discussion groups; to give some form of creative expression, as in dramatics for children and adults; or to build character, especially through emphasis on sportsmanship and fair play in athletics. They hoped not only to entertain for the moment and to keep young people out of mischief, but to give to them resources upon which they could draw in the future.

These programs of activity proved attractive to the younger children. The children's theater and dancing group at Greenwich House always had a full enrollment and acquired a city-wide reputation for the quality of its work. Those children who were sent to the centers to be kept out of mischief could be interested in various crafts or other specialized activities. But the boys and girls in their mid-teens and older were much harder to hold with activity programs — chiefly because these programs ran counter to the recreational habits of the community. The centers assumed that some types of recreation were better than others. Those which involve 'creative' activity stood at the top of the list, while those which involved the element of chance stood lowest. This rating was almost directly opposite to that of the community.

The weight of inertia, which made 'hanging around' the neighborhood's most characteristic leisure-time pursuit, dampened the appeal of 'creative' activities. Even those who attended the centers often used them simply as places to hang around, to the dismay of those in charge. Boys frankly stated that they regarded a center as a place to hang around, since going home was out of the question and they did not have money to go elsewhere.

From time to time all the recreational centers endeavored to put on some sort of intellectual program, either in the form of discussion groups, lectures, or classes. With the exception of dramatics, these recurrent efforts consistently met with poor response. Only the small group which had had some college training, but did not have sufficient money to join a professional or other club, supported intellectual or semi-intellectual activities. Most of those who had not gone to college were not interested, and those who had gone felt too superior to the recreation centers to attend. Again, the workers ruefully reported that intellectual programs had had more appeal in the past, but they had no definite evidence. The statement may well have been true of the Irish, for those with intellectual interests had come to look down upon the recreation centers as places where lower-class people went, and in 1930 almost all the support for intellectual activities at the center where the membership was mixed came from Italian, not Irish, boys and girls.

While recreation centers struggled against the negative force of inertia, they waged a positive attack on the universal habit of gambling. By specifically prohibiting craps, they tried to outlaw the practice in its crudest form. By building up an attitude of sportsmanship, they sought to provide an alternative.

In instilling sportsmanship into those who were regular in attendance, some of the centers were outstandingly successful. The girls' basketball coach at Greenwich House was able to report proudly on the attitude displayed by her team when it lost the final match in an inter-settlement tournament. At the end of the game the girls cheered the opposing team and forgot to ask the score. It was only on the way home that they remembered to ask what the score had been, and greeted the news that they had lost with, 'Never mind. It was a good game.' But in spite of such signal achievements as this with their own members, the recreational centers made no apparent dent on the standards of sportsmanship in the community. Independent local teams were as ready to abscond with the stakes, or to start a fight, as they had been ten years before.

The Boy Scout movement was the first to tackle the problem of juvenile delinquency on a national scale through recreation. But no program of activity was at sharper variance with the habits of the community or less attractive to the rank and file than that of the scouts. Scouting never flourished in the area. Troops existed at some of the recreational centers and churches from time to time, and independent troops met at different places within the district. When one of the small local settlements closed its doors, the building was given over to the Boy Scouts, but they found the district so unfavorable to scouting that it was hardly worth while to use the building. Such troops as had been organized showed a tremendous turnover of membership and troops themselves had been short-lived.

Neither neighborhood conditions nor neighborhood attitudes were favorable to scouting. Studies in other communities have shown that those who go into scouting tend to be a selected group made up on the whole of the more ambitious, the more well-to-do, and of those to whom outdoor programs appeal and whose background and home training coincide, at least in a measure, with those scout ideals upon which the organization lays stress.[1]

To the scout leaders, local boys were 'bad scout material.' In no uncertain terms they condemned the typical Italian boy of the

[1] Information supplied by research division of National Boy Scout Headquarters.

locality as a filthy-minded rotter, with low taste and no moral fiber. The neighborhood boys retorted in turn that 'scouts are sissies.' Although the local boys were eager to get out of the city and to go to beaches, they were not attracted by the outdoor program of the scouts — by 'nature and that kind of silly stuff.' Their home and community standards were very far from coinciding with those stressed in the scout program. The Boy Scout's 'good turn daily' was hardly compatible with the demands for tips which rose instinctively to the lips of the local boys on every occasion; even when a pedestrian had already picked herself up out of a mud puddle before the boys on the sidewalk reached her side, they were sure to be ready with the inevitable 'tip for helping you up, lady?'

The most fundamental clashes between the programs of organized recreation and the habits of the community arose over the neighborhood's attitude toward women. Obviously, no center approved the neighborhood's view that women were a species of game to be hunted. They were, however, not very successful in combating this point of view. While wishing to promote an easy play relationship between girls and boys, they continued to maintain quite separate boys' and girls' departments and activities, they promoted few joint ventures other than dances, and one of the girls' workers even took the attitude that she did not want the boys' groups at her center to meet with the girls because she had taught the girls standards of behavior above those of the boys. 'When they have learned to act decently, they can come and meet with my girls.' Even at dances girls and boys had nothing to say to each other and separated into groups of boys and of girls on opposite sides of the hall the moment the music stopped; except in dramatics they engaged in little joint activity. At the religious centers, small groups of older boys and girls met together, usually for serious discussion. According to the report of one center the boys and girls five to ten years before had gone out in groups and had played together more in the manner of which the center approved than did their girls and boys in 1930. The change may have reflected either the change in nationality of members or the greater sophistication of the post-War generation, which rarely went out in groups but only in pairs.

While the centers which furnished a program of activities were

working to equip individuals with resources upon which they
could build an avocation or interest, other agencies, chiefly two
centers for boys on the outskirts of the area, followed the group
approach. Those whose club program was of chief importance
recognized that, in proportion as positive interests were weak, individuals would depend upon group association to bolster themselves up and keep themselves diverted. They set out to attract
the comparatively resourceless group whose attitude was, 'We
would not go to the neighborhood house because they tried to put
us all in different activities, and wherever we go, we go together.'
The programs of these centers were somewhat closer to the habits
of the unsponsored groups in the community. Clubs of all sorts
came in, and the effort was primarily to deflect them from anti-
social conduct, without struggling as hard as the other type of
center to effect an 'improvement' in their recreational taste.

The group approach was carried farthest by one organization
which believed in going to the boys and girls on the blocks where
they played, working with them there in the groups in which they
found them. This organization took the position that a different
code of conduct built up inside a neighborhood house or school was
more likely to produce dual attitudes on the part of the girls and
boys than to modify their habitual conduct. Its work was new and
was confined to one block, so that it could not be compared with
that of the more established agencies. It was correct, however, in
thinking that the children associated the more formal centers with
school rather than with their unsupervised play. These organized
centers ran their programs according to the school calendar, closing down during the school vacation and curtailing their activities
on Sundays. Instead of functioning at their height during the
time when the young people had the greatest leisure, they functioned as a supplement to the school program. The suggestion
made to one center that the very time when it should be active was
the time when school was not in session was met with the statement that 'the children do not look at it that way. They expect
that when school closes the house will close also.'

Like all the other community institutions of this area, recreational institutions, either those provided publicly or those made
available by private funds, were patronized almost exclusively by
the local people and scarcely at all by the Villagers. The only ex-

ceptions were the professional women's gym class and the Italian class, a class in pottery and a theater group, all sponsored by Greenwich House, and the young people's society at the church house of a Fifth Avenue church. For the rest, the recreation of the Villagers was supplied commercially or else was self-directed.

2. SPONTANEOUS ACTIVITY

Entirely independent of the recreation centers were privately organized social clubs — the characteristic social form for boys between the ages of eighteen and twenty-four who were working and had money enough to acquire clubrooms and maintain club activities. These clubs, of long standing among the Irish, were of comparatively recent date among the Italians, largely because the second generation Italians only reached the club-forming age in the 1920's. The life of these clubs was apt to be confined to a few years during which the original members grew up and dropped away. A number of Irish clubs — dead at the time the study was being carried on — were remembered, though they had been out of existence for some time. The Italian clubs, on the other hand, were much more numerous in 1930 than the Irish, but none was more than six years old, and there were few which had existed earlier of which any memory was retained. Very occasionally an older group passed on its club organization to a younger group when it disbanded, but only one such case was found.

The distinguishing feature of a formal social club was the possession of a clubroom. Occasionally such clubs used the facilities of a recreational center and ran their parties there, but the independent clubroom which did not have to be shared with others was very highly prized. While the centers had the greatest difficulty in keeping their patrons from damaging the centers' property, the independent clubs treated their rooms with pride and care.

Such of these social clubs as maintained athletic teams centered their activity and interest around athletics. An example of this type was an Italian club of soccer players which had taken for its name that of the champion soccer team in Italy, and which was held together around this interest. In the clubs which were not athletic, the meetings were chiefly devoted to a consideration of how to pay the rent on the clubroom, so prized as a hangout.

The principal means of raising money was the giving of dances, sometimes at the clubroom itself, occasionally in the hall of one of the neighborhood centers, and not infrequently at a public hotel or hall. Virtually all social clubs had an annual money-raising dance, while some ran a series of dances so frequently that dancing became a principal form of their activity.

Though Irish and Italian clubs were essentially similar, the Irish had one distinctive type, the rowdy, hoodlum club whose members got drunk every night, broke up the premises, and were repeatedly being put out on the street by irate landlords. The Italian clubs never went in for rowdyism in the way that some Irish clubs did. When they ran foul of the authorities, it was because of the sale, rather than the consumption, of liquor, or because of gambling or women.

The number of these clubs at one time was difficult to estimate, because they came and went so fast, because they were sometimes found connected with a neighborhood house and sometimes not, and because some of those which were small and new did not have conspicuous clubrooms and were difficult to find. During the time when the study was being conducted, some dozen such clubs, apart from those affiliated with neighborhood centers, were found, while a number of others met on the blocks adjoining the immediate area of study. Owing to the number of these clubs and the fact that all held dances more or less frequently which were open, not only to their members, but to the public from whom the club raised its funds, they furnished the principal dance facilities of the neighborhood. Local boys attended these dances and those run at the recreation centers rather than public dance halls. Only one recreation center consistently confined its dances to its own members instead of opening them to the public and charging admission, while others at different times held both open and closed dances.

Private social clubs were boys' organizations. In a few cases, however, girls were taken in as members to help pay the rent. This was the case with two Italian clubs, in each of which the girls had a separate organization. They did not use the clubrooms to hang around in as did the boys, but had the use of the rooms for meetings at specific times. In both cases girls had not formed spontaneous groups, but had been brought in as friends of the boys and had been formed into a group of their own at the instigation of the boys.

Each club tended to disintegrate as soon as its members started 'keeping company,' although the strong athletic interest in one club continued to hold the boys together after they had acquired girls. As one after another of its members deserted, the club would eventually disappear and its place be taken by an organization of a younger group.

The private social clubs and the organized recreation centers held each other mutually in disregard. To the recreation workers, and the clubs at the recreation centers, the private social clubs were made up of a low type, assumed to be irresponsible, and either connected with politics or likely to use their clubrooms as a place to gamble or to bring women for immoral purposes. The social clubs, in their turn, preferred their independence and considered themselves more responsible than those who enjoyed the paternalism of recreation centers.

The Crime Prevention Bureau shared the attitude of the recreation centers toward the private clubs, assuming that they fostered vice and seeking to have them closed up. The local police, on the other hand, were sympathetic with their existence and had no desire to molest any but the few with a membership of rowdies or criminals. The clubs of the neighborhood which were in existence in 1930 showed the contentions of both sides to have some basis in fact.

There were a few evidences of political connections and some of the social clubs ran into difficulties because of evidence of gambling and vice which the police found there. The latter represented the tougher type of club which ran a poolroom and gambling joint of its own instead of patronizing commercial places, and was largely composed of cab-drivers and idle toughs. Only one such club was definitely located in 1930, while one or two others showed some of the characteristics.

On the other hand, some of the clubs contained a very reliable element. They showed an attitude of responsibility for the younger members of the community, initiative in sponsoring play groups of younger children on their own blocks, and a willingness to assume leadership which was in contrast to the acknowledged absence of such leadership in the organized recreation centers. Some clubs, moreover, stood high in community esteem. One of the Irish clubs in 1930 was the chief independent organization of the younger Irish in the community. The still younger boys looked up to this club as their ideal, and young and old alike, even the parents, turned out to the club's annual affairs. Only a political banquet or a church social could get out such a crowd as this club did.

For the boys and men of the locality, the more typical form of recreational organization was neither the recreation center nor the formal social club, but the informal, 'hang-around' group which hung out at a candy store, ice-cream parlor, cigar store, in front of a laundry, in the park, or on the street corner. Barber shops discouraged their presence by their signs, 'If you have nothing to do, don't do it here.' The groups which hung around together were all more or less exclusive affairs and the places which became their hangouts tended to be inaccessible to others. A young East Side pugilist, who was a stranger to the community, but knew his way around poolrooms, made the rounds of the poolrooms in the neighborhood. In each he found the same situation. As soon as he came in, all conversation ceased and he was eyed with suspicion bordering on hostility. 'It's very hard to get in on these places,' he reported, 'because the people there have always known each other and they resent a stranger.' Another East-Sider made the rounds of the candy stores, and came back with a similar report. 'When a stranger goes into a candy store, the fellows all stop talking, even though all they have been discussing was the last picture at the local movie house.'

The 'hang-around' groups drifted together usually because of proximity, but each group tended to be fairly homogeneous. An occasional individual of a different sort might be found attached to a given group, as, for instance, a college boy who hung around with his old school playmates at the nearest ice-cream parlor because there were not enough like him to constitute a group with him, and because he lacked the money to go elsewhere. The observant boys of the neighborhood distinguished among the 'hang-around' groups between two principal types — the care-free and the tough. In almost identical words, several intelligent local boys from several groups described the ice-cream parlor, street-corner gangs as the boys who took things as they came along without ever thinking ahead, careless in the sense of being without imagination and without ambition, drifting from one day through to the next. This was the type which was found to make up most of the thirty 'hang-around' groups investigated in the course of this study. These groups were not tough, although they might contain some 'wise guys' who liked to swagger and appear tougher than the really tough ones. Such groups, largely because of their inertia, were not likely to contain members who had been in trouble with the police or were likely to get into trouble in the immediate future.

The tough type of group was apt to be drawn from a somewhat wider geographical area than the carefree type because its membership was more distinctive. It was found primarily in poolrooms, sometimes in cigar stores, outside of speakeasies, or in gambling joints. It was likely to be slightly older and to contain professional loafers, a backbone of cab-drivers, and even an occasional criminal. Much harder to reach, these groups were not investigated with anything like the detail of the other type. They were located, however, sufficiently accurately to indicate that their number in 1930 was certainly much smaller than that of the 'hang-around' groups. Local residents agreed that this had been the case ten years before.

In addition to these two types — the carefree and the tough — a very occasional group of more ambitious boys was to be found where the members were attending high school or, once in a while, college. Like the tough type, these groups tended to be drawn from a wider area than the local block.

Hanging around — i.e., doing nothing in company — was the principal form of local recreation, not because of any positive choice, but by reason of lack of initiative and, especially, of money. Since much recreation required money, and what did not require money called for imagination, or at least space — which, in turn, required money in the city — these circumstances largely forced the boys and young men into inactivity.

All in all, hanging around was not very exciting to the hangers. Doing nothing, chatting, joking, and 'passing remarks' at the passers-by occupied the empty hours. It was hard to find things to talk about for hours on end, for even the perennial topics of sports, women, and the movies became well worn. Somebody might join the group who was ready to place bets; occasionally a pack of cards would come out. Sometimes, if the night was cold and the hangout out-of-doors, the group would go tramping around the neighborhood. Those groups which met in the park were apt to find girls there for horse-play. Once in a while somebody had a friend with a car and the gang would go riding to Brooklyn or Jersey. In the summer time, there was Coney Island. Sometimes, if they had money, they might go to a prize-fight. In one of the fellows' houses they might listen to fights, baseball games, or detective stories over the radio, or, rarely, play cards, but boys were not usually encouraged by their parents to bring their gang to the house. An occasional stroll around the neighborhood, a show on Sunday night if one had money, and, again if there was money, a girl to take out on Saturday night and an occasional dance, completed the groundwork of leisure-time activity for the bulk of ordinary local boys who made up the 'hang-around' groups. The bitter comment of a member of one group, 'It's more like frustration than recreation,' appeared to the observer to be a valid characterization.

Among the younger boys, the organization which corresponded to the 'hang-around' group was the street-play group. The boy gang has received much consideration from sociologists and social workers, as well as from the police, and to the general literature on that subject the present study can contribute little. Some thirty groups of younger boys and another thirty groups of older boys existing in the neighborhood at the time the study was being conducted were canvassed and the history of each group and something of its membership was ascertained. The outstanding characteristic of all the younger groups was their essentially play character. They did not conform to the picture of the close gang which has been built from a study of delinquent boys and they reinforced the conclusions already reached by others that the closeness of the group increases with its anti-social character.

Of the thirty groups examined, only four had clearly anti-social characteristics, and only one was actively anti-social as a group. Of these four, one was led by a boy who had been in court, whose brother was a gangster, and who ruled the club with the iron hand of the gang leader, 'If you tell my real name I will kill you, and I mean it.' When this group was invited to go swimming, the members were eager to go and started to follow the person who had invited them. The leader, distrustful, would not go, and, glowering at his followers, challenged them with an emphatic 'I am not going. Are you?' The others wilted, although they longed to swim. This group was known to the police as a group and had been picked up for joint predatory activity.

The second group was more potentially than actively predatory, its chief characteristic being apathy. One of the older boys on the block who had tried to arouse the group complained that it never turned up to play a game when the date had been made. In contrast to the rest of the play groups which were approached, all of which were friendly and eager to talk about their group, this group met the advances of the investigator with indifference and obscenity. The neighbors had observed this gang and were worried by it.

In a third group, the leader was a confirmed thief — anything and everything which he could lay his hands on by house-breaking, shoplifting, or just helping himself around his home and the neighborhood — and his lieutenant was a misfit at school who had been placed in what the boys called the 'crazy' class and who played truant. In this case the group followed the leader because of his vigor and resourcefulness, but did not share his predatory habits — except in little matters such as 'finding' paint-brushes so that they could help fix up their hangout in an empty house which was lent to them.

The fourth group that showed positive anti-social features did not do so as a group, although two of its members had been in court for store-breaking. This group was one of the most active in the locality, had found a hangout in an abandoned water-tank on the roof of a tenement, played a lively game of punchball on a street with a trolley line, and tramped the neighborhood looking for excitement. It was the clearest example of the likelihood that normal good spirits and resourcefulness on the part of smart, active boys in a congested district of this type might bring such a group afoul of society and the law.

The rest of the groups were all purely play groups. Whatever mischief they might get into was incidental. The 'smartest' acts of which they boasted were nearly always skillful ball plays. Their 'bravest' acts usually involved such things as climbing over roofs or standing up to bigger fellows in a fight. They were, in fact, inclined to be careful to keep from their membership boys whom they thought likely to get them into trouble unless those boys were especially proficient in sports. The leadership which they followed was not the type of gang rule exercised by the leader of the predatory group described above. Their leader was usually the best ballplayer, and quite strikingly was frequently a member of another race or color, one who would not otherwise have rated in the group.

In the general setup of play groups and older boys' groups there had been no appreciable change. Fads in games came and went. Brick-throwing was less in vogue than it had been ten years before. But the essential qualities of play organization remained substantially unchanged.

There were no records to tell what proportion of the boys and young men of the neighborhood were to be found at recreation centers, in social clubs, or in informal groups, or how the proportion had changed. None of the recreation centers kept accurate records, there was overlapping of membership between formal and informal groups, and the latter kept no records at all. Most of the boys and young men, perhaps four fifths, belonged to something. Among the younger boys there was a small number whose parents would not permit them to play on the street and who were, therefore, not members of block groups. Some of these were sent to recreation centers, while others were not. Among the older boys, the few who were attending college or night school and the few who had money enough to go elsewhere or, rarely, a special interest or skill such as music, constituted the small element which did not join in any local group recreation.

A large proportion of the boys — certainly well over half — had at some time had some contact with one or another of the local recreation agencies — settlement, mission, church, scouts, school. A small proportion — perhaps three or four hundred out of a population between the ages of ten and twenty of 4845 in 1920 and 3186 in 1930 — were really active members for whom the recreation center filled an important part of their lives and directed their activity. The number in independent social clubs was considerably less than those who patronized the centers, if the clubs which met at the centers were included in the latter rather than the former count. As the numbers attending the centers did not decrease with the population, larger proportions of the young people were, obviously, in touch with the centers in 1930 than in 1920.

Unlike the boys, the girls did not form independent social clubs, except as occasional adjuncts to those of the boys, nor were they to be found in constant informal groups. Their only hang-outs were the steps of their own houses. This situation supported the observations made in other studies that girls do not tend to gang together in anything like the way that boys do. Though among the smaller children little girls were sometimes included in gangs with little boys, the club or gang idea was only occasionally to be found among the younger girls. Many girls had as their only leisure-time activity 'sitting,' and 'sitting' was an essentially solitary procedure whether indoors or on the steps, in contrast to 'hanging around' which assumed a group. Though more girls were enrolled at the centers than in 1920 and the type had changed, the whole number in any sort of recreational group in 1930 still constituted a very small proportion of the local girls.

While recreation held a central place in the lives of the young, it played a negligible role in the lives of the local adults. Recreation centers contained no services for men and had only begun to serve more than a few of the women. The familiar American 'joining' habit did not characterize this district. The area did not abound in lodges and women's clubs so familiar in small or suburban communities. A few men's clubs existed in the locality and their number was on the decrease. The Italian mutual benefit societies were fast dying out and few had ever furnished much in the way of social activity. Several of the principal fraternal orders, e.g., Masons, Moose, and Odd Fellows, inaugurated, in the early years of the century, specifically foreign lodges. In New York City the Italian lodges constituted the principal foreign units of the Masons — thirteen out of the twenty foreign lodges in 1930 — and the only foreign body of the Moose was Italian. All of these lodges had grown in membership between 1920 and 1930, but they had grown from outside of the Village, not from the local area. The total number of new enrollments from the neighborhood in the Masonic lodges between 1920 and 1930 was twenty-five.

The lodges which formerly had had their meeting place in the locality were meeting at some central hall or in Brooklyn, and dispersion of the population from the neighborhood had put a stop to local lodge activity. The people in the locality insisted that Italians in general had stopped joining lodges, but as far as the Masons were concerned, the evidence of their membership list showed a very substantial increase in all the Italian lodges between 1920 and 1930, indicating that Italians had not stopped joining, but that lodge members had left this locality. The secretary of the Moose reported that Italian members were joining all the time.

The absence of distinctive forms of recreation from the culture pattern of the Italians gave less basis for the survival of Italian recreational institutions than those of some of the other immigrant nationalities. In contrast to German and Slavic immigrants, the Italians had no kind of recreational activity to which they were devoted and which they consequently made efforts to keep in America. The same was true of the Irish, whose distinctive recreational forms largely died as far as the group in this locality was concerned. Although Irish dances and songs were sung in some few families on such occasions as Christmas celebrations, traditional Irish forms of recreation rarely engaged the adult Irish population of this neighborhood.

Informal groups of men had their hangouts as did the younger men and boys. For a certain group of Irish, and a smaller group of Italians, the political club served as a social center and a hangout. The Italians had not come to use the political clubs to anything like the extent that the Irish did, for their clubs never had more than a handful of people sitting around, while there was always a group coming and going at the Irish clubs. With the passing of most of the old saloons, the Irish were left without their old haunts, and they made certain cigar stores and real estate offices their hangouts, while the Italian men continued to use their Italian cafés. Each café had its own clientèle, chiefly of older men or those recently out from Italy, who spent the evening playing cards and talking. The café, the equivalent of the coffee house or sidewalk café in Italy, remained a distinctive symbol of the Old World, as rarely used as a hangout by the American-born as was the American ice-cream parlor by the older group.

While men and boys attended recreation centers, formed social clubs, and hung around cafés and ice-cream parlors, leisure and recreation were not expected to play much part in the women's lives.

Social life outside the home was not so new to the Irish women as to the Italian. Irish women's clubs at recreational centers were as much as twenty-five years old. In the old days when the neighborhood was a neighborhood, they took part in church parties and in affairs run by the political clubs. Each parish had its group which combined religious and social activity and ran the affairs of the parish and of the parish clubs. After the advent of women's suffrage, they increased their social activities at the political clubs. A local court of the Catholic Daughters of America was chiefly Irish in membership. The worker in charge of one of the Irish women's clubs at a recreation center complained that it was hard to get the women out to club meetings nowadays because the women had so many other forms of social activity which engaged their attention. The president of a religious society at one of the churches had found the same difficulty with her women. The Irish women who were involved in these activities were neither the down-and-out of the waterfront nor the prosperous political group. They were rather the substantial lower middle class element whose married children had moved out, but who had remained interested in and loyal to the old neighborhood.

Except for a very few Italian women who had belonged to the mothers' club of a neighborhood house, organized recreation was new to Italian women during these years. Starting around 1924, with the Protestant centers and extending to Catholic churches, health center, recreation center, and political club, one club after another was organized for Italian women. The development of these club activities for Italian women involved a changed attitude toward recreation for women on the part both of the women themselves and of their husbands.

For most of the Italian and Irish women of the locality, and for many men, family affairs rather than formally organized or even informal groups offered the principal source of recreation. Among the Italians, weddings were especially the occasion of great festivity, not only to the immediate family, but to friends and

neighbors as well. An Italian wedding which was not so arranged
as to give the guests at the wedding a good time was sure to be
criticized for this shortcoming in no uncertain terms. In discussing a recent local wedding, one of the Italian women plainly
set forth the recreational role which weddings were expected to
perform. At the wedding in question the bride had 'come in' so
late that after the ceremony had taken place there was only time
for the guests to greet the bride and to present their gifts of money
to her. There was hardly any time for dancing and for the guests
to enjoy themselves. The women agreed that this wedding had
not been a success.

All possible events — engagements, christenings, graduation,
or home-coming — were made occasions for appropriate parties.
If someone became in any way distinguished, it was an excuse for
a party in his honor, such as the one held at an uptown hotel in
honor of two local young men who had been appointed as internes
in one of the better hospitals. Among the Irish, funerals continued to hold an important place. Although wakes were said to
be becoming less general than they had been a decade before,
the number which were held while this study was in progress
indicated clearly that the practice of holding wakes had by no
means disappeared, nor had they lost their character as social
events. One of the district political leaders had the reputation
of always turning out for all the wakes — a practice to which
much of the loyalty to him was attributed. Christmas, of course,
brought families together for merrymaking and was one of the
most important festive days during the year both for Italians
and Irish. For Jewish families, festivals and High Holidays
constituted corresponding occasions for family reunions and
celebrations.

For those who did not take part in clubs, these family affairs
constituted the chief, often practically the only, form of recreation, especially for people who scorned to spend their time in
gossip with neighbors. Though the growth of club activities for
women enlarged the field of recreation for many, the majority
of the Italian women of the locality were still to be numbered
among those whose chief recreation consisted of family parties
and Christmas celebrations.

The principal innovations of the years did not come in the

form of organized recreation, offered by recreation centers or indulged in by spontaneously organized groups, but rather in the extension of the commercial forms — especially the movies. For this district the movies became not only the most universal form of recreation, but a major source of ideas about life and the world in general. It would have been highly desirable had this study been able to examine the moulding effect of the movies upon the habits of the people of the neighborhood, but the problem was too difficult to tackle within the compass of available time and effort.

Movie attendance had become practically universal. The community boasted two small neighborhood movie houses patronized by the children of the locality, sometimes in the company of their parents and sometimes alone, charging ten cents for children and twenty cents for adults and showing serial films. Each of these cheap places was known to the young people of its immediate neighborhood as 'The Dump' because of its noisy, disorderly, odorous, and dirty character. These two neighborhood houses had served the neighborhood for years; a third was torn down to make way for a new building.

In addition to these 'dumps,' patronized by children almost entirely, the district formerly boasted a large, well-established neighborhood movie house that was frequented by adults as well as children, and was an important feature of the life of the community. Although located in the heart of the Italian neighborhood, this house practically never showed Italian films because, as the manager put it, 'for a neighborhood house you have to count on the people that come several times a week. The older Italians who are interested in Italian films don't go to the movies that way.' When this house was destroyed to make way for the subway, it was missed in the locality, and three years later it was still being described as one of the old landmarks and a neighborhood institution whose loss was regretted. Coincident with the passing of this neighborhood movie house came the establishment in the district of one of a chain of movie palaces, charging much higher admission than the local 'dumps' and patronized largely on Saturday nights by young men with their girls or on Sunday nights by the whole family. This house was also patronized by the Villagers, as the others never were.

Movie attendance was governed by habit and by the status of different movie houses rather than by the particular film which was playing. Young people outgrew the 'dumps' which they attended as children, not because they were any less attracted by the Wild West or gangster films and the lurid posters which these houses featured, but because they 'wouldn't be seen there.' Even the new movie palace, and the series of large movies on the business thoroughfare which bordered the northern edge of the district, were not rated as the most desirable places at which to be seen. Any boy who could afford the extra quarter necessary to take his girl to a Times Square theater did so, even to see the same picture, for he thereby displayed his willingness to spread himself for the girl. The distinction between taking a girl to Times Square or to the local house was pointed out by one young man, who carefully explained that if you took a girl to a Times Square movie, you could try to kiss her good night, but if you only took her to a local movie, it would be presumptuous to attempt to kiss her.

The glamour which surrounded the movie and entertainment world in the eyes of the whole country during these years was positively dazzling to local young people. Boys and girls at Greenwich House experienced the crowning event of the year — perhaps of their lives — when the great Roxy, he who had made the movie palace into a 'cathedral,' not only sent one of his men to coach a show at the House, but came down himself to one rehearsal. No prince or potentate could have thrilled them so by his presence. Not even Primo Carnera, the boxing champion, whom a political aspirant brought to his club to give it prestige, could make such a stir — nobody, probably, except some other great name or face from the movie world.

The majority of the Villagers did not find it necessary to organize for purposes of recreation because of the forms which their leisure-time activity took and the fact that they could use their homes for recreation as the local people often could not. Out of a sample of 300 villagers, only 32 per cent belonged to any sort of organization or club which could serve a recreational purpose, either by providing associates or facilities as would a college club or Y.M.C.A., or by engaging in specific activities as would a dramatics group or a walking club. Apart from a club attached to one of the local tea-rooms, to which 2 per cent belonged, all these organizations were city-wide rather than local. Four per cent belonged to professional or civic societies, while 64 per cent were members of no organized society or club.

The types of leisure-time pursuits which most of the Villagers preferred were either essentially solitary or informally social and called for no organized activity. Among a sample of 90 Villagers, reading headed the list of ways in which they preferred to spend their leisure for 50 per cent of those answering, while 93 per cent reported that they actually read a great deal. Thirteen per cent liked to engage in creative or contemplative activities, which, too, were solitary. For the 21 per cent that preferred some form of 'sociability' — conversation, dancing, drinking, or rarely, cards — their own apartments, or the commercial facilities of the city served their need. If they, and the 9 per cent whose favorite diversion was the theater, did not have the necessary money to use commercial facilities, they scanted on their food and clothes to attend the theater or to buy liquor for a party. The 9 per cent whose recreational preference was for some form of athletic or outdoor activity were the only ones who found it necessary to join organized groups, although some of the young people who were strange to the city or community, and liked sociability but did not like to make their friends through speakeasy pick-ups, voiced a desire for organized means of meeting new people.

With so large a proportion for whom reading was a principal pursuit, the public library would seem to have been the one local institution in a position to serve the Villagers' recreational needs. Only a third of the 198 people reporting on the use of local facilities, however, used the public library. Among 90 interviewed, only 18 per cent used the local library. It served the local people in the earlier years, and after the construction of new office buildings the daytime population almost made up in new cardholders for the old residents who had moved away. A study of the reading habits of a sample of 75 Villagers [1] showed that only 16 per cent preferred to obtain their reading matter from the public library, in contrast to 38 per cent of a corresponding group in a town. Forty-five per cent preferred to purchase their books

[1] Moshier, L. M., *op. cit.*

while the rest used rental libraries or borrowed from friends.

The reason for the preference was probably revealed in the type of reading, for the Villager group, in contrast to the town group, read more recently published books that would be less likely to be available at a library than the kind of works that made up the town groups' reading matter. Their taste in novels ran, as would be expected, to those with literary quality, the psychological and the sophisticated rather than to the romances, historical novels, and detective stories that were the town's favorites. They selected their reading on the basis of their knowledge of the author or reliance on book reviews, scorning the study-club programs and book-club selections upon which the townspeople more largely relied. And while 34 per cent of the townspeople found the movies and the radio seriously competing with reading for their leisure time, these activities offered rival interests for only 12 per cent of the Villagers. They averaged approximately seven hours of book reading each a week.

The list of magazines read by the group showed a predominance of quality and liberal journals, while the mass magazines which were so extensively read by the town group, and by their neighbors in the Village, where they made up 62 per cent of the newsstand circulation of weeklies [1] and 81 per cent of monthlies, were read only by some of the younger men.[2] For those of the Villagers for whom reading rather than parties was the principal form of leisure-time activity, their recreation was thus part of their serious life rather than an avenue of escape.

The recreation of Villagers and of local people differed substantially in that for the former it was either an escape from or an integral part of a crowded and swift-tempoed life while for the latter it was often a none-too-satisfactory way of filling empty hours.

[1] The *New Yorker* accounted for 35 per cent of newsstand sales of weeklies.
[2] Cf. Table XII, Appendix F, pp. 468, 469.

XIII. SOCIAL WELFARE

NOTHING was more characteristic of the social organization of this community than the multitude and variety
of the agencies for social welfare which served it. There
was no possibility of estimating the cost or even the total personnel engaged in furnishing the thirty-five thousand people of
this community with protective, remedial, or ameliorative services. An attempt simply to enumerate all the agencies, both
public and private, which touched the members of the district
in 1930 reached the number of two hundred without going beyond
those actually located in the district and the most obvious of the
city-wide agencies. Among the two hundred were twenty-seven
agencies interested in family welfare, forty-nine working in one
way or another with children — protecting, preventing or cor-
recting, giving maintenance, institutionalization, nursery care,
or vocational service; fifteen were devoted to protective work
with adults. Recreation claimed the interest, in whole or in part,
of twenty-nine agencies working for children and adults, and
health the efforts of twenty-two. Others provided for a variety
of community interests, including residence needs and employment services. It would be difficult to pick out any field of social
work which was neglected in this area.

The bulk of the support for these multitudinous agencies came
from outside of the district. With the exception of the parishes,
particularly the Catholic, in which members were assisted by the
funds and efforts of fellow parishioners, the social welfare services
of this community were the product of organized philanthropy,
administered from outside, rather than the community's expression of its own responsibility. The multitude of these services
reflected the failure of the city, of which the district was a part, to
produce the kind of life which the standards of the city demanded.
While some of those who served it had made the district their

home and acted as its spokesmen on civic questions, even they had come in with the points of view and experience gained elsewhere, bent upon moulding the life of the community closer to the way of living which they had conceived in other settings. The larger community imposed itself upon the local area so thoroughly through the channel of social work that some of the local social workers in 1930 considered it a matter for boasting that there was not a family within the local tenement district which had not been reached by some social work agency. The accuracy of this statement was of less moment than the attitude which it reflected.

In the face of the feeling of those who conducted various social work activities that they 'possessed' the district, it required a positive effort to see the community as something other than so many clients or patients or members of this or that agency — so many people to be adjusted, inoculated, re-created, or what-have-you. When the present study was undertaken, every effort was made to avoid approaching the community through social work channels, in order better to see it in its own terms. The ubiquity of the social agencies made it very difficult to carry out this effort.

The attitudes which underlay the practice of social welfare activity in the Village during these years reflected a variety of assumptions, chief among which was a sense of responsibility combined with a sense of superiority. Historically the practice of social work, of which the manifold examples in this decade were the current representatives, stemmed from the Puritan tradition of moral responsibility. Although the professional standards of certain of the social work agencies were based upon radically different concepts, the point of view of many of the social workers, and certainly of those who contributed the funds which supported the local social work, was not far from the traditional view. A sharp gulf separated server and served. Those who administered came from a different world. Those served were always 'they,' never 'we.' Whenever 'we' was used, as it was by those who theoretically believed in genuine social action by the community, it could hardly escape striking a false note. A complaint of one of the workers who had served the community longest was not typical of all local workers, but was representative of the attitude of a substantial proportion. 'Times have changed,' she complained in 1930. 'In the old days, people used to be so grateful for what you did for them. Now they don't seem grateful any more.'

In the history of social work, three major attitudes have, roughly, succeeded each other as the basis for social work activity. The first was strongly moralistic, growing as it did out of the Puritan concept that material success was a sign of virtue. The poor and unfortunate were to blame for their position; laziness and intemperance were presumed causes; the poor were to be not only aided but 'corrected.' In this, the churches, of course, had an important part as the guardians of the morality of the community. While this attitude had ceased to dominate the leaders of the social work profession by the early years of the twentieth century, it still survived in individual workers and in the attitude of some of their agencies. In spite of the official views of most agencies, a stigma of blame still attached to those receiving philanthropic aid.

Near the turn of the century, the moralistic concept gave way to a stress upon the social responsibility of the community for the conditions of the poor, and the environment received the blame for much which had formerly been attributed to the defective moral sense of the unsuccessful. Improvement of the community was the imperative contained in this philosophy, and the motivating factor in the program for social action and community betterment adopted by the settlements and those Protestant churches which became imbued with the 'social gospel.' After thirty years, both settlements and churches were on the defensive for not having achieved the community improvement called for in their programs, and both were still in the vanguard of those working for civic betterment. It was among this group that distrust of public agencies was least strong, and concern over such problems as housing, playgrounds, or street safety was greatest. A few of its members regularly represented the section of the city on all city-wide projects, sponsored all community efforts, served as the guiding spirits and executive secretaries of all co-ordinating bodies.

The third attitude was new and growing during the post-War years. This was represented by those who regarded social work as a therapeutic process chiefly directed toward the treatment of the maladjusted individual according to the techniques of the professional social worker. Important among these techniques, and increasingly featured during the period, was the psychiatric approach to problems of maladjustment. Difficulties arising out of the individual's personality rather than those resulting from the economic or social system of which he was a part, or from the weakness of his moral fiber, were the object of this group's concern and effort. This point of view represented the attitude of the family case-work agencies rather than of the community or health centers. Theoretically, it was completely free from moral judgment. Actually, its exponents carried over some of the moral blame formerly attached to the fact of poverty and applied it to those who were not susceptible of regeneration in response to the techniques applied. The presence of 'begging tendency' as a possible problem to be checked on a case worker's record card reflected a survival of the moral judgment. This group was less concerned with the problem of changing the social and economic environment of the individual than with enabling the individual to live happily within the confines of any situation which he might have to meet.

These three main social work attitudes represented the three major successive stages in the development of the profession out of the basic Anglo-Protestant American tradition. All survived in this locality and added a confusion of intent to other factors of confusion in the community. In contrast to them all stood the point of view of the Catholic group — namely, that almsgiving was a duty; the poor would always be with us and call for help as a Christian service; no particular stigma attached to poverty or misfortune; the necessity of reforming the community was less than that of caring for the spiritual welfare of the individual, and, except in the spiritual sphere, there was no process of rehabilitation in the psychiatric sense involved. The Catholic group gave aid to people in distress simply because they were in distress, without bothering with any elaborate professional technique. 'Pauperization' never aroused the fear among the Catholics that it had and still did among the American Protestants. The professionalized agencies regarded the traditional Catholic social services as sentimentally and sloppily administered.

In the post-War years, the organization of the Catholic charities to supplement the work of the local Saint Vincent de Paul societies in each parish brought into Catholic social work the professional case-work techniques which characterized the more recent of the social work attitudes. The leaders of the Catholic charities, trained in the same schools as the workers of other agencies, made headway during these years in introducing standards of work which made them resemble other case-work organizations. They continued to distrust, however, the psychiatric approach, especially when it was administered by a non-sectarian or Protestant agency.

The many agencies co-operated through a Lower West Side Council of Social Agencies which met periodically to discuss problems of common interest — housing, recreation, the continuation school, crime prevention. Agencies working in the same field established boundaries of the districts which they were to serve and allocated problems.

The circumstances within which the several agencies operated, however, made their co-operation difficult. The necessity of showing a good quantitative record in order to attract donations practically forced agencies to compete for the possession of clients. The very danger of losing their jobs and salaries pressed the workers of the various agencies into efforts to bring as many people as possible on the rolls of their organizations, which, in the face of a declining population, tended to produce a proprietary attitude toward clients. It was back of the increased difficulty which the Protestant missions experienced in finding new members who were not tied to another agency; it was reflected in the complaint of one worker: 'These people know pretty well what is offered in the neighborhood. They shop around from agency to agency to see what they can get.' In this situation, it was not surprising to find some of those who patronized certain institutions taking the attitude that they were doing a favor to the workers in the institution by their patronage. The rivalry and the proprietary attitude was, of course, much more intense among the local agencies than among city-wide agencies serving the locality, for the latter did not depend upon local patronage for survival.

Differences in standards between agencies which were necessarily competing often made them critical of each other. One agency objected to including on a recreation committee the head of an agency which was, according to all observable standards, doing an outstanding recreational job. Although the line was supposed to be drawn between bedside nursing and health education, agencies in these respective fields feared that their domain was being invaded by the other. Private agencies frequently doubted the professional quality of public services. Catholic agencies distrusted the Protestant ones, while the latter were not sure that the Catholics were doing a good job. Case-work agencies alternately accused the settlements and recreation centers of meddling in case work when they did not know how and blamed them for not doing their job well because they did not carry on case work along with their other activities.

In this situation, the social welfare activity carried on in this community reflected the personality of a few outstanding workers rather than a definite community program. While the majority of the social workers in the locality at any time were transient, and the turnover of case workers, recreation leaders, or nurses was heavy, most of the welfare organizations contained one or more individuals who had served the locality for some time, who dominated their agency's work, and, in one way or another, set the stamp of their personality on the community. Their manner of approach and the nature of their relationships with the people whom they served varied greatly. One maintained a highly efficient organization, but herself remained an impersonal force; another did the bulk of the actual hard work for her own agency and for every sort of local welfare committee; another formulated for the community the needs of which it was often as yet unaware and stood for the locality in dealings with the outside world; another built up so much personal prestige and confidence that the police brought local disputes to her to settle. These and other dominant figures introduced a quality into the life of the community which was not accounted for by the character of the local people or the nature of the welfare or other institutions, and which depended on the continued presence and activity of these personalities.

In dealing with the community, all welfare agencies encountered a more or less serious confusion between server and served as to the nature of their mutual relationship. The nurses and other health workers were clearest in their approach because they had a specific job to do and a rigorous technique which eliminated confusion on moral issues. The local director of the visiting nurses' service was able to report that no single case of cross-infection could be traced to her nurses. But other agencies had no such definition of function and standard of performance for their jobs.

Even the health agencies, moreover, contributed to some of the confusion between client and worker which other agencies encountered. The local health center serving a section of the area prided itself upon the fact that it had trained its families to turn to the center in all sorts of situations — not to try to doctor the baby themselves but to bring it to the clinic. The case-work agencies, in their turn, complained that the people of the district were hopelessly dependent; once a family had been taken on as a case, it was impossible to put it back on a self-sustaining basis. The people themselves were in a quandary. One set of 'ladies' from the mysterious world outside of their own came into their homes and insisted that they rely upon them and turn to them at all times. Another set, who looked essentially the same as far as the Italian mothers could see, blamed them for acting in the way that the first set of ladies urged them to act — condemning them for their 'begging tendency' and regarding them as hopeless 'cases.' One case worker reported that her agency was taking on as few cases as possible from the neighborhood because it had such a hard time getting rid of them, and it was closing out its old cases whenever possible. 'You'd be surprised,' she concluded reproachfully, 'how these families somehow manage to get along when we stop carrying them. Their dependency is more a habit than a condition.'

To those who had learned from their years in America that everyone should try to get as much for himself as he could, the process of getting as much as possible from a social agency was the most natural thing in the world. Both teachers and social workers complained that if anything was being distributed free the Italian families were sure to turn up asking for it, whether they needed it or not. If it was shoes for school children, well-shod Italian children would demand their pair; if free lunches, children of well-dressed Italian parents were sure to be found in line with the rest. Even those social workers who had learned about cultural conflicts and who had abandoned the moralistic approach to problems of poverty still attached a stigma to the acceptance of charity. Those who did not recognize that stigma, and did not seek to avoid it by vigorous efforts, actually fell under the moral ban which formerly applied to all the poor.

Within these conditions which characterized the social welfare services of the community throughout the post-War years, some trends were noticeable. More services were being furnished, especially for health and recreation. Since the population was decreasing very fast, the volume of services per capita mounted rapidly. Apart from the actual drop in number of persons to be served, there was a slight decrease in the need for social work. In terms of income, congestion, mortality and morbidity rates the trend was toward an absolutely smaller volume of need. But there was no evidence of a greater or less call for aid in social adjustments. It was the opinion of some of the social workers that those better able to adjust themselves had been the ones to move to more attractive neighborhoods, leaving more problems in proportion to population than had been the case in 1920. Others thought that the most needy had moved to lower-rent sections of the city as the rents in the locality had mounted. There was a definite trend in the professional standards according to which social work was carried on, but none that could be discovered in the attitude of the community as a whole or of the individual client toward social services.

1.   HEALTH

Outstanding among the services which were extended during the post-War decade were those affecting health. Community conditions both made these services necessary and stood in the way of their success.

Living conditions in the Village were far from favorable to the health of the inhabitants. Although by 1930 the area was less congested, ill-housed, and subject to the various health menaces of the city than some other parts of the metropolis, in absolute terms, it could not by any stretch of the normal imagination be regarded as a healthy district. The number of tenements of the 'railroad' type condemned in 1880 was small, but the bulk of the local tenements had been regarded as unfit by the state legislators in 1901. In many of these houses, the basements, whose occupancy was forbidden by law in 1930, were still occupied and the landlords were fighting against having the prohibition on basement occupancy enforced. Hall, and sometimes yard, toilets served several families, and were, as a result, characteristically ill-kept. The streets in which the children played were usually filled with filth and grime. On some, refuse from pushcarts littered the gutter, on others, only the banana peels, papers, and other odds and ends thrown on the sidewalk or the streets by people who did not see the necessity for walking up four or five flights of tenement stairs to find a waste-basket in their homes. Although the schools engaged annually in the city-wide anti-litter campaigns, their training was undermined by the absence of waste-cans on the streets where children played, and where adults, in warm weather, spent their time. The presence of factories scattered through the residence blocks contributed a variety of odors and sounds. A mattress factory frequently filled the air of one block with feathers. Sunshine was scarce — although the large proportion of low houses made the district less sunless than the 'rich men's slums' of Park Avenue — and there was plenty of damp mustiness in the 'cold-water flats.' One had but to walk through the district on the first warm days of spring to smell the dank tenement air as it poured into the street through newly opened windows. Though there were less-healthy spots in this and other metropolitan communities the world over, local conditions were sufficiently unfavorable to invite the health services of those who were looking for need and to discourage those who objected to a patching process on the top of a rotten foundation.

Like all the rest of the city, this district profited from the vigorous policy of the City Health Department, which developed strikingly during these years. In addition, extensive new health services supported by private funds were either separately established in this community or added to the work of welfare agencies already located in the area. In 1920, the district was directly served by the out-patient department of a local Catholic hospital, by a dispensary which had been operating at the same site for nearly a hundred years, and by a visiting nursing service. In addition, the various day nurseries and kindergartens had the services of doctors and nurses for the children under their charge. That year marked the beginning of the public health drive in the city — evidenced by the inauguration of 'health day' in the schools — and, in this community, a change from health services primarily directed toward the care of the sick to those which worked for the preservation of health. A local settlement opened a baby clinic, a cardiac class, and a pre-school clinic. The following year a new health center was established which launched a frontal attack on the high rate of infant mortality in the district and undertook to 'Americanize the health and life habits of this foreign-born element so that their children might become future American citizens, physically and industrially efficient.' [1]

In the promotion of public health during these years private agencies of the locality pursued policies closely in line with those of the public. They joined vigorously in health education programs, and concentrated their efforts on disease prevention, pre-natal and infant care and the care of pre-school children. In certain fields the local private agencies went further than the Health Department, especially in incorporating mental hygiene into their programs.

The relation between public and private health agencies was somewhat clearer and closer than that between public and private bodies in other fields of public welfare. When the Health Department had been effective, as for instance in its campaign for the prevention of specific diseases, the private agencies slackened their main effort and simply co-operated under the lead of the public body. Their preventive work took the more general form of posture classes, fresh-air summers, lamp treatment, and pre-natal care. In fields which were still too experimental for the public department to enter, such as mental hygiene, the public agency offered only verbal encouragement while the private centers undertook more or less extensive work. In fields which public agencies were in a position to enter but not to carry through effectually, such as pre-natal, infant, and pre-school care, public and private efforts were intertwined — Health Department doctors serving in clinics housed by private agencies which furnished nursing and social service staffs. On all policies, the public department tended to serve as organizing and propaganda center, disseminating accepted policies, often leaving the actual service growing out of those policies largely to private agencies. Theoretically, the line of demarcation between public and private efforts was marked out

[1] Judson Health Center, *Annual Report*, 1927, p. 22.

by conference between the health department and private agencies, but actually the several private agencies of the locality pursued fairly independent courses.

In 1920, the main concern of the New York City Department of Health was with the problems of smoke control and protection against European epidemics; by 1930, it had developed a complicated, city-wide machinery to prevent disease by immunization, to spread health education, and to give millions of babies scientific medical care and training. Especially since 1925, public health policy tended strongly in the direction of disease prevention and health education.

The most intensive of its disease-prevention campaigns was the attack against diphtheria. Starting with the use of Schick tests and toxin anti-toxin in the city schools in 1919, the campaign was extended to pre-school children after 1924. In 1928, a Diphtheria Prevention Committee inaugurated a city-wide campaign, using newspapers, leaflets, and billboards to educate the public, and establishing special clinics. The record of the number of deaths from contagious diseases tells the story of the success of these efforts and shows Greenwich Village sharing the experience of the whole city. There were only a fifth as many deaths from diphtheria in New York City in 1930 as there had been in 1920, a rate of 2.8 per 100,000 of the population as compared with 18.4 ten years before. Deaths from all the principal contagious diseases in 1930, exclusive of tuberculosis, were less than a third of what they had been ten years before, falling from a rate of 50.6 per 100,000 to 12.4. In Greenwich Village deaths from contagious diseases dropped from a rate of 81.5 per 100,000 from 1920 to 1922 to 35.5 for 1928 to 1930.[1] Deaths from tuberculosis dropped in the city from a rate of 108.5 in 1920 to 64 in 1930, and in Greenwich Village from 162 from 1920 to 1922 to 100 from 1928 to 1930.[2]

Health examinations were vigorously encouraged by the public health department and were extensively carried out by Village agencies. One of the local centers pointed to the increase in the number of examinations as a strong evidence of the success of its program between 1927 and 1929. Since physical examinations were required of the children sent to fresh-air camps or homes

[1] Numbers are too small to make rate figures on the basis of a single year.
[2] Cf. Table XIII, Appendix F, p. 470.

during the summer, the extension of fresh-air work to include a large proportion of the children of the neighborhood meant that at least a partial examination had become general by 1930.

Health education steadily increased in importance in the work of the city health department and of the local agencies. The public program was directed not only toward the prevention of specific diseases, such as tuberculosis, diphtheria, or smallpox, but also toward raising the general level of the community. In 1920, the Bureau of Child Hygiene supported its recommendation for school health education with the contention that 'The child who knows how to keep well and who, moreover, is so trained in health habits that he demands the type of environment that will make such habits possible, has provided not only for himself but for the community at large those standards of healthful living which make for the prevention of all disease, and for raising the standard of individual and community health.' [1] In establishing the Bureau of Public Health Education in 1925, the department expressed the hope that it would improve the individual and community life of the future.[2]

The stress on health education meant that the New York public during these years was made health conscious, by a mounting barrage of health propaganda. In the local community, all the private agencies increased their health education services by means of classes and clinic and home visits. They supplemented the wholesale propaganda of the city health department by direct personal contact with often illiterate or non-English-speaking women, and, especially, with children. Local centers used both the device of individual instruction of children and mothers in the course of daily clinic service and that of forming classes for mothers on nutrition and child care.

One center, whose everyday clinic practice included carefully worked-out health education, felt that it had been successful through this method in arousing health interest in the district. A foundation, in granting funds to this center for the extension of its work, specified 'the study of methods best adapted in teaching hygiene and health to the people of a congested district.' The methods included very full co-operation with both public and

[1] New York City Department of Health, *Annual Report*, 1920, p. 186.
[2] *Ibid.*, 1925, p. 51.

parochial schools, with dental service, posture work, and nutrition classes. Through the efforts of the center, both teachers and pupils in the two schools served were made thoroughly health conscious.

In addition to extensive health education at the schools, an experiment in intensive instruction was provided to a small group of mothers and children through a nursery unit where the children were given all-day care and the mothers had to come for a certain amount of time each week to observe the methods of care employed at the nursery. Classes in nutrition and child care were provided for 'little mothers' — older girls who had had to assume responsibility for the care of their younger brothers and sisters. After experimenting with this intensive form of parental education, however, the foundation which had supplied the funds came to the conclusion that this method was too expensive to be feasible.

Other health agencies similarly stressed health education increasingly, with emphasis on nutrition, especially the feeding of younger children. A settlement house added classes in home-making for younger mothers and older girls to the regular nutrition work of its pre-school clinic. The visiting nurses, in the course of their daily visits, emphasized 'instruction in personal hygiene, sanitation, and the prevention of disease.' Education in nutrition was added by a welfare school and recreation center in 1929.

Pre-natal and infant care reflected the public drive to cut down infant mortality which gained momentum after the organization of public pre-natal clinics in 1924. The local health agencies, with the exception of the local hospital, stressed pre-natal and well-baby work increasingly, and in 1930 the hospital started to build a new dispensary which was to include pre-natal and infant clinics.

With a sharp falling-off in the number of births in the locality annually, resulting from a decline in both population and birth rate, the combined services of visiting nurses and clinics were sufficient to see that every mother and baby was under observation and care. The clinics and nurses made an effort to locate the women who were pregnant and to bring them to the clinic if they did not come on their own initiative. Hospitals reported births to the nurses or well-baby clinics of the district, and these, in turn, sought out the mother and urged her to bring her child to the clinic for regular inspection. Whereas in 1920 a large part of the 1235 babies born in the district were born at home, with the aid of midwives, and raised on the basis of the grandmother's advice, in 1930 most of the 462 mothers had received clinic care and instruction, a large proportion of the babies were born at a hospital, and nearly all were raised under the watchful eye of the clinic doctors.

To be sure, in 1930, there were still a half-dozen midwives in the neighborhood and others within reach who tended local women. But these had lost so much business that they had either turned to bootlegging contraceptives and performing abortions or else they professed to be eager to retire, ill, or reluctant to take cases. Many Italian women, too, continued to patronize an Italian doctor who had an enormous obstetrical practice — a would-be interviewer found the way to his office blocked by two waiting-rooms full of patients and a line extending into the hall and down the stairs — and who was the despair of the hospital where he took such of his cases as he did not deliver at home because even there he could not be persuaded to take the usual antiseptic precautions. Most of the local doctors, however, complained that the clinics had taken away the bulk of their maternity and infant business.

The extension of these services was vividly reflected in the declining rate of infant mortality. For the city as a whole the rate per 1000 live births dropped from 85 in 1920 to 57 in 1930. In the local district it remained higher than for the city but dropped proportionately, from 107 in 1920 to 71 in 1930. In the latter year it was below the rate of 74 for Manhattan, whereas in 1920 it had been above the Manhattan rate.[1]

The increased emphasis on nutrition work by the local private agencies was reflected in the decrease in the infant deaths due to diseases of the digestive tract from a rate of 17 per 1000 for 1920 to 1922 to 8 during 1928 to 1930. Most noticeably, the decline occurred in the part of the area intensively served by the two agencies maintaining baby clinics. In the waterfront section to which the clinics were less accessible, the rate remained 18 per 1000, while in the section served by the clinics, the most congested part of the Village, it had fallen to 2 per 1000.

When the figures of infant mortality are examined in detail, they tend to show the same story as those for the rest of the city;

[1] Cf. Tables XIV, XV, Appendix F, p. 471.

namely, that infant care had gone farther than maternal care in eliminating fatalities. Deaths within the first month, which accounted for only 39.2 per cent of the deaths under one year between 1920 and 1922 amounted to 48.4 per cent in 1927 to 1929. Though the number of maternal deaths was too small for reliable comparison, the increase from 3.5 per 1000 births in 1920 to 1922 to 6.7 in 1928 to 1930 was discouraging.[1]

Emphasis on dental work also reflected a general city-wide interest, but it was particularly characteristic of local agencies. One installed a dental clinic in 1921; another introduced dental equipment into a public school in 1925 as well as continuing the dental work at its clinic and lent a dentist and dental hygienist for periodic clinics at another agency. Still another general clinic concentrated the bulk of its attention on dental work after 1924, until by 1930 it had six doctors and 412 weekly hours devoted to the care of teeth. A day nursery installed a dental clinic in 1930. When one of the local centers decided to minimize the work of its treatment clinics in order to concentrate on health education and preventive work, it did not feel that its dental work could be suspended or cut down.

The principal type of activity in which the local agencies went ahead of the public department was in mental hygiene. The health department recognized the importance of mental hygiene and recommended to the department of education as early as 1924 that it encourage mental hygiene with pre-school children, but it did not feel itself in a position to include mental hygiene in its own health work.

Among the local private agencies, one established a mental hygiene clinic which handled adjustment cases of both children and adults. It took up habit and adjustment problems in connection with the schools, in order to correct the influence of poor parental discipline so frequently in the district where, according to the center's report, 'mothers are noted for their overindulgence of children.' Truancy cases were referred to the center by the attendance supervisor. Another agency introduced psychological tests for its nursery-school children in 1922, added a psychiatric social worker to the clinic in 1924 and a consulting psychiatrist in 1930. Yet another agency recognized the need for mental hygiene in the institu-

---

[1] The rate for the city remained constant, 5.3 in 1920 and 5.4 in 1930.

tion of its country home for emotionally unstable boys. Mental hygiene was added to the technique of the visiting nurses in 1929.

More and more during these years, public health came to be looked upon as a problem to be handled on a local community basis. Reflecting this trend, the Health Department began in 1929 to publish its cases of reportable diseases by districts, and a Committee on Neighborhood Health Development, privately supported but located in the department, was established. The problem of this committee was to appraise the health needs and services of the various parts of the city with a view to setting up neighborhood health units. Its first analysis of health conditions showed the section which included the Village to be one of the worst in the city. The high mortality and morbidity rates reported reflected chiefly the waterfront conditions rather than the blocks most directly served by the local health agencies.

According to the basic idea of community health service, neighborhood facilities should be pooled and made jointly available to those in need. On this basis, local agencies divided the territory and allocated functions among themselves. Agreement as to the essentials of the job to be done and division of territory and function, however, did not prevent the rivalries and jealousies characteristic of groups actually working at cross-purposes. The investigator for this study had the frequent experience of being asked by one agency to find out what another was doing or of being treated with suspicion by one agency because of having association with another.

Taken as a whole, the health services available to residents of the locality, apart from the practice of private physicians, grew in number and variety. A rough estimate places the proportion of the population served by local health units in 1920 at 14 per cent, in 1924 at 23 per cent, and in 1929 at 32 per cent.[1] Those served by the health agencies were almost entirely the local people rather than the Villagers. The visiting nurses reported that they were very rarely called by Villagers, although they knew that the latter often needed nursing service and could not afford private care. One or two of the Villagers were beginning to bring their babies to one of the baby clinics in 1930.

[1] Cf. Table XVI, Appendix F, p. 472.

The effectiveness of the local health services was reflected in the declining mortality rates during these years, chiefly in the lower age groups and for causes involving contagion, tuberculosis, digestive disorders, and, to some extent, pneumonia. That the services in question were genuinely responsible for much of this improvement appeared from a comparison of the district immediately served by the clinics with the rest of the area and especially by following those cases under care. In the district covered by the local office of the visiting nurses, forty per cent of the pneumonia cases in 1930 were fatal. Not one of the seventy-two pneumonia patients cared for by the visiting nurses died. Only certain health problems were tackled during these years, however. As in the rest of the city, the death rate from cancer and heart diseases continued to rise and the volume of venereal disease showed no decline.

The effect of the development of clinical services upon the local doctors was to deprive them of much of their private practice and to send them into the lines of work not covered by the clinics. Although one of the health centers made a definite effort to secure the co-operation of local doctors and to include them in its health education program, it found them very hard to approach. Those with empty waiting-rooms in 1930 spoke bitterly of the clinics — 'After all,' they said, 'we doctors took care of poor people for low fees, or even free, and once the clinics get people in, they send them around to be treated for this and that until they have paid as much in clinic fees as they would have paid to a doctor.' Some of the doctors found no fault with the clinics for treating the really poor people, but objected that they accepted people who could afford to patronize a private physician.

With the care of children, and to a considerable extent women, out of their hands, one after another of the local doctors specialized in venereal disease. The Italian doctors in particular who continued to practice in the locality had nearly all become venereal disease specialists by 1930.

Of all the programs undertaken in the local community during these years, none brought so co-operative a response from the local people as the campaign for health. A health center could point with satisfaction to the increasing success with which it was able to maintain contacts with its clients. When it started to work in 1921, it found that Italian women would only turn to a doctor in a crisis, they considered it indelicate to inquire into a physical condition unless it was acute, they regarded the hazards of child-bearing fatalistically, and they retained superstitions about pregnancy and child protection. In 1929, it reported that many families kept in touch with the clinic from year to year, several members of each family were under health supervision, and the center had been able to discontinue some of its treatment clinics in favor of preventive and educational work. The local undertaker reported that he not only had very many fewer children's funerals, but that he rarely saw the evidence of lack of nutritional or other care that used to be so apparent in the children he was called on to bury. The part of the school program which 'took,' while much of the rest did not, was the stress on health.

In fact, one of the sharpest ironies of this community was the success of health education in an area where housing and living conditions were basically inimical to the health of the inhabitants.

2. DEPENDENCY

When a family in Greenwich Village fell below the level of social self-maintenance, there were a number of agencies ready to help it out. The principal organizations equipped to give family aid were the various city-wide private case-work agencies. The city's Public Welfare Department was on hand in case of destitution and its Board of Child Welfare administered mothers' pensions to widows. Home visitors connected with the local health agencies or settlements might assist with advice. The Protestant churches each maintained poor funds, but habitually gave very little relief. The Catholic parishes, traditionally responsible for the care of their poor, dispensed aid through their Saint Vincent de Paul conferences and their Ladies of Charity as well as out of the pastor's pocket. The political clubs furnished such various forms of assistance as appeared to be politically expedient.

It was almost impossible to secure even an approach to an accurate picture of the volume and character of social case work carried in this locality during the post-War years because records of such work were not kept at all by many agencies. Where they were kept, they were frequently not classified in such a way that the cases from this area could be sorted out, and where they were actually available, they were so subjective and incomplete as to give a very unsatisfactory picture of the work which they represented. The only records which could be used, those of the city-wide private case-work agencies, revealed changes in the emphasis of the agencies' work rather than changes in the actual problems offered for case-work solution or in community needs.

The practice of social case work underwent a series of changes during these years in the explanation of social problems, in the philosophy of treatment, in the set-up for treatment, and in the technique and training of the social worker. The social case workers recognized increasingly that each social problem was likely to be the product of many factors which defied a single solution. They tended to regard problems as the product of conflict situations rather than to attribute them to the inadequacy of any one element, either hereditary or environmental. They regarded the individual's emotional and physical needs as the central factor, largely determining his behavior and the circumstances which he ought to be required by society to meet. If environmental conditions beyond his control were the cause of his maladjustment, they considered it society's responsibility to modify those conditions.

Techniques for treatment, naturally, followed changes in the explanation of maladjustment. Treatment was increasingly geared to the whole person rather than to any particular aspect of behavior, since to tackle the latter was to treat a symptom, not a cause. Every effort was made to get the client to do things for himself, on the assumption that only by drawing on his own potentialities could any permanent adjustment be made. Because of the belief that behavior was so easily conditioned, treatment was extended to the very youngest age groups. The field of social treatment was enlarged beyond the bare necessities for survival to include provision for both physical and mental health, recreation and the use of leisure, vocational adjustment and cultural development. The increased stress on society's obligation to alleviate conditions, not as charity but as a measure of social justice, brought an increase in the number and variety of public welfare agencies. Where some difficulty in the individual's personality was involved, rather than a condition outside of the individual's control, the private rather than the public agency continued to be regarded as the proper one to handle a case. The latter's function called for technical equipment to do highly skilled, intensive work, to render the best possible service to the client and to pioneer with research and demonstration projects.

In line with the increasingly specialized character of the cases handled by private agencies went their insistence upon professional training, an objective, clinical attitude, and certain standardized procedures. The status of the case worker became more professional, both in relation to her superiors and in the professional associations organized during these years. Her training became more varied and at the same time more specialized. Certain routinized procedures as the basis for treatment were built up, record keeping was emphasized in relation to both treatment and research, and case loads were diminished to allow for individualized treatment and wider responsibility. Training for this type of work was developed first and farthest among New York agencies by the Charity Organization Society and it penetrated by way of its school of social work into the other organizations.

The Greenwich district was served by the workers of the three major case-working agencies, who, to a greater or less degree, adopted these attitudes toward their work and their clients and used the corresponding techniques.

The social attitude underlying the newer techniques were, however, the product of the professional group of social workers rather than of the community which supported the agencies. The professional bodies thus had a dual problem of maintaining high standards for their workers and of educating the community to appreciate those standards and to accept the attitudes back of them. Control over the two non-sectarian agencies lay in the hands of men of wealth and prominence who served on the boards of the organizations for life or for long terms and whose chief function was to raise funds. The professional staff in one agency attempted to use the board as a channel through which to educate the stratum of society which its members represented, and took care that the personnel of the organization with whom the board came in contact was not of the sort which might irritate men of wealth by 'obstreperous' views. It also used volunteers drawn from the same social level as a means of educating the community and developed a special department for their training. It devoted part of the bulletin which it sent to its members to efforts to break down prejudices against certain racial groups, employing such devices as that of telling the story of a case in such a way as to arouse the sympathy of the reader and waiting until the end of the story to note that 'this family recently arrived from Italy.'

Up to 1930, however, the agencies did not reach the point of putting into practice their professional theory that representatives both of the professional workers and of the group which was being served should actually participate in the direction of an agency's policy. In one agency, even the presence of the executive at a board meeting was an innovation during these years. In another an approach to participation was made by district committees set up to draw in members of local communities in order to make the work an integral part of the community's life. In the Village district, the committee contained a variety of local people, with a nucleus of social workers connected with other local agencies, Protestant ministers, one or two doctors and professional social workers who happened to be Village residents. When the Greenwich district was discontinued as a separate unit in 1928, the five members of the local committee who were retained to serve on the committee of the newly consolidated district were two Protestant ministers, two health workers, and a visiting teacher.

The Catholic agency was under the jurisdiction of the archdiocese of the Catholic Church, with the actual direction in the hands of the chiefs of the professional staffs. In this case there was not the difference in social attitude between the workers and those who supported their organization that there was in the other case-work organizations. Contact with the local community came through the local pastors who had the decision as to whether to try to handle a case personally, to call in his parish Saint Vincent de Paul Conference or Ladies of Charity, or to refer it to the Catholic Charities or a non-sectarian agency.

Although the three major case-work agencies moved in the same professional direction during these years, they differed substantially in their approach. The dictates of case-work technique were the governing factors for one agency with respect to both social attitudes and procedure. In spite of the non-union attitude of the bulk of its board members, it did not refuse aid to a striker's family simply because the man was on strike. On the other hand, it did not make a practice of referring Catholic clients to birth-control clinics because its standard of case-work practice precluded advising anything which ran counter to the religious standards of the group to which the client belonged. Alcoholism was regarded as a symptom of conflict rather than as evil in itself and such cases were accepted. This agency only refused or abandoned a case when it considered it hopeless from the point of view of rehabilitation. It did not believe that it could reform the world and was willing to leave action for social reform largely to other agencies. It maintained increasingly high professional requirements, used the district offices as training grounds for students attending its social work school and kept its older staff members in constant touch with new developments through continued study at the school. Its interest and emphasis during these years turned increasingly to behavior problems and mental hygiene.

The other non-sectarian agency had not followed the advance wing of the professional social workers to the point of giving up the idea of individual responsibility and of absolute right and wrong in favor of a notion of psychological determinism. Although a rigorous supporter of social action, it stressed primarily child care, social hygiene, widow's pensions, old-age security, and various health measures. It gave less support to forms of social action involving changes in labor conditions or moral concepts and hesitated to accept a wide interpretation of state responsibility for social problems. This agency was less strict in the professional qualifications of its workers, encouraging them to acquire additional training, but not putting pressure on them to do so. It strengthened its emphasis on health in this period and set up a mental hygiene clinic and vocational guidance service. It showed, in particular, a growing interest in the aged, choosing to use a country estate which was donated to the society as a home for old people instead of as a camp or a convalescent home for mothers and babies.

The Catholic agency reflected the principles of the Church in its program, developing a new technique but not a new attitude. Although some of its field workers and supervisors took mental hygiene courses and the organization maintained a small mental hygiene clinic, it did not accept the stress on the supreme importance of the individual personality which the mental hygiene approach featured. It took no stock in the move to discard sharp distinctions between right and wrong and to abandon the sense of sin to which the vanguard of the professional group gave at least lip service. Since it did not make the psychological adjustment of the individual the only criterion, it was more willing than the first agency simply to carry cases along when there seemed to be no possibility of effective rehabilitation. It had been traditionally in favor of apprenticeship on the job rather than formal training, and although it sent its key people to be trained in the school of social work, the stress upon the spiritual side of its work made professional social work training an incomplete preparation. The directors commented with amusement on the way in which workers trained by the non-sectarian agencies acted as if they knew just how to run the Catholic Charities. Although the case-work techniques penetrated the Catholic Charities as more and more positions in the organization were filled by graduates of the School of Social Work, the philosophy back of those techniques remained essentially foreign to the Catholic Charities' approach. The emphasis in its work remained unchanged except as it reflected the necessity of meeting varying economic conditions.

These three agencies served an undifferentiated assortment of Greenwich Village families faced with essentially similar problems.[1] It was largely a matter of chance whether a family in distress fell into the hands of one or another of the agencies, to be classified as a behavior problem, a health problem, or in need of spiritual guidance. Actually the records of local cases would indicate that it did not make such a great deal of difference, for the bulk of problems presented to all the agencies appeared on their records as problems of poverty or ill health.

The largest number of cases involved physical difficulties, with economic inadequacy a close second. Much less numerous were problems arising out of increasing family burdens or such disruption of families as would make the carrying of ordinary family burdens impossible— e.g., old age, broken homes, desertion; imprisonment; mental difficulties and behavior problems; bad management of existing resources — e.g., bad housekeeping; and cases

[1] Cf. Table XVII, Appendix F, p. 473.

whose description carried a note of moral condemnation — e.g., intemperance, begging tendency, immorality.[1] Problems arising primarily out of community conditions were rarely recorded by the case worker, presumably because social agencies took for granted the unfortunate community conditions that their clients had to face — they would have had to record them for practically all cases — or else their emphasis on individualized treatment produced a statement of problems in individual terms.

The proportion of cases involving health problems remained approximately the same throughout the period, amounting to about twenty per cent of the cases handled by each of the three agencies in the early, middle, and late years of the decade. Economic insufficiency figured more largely in the early and late years of the decade than in the mid-years. It was involved in approximately twenty-four per cent of the cases in 1920 to 1922 and 1927 to 1930. In 1923 to 1927 it amounted to approximately eighteen per cent. Old age figured in a small proportion of the cases — approximately three per cent of the whole number during the entire period. Problems involving illegitimacy, desertion, death, or imprisonment constituted a negligible proportion of the total and showed no noticeable variation among agencies or from the early to the later years. The recognition of mental difficulties and behavior problems reflected the growing emphasis on the psychiatric approach on the part of the more progressive of the non-sectarian agencies, the largest proportion of this type of cases appearing in its records during the late years of the decade. Cases involving a moral judgment appeared in both of the non-sectarian agencies, in spite of the psychiatric emphasis. 'Intemperance' recorded the persistence of a moral attitude in the conservative and 'begging tendency' the goal of rehabilitation of the more progressive.

Differences among the nationalities which were served showed some consistency from year to year and between the several agencies. A smaller proportion of the Italian cases involved economic inadequacy than did those of the Irish, American, or other scattered nationalities. Physical problems ran fairly evenly through all groups. Old age appeared among the Irish, especially those served by the Catholic Charities, in twice the proportion of cases

[1] Cf. Table XVIII, Appendix F, p. 474.

that it did among the Italians. The group of miscellaneous nationalities most of which came from the waterfront section, furnished the largest proportion of desertion cases. Mental and behavior problems showed more variation among agencies than among nationalities. Cases involving moral judgment reflected some difference among nationalities, with 'intemperance' attributed to the Irish and 'begging tendency' to the Italians.

Changes in the activity of the public agencies were responsible for certain of the trends observable in the statistics of private agencies. With the increased activity of the Board of Child Welfare, problems arising out of widowhood became less the concern of private agencies. With the introduction of old-age pensions in 1930, cases of old age began to pass out of private hands.

The records gave a wholly inadequate picture of the services rendered in the treatment of these problems, because a case worker would do many things for a family at once, but only record certain of those things in her statistical report. The chief services recorded by these agencies were various forms of health assistance and some economic aid and child aid. It was completely impossible to secure an estimate of the amount of relief given or even the number of the cases in which relief was actually disbursed. In comparison with the number of cases presenting economic problems, there were few cases in which employment was found, vocational adjustment made, or wage increases secured. The strengthening of church connections appeared frequently on the cards of the Catholic Charities and also on six per cent of the cards of one of the non-sectarian agencies.[1] In the absence of any data as to how long cases were carried, when and why they were closed, and what happened to the clients subsequently, these records gave only the most superficial indication of what it meant to these 1064 families to come under the care of case-work agencies.

The families themselves had remarkably little to distinguish them from the rest of the local people. As a whole, the group was made up predominantly of unskilled workers. Some two thirds of the cases gave occupations which fell into the unskilled class. Other samples of tenement families showed 40 to 45 per cent skilled workers. The low occupational status, however, did not

[1] Cf. Table XIX, Appendix F, p. 475.

account universally for a family being a social agency's client. In this respect there was a striking difference between the Italians and the Irish. Only 57 per cent of the Italian cases were the families of unskilled workers, while 79 per cent of the Irish were drawn from the unskilled class. The fact that 33 per cent of the Italian cases came from skilled and clerical ranks and 10 per cent from business and professional, suggests that a somewhat different group was reached by the case-work agencies among the Italians than among people of any other nationality. The wage-level of the group could not be determined. The majority of those reporting their wages gave a figure somewhere between $25 and $35 per week, but this was as likely as not to be the wages which they would have been getting if they had been working. The figures had only slight value in indicating that the private case-work agencies did not serve, exclusively at least, those whose earning capacity habitually placed them in the lowest economic group. This conclusion was supported by the evidence of rent paid. Both the average rent paid and the range of rents resembled a cross-section of the lower-priced housing of the locality. Again the Italians stood out in contrast to the others with a consistently higher average rent. The Irish represented the other end of the scale with the lowest average rents and the largest proportion working as janitors in order to get their rent free.

There was some slight evidence that family size was responsible for pushing families below the self-maintenance level. In the 1927 to 1930 period, 34 per cent of the families served had three or more children, while the census of 1930 showed only 17 per cent of the local families with three or more children and 5 per cent with five or more.[1] In the 1919 to 1922 period, 49 per cent of the case-work families had reported three or more children and 20 per cent reported five or more.

The case-work families represented a larger proportion of broken homes — widowed, separated, divorced, deserted — than was characteristic of the total population, but again there was a serious source of error in that the census did not report cases of desertion, and frequently not of separation. The number of desertions among the case-work families, however, was not large.

[1] *U.S. Census, 1930.* Not exactly comparable — three or more children presumed to exist in families of five or more members.

Thirty-three per cent of the homes visited by case workers were 'broken,' in contrast to only 4.9 per cent of the men and 12.2 per cent of the women in the district in 1930 who were widowed or divorced. The smallest proportion of broken homes was among the Italians, the largest among the miscellaneous nationalities chiefly on the waterfront. The Irish and the American groups were chiefly responsible for the number of widows. Separations as well as desertions were more conspicuous among the scattered nationalities than among those more solidly represented in the locality.[1]

There is little evidence to suggest that it was the newer arrivals in the country who needed the aid of social workers to help them in their first adjustments. Some 40 per cent of the clients in the early period and more than 60 per cent in the later period had been in the United States for twenty years or more. Only approximately 17 per cent in the early, and 15 per cent in the later, period had been in the country for less than ten years. Here again, the group of case-work families looked like a cross-section of the families of the locality.[2]

When the study of these records was undertaken, it was hoped that they would contain evidence which, combined with other knowledge of the community, would contribute to an understanding of the problem of dependency in an area such as this. But the one significant fact which stands out is that there was nothing distinctive about this group of a thousand families as far as any of the gross measurements used could show. By and large, they were a very ordinary sample of the local population.

How, then, did they come into the hands of case workers? The great bulk were referred to case workers by some other welfare agency. Churches, settlements, and nurseries referred 19.1 per cent, public agencies, 5.4 per cent, and other social agencies, 14.3 per cent — making a total of 38.8 per cent. Physicians and medical agencies referred 18.1 per cent. Only 6.3 per cent came

---

[1] Were the total numbers not so small, the evidence might at least raise the question as to whether desertion and separation took place more readily where families lived apart from their own group than where the pressure of the group held them to more regularity.

[2] So large a proportion of the cases failed to report whether the client was a citizen or an alien that little light is available on this point. On the basis of the fragmentary evidence of the cases where the fact was noted, it appears that approximately half of the cases of foreign-born were aliens in the early years, 40 per cent in the middle years and 35 per cent toward the end of the period.

through schools or other children's agencies, suggesting that problems of dependency were not detected primarily by the schools. Case-work technique laid stress increasingly upon a personal application from the client. For the whole period, 21.4 per cent of the cases came through personal applications, while 15.3 per cent were brought in through other individuals or private connections. The agency most insistent upon case-work technique received 28.6 per cent of its cases through personal application — 36.6 per cent in the later period — as against 12.3 per cent of the Catholic Charities cases.

The variety of the sources of referrals would indicate a working relation among social agencies of the community, and also that the case-work agencies had become sufficiently familiar to the residents of the community so that they turned to them of their own accord for aid.

In the absence of statistical evidence that the dependent group had a distinctive character, the experience of the case workers in the district was sought as a supplement. Most of the field workers who were carrying cases in the community in 1930 had little familiarity with the district. They were new to the area, often to the city, served a wide area and had few cases within the locality. No case-work agency maintained a district office in the neighborhood. One had done so, but the local office had been consolidated with another on the West Side in 1928 and the staff was scattered.

Those in charge of the case work which was carried on in the district were willing to generalize as to the nature of the problems with which they had to deal, but their generalizations coincided so little with each other that they indicated a subjective bias rather than the case workers' objective diagnosis. According to one agency, the Italians of the Village compared very favorably with those of the East Side; they had intelligence and initiative; they had become more Americanized and easier to work with during these years. Another agency, by contrast, regarded the local Italians as very poor human material — they were a low type compared with other parts of the city and offered little or nothing to take hold of for rehabilitation.

The workers agreed in some measure as to which problems they were most likely to find, which were most difficult to deal with, and how the principal nationalities in the locality compared. They agreed that health habits could be modified with relatively little difficulty except when it came to food, but that food habits were especially hard to change. They recognized that certain practices which were at variance with American customs were not regarded as problems by their clients. Bootlegging, carrying firearms, and extra-marital relations were the principal Italian customs which they accepted as falling within this category. Hard drinking they accepted as a recognized Irish practice. They tended to treat these practices much as they did the neighborhood fact of bad housing, as general conditions which did not need to be recorded or tackled in each instance.

Their experience had led them to expect closer family ties among the Italians than among the Irish, with fewer homeless men and unmarried mothers. They regarded the Italians as less ready to turn to institutions than the Irish — unlikely to have recourse to law, loath to go to a hospital, and eager to withdraw their children from school as soon as possible. They agreed to some version of the observation that the Irish did not seek relief until they were down and out, while the Italians were glad to get it at any time. To one this meant that 'the Italians are born beggars'; to another, that 'the Italians think that they have a right to relief'; to another that they 'carry over the business attitude.' They did not agree at all on the question of the prevalence of mental hygiene problems.

The generalizations of the social workers did little more than support the conclusion that case-work records were likely to reflect the social workers at least as much as they revealed the clients, and that the practice of social work was a long way from that scientific objectivity prescribed by the case-work techniques developed during these years.

3. DELINQUENCY AND CRIME

It was the general opinion of the neighborhood that 'there are just as many people out of jail that ought to be in as there are in jail. I'm not mentioning any names, but ——.' Landing in jail was a matter of accident, and, though unfortunate, was to many no serious blot on a person's reputation. It was the neighborly thing to inquire when a woman expected her son 'out,' as one would inquire about a boy away at school. Mothers took the initiative in bringing a conversation around to their boys in jail so that they could explain that it was really the fault of the rest of the crowd, but the others had connections, so they got off and their poor boys had to serve time. A college boy could coolly sit down to discuss how it had happened that his brother had landed in jail while he had landed in college — both in careers that were out of the ordinary.

It was not in the least unusual to know people who were in jail or who had been there. A quiet young man who went with an educated, responsible group, not with the rougher element, could list over one after another of his boyhood friends — the one that was 'sent up' for dope-peddling; the two brothers who were caught housebreaking and who went back to jail a second time because both broke their parole; the one, just down from Sing Sing, who was working in the gambling place run by another friend who had got out some time before; the one who had stopped the petty 'jobs' he had been doing and was waiting around for a silk 'job' on the docks that would bring him good money.

The matter-of-fact attitude toward law-breaking applied to people, young and old, who were guilty of both sorts of offense, those which were technical breaches of the law but did not violate the neighborhood code, and those which were violations of the local code as well as of the law. Entering an empty house, an offense for which local boys were frequently arraigned, was not a locally recognized offense, but was anybody's fair game. Breaking into a locked store, on the contrary, was an offense which the neighborhood as well as the courts regarded as outside the pale.

The actual amount of juvenile delinquency and adult crime in the community could not be measured with accuracy. It has been amply demonstrated [1] that court records do not give a valid measure of recognized delinquency, let alone of the volume of such conduct which has gone unobserved and unapprehended. The numbers of those from this district who were arraigned in the children's court were too small to give a valid rate even for such cases or to show significant variations in number, geographi-

---

[1] Cf. unpublished study of delinquency rate-making on basis of 1930 juvenile offenders, made by Sophie M. Robeson for the New York City Welfare Council.

cal distribution or type of offense from year to year. The offenses followed closely those of the rest of the city, with stealing and the violation of local ordinances by such activity as hitching on backs of street cars predominating for the boys, and the few girls — only thirty-eight in the course of ten years — brought in for sex offenses almost exclusively. More than a quarter of the boys brought to court were dismissed, and the tendency was toward dismissing a larger rather than a smaller proportion in later years. Something less than two thirds were placed on probation, with a trend in the direction of fine rather than probation in a larger proportion of the cases. A smaller proportion of the girls were discharged or given suspended sentences than the boys and a larger proportion were committed to institutions. A majority of the boys were brought into court by local citizens, while the girls were as frequently brought in by their parents or by the Children's Society. The police rather than the neighbors were bringing an increasing proportion of the offending boys to court.

The boys themselves were not a distinctive group, but, in all external characteristics, resembled any sample of the boy population — predominantly Italian in about the same proportion as the rest of the local boys, tenement dwellers of low to fairly low income range, most numerous in the most populous blocks and the most populous houses, and drawn from families of all sizes, and from broken as well as complete homes.[1] There was some slight evidence of a decline in apprehended delinquency in that the drop in court cases was greater than the decrease in the boy population of the area.

Adult criminals were even more difficult to identify because the habit of giving false addresses was stated by correction officers to be so common that court records could not be used to discover local offenders. The parole officer in charge of the area reported that he always had plenty of cases, that they were chiefly located in the more populous part of the Italian district, and that he had more trouble with second generation Italian young men than with the foreign-born. Apparently a large number of local men were serving terms in Sing Sing. A canvass of a single block had shown eight men in Sing Sing at one time. When one of the school

---

[1] Examination of the reports of the probation officers on their visits to families and homes did not reveal distinctive home conditions, but homes and families of all types.

nurses visited the prison, she found that so many men who had attended one of her schools were serving terms that they had organized a large club named after the school. Since this school was in the Irish section, the presumption was that these men were chiefly Irish.

Several of the blocks were known for the particular type of criminals which were to be found on them. If an automobile was stolen or property destroyed, the police automatically suspected the crowd on one block. Another was a center for dope-runners, and the boys who had grown up there had stories of the way in which the dope-handlers had tried the youngsters out as delivery boys. An adjacent block was reputed to contain the lone-wolf type of criminal who did not go with a gang, while the next contained organized gangsters. Certain at least of the gangsters were known, but the neighborhood tried to avoid being mixed up with them. When one of the best-known gang figures came to tell the head of a settlement what he thought of the way his child had been treated, the cook brought her dish-wiping into the hall outside of the director's office and stood by with a dishpan full of substantial cups to use as ammunition in case the gangster got ugly with her chief. When a child at a day nursery announced blithely, 'My daddy's got a machine gun at our house,' and then clapped her hand over her mouth, exclaiming, 'Oh, he said I mustn't tell,' the workers at the nursery took pains not to notice the episode.

One policeman was particularly uncomplimentary about the people on his beat. 'My opinion of the people on this street is that from five years up to sixty they all are thieves. They're all born criminals; I wouldn't trust any of them over three years old. You try and do something with them! It's no use; you might as well work on that sewer out there. You see the tin water drains on the church there? Well, they were all copper once, but the kids stole them all, and when the priest tried to chase them, they threw stones and broke the church windows. In ten years they'll all be gunmen and gangsters. If I had it to say, I'd send them all up to Sing Sing. I wouldn't build no playgrounds for them; that won't do any good. I've been on this beat for twenty years and I ain't seen no change yet.'

But though there were enough professional criminals and

enough lawlessness in the community to elicit even such an exaggerated statement as this, the gangster was not the ideal of most of the local boys. The bootlegger frequently was, but, even among the multitude who reveled in gangster films, the gangster was not. In an effort to check up on the attitude of the youngsters, an older boy went around to all sorts of street play groups, even those on the uncomplimentary patrolman's beat. He got the boys talking about what they would like to do and frequently found them eager to get into the liquor business and envious of the local bootleggers. Then he picked one of the boys, a fat boy if one was handy, and tried to compliment him on being like Al Capone — that gang chief was then still at the height of his prestige and power. But he could find no group which would accept the compliment. A bootlegger was one thing. But a gangster was something different. No, they didn't want anything like that. Force of circumstance might thrust them into law-breaking. Some laws were meant to be broken anyway. But a life of crime did not appeal to the majority of those who were growing up in this neighborhood.

XIV. THE FAMILY

1. PATRIARCHAL, ROMANTIC, EXPERIMENTAL

AS EACH of the community's institutions lost much of its
ability to provide social organization, standards of conduct, or effective social control to the people of this locality, the family remained the fundamental institutional unit. For
many of the Villagers, moreover, not even the family continued to
function socially.

Three distinct family types, the patriarchal, the bourgeois-
romantic, and the experimentally individualistic characterized
respectively the Italian tradition, the old American tradition, and
the new efforts of the Villagers. Others in the community approached one of those three types. The patriarchal form was
closely adhered to by the Spanish, and certain of its elements were
retained by Irish, Jews, and Germans. The large, close family
was traditional to Irish and Jews, but the mother, so far from being completely subordinated to male domination, often came near
to ruling the family themselves, while masculine dominance was
the chief patriarchal feature of the German form.

The bourgeois-romantic type, represented by the Yankee
Ninth Warders and a few of the more conservative of the Villagers, was the form toward which the younger generation Irish
and Italians were approaching and from which the Villagers
were often fleeing. Just when many old Americans were repudiating this pattern — the small family of parents and two children supported by the earnings of the father in a suburban home
fitted with the latest in kitchen equipment — it was becoming the
one traditional American institution which the newcomers were

adopting most heartily. The Villagers, in their turn, attempted to build their experimental family around the principles of the maximum of individual freedom and self-development.

With respect to each of the stages in the cycle of the family and each of its traditional functions, differences among the several types affected the social life of the locality.

Contacts and courtship leading to marriage were not supposed to be necessary in the patriarchal family because the arrangement of marriages was a responsibility of the parents. The conservative Italians and Spanish continued to regard such contacts as unnecessary and undesirable. The Italian girls, under the watchful eyes of parents and neighbors and living in congested quarters where they could hardly entertain men, could only meet men with the greatest difficulty, at work or secretly on the street corners. Courting had to go on at the movies, at dances, in the park, on the street, or occasionally in the dark entrance-ways of the near-by factory district — but a girl who valued her reputation must not be known to be willing to go on these streets at night, and even the tougher of the local boys hesitated to start a girl on the downward path by taking her there.

At the same time, the inability of their parents to arrange their marriages sent Italian girls hunting for men by hook or crook. Various places at which dances were held were rated according to the kind of crowd — i.e., the chances that one might have of finding a good match. In the summer time, beaches and uptown swimming pools were attractive for the same reason. One girl, who thought herself very superior to the neighborhood, gave the situation away in discussing the Sunday excursions which she and her girl friend made to a certain lake in the country. It was a long, hard trip, but they went there rather than to nearer places — 'And you don't think we go there just for the swimming, do you? That's the place where you meet swell men,' and she launched into an account of the Packard car driven by the ones they had picked up the week before.

Out of a sample of twenty-two young married Italian women in 1930, only three had ever been out alone with any man except the one that she married, while six more had been out with other men in groups but not alone. Seventeen, however, had gone out with their future husbands before they were engaged. Seven had met

TABLE XX. RELATIVE POSITION OF DIFFERENT FACTORS IN
EXPERIMENTAL FAMILY FORM APPROVED BY VILLAGERS

PER CENT OF VILLAGERS DIRECTLY QUESTIONED APPROVING OR
DISAPPROVING FOLLOWING PROPOSITIONS [1]

	APPROVE	DISAPPROVE	DOUBTFUL
Married women should have independent interests.	86%	12%	2%
Every effort should be made to keep the family intact.	81%	19%	0%
It is not wrong for unmarried couples to live together.	76%	22%	2%
Divorce should be made easier.	73%	25%	2%
Husbands should share in household tasks.	70%	23%	7%
Married women should be self-supporting.	65%	34%	1%
Children are not necessary to a successful marriage.	59%	31%	10%

their husbands through their families, six had picked them up on
the street, at a beach, or public dance, three had been neighbors,
two had met at work, three had met through friends, and one at a
settlement. Seventeen went to the movies, the park, bus-riding, or
walking with their fiancés. Only four reported associating with
them at home or at a friend's home, while one had no association
before marriage.

Italian young men continued to expect the girls whom they
married to be virgins, though they occasionally took the attitude,
'It's pretty hard to find one these days.' They were apparently
not as careful to make sure as they had been, for they took it for
granted that a girl who got into trouble would go to some other
community where her reputation was not known and would have
no difficulty making a good match.

Association and courtship before marriage were part of the
bourgeois-romantic ideal, but chastity on the part of the girl was
strictly called for. The Irish young people were expected to go out
together, as were the old Americans, and some, but not all, of the

[1] Eighty-five persons. Where all did not answer question, per cent of those answering
recorded. Sample overweighted with conservative element because these were easier to
find at home.

Germans. Girls were expected to know how to 'take care of themselves' and to make the men keep their distance. Men expected their wives to be virgins, and would not consider marrying a girl who had slept with them before marriage, though a few boys were not so insistent upon the latter point and mentioned certain of their friends who had slept with their wives before marriage.

The attitude of the man was distinctly possessive, and it was assumed by the Irish, by those of the Italians who had adopted the romantic pattern, and by others among the local people who fell within this mould, that as soon as a couple started 'keeping company' the girl should stop associating with other men and that other men should keep away from her. 'We don't go to dances any more,' explained three girls, 'we only go to balls, the church ball, for instance, with our escorts. You see, we are all keeping company now.' A girl still had to be careful not to go too much with one man if she wanted to avoid the restrictions and responsibilities that went with it, but it was more the code to go out with a series of different men before settling down to one man than it had been ten years before.

The experimental pattern of the Villagers not only assumed much free contact among young people, but expected neither husband nor wife to enter marriage as virgins. The living arrangements of the Villagers were peculiarly well suited to free association. Neither parents nor community eyed young people's conduct critically. Many had come to the Village to escape just such supervision and had acquired apartments of their own where they could entertain whomsoever they pleased. They could follow up contacts made at work — through friends, or in any other way, as the local boys and girls could not. 'Keeping company' was not part of this code, for the possessive attitude of the other forms was absent and the most intimate association did not convey priority rights.

Marriage itself, in the patriarchal institution, was a union of families rather than simply of individuals. In the Catholic view, it was an indissoluble sacrament. In the Italian tradition, it was governed by fate. The older women were almost completely dominated by a fatalistic attitude, and though those of the younger Italian girls who had taken on the romantic attitude regarded marriage in quite a different light, there were many who continued to feel that they were instruments of something beyond their control. Health clinics encountered this fatalistic attitude; it was apparent in the statements of the more conservative of the girls; it was registered in the eyes of the young brides whose pictures filled the windows of photographers' shops. The girls who faced the camera on their wedding day with that characteristic expression of impersonal and fearless resignation bore eloquent testimony to the persistence of the outlook on marriage which their mothers had had.

The foundation of romantic marriage, as none who attended the movies or read the mass magazines could fail to note, was love. It was a union of individuals, not of families, which might retain its sacramental character if the couple was Catholic or it might not. It was assumed to be permanent, but since it was supposed to be held together by love, infidelity was recognized as a cause for divorce by the non-Catholics, and even by some of the less observing Catholics. This was the form which marriage took for the old American and Irish young people. The Italian young men approved it verbally, but there were grounds for suspecting that some of the latter actually took the patriarchal relationship more for granted. It was becoming increasingly the ideal of the Italian girls — so much so that an Italian social worker, who was closer to the minds of her people than, probably, any other social worker in the community, was very much worried by the romantic attitude of the girls. 'They see the movies and read the love-story magazines and get their adolescent minds chock full of romantic notions, and they have nothing to take hold of.'

Marriage in the experimental form which the Villagers approved was not a sacrament, but a purely temporal arrangement. Even its legal aspects seemed to many to be wholly superfluous. It attempted to be a relationship in which there was no subordination. Neither fate nor romance was responsible, but the intelligence and the physiology to two very mundane people. It was based upon a mutual relationship of which love, no longer romantically but rather psychologically conceived, was one element, and it was terminable at will when the partners found themselves no longer compatible. Villagers differed in the degree of permanence which they assumed. At one end of the scale were the young couples who were living in the Village until they had enough money to move to the

suburbs and bring up children and who were closer to the bourgeois-romantic than to the experimental form. At the other end
were those who made a point of the impermanence of marriage.
Most were trying to work out the best sort of personal arrangement
that they could manage without subordinating their own interests
and egos. The vast majority of those directly questioned believed
in making every effort to keep a family intact, though they did not
believe in the obligation of permanency.[1]

The relation between husband and wife in the patriarchal family rested upon the complete subordination of the woman. Although many women actually ruled the house, the show of masculine authority was maintained. It was not an unusual sight to see
an Italian father stand at the foot of the tenement steps and
sharply order his wife and children to go up before him, arrogantly
bringing up the rear himself.

In the bourgeois-romantic family the woman was less subordinated and had her own sphere of responsibility and authority.
In this family, a division of function by which the husband
brought in the income and the wife assumed responsibility for the
home and children often gave the mother the last word in matters
affecting the children and the internal organization of the home.
The sphere of interest of husband and wife were expected to be
wholly distinct. Among the young people for whom this was the
ideal, the possibility of any common interests between husband
and wife and any companionship between them was an altogether
foreign notion. A group of Italian girls struggled valiantly to get
the drift of an interviewer's questions about possible common interests. ' I suppose,' one of them finally suggested, 'that a girl might
read the paper after her husband goes to work and find something
to show him when he gets home.' This was the limit of their
imagination.

The experimental couples started with the assumption of common interests, or of independent interests outside as well as in the
home, for which each had respect. Whereas the home was the
woman's sphere in the patriarchal family and her job in the bourgeois form, it was an incidental interest to the experimental woman.
Theoretically both home and children were as much the man's concern as the woman's, if the woman's interests happened to be more

[1] Cf. Table XX, p. 406.

strongly outside the home than his. Actually, in the families of Villagers, the burden of the home and children tended to fall much more heavily on the woman than on the man because, when both were drawn by interests outside the home, it was much easier for him to avoid home responsibilities than for her. The experimental family thus broke down the division of function of the bourgeois household, bringing both man and woman into the sphere occupied by the other. Among those Villagers expressing themselves directly on the subject, a slightly larger proportion stated that the husband should share in the household duties than thought that the wife should be self-supporting. The practical effect in the homes observed, however, and in those reported upon by teachers in progressive and nursery schools, was that the women went out to earn more often than the men took the responsibility for tending the baby and washing the dishes. The burden and responsibilities of the woman were often increased to the point where the entire home rested on her shoulders.

The ideal of the patriarchal family was as many children as possible. Among the older Italians large families were conspicuous, furnishing a large proportion of the children who played on the street and who attended settlements and other centers. They did not constitute so large a proportion of the local Italian families, however, as their prominence in public places would suggest.

The census of 1920 gave the average number of children per family in the Italian section, surviving and living at home, as 2.5. In 1930, the average was 1.7. Only 21.4 per cent of the families in this section in 1930 contained more than four persons — i.e., if both parents were living, more than two children. Only 6.5 per cent contained five children or more.[1] A sample of 1221 specifically Italian families drawn from the census of 1925 on a series of Italian blocks showed 36.7 per cent with more than two and 12.4 per cent with five or more children.[2] In all these cases, the number of children alive and residing at home was reported; neither those who were grown and had left home nor those who did not survive appeared in any of these counts. A canvass of Italian houses in 1930 supported the evidence of the census to the effect that the Italian family with more than four surviving children living at

[1] Cf. Table XXI, Appendix F, p. 476.   [2] Cf. Table XXII, Appendix F, p. 476.

home was the exception rather than the rule. Among 310 families in twenty scattered houses in 1920, the average number of children living at home was 1.9 per family. A quarter of these families had no children living at home. In the house which contained the largest proportion of children, the average per family was 3.1.

While these samples may have been weighted with older couples whose children had grown and moved away, records of the families with young children attending a pre-school and a baby clinic told the same story. The average number of children per family at the pre-school clinic from 1921 to 1924 was 2.9 and from 1926 to 1929 was 2.6; at the baby clinic in 1929 it was 2. Though this evidence, in turn, is obscured by the heavy infant mortality in the early years, and the fact that the young mothers were the ones to be attracted to the clinic, it seems clear that the idea of large families was more prevalent than the fact. Although there was not enough accurate information for 1920 to indicate how much of a trend toward smaller families there had actually been, the evidence of the number of young children in proportion to the Italian women of child-bearing age showed a decline of 26 per cent in the number of children under ten per thousand women between fifteen and forty-four years of age.[1]

The Irish families of the previous generations were reputed to have been large — six to ten was the usual number in the years before the War in the opinion of fifty Irish people questioned. Evidence of available samples indicated that the Irish families in the district had continued larger than the Italian. The proportion of large families in the waterfront section where the Irish predominated was greater in 1930 than in the Italian section, and in both 1920 and 1930 the ratio of children to women of child-bearing age was higher. The Irish families patronizing the pre-school clinic were larger on the average than the Italian — containing 3.3 children in both the early and the later years of the decade. The Irish families in the hands of case-work agencies also contained a larger proportion with many children than did the Italian.

Though the Germans had retained the masculine authority of the patriarchal family, they had not continued the large family, for the families of those Germans who remained in the locality

[1] Table XXIII, Appendix F, p. 477.

numbered one to three children and even the older generation did not favor many children.

The bourgeois-romantic family did not measure its success in numbers as did the patriarchal, and those among the old American, the German, and the Irish who adopted this attitude sought to keep their families down to the size which could be easily supported. By 1930, two children, preferably a boy and a girl, had become practically symbolic of the family type, whether among the Irish, the young Italians, the Germans, or the conservative Villagers. This stereotype, which had the sanction of the Century of Progress Exhibit along with the advertisements in all the home magazines, was fully accepted by the younger element in the community.

The experimental family was likely to be still smaller than the bourgeois-romantic. Whereas the latter called for children to complete the home, the experimental form might be childless if the tastes of the couple so dictated. It might have one, two, or three children, rarely more, though if there were sufficient means and interest on the part of parents, there was nothing in the pattern to stand in the way of a larger number. Practically, the financial and social strain of urban living kept the experimental families in the Village down to one or two children. Two families of four children were known and were very generally commented upon in the community. Among eighty-nine married Villagers interviewed, sixty-one had no children.[1] Half of the twenty-eight families with children contained one child only. Eight families had two children, four had three, and two had four. Among the families sending their children to a local progressive school, the average of 1.78 children per family was very close to the average of 1.7 in this sample of twenty-eight families with children. Inclusion of the childless families in the sample brought the average down to .56 children per Villager family. In ten houses containing 452 apartments occupied by Villagers, a total of only thirty-one children were found in 1930.

In the patriarchal family, all members, and especially the children, were subordinated to the family group. The relation between parent and child was one of absolute obedience on the latter's part and responsibility toward the group for support and co-operation. Children took it for granted that the support of their parents

[1] Seventeen of these had been married less than a year.

would be their responsibility. 'They sacrificed for us when we were little. It is only fair that we should support them in return.' In a patriarchal home, children had no 'rights,' only duties. Until the Italian home was broken by the impact of American institutions, this attitude remained, and nothing in the whole process of adaptation served more to cast the younger Italian adrift than the undermining of this assumption.

In the bourgeois-romantic family, responsibility was on the side of the parents rather than of the child, the parents being obligated by the fact of bringing the child into the world (presumed to be their responsible act rather than an act of God) to support and rear the child and to give him all the 'advantages' within their power. The child continued, as in the patriarchal family, to owe obedience and respect to the parents, however. One of the Catholic priests aligned the Catholic Church on the side of the patriarchal filial relationship and the Protestant churches with the bourgeois-romantic in the statement: 'There always was a difference between the Catholic families and the Protestant families. Catholic parents have children so the children can take care of the parents — that is always the idea. Protestant families, on the other hand, were entirely different. Protestant parents took care of their children; even gave them a little money so they could get married.' The Irish carried the responsibility of children toward the family group into the romantic family as they developed it in this community. The Germans carried over the strict obedience of children, with less insistence upon the subordination of their interests to those of the family group. Among the younger people of all groups the emphasis on giving to the child rather than expecting services from him was general.

In the experimental family, the child had rights rather than duties, except as such duties might be developed as part of an educational process. The parents' responsibility extended beyond support to the provision of the most favorable environment for the development of the child's personality. The experimental family became preoccupied with problems of child psychology and, with the aid of the progressive schools, which became almost as much educational centers for parents as for children, attempted to organize the family life along the best psychological lines.

The net result of the differences among these families was to make the home a very different sort of institution. For the patriarchal family, it was the family group itself and the functions which it performed which made the home. The place was of secondary importance if the relationships and functions were there. This made the Italian and Spanish families relatively indifferent to their physical surroundings. To a somewhat less degree the older Irish shared this attitude.

In the bourgeois-romantic family the physical home was the focus. Far from being a matter of relative indifference as it was to the patriarchal household, the house and its furnishings *was* the 'home.' For this type of family, a high material standard of living was all-important. The 'lovely home' which the Irish and Italian young people craved was symbolic of their adoption of bourgeois-romantic values.

In the experimental family of the Villagers, the physical home had lost its symbolic importance and had ceased to be an end in itself. The experimental families attempted to make home a psychological state which would provide security for members of the family, especially the child. They sought to make it serve as a bulwark against the pressures of city life.

The functions performed by the several family types differed, as did their forms. The patriarchal family definitely gave status to its members in Italy and continued to do so, to a less extent, in this community. The Irish family, perhaps more than the Italian, retained a status-giving function, partly because the families established their reputation when the community was closer and partly because, in the political system, family loyalty played an important part. City conditions were such, however, as to take away even from the patriarchal family much of its status-giving function. The bourgeois-romantic family gave status to its members to a very much smaller extent, partly because the unit in this family was the single group of parents and children rather than the wider kin group. In the experimental family, status-giving was abandoned altogether. Since the Villagers in no way acquired their position in the local community because of their families, they had no inherited family status to hand on to their children. The assumption of possible impermanence in these families, moreover, directly negatived any status-giving role which they might perform.

Within the family group, all three types furnished a measure of security, protection, and mutual aid. The loyalty within the Italian family made it impregnable against the assaults of the world — again until its foundations were undermined by the process of adaptation. Protection and mutual aid were rendered, not only within the immediate family, but for the wider group of relatives. Similarly, among the Irish, 'when someone is a relative, no matter how distant, and you know they are alive, you can't help wanting to do something for them.' Protection of children, however, rarely involved an attempt on the part of the family to stand between them and the experiences of life about them. The families which exercised oversight over their children in the attempt to give them this sort of protection were more apt to be those which had adopted the bourgeois-romantic attitude of parental responsibility rather than those within the patriarchal mould.

Though the bourgeois-romantic family was less solid than the patriarchal, the man's role of protector was carried over both in a chivalric attitude toward the wife and in relation to the children. The security within this family type was primarily that of physical safety.

In the experimental family, the effort, often unsuccessful, to provide psychological security for the children was a prime consideration — stressed, perhaps, because of the frequent absence of it for the parents whose relationship often lacked the security of the more stable forms. There was practically no carry-over into the experimental family of the protective function or chivalric attitude on the part of the man toward the woman. Mutual aid was part of the reciprocal relationship, but it had to compete with personal interests as it did not have to in families of the other types. On the other hand, the experimental families went far beyond either of the others in attempting to shield the child from an unfavorable environment. Difference in economic status which made it much more possible for Villagers to control the environment of their children was largely responsible, but the family attitude was a secondary factor.

Economic functions had been lost by all types of city families as far as production was concerned. Except for the Jewish, Italian, and German storekeepers' families, where wife and children helped in the store, there was no co-operation in actual productive activity, whether the family was patriarchal, bourgeois-romantic, or experimental in type. Families varied, largely with economic status, in the economic functions carried on within the home. In the preparation of food, households ranged from the Italian families who made their own tomato paste and mixed their own bread — to be baked by a local baker — through those who bought bread, but rarely used canned or prepared foods, to the Irish who relied much more heavily on canned foods than did the Italians, who scorned them, and to the Villagers, who patronized delicatessen stores and frequently ate out. The new apartments and remodeled buildings that provided a minimum of kitchen facilities recorded the passing of food-preparation as a home function. Laundry remained a function of the poorer homes, supplemented by the 'wet wash,' while the Villagers depended upon the multitude of laundries and cleaning establishments which followed apartment building into the area. Among the Villagers, the home as a producing unit was reduced to the barest minimum, leaving practically no economic functions for the woman who stayed at home. In part this situation arose from the 'friction of space' characteristic of a congested city district [1] which reduced living quarters to the minimum, but partly it reflected a definite effort on the part of the experimental families to minimize the physical aspects of the home. For the woman of the experimental family, the kitchen was often the symbol of the type of life from which she had freed herself.

The three types of families remained economic units in varying degrees, however, for purposes of consumption. The patriarchal family expected that all earnings would be pooled and used for the benefit of the group. Both the Italian and Irish families retained this characteristic of having their members 'working for it,' though the practice of having the working children pay board and keep the rest of their pay was becoming more usual. The older Irish women felt that it didn't seem right 'to make a boarding-missus out of the mother,' but were coming to accept the practice.

The bourgeois-romantic families, with their stress on the father's responsibility for the support of the family, did not commonly look to the children for contributions to the family, except

[1] Carpenter, Niles, *The Sociology of City Life*, New York, 1931, p. 127.

such as were involved in having grown children 'pay their way.' In spite of many patriarchal features, the Jewish families displayed this attitude, quoting the proverb, 'Better to be under the ground than dependent on one's children,' but at the same time insisting that a grown boy must support himself.

The experimental families were often not even self-maintaining. They expected no contribution to the family income from the children and laid considerable stress on the economic independence of the woman, so that the incomes of husband and wife were not only separately earned, but sometimes separately spent. In a substantial number of the Villager families, moreover, the family was dependent on contributions from parents, on legacies, or on other supplements to their income. This was the situation among twenty per cent of the patrons of a progressive school.

The combination of differences in the economic organization of the family itself and in the background from which the families came often resulted in a greater economic strain in the families of the Villagers, in spite of their higher income level, than among the local low income families. The Italian and Irish families which could depend on their children's earnings could look to an increasing income and a corresponding increase in their standard of living. Their costs of living, moreover, were relatively low, for they availed themselves of public facilities for all except their basic needs, with the cost of education carried by the state, and the cost of health and much of the cost of recreation borne outside the immediate family. Measured from the basis of the previous generation, the improving economic status of these families placed them under relatively little economic strain.

Villager families brought into city conditions, where certain levels of health and comfort were very difficult of attainment, the standards of their parents' homes. The burden of educational and other costs rested heavily upon them, for educational expenditure, once the principles of progressive education had been accepted, did not stop with the ordinary school session, but included such extras as music lessons and almost certainly included taking the children to the country. They did not use the public facilities, such as schools, churches, public playgrounds, and day nurseries, but instead provided a duplicate set of facilities out of their own pockets. They retained responsibility for many of the family functions which had been taken over by the public, but carried them financially instead of performing them personally. Since these families had characteristically repudiated the bourgeois money drive, they did not direct their energies toward making sufficient money to carry the heavy cost, but solved the problem by relying on their parents' assistance, exploiting the earning resources of the wife, and limiting the family size to a minimum. In turn, they expected to continue to aid their children financially when these should found families of their own. The sequence set up in this family form was thus toward the maintenance of a standard of living set by the preceding generation, an increasing level of expenditure necessary to maintain it, and decreasing resources.

No families performed the educational role which was traditional before the days of public education, but all retained some measure of their educational function. The families differed again, however, in the aspect of education which they carried as their responsibility. The Italian and Irish families were primarily concerned with instructing their children in standards of behavior; the Villagers devoted themselves to transmitting to their children a heritage of literate culture.

Impeded by their illiteracy and by the fundamental incompatibility between their culture and the local environment, the Italian families made little effort to transmit an inherited culture to their children, but they did undertake to mould and control the behavior of their children even along lines which were at variance with the local community. Outside agencies differed in their policy of backing up or ignoring these parental efforts, a minority making a point of supporting the parents in disputes with their children, wherever possible, or of praising parents to their children whenever the opportunity presented, the majority disregarding the home on the ground that, since the child had made a break from the home culturally, nothing was to be gained by trying to bridge the gulf in matters of conduct and discipline. In many Italian families, in fact, the process of cultural education was reversed, the children teaching the parents, rather than *vice versa*. The attempt to enforce behavior standards in the absence of cultural ties often met with such obstacles in the attitude of the children, as well as in the conflict with outside influences, that the families where the children had done most to educate the parents culturally had the greatest success in their efforts at controlling their children's conduct, since they could meet their children more nearly on the latter's terms and could command their respect.

The Irish families were in a much better position both to transmit a cultural heritage and to maintain standards of conduct because they were supported in both these educational efforts by the institution of the Church which was integral with so large a part of their culture.

The Villagers took much less direct responsibility for instilling standards of behavior into their children, apart from the fundamentals of habit-forming, than for cultural transmission. Since they were largely drawn from among the intelligentsia, literate culture was their *métier*. The time which they set aside from their other preoccupations for association with their children was devoted to enlarging the child's experience rather than to supervising his conduct. Since they wished their children to acquire the power to discriminate and choose rather than to follow any rule of thumb, they were much less interested than were their Italian and Irish neighbors in adult standards of behavior. They were, in fact, ready to hand over to others any responsibility for conduct which they might have, and placed their children in nursery school at an early age.

Although much of the educational function had been assumed by outside agencies for all the local family types, the Villagers were in a position to select the educational influences to which their children should be subjected, while the Irish and Italians had only the choice between the alternative forms of general education offered by Church and State.

For the adults among the local people, the family continued to perform a recreational role, but not for the younger members. The local young people virtually never used their homes to entertain their friends or as places in which to play. All the recreational groups in the community were specific age groups. Only at weddings or when the 'uncle from Jersey' took the family to ride in his car, and very occasionally at the beaches, did the whole family take its recreation together. Among the Villagers, for whom reading and parties were principal forms of recreation, the physical home figured importantly, but the family little if at all.

While these three types of family existed in the Village throughout these years, their proportion changed as the mobility of population brought in some elements and drew others out; as the same group of people shifted from one type toward another; and as the types themselves underwent certain modifications.

The supplanting of Italian and Irish by Villagers meant definitely the substitution of the experimental for the patriarchal or, to some extent, the romantic family type in the community. Among the Villagers themselves, the group which was less experimental and more sympathetic to the bourgeois-romantic form was relatively new to the community, but there was no substantial evidence that the Villagers as a whole were becoming more romantic and less experimental.[1]

Among both Italian and Irish young people, the trend toward the romantic form was strong, while the Jewish young people, partly because of their college experience, were the only ones among the local population to entertain the experimental form in their imagination — even if they did not put it into practice.

Many Villagers repudiated family relationships altogether. The district abounded in single people living alone or in groups. For these bachelor groups, both of men and girls, the district was peculiarly well suited because of its small apartments and because of the looseness of its social organization. In contrast to single people living alone in the suburbs who found suburban society geared to the family group, those in the Village found no such situation, but rather everything favorable to them. A sample of twenty-five households of single or formerly married people showed no type situation, but a range from the very flexible and impermanent to those which had been in existence for years. There were single women who had lived together for many years and had made every effort to create a 'home,' even to the point of adopting children in a few cases. There were young people who expected to give up their bachelor ways and settle down to family life, usually of the experimental type. There were others of all ages, both men and women, who repudiated everything which had to do with home and family and made no attempt to turn whatever living arrangements they might make into any substitute for the

[1] Comparison of those who had been in the Village less than five years with those who had been there more than five showed the newer residents to be slightly less experimental, but the size of the sample was too small for the difference to be significant.

family and home life which they had discarded. Fifteen out of the twenty-five in the random sample were made up of men or women under thirty.

There were many among the Villagers whose experimental families had proved unsuccessful and who, either divorced or separated, had come to the Village for escape. Although the Census of 1930 showed only a slightly higher proportion of divorced persons in Greenwich Village than in Manhattan — .7 per cent of the men and 1 per cent of the women as compared with .4 and .7 per cent respectively — 12 per cent of the 209 persons replying to a questionnaire were either divorced or separated.[1]

For many of the Villagers, no institution, not even the family, retained a significance in their lives. Among most of the local people, the family remained the chief agent of social control. Time and again, efforts to trace differences in conduct or attitude to their source led to the peculiarities of the individual family — not even to the type of family but the personal factors in the particular family situation. But in many families the gulf between the first and second generations left many of the younger generation without even this effective guide.

[1] The census did not report those who were separated. There was no reason to think that the sample was biased in this direction. Neither census nor sample indicated those who had been divorced and remarried.

CONCLUSION

THIS study of Greenwich Village has shown that the social factors dominating this community were those which led toward social disorganization and cultural confusion. In the post-War years, stabilizing influences were hard to find, while those which either reflected or promoted social instability were apparent on every hand.

No social cement bound into a social whole the fragments of old cultures — immigrant and old American — which were thrown together in this community. Nor were there any distinguishable signs that forces were at work to shape new cultural patterns out of fragments of the old. The most diligent search brought forth no evidence that the direction of social evolution in this community was toward a social order for twentieth-century America, but only that it was away from the social orders of the past. The impact of the depression, frustrating the money drive and undermining its traditional sanction, cannot fail to have added a further disintegrating pressure.

To most of the people of the community, the daily details of living — household habits, the rhythm of work, personal relationships, and concrete observations — made up the texture of their lives and preoccupied their thoughts as well as their actions. Considerations of the type here discussed were present to the minds of only the most thoughtful. Yet, wherever the articulate and inquiring young people expressed themselves, it was to stress the confusion rather than the order of their lives.

'We have no one that we can look to,' they explained. 'What help are our parents when it is we who are in a position to tell them what to do, not they us? How can we rely on the schools when we don't believe that they understand the real problems which we have to face? The priests can instruct us in our religious duties, but where does that get us? It's pretty hard to have respect even for judges when you see the way that some of them come out of the speakeasies. I guess we've just got to figure it out for ourselves. But tell us, do we ever actually get that "American standard of living," or must we just hope for a "break"? Have we got to play ball with the political machine and the rackets if we don't want to get left? And do you think we'll ever really get by as Americans, or are we bound to stay "wops" and "kikes" for the rest of our lives?'

Most of the younger Villagers looked upon their life in the Village as a temporary phase, yet had no clear idea where it might lead. They had turned their backs upon the Main Streets from which they had come, and on the values which governed these communities, but had set their faces toward no alternative way of life.

The Irish, alone, among the social groups of this locality, continued to find the main parts of their social structure relatively intact, and to accept political jobs, nice homes, and bourgeois respectability as a satisfactory framework within which to order their lives.

The significance of Greenwich Village as a commentary on American civilization during these years is not due to any qualities which made it unique. It lies, rather, in the fact that the Village presents, though in a somewhat exaggerated form, social problems and social processes common to other urban communities. The people who lived in the Village were an ordinary collection of forty to fifty thousand individuals, equipped with the physical needs and psychological drives that are dominant in this or any other time or place; the daily round of getting and spending, eating and sleeping, making merry and suffering went on here as elsewhere.

On the basis of these daily repetitions, the district could be dismissed with the thought that 'people lived here as they have lived before and as they live elsewhere.' But the organizing factors which make or fail to make a social whole out of the life habits of any community are what determine its social development. The compelling social fact of this community was the failure of traditional controls to operate and of traditional patterns to produce a coherent social life. What new patterns may develop to replace the rampant individualism which finds few outlets in the urban life of twentieth-century America except in predatory action or escape? Whence may come organizing forces which will canalize individual energies and give them social form?

THE END

APPENDICES

APPENDIX A

NOTE ON METHOD AND SOURCES

In the field of the social sciences where such diversity of method reigns and such a multitude of techniques are clamoring for approval, each new study calls for a statement of the method employed. For this volume, such a statement is particularly imperative, since the nature of the materials has made it largely impossible to show by direct references in the text the sources from which many of the statements have been drawn.

Two cardinal principles have underlain the method of this study: first, the conviction that the student of any human situation must bring to his study a fundamental and genuine respect for the people and institutions studied and a determination to view them first and foremost in their own terms; and, secondly, the assumption that all types of material, whatever their source and form, may shed light on a problem if they are regarded as evidence and are subjected to the tests and criticism which all evidence demands. Within the limits laid down by these two principles, a completely opportunist approach has been employed for using whatever sources of information have been available.

The social scientist cannot have recourse to the complete detachment of the natural scientist. The material of the natural scientist occupies one world; he lives in another. The social scientist can never forget that the objects of his study are creatures of his own world; nor should he forget, for to do so would be to distort his view by making of his subjects creatures of another sphere. In view of the necessity of his identifying himself with his subjects, but of not projecting onto them his own values, convictions, and prejudices, he must consciously recognize that some definite state of mind is inevitably involved and he must include such a state of mind as part of the controlled technique.

In this study, a constant effort has been made to see in their own terms, and with respect, the wide variety of people and of institutions which made up this community — people who lived within the law and without; who were intellectuals or illiterates; institutions divergent or opposed in aim and widely variant in method. It was not easy, however, to convey to those who were being studied the idea that to examine was not to criticize and to describe was not to blame. Again, the objectivity of the natural scientist was of little avail, for human dignity does not like to be treated as a laboratory specimen. Bafflingly typical was the attitude of the school principal who declared, 'I am going to take every single "white rat" question out of this school questionnaire,' and ended by throwing out practically every question. The location and composition of the district intensified the problem. A city population is too aware of differences from itself not to be on the defensive about its own position, and this area was peculiarly distrustful and on its guard against the world.

Every effort was made to avoid the situation into which much social investigation is driven by the human resistance to being studied, namely, over-reliance upon the exceptional, upon those who are sufficiently educated and able to be objective about themselves and will co-operate consciously — students, for instance — and those who have diverged in such a way as to place themselves in the hands of some remedial agency which can then exploit them for purposes of research. Patients in clinics, clients of relief agencies, prisoners in jail cannot protest effectively against being treated like 'white rats.' But in between those who understand and co-operate and those who are in the hands of agencies lies the great mass of society which cannot understand that to be viewed dispassionately is not to be relegated to the realm of the lower animals, and which is in full possession of the freedom of action necessary to escape being so treated. A community study such as this should reach this great mass if it is to avoid the pitfall of generalizing from the exception which has attained notice by reason of its very divergence.

Although it has been necessary in certain instances to rely on evidence of the above types, such evidence has been heavily discounted for the bias which it represents, and the study has erred on the side of refusing agency leads which might have proved valuable rather than of depending too much upon them.

The effort to view institutions and individuals in their own terms has led to the necessity of describing them in relation to their aims, standards, and assumptions. What is consciously thought about in any community is only the smaller and less general aspects of life in that community. But the unstated assumptions which govern most thought and action lie embedded in the tradition of the group and yield only with greatest difficulty to the direct attack of the investigator. It has, therefore, been necessary to analyze, in their general aspects, the traditional behavior or culture patterns of the groups and institutions represented in the community. The historical development of these patterns had to be indicated, though sketchily, for a cross-section of a culture pattern at any time is infinitely involved and, even at best, reveals inconsistencies and contradictions which are only explicable in the light of their historical development.

If a total study is to have coherence, however, the situations which have been viewed in terms of their several patterns must then be considered, together with their patterns, in the light of some still other considerations, common to all, external to all, or reciprocal among several.

The co-ordinating point of view which has been brought to bear upon the diverse elements here studied is the question of the place which this community — and the various elements in it — occupies in the development of American culture.

With this approach, the first practical problem was to decide which were the dominant groupings in the community. An attempt to study this community primarily in terms, for instance, of such a class alignment as would be typical of an English town, or even the 'working-class'-'business-class' distinction found in Middletown, would have resulted in a distorted and unrealistic view of the whole social structure. A first rough survey quickly showed the importance of the social gulf between the local population — largely but by no means wholly tenement dwellers — and those who had moved into the neighborhood after it had begun to be reclaimed. Among the former, ethnic groupings were clearly dominant and among the newcomers self-selected groupings.

The second problem was to find the relation of individuals to the patterns of their respective groups. Certain key features of each group pattern were selected and used as touchstones. In respect to each pattern, characteristics were chosen which represented either end of the scale of conformity — the first and the last feature to be abandoned by someone abandoning the ways of the group — and these were used as short cuts which made it possible to eliminate many questions. For example, if a Catholic is married outside of the Church, it is not necessary to look at the frequency with which he attends Mass or at much of anything except whether he sends for a priest on his deathbed, while if he goes to confession every month it is probably safe to assume that he observes the Holy Days of Obligation. If a Jew fails to have his son circumcised, it is hardly necessary to inquire whether he keeps a strictly Kosher house, and if he refrains from cooking on the Sabbath, he is pretty sure to have his son confirmed.

By thus bracketing the individual in relation to the group pattern, it is possible to indicate much about him in his social relationships without attempting the virtually impossible task of covering the whole range of his experience, behavior, and attitudes. In this study, this device has been used in preference to the full-length case study, since the interest has been social rather than psychological and since it has not centered upon a specific behavior problem such as delinquency.[1] The more a person diverges from the pattern to which he is being referred, the further his conduct must be probed, unless there can be discovered some other pattern to which he has come to conform.

To assume the rest of a pattern where there is conformity on key points

---

[1] Cf. Appendix B for schedules and page 431 for account of framing of Italian schedule.

is only safe if watch is constantly kept for shiftings of patterns and of boundaries between groups, or for realignments within old groups and the cutting across old lines by new groupings. The danger of forcing people into a mould and keeping them there is greatly enhanced by the usual point of view of informants, since people who are part of a shifting scene tend to think and talk in terms of the old alignments, while it is the very process of breakdown and regrouping which is of greatest interest to the student of social change.

The specific techniques used for securing the data called for in the above statement have been governed simply and solely by the problem of availability. No techniques were ruled out by the nature of the approach, but many were eliminated or restricted by the practical limits of the situation.

Virtually no satisfactory statistical sources or means of statistical measurement were at hand. In securing the commonest type of basic social data — statistics of schools and agencies, building operations, assessed valuations, etc. — enormous effort was involved, and the results were far from rewarding because of the constant necessity of making estimates. Scarcely any two administrative districts in New York City coincide, nor is there any uniformity in the data available for various institutions and various periods. The district studied coincided with six census tracts ('Sanitary Areas'), so that population data was in a usable form. Data on districts which did not coincide with these census tracts — namely, political, school, police, social agency, parish, assessment, library, etc., all of which differed from the census tracts and also from each other — had to be manipulated to apply as nearly as possible to the census areas, or the records had to be searched according to a street directory and the individual cases collected. In many respects, the small number of cases involved made statistical treatment of the results of questionable validity. As far as was reasonably possible, such recorded sources as existed were exploited and were subjected to such treatment, statistical or otherwise, as their character permitted.

Written questionnaires susceptible of statistical treatment were hardly suitable, for a large part of the population was either actually illiterate, or semi-literate, and not capable of responding to the questionnaire approach. A very substantial amount of literate intelligence and habit is necessary to the answering of even the simplest sort of written questionnaire. Such a condition did not obtain among the majority of the people here studied. Those who were sufficiently literate could not be reached, for there were very few organized groups such as Parent-Teachers' Associations or clubs, through which they could be approached. The one place where it might have been possible to use questionnaires effectively, the schools, could not be used because of the attitude of the school authorities who were at the time threatened by a legislative investigation. The notoriously uncertain device of mailing was tried for a random sample of Villagers with the meager result expected — a ten per cent return with all the bias of self-selection involved. It was virtually impossible to secure from any group enough formal interview questionnaires for statistical treatment, for the part of the community which contained bootleggers, dope-runners and gangsters could hardly be canvassed, schedule in hand, while the large number of single or childless working people, living at a fast pace, could rarely be found at home during waking hours. Dozens of unanswered doorbells at all hours of day and evening testified to the habits of this group.

It became necessary, therefore, to resort to various types of interviews and observations, not uniform in either method or results, and to devise ways to secure such interviews or observations and to utilize such non-statistical results. Interviewers were selected for each contact on the basis of their ability to elicit the particular type of information sought, which meant, in general, those who were as closely identified as possible with the group studied. To study the Italian group, for instance, knowledge of the verbal language was insufficient without such a knowledge of the language of implication as is possessed by those bred in the tradition of the group.

Every effort was made to take advantage of the insider's insight in dealing with all groups, not alone where, as in the case of the Italians, language made this procedure imperative. In selecting college students to investigate street-corner loafers, those whose own backgrounds were similar were chosen in preference to boys from more refined localities. A red-haired Irish girl, 'with the map of Ireland written all over her face,' was sent to draw out even second and third generation Irish. When the reputation of the area for social freedom and unconventionality was to be tested, a person with great personal charm was sent out as a sort of magnet to attract, if possible, the kind of proposals which were supposed to be current.

The insider was of especial value in catching the implications of things casually or incidentally said, of varieties in phrasing, or of the omissions which are often most eloquent of all. As one of the local boys was at pains to explain, unless you knew how this neighborhood did its swearing you could not tell when a boy was really swearing, when he was just talking the language of his street, and when he was giving himself away as a stranger or greenhorn by using the unapproved expression.

In using the insider as an interviewer, however, a genuine difficulty presents itself. Though he senses what he hears and sees as the outsider cannot, it is not always easy or possible for him to articulate it in terms which others can understand, and he does not always notice consciously those things which are most part of his assumptions. Often he in turn must be drawn out by an outsider before his interview experience is made fully useful. It was frequently necessary in this study for the director to probe the interviewers in order to amplify their direct reports. The ideal interviewer is the one who is sufficiently of the group to recognize implications and is at the same time either detached and articulate or in some way outside the group as well as inside it. One such, a Jewish college student who had grown up among the neighborhood Italians and associated constantly with them, proved invaluable by virtue of being both in and out of the group and at the same time observant and articulate.

Sometimes, however, it is not the insider who can elicit the most from the subjects and situations studied, particularly when the source to be tapped is a highly articulate person whom one wants to draw into as full an explanation as possible. A situation in point arose when it came to studying the parochial schools. A choice had to be made between using an Irish Catholic who knew the system, or a Jewish woman who knew nothing whatever about the parochial system, though she was well acquainted with public and progressive schools. The latter was selected in a desire to induce those in charge to be as explicit as possible. They would have taken too much for granted in talking to a Catholic. A Protestant might have put them on the defensive. But a Jew could be as inquiring as she pleased. In this situation, the outsider was used to do the actual interviewing and the insider, the Catholic, was used to check the results.

Throughout this study, the data-gatherers were on the alert for evidence other than that directly sought, and were at pains to capitalize their efforts on the frequent occasions when they did not find what they sought. Much effort which did not bring the intended fruit was salvaged by a recognition of other significances which the materials contained. An unsuccessful effort to introduce a questionnaire into the schools, for example, brought to light the fears and prejudices of persons in the school system and revealed things about the relation of the schools to the community which were of great value and would have been difficult to obtain directly.

The material has been analyzed by applying the critique of evidence which is the historian's constant tool. The historian is constantly dealing with materials of just this type, never uniform or complete, never produced under controlled conditions, always subject to the bias of recording and the accident of preservation, and always complicated by the problem of whether a silence shelters a commonplace or something which does not exist. Everything, quantitative and qualitative, has here been regarded as evidence and has been treated accordingly. It has been tested and discounted for bias, examined for internal consistency, and subjected to external checks, weighed for completeness and searched for the meaning of omissions.

A full, critical appraisal of any fragment of evidence, however, rests upon a knowledge of all the rest of the evidence. Only in the light of the whole is it possible to see the relevance and significance of any part, and to answer the crucial question, 'Evidence of *what?*' The practice used in some studies of presenting excerpts of material, apparently on the assumption that the reader is in a position to interpret the material, fails to recognize the basis necessary for interpretation and relieves the author of a responsibility which is rightly his. Nobody is in so good a position as he to analyze and interpret the material, for he has on hand more evidence than anyone else to aid his critical understanding. So-called facts do not speak for themselves out of the material; they are wrung from reluctant sources by a painstaking process of scrutiny and examination. It is the author's task to present, not fragments of evidence of whose validity and representativeness the reader is in no position to judge, but a considered, fully digested, and interpretive study.

The nature of the material used in this study makes detailed documentation impossible except where the material can be thrown into tabular form. It is not possible to refer in a footnote to a verbal statement, as to a page in a book, for the circumstances in which the statement was made — in response to what question, put by whom, how, in what atmosphere, and following what conversation — are as essential as the statement itself. References have, therefore, been made only to tables and to printed material. The following list of oral sources (pages 434, 435), with a guide to the parts of the book in which they have been principally used, will indicate the largest blocks of material. Much evidence cannot even be indicated in this way, however, for it is cumulative — a few sharp situations or statements making clear what had been already indicated from many directions.

Type of Approach	Number	Persons Studied	Interviewers	Chapter in Which Material is Chiefly Used
Mailed questionnaire	212	Villagers	—	II, 3, IV, VIII, XIV
Interview schedule	100	Villagers	Sophisticated young woman	II, 3, IV, VIII, XIV
	144	Italians	5 Local Italian young men	IV, V, VI
	60	Irish	Irish girl	IV, V, VII, IX, X, 2
	50	Spanish	College student from Panama	V, VII, 2
	12	Jewish	Local Jewish man	V, VII, 2
	19	German	Staff interviewer	IV, V, VII, 2
	22	Young married Italian women	Public health nurses	VI, XIV
	27	Villagers living in non-family groups	Women college students	VIII, XIV
	20	Apartment-house superintendents	Home economics student	II, 2, VIII
Informal interviews	50	Italians	Italian girl	II, 3, IV, V, VI, XIV
	35	Prominent Italians	Staff inteviewers	IV, V, VI, XIV
	47	Italian girls	Staff interviewer	VI, XII, XIV
	15	College students	Staff interviewer	IV, XI, XII
	15	Young married people who had moved away on marriage	Staff interviewer	IV, V, XIV
	19	Italian families moved to Brooklyn	Staff interviewer	II, 3
Information schedule	57	Pre-Volstead Saloonkeepers	Local Irish woman	III, 1
Group contacts	30	'Hang around' groups of older boys and young men	College student	IV, V, 2, XII, 2, XIII, 3
	30	Street play groups of younger boys	College student	IV, V, 2, XII, 2, XIII, 3

Type of Approach	Number	Persons Studied	Interviewers	Chapter in Which Material is Chiefly Used
Informational interviews with key people		Artists and writers	Staff interviewer	VIII
		Real Estate Dealers	Staff interviewer	App. C
		Political Leaders	Staff interviewers	IX
		Protestant ministers	Theological student	X
		Catholic Priests	Catholic student	X
		Superintendents and Principals of public, parochial and private schools	Psychiatric Social Worker	XI
		Settlement, mission, recreation center leaders	Staff interviewers	XII
		Health workers	Staff interviewers	XIII, 1
		Social Case workers and supervisors	Psychiatric Social Worker	XIII, 2
		Probation, Parole, Police and Crime Prevention Officers	Staff interviewers	XIII, 3
Groups canvassed		Factory Managers		App. D
		Storekeepers		III, 1
		Docks		III, 1
		Service industries		III, 1
		Newstands		XII, 2
		Superintendents of new apartment houses		II, 2, IV, 1
		Sample of 20 tenement houses		II, 3, IV, 1, XIV
Participant observation		Churches		IX
		Settlements		XII
		Tea rooms, cabarets		III, 1, VIII
		Hangouts		VIII, XII
		Speakeasies		III, 1, XII
		Streets		V, 2

APPENDIX B

FORMS OF INTERVIEW SCHEDULES

THESE schedules were used for purposes of recording, not as direct questionnaires. They were designed to bring out the process of cultural distortion. The questions attempted to define the issues in terms relevant to the culture of the group. Each schedule was worked out carefully with people who knew the culture and problems of the group.[1] The interviewers used either direct or indirect questioning as the circumstances dictated, making every effort to check the authenticity of each view before recording it. The interviewers in turn were checked to make sure that they were not imposing their own attitudes upon the persons interviewed.

Only those questions on the original schedules which dealt with social attitudes are included here. For each person interviewed, such relevant social data as age, sex, marital status, nativity, national origin, years in United States, occupation, education, were secured.

ITALIAN

INTERVIEW SCHEDULE FOR SOCIAL ATTITUDES

Should a girl choose her own husband —— or be influenced by her parents' choice? ——
Should every girl marry? ——
What are the most important considerations in choosing a husband: family reputation? —— money? —— occupation? —— health? —— steady work? —— love? —— character? —— other? ——
What is most important in choosing a wife: family reputation? —— beauty? —— intelligence? —— dowry? —— housework? —— other? ——
Would you object if your daughter (or sister, brother, self) married: Irishman? —— Frenchman? —— American? —— Jew? —— Protestant? —— Italian from other part of Italy? —— Italian born in Italy? ——
Do you favor large families? ——
Can a marriage be considered successful without children? ——
Do you approve of divorce? —— on any grounds? ——
Should husband have complete authority in the home? ——
Would you allow your daughter (or do you think parents should allow their daughters) to: bring boy friends to house? —— go out with group of boys and girls? —— go out with man if not engaged? —— go out with fiancé? —— go out with other girls? ——
Should children obey their parents absolutely? —— to what age? ——
Should children continue to be guided by their parents after marriage? ——

[1] Cf. page 431 for account of framing of Italian schedule.

Should parents expect a child to sacrifice his own interest or ambition to promote the welfare of the family? ——

Should working children bring home all their pay envelopes? —— part? —— none? ——

What should a son's allowance cover? ——

What should a daughter's allowance cover? ——

Should you prefer a girl to work in office? —— as servant? —— in factory? —— not at all? ——

To which occupation would you object? ——

Should you prefer a boy to work in factory? —— at skilled work? —— as waiter? —— in office or store? ——

To which occupation do you object? ——

Should a son follow his father's trade? ——

Should you prefer that a boy learn a skilled trade or continue his general education (high school)? ——

Do you prefer parochial or —— public school? ——

Do you attend church on all Holy Days of Obligation? ——

How often do you go to confession? ——

Do you think that the Church is gaining or losing in influence? ——

Is it well to protect a baby with charms? ——

Must an expectant mother eat whatever she wants, to be sure that the child is not disfigured? ——

What are your three favorite Italian songs? ——

What two operatic selections do you know? ——

Can you dance the quadrilla —— or tarantella? ——

Name the two greatest Italians ——

Name an Italian artist —— musician —— scientist ——

Is America a good place to live? ——

Is it the right atmosphere for raising children? ——

What is your ambition for your children: boys —— girls ——?

Should you like to return to Italy? —— to visit? —— to remain? ——

Do you associate with people from other parts of Italy? ——

Are people from different parts of Italy becoming more friendly? ——

Do you prefer to live in an Italian neighborhood? —— or where there are other nationalities? ——

What American ways do you like? ——

What Italian ways do you wish to retain? ——

What have been the greatest changes in Italian life in this district during the last ten years? ——

Are you glad —— or sorry —— to see these changes?

What changes do you hope for in the future? ——

VILLAGERS

INTERVIEW SCHEDULE FOR SOCIAL ATTITUDES

Do you consider it wrong for an unmarried couple to live together? ——

Should divorce be made easier? ——

What should be the grounds? ——
Should every effort be made to keep a family intact? ——
What makes for a successful marriage? ——
Are children necessary? ——
Should married women have interests independent of their husbands? ——
Should a married woman be self-supporting? ——
Should she give up work which interests her when she gets married? ——
Should husband share in household tasks? ——
What should determine the size of family? ——
What do parents owe to their children? —— support? —— social prestige? ——
education? —— autonomy? —— other? ——
What has a parent a right to expect from a child? —— respect? —— support?
—— obedience? —— other? ——
Until what age? ——
What should determine whether a girl can go out alone with a boy? ——
Would it distress you if your daughter married: Italian? —— Jew? ——
Irishman? —— Spaniard? —— Catholic? —— Protestant? —— Negro? ——
other? ——
Which would you strongly oppose? ——
Would you prefer a son or brother to enter: business —— or profession ——; be
a salesman —— or learn a mechanical trade ——; public service (fire, police,
etc.) —— or industrial worker ——
Should all parents try to send their children to college? —— Why? ——
Is the Church an important factor in modern life? ——
Should it be? —— Why? ——
Should churches adapt their doctrines and their practices to modern conditions?
—— Why? ——
Do you disapprove of dancing and card playing on Sunday? ——
If your income were curtailed, what would you cut down on first? ——
What would you find hardest to give up? ——
Would you save on food for: rent? —— theater tickets? —— travel? ——
study? —— books? —— clothes? —— radio? —— furniture? —— automo-
bile? —— other? ——

IRISH

INTERVIEW SCHEDULE FOR SOCIAL ATTITUDES [1]

What occupation do you most favor for a boy: civil service? —— profession?
—— stenographic? —— priest? —— business? —— skilled trade? ——
other? ——
What occupation do you most favor for a girl: civil service? —— teacher? ——
office? —— skilled trade? —— nun? —— nurse? —— domestic? ——
other? ——

[1] Since only a small number of Irish were to be interviewed, this schedule was designed
for the double purpose of discovering the attitude of the individual and getting information
about the community. It therefore contains questions of two distinct types.

Do you prefer parochial —— or public —— education?
Are Irish-Americans mixing with more kinds of people now: Italians? ——
Spaniards? —— Poles? —— Germans? —— Jews? —— other? ——
Has there been more intermarriage with foreigners? —— Protestants? ——
Would you object if your daughter (or sister, brother, self) married: Italian? ——
Spaniard? —— Protestant? —— Jew? —— do you know cases? ——
Would you allow children to be raised Protestant? —— do you know cases? ——
Do Irish-American families stick as closely together as before the War? —— im-
mediate family? —— grandparents, aunts, cousins, etc.? ——
What was the usual number of children before the War? —— now? ——
What is the ideal number of children? —— Why? ——
Is divorce permissible on any grounds? ——
Should children bring home all of their pay? —— part? —— none? ——
Do they bring home as much of their pay as they used to before the War? ——
Should children place family interests before their own ambition? ——
Should children obey absolutely? —— to what age? ——
Do girls have too much freedom? —— in what ways? ——
Do girls work more after marriage? —— how long? ——
Should they work for: need? —— a better standard of living? —— independ-
ence? ——
Is husband recognized as head of the house? —— should he be boss? —— or
share fifty-fifty? ——
Is the Church gaining —— or losing influence? ——
Are you as strict in church observance as your parents? —— as your older
brothers or sisters? —— as you used to be yourself? ——
Is interest in politics greater? —— or less —— than it used to be among older
men —— younger men —— older women —— younger women ——
Are you interested in Ireland? —— in Free State politics? —— Irish stories? ——
songs? —— literature? ——
Do you wish to return to Ireland: to visit? —— to remain? ——

SPANISH

INTERVIEW SCHEDULE FOR SOCIAL ATTITUDES

Do you strictly observe Holy Week here in America? ——
Would you go to work on Good Friday? —— on any other important religious
day? ——
Which in your opinion is the more important: Christmas? —— Good Friday?
—— Mardi Gras? ——
Do you ever go to an Irish church? ——
Would you permit your daughter to marry a man of her own choice? ——
What are the most important things in choosing a husband for your daughter:
character? —— money? —— occupation? —— health? —— family reputa-
tion? —— family social standard? —— love? —— steady worker? ——
Would you be willing for your daughter to marry: Italian? —— Irish? ——
American? —— Jew? —— Chinese? —— Spanish Mestizo? —— Negro? ——

Would you allow your daughter to go out unchaperoned: with boy friend? ——
with fiancé? —— in group? ——
Would you be satisfied with only a civil ceremony in marriage? ——
Do you approve of birth control? ——
Do you think divorce permissible on any grounds? ——
Do you consider infidelity of men a serious offense? ——
Should the wife obey her husband in all matters? ——
About how long would you mourn for a: son? —— cousin? —— brother? ——
mother? —— husband or wife? —— Which would you mourn for a longer
period if you were in Spain? ——
Would you have a wake and 'novena' if a member of your family died? ——
Would you prefer to live: in a Spanish neighborhood? —— in neighborhood
where not many Spanish people live? ——
Do you know Spanish people in other parts of New York? ——
Do you associate with: Spaniards? —— South Americans? —— Central Ameri-
cans? —— Mexicans? —— Porto Ricans? —— Cubans? ——
Do you know any: Spanish songs? —— Spanish dances? ——
Do you consider America a good place to live? ——
Are you planning to return to your own country? ——
Are you anxious to improve your English? ——

JEWISH

INTERVIEW SCHEDULE FOR SOCIAL ATTITUDES [1]

How often is synagogue attended: High Holidays? —— Saturday? —— Holi-
days? —— Daily? —— Not at all? ——
On which of the following days do members of the family stay at home from
work: High Holidays? —— Festivals? —— Saturdays? ——
Which of the following things are not done on Saturday: Carrying money? ——
Riding? —— Writing? ——
Do men in the family: Fast on Yom Kippur? —— Pray daily with Tfillin? ——
Wear Tzitzith? ——
Will any member of the family eat meat outside of home unless certain it is
Kosher? —— eat bread on Passover? —— eat milk with meat? —— eat pork
products? ——
Are the following holidays celebrated at home: Passover? —— Succouth? ——
Purim? —— Chanukah? —— Shovuoth? ——
Has the family separate dishes for meat and milk? —— separate dishes for
Passover? —— a mezuzah on every door? —— or on entrance only? ——
Do women light candles on Friday night: with blessing? —— without bless-
ing? ——

[1] Designed to discover both changes in traditional Jewish practices and relation between adherence to tradition and loyalty to Jewish group. The number of families who could be reached was too small to make this study of general value, but the schedule is included with the schedules of other groups in order to complete the series.

Are any lights lit from sundown Friday to Saturday? —— Is any cooking done on Saturday? —— Is telephone answered on Saturday? ——

Do parents observe following customs: have sons circumcised by mohel? —— or by doctor? ——; have eldest son redeemed? ——; have sons Bar Mitzvah? ——; have marriage ceremony performed by: orthodox rabbi? —— conservative rabbi? —— reformed rabbi? —— civil officer? ——; arrange strictly Jewish funeral? —— observe Shivah? ——; observe Kaddish: for year? —— less than year? ——; observe anniversary of death? ——

Which of these customs do children expect to observe? ——

Is there strong objection to intermarriage with Gentile on the part of parents? ——

Are children allowed to go to the homes of Gentiles? —— Are they allowed to bring Gentiles to the house? —— Are girls —— or boys —— allowed to go with Gentiles? ——

Has any member of family ever married a Gentile? ——

Has any member of family ever changed his name? —— Is this considered desirable? ——

What age is thought desirable for a girl to marry? ——

Is shadchem approved? ——

Is a large family considered a blessing? —— What is considered ideal size of family? —— Should girls work after marriage? ——

What occupations for girls are desirable? —— undesirable? ——

What occupations for boys are desirable? —— undesirable? ——

Are children being trained for the professions? —— If not, are they being sent to college? ——

Are children being given a musical education? ——

Does the family belong to: an orthodox congregation? —— a conservative congregation? —— a reformed congregation? —— no congregation? ——

To what Jewish organizations do members of the family belong: father? —— mother? —— boys? —— girls? —— To what non-Jewish organizations does any member belong: Organizations? —— Who belongs? ——

What Jewish newspapers —— or magazines —— are read regularly in the home? What other magazines —— or newspapers —— are read? What languages are spoken —— or read —— by: father? —— mother? —— boys? —— girls? ——

What Hebrew education have children received? ——

APPENDIX C

GREENWICH VILLAGE AS A REAL ESTATE DEVELOPMENT

SINCE the real estate factor seemed to many of the people of the locality to be the dominant one, and since the corresponding developments in other cities are inevitably bound up with real estate conditions, an attempt was made to analyze the local situation from a real estate point of view.

Expenditures for the alteration of old, and the construction of new, buildings in the Village appear to have been independent both of other building on Manhattan and of general conditions in the building industry. The annual volume of construction in the Village shows no correlation with the index of construction for Manhattan as a whole or with changes in construction costs and in the price of building materials. The conditions, discussed in the text, which made for a residential backflow and determined the suitability of the Village, were the governing factors.

The state of the real estate market cannot be accurately determined, for the prices at which sales take place are not made public and only the assessed valuation is reported. On the basis of the latter, however, it appears that the reconstruction of the area brought a very substantial increase in property values. The average increase from 1920 to 1930 in the assessed value of the land amounted to 75 per cent as compared with 69.5 per cent for the Borough of Manhattan.[1] It may be fairly assumed that in this district the usual relationship between increases in market and assessed values has obtained, namely, that assessed values have followed the upward course of market values, lagging behind, but moving more nearly in accord with market prices than if the latter had been on the way down.[2]

Land within the Village changed value at a very uneven rate, some blocks changing little, while others tripled in value between 1920 and 1930. Most of the increase occurred within the central portion of the Village where a large proportion of the blocks more than doubled and all except two increased at least 50 per cent. Few in the waterfront area and in the tenement district south of Washington Square rose as much as 50 per cent, but none failed to increase. Lots fronting on Seventh Avenue at the

[1] For Manhattan, taxable land only; property exempt from taxation excluded.

[2] The absolute relation between market and assessed values is of no importance to this discussion, though the length of the time lag is.

principal intersections rose most, while those under the elevated structure on Third Street increased less than 10 per cent.[1] Even the blocks which rose the least, however, increased more than the average of 9.4 per cent for the corresponding tenement section of the lower East Side which remained unreclaimed. The most extreme increases in the Village, on the other hand, were less than the average increase of 518 per cent for the reclaimed area of the East Fifties.

Although the Village shared in the real estate boom produced by the backflow of population onto Manhattan, it clearly did not experience the full force of that backflow, as did the mid-town area. Comparison of a sample of fifteen blocks in the Village, the lower East Side, and the East Fifties, which were assessed in 1920 at the same basic rate per front foot, showed the combined effect of the decreasing value of tenement property and the rise brought about by reclamation. Prior to 1920, the decline in the value of tenement property had already set in, for the East Side blocks had decreased between 1917 and 1920 by an average of 14 per cent. The effect of the residential backflow, however, was not felt until after 1920, for neither the Village nor the mid-town blocks showed any increase between 1917 and 1920. From 1920 to 1930, the increase on the selected Village blocks ranged from 19 to 131 per cent, averaging 67 per cent. By contrast, half of the East Side blocks showed no change, the remainder varied from a 2.5 per cent decrease to an increase of 47 per cent, and the whole sample showed an average increase of 8 per cent. The blocks in the East Fifties, on the other hand, showed a very much more precipitate rise than the Village — increases ranging from 67 to 650 per cent, and averaging 269 per cent.[2]

The scattered and sporadic character of the Village rebuilding is reflected in the irregular distribution of the increases in the value of buildings. While increases in land values radiated on the whole from points of maximum accessibility or residential attractiveness, building values showed no such systematic rise.[3]

The larger part of the increase in property values appears to have been due to location rather than to investment. The amount invested in building activities amounted at the most to only 44 per cent of the increase in improved value, leaving the factor of location to account for 56 per cent.[4] If allowance were made for depreciation in the value of existing buildings due to obsolescence, the proportion of the increase attributable to location would be considerably greater — as much as 64.5 per

[1] Cf. map, Appendix G.
[2] Tentative Land Value Map, prepared by the Department of Taxes and Assessments, 1917, 1920, 1930.
[3] Cf. map, Appendix G.
[4] Table XXIV, p. 444; Charts X, XI, p. 446.

TABLE XXIV. CHANGE IN VALUE OF PROPERTY DUE TO LOCATION
RATHER THAN TO BUILDING ACTIVITY [1]

(IN MILLIONS)

	VALUE (IMPROVED) 1920	VALUE (IMPROVED) 1930	INCREASE IN VALUE, 1920–30	EXPENDI-TURE ON BUILDING ACTIVITY, 1920–30	INCREASE IN VALUE IMPUTED TO LOCA-TION, 1920–30	
					VALUE	PER CENT
Eastern section (east of 6th Avenue [2])....	$ 9.7	$ 15.0	$ 5.3	$ 1.4	$ 3.9	73.6%
Central section .	35.1	75.0	39.9	22.0	17.9	44.9
Western section (west of Hudson Street)...	15.9	26.2	10.3	1.2	9.1	88.5
Entire district..	60.7	116.2	55.5	24.6	30.9	55.6

cent if an annual rate of 2 per cent for depreciation were allowed. The
influence of location was particularly apparent in the waterfront section
where new investment amounted at most to only 10 per cent of the increase in value. A comparison of the properties facing or accessible to
Seventh Avenue — the thoroughfare of the new Village — with those
facing Bleecker Street — the 'Main Street' of the old — shows the
diffusion of the increase through the neighborhood beyond the particular
place or amount of building. Property values on these two streets kept
close together until 1926 and diverged importantly only after a number
of large apartment houses had been erected along Seventh Avenue.

But though the rise in property values greatly exceeded the amount
actually spent for building, the net effect was to increase the value of improvements on the land even more than the value of the land itself. If the
value of the buildings is compared with the land upon which they were
located, to determine how far the district might be regarded as 'built up'
and how heavy a superstructure of improvements the land was bearing,
the buildings are seen to amount to considerably more in 1930 than in
1920. By 1930, the building made up at least a quarter of the total value
of land and building combined on 55.6 per cent of the 2500 lots [3] as com-

[1] Compiled from Tax Assessors' list as published in the *City Record* and building permits
reported in *Real Estate Record and Guide*.

[2] City block 552, on west side of Washington Square, included in central section.

[3] Cf. Chart IX, opposite.

CHART - IX

REAL ESTATE DISTRIBUTED ACCORDING TO PROPORTION OF VALUE REPRESENTED BY IMPROVEMENTS

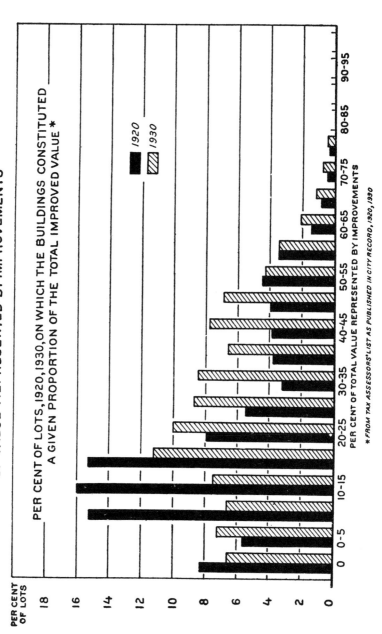

PER CENT OF LOTS, 1920, 1930, ON WHICH THE BUILDINGS CONSTITUTED A GIVEN PROPORTION OF THE TOTAL IMPROVED VALUE *

1920
1930

PER CENT OF LOTS

18
16
14
12
10
8
6
4
2
0

0   0-5   10-15   20-25   30-35   40-45   50-55   60-65   70-75   80-85   90-95

PER CENT OF TOTAL VALUE REPRESENTED BY IMPROVEMENTS

*FROM TAX ASSESSORS' LIST AS PUBLISHED IN CITY RECORD, 1920, 1930

pared with 33 per cent of the lots in 1920. The sites where the buildings added nothing to the value of the land were only half as numerous in 1930 as in 1920, in spite of the fact that a number of new sites had been razed in the process of subway construction.[1] The relative decrease in amount of obsolescence or near obsolescence in the district is all the more noteworthy in view of the fact that the land itself increased on the average 75 per cent in value during the period.[2] The larger proportion of the total value represented by improvements thus allowed for a corresponding increase in value of buildings before a difference in the proportion of the total furnished by the building, as compared with 1920, would appear.

It is virtually impossible, however, to determine how good an investment Village realty actually was during these years. In the early days of the Village's development, figures were frequently published by realtors to show that there was a profit to be made in remodeling. There is no reason to think, however, that such figures were representative, and at best they showed only gross return on new investment, making no allowance for interest charges, amortization, taxes, or other costs, or the percentage of vacancies. In respect to later developments, no comprehensive estimate, however rough, could be made. In the middle of the decade, realtors disagreed, at least in their published statements, as to the terms upon which local real estate could be made to yield a return. Industrial property in the center of the area appeared to have become unsuitable for such use. Two loft buildings had been converted into apartments, two more owners were planning in 1930 to make a similar transformation, and a local chamber of commerce stated in 1930 that most industry could not pay the rents which the valuation of Village property called for. It was a common cry of landlords that they were being taxed into the necessity of converting tenements into more income-producing forms. Taxes were accused of driving the old residents out of their homes by forcing remodeling.

The contention that high taxes, which reflected primarily the higher assessments on increased land values, not an increased tax rate, were forcing remodeling was also hard to check. A sample of the tenements scattered in different parts of the district showed their landlords paying from 13 to 77 per cent more in taxes in 1930 than they had in 1920 — on the average 54 per cent more. As these taxes ranged in 1920 from 10 to 20 per cent of the amount received in rent and averaged between 15 and 20 per cent, the amount of rent increase which would have reflected added taxes would have ranged from 2 to 17 per cent, and would have averaged 10 per cent. These computations are based on the assumption of only 10

[1] Twenty-eight hundred lots in 1920 reduced to 2468 in 1930 by the city's taking properties for streets.   [2] Cf. Chart.

per cent of vacancies. One suspects that landlords blamed taxes for forcing remodeling, not because they could not have met the added taxes out of rents if their houses had been full, but because they could not keep their houses occupied.

Whether the benefit of rising property values was reaped by old residents or by new investors cannot be determined because there is no way to discover the prices at which properties changed hands. There was, however, a heavy turnover in ownership accompanied by changes in the type of holders in the district. The latter involved principally a shift from individual to corporate holding and the rise of a number of local Italians to positions as property-owners.

TABLE XXV. CONTINUITY OF OWNERSHIP

NUMBER OF INDIVIDUALS AND ORGANIZATIONS HOLDING PROPERTY IN 1920 AND 1930 [1]

	NUMBER OF OWNERS			PER CENT OF 1920 OWNERS STILL OWNERS IN 1930	PER CENT OF 1930 OWNERS WHO HAD BEEN OWNERS IN 1920	PER CENT OF 1930 IMPROVED VALUE HELD BY OWNERS WHO HAD BEEN OWNERS IN 1920
	1920	1930	COMMON TO BOTH 1920 AND 1930			
Real estate corporations [2]	56	217	14	25	7	11
Business companies..........	83	75	20	24	27	52
Institutions......	38	42	29	77	69	93 [3]
Individuals						
Italians.....	177	333	86	49	26	31
Others......	1,323	837	362	28	43	50
Total..........	1677	1504	511	30	34	41 [4]

Roughly measured, the turnover in ownership amounted to 59 per cent of the property in the district.[5] Only 41 per cent in 1930 was owned by individuals or corporations who had held any property in the area in

[1] Compiled from Tax Assessors' lists, 1920, 1930, as published in the *City Record*. See Table XXVI, p. 447, note 1, for accuracy of data.

[2] Corporations with different names separately counted, although some may have been subsidiaries of other companies.

[3] Income-producing property only.

[4] Excluding tax-exempt properties.

[5] Measured in improved, assessed value; cf. Table III, Appendix F, p. 464.

CHART-X

VALUE OF BUILDING ACTIVITY DIVIDED BETWEEN ALTERATIONS AND NEW CONSTRUCTION*

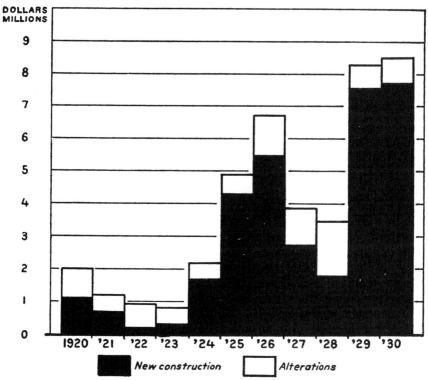

DOLLARS
MILLIONS

New construction ▪   Alterations ☐

*REAL ESTATE RECORD AND GUIDE; VALUES STATED IN BUILDING PERMITS. DECLINE 1920-'21
REFLECTS DROP IN PRICES; OTHER CHANGES REFLECT VOLUME OF OPERATIONS.

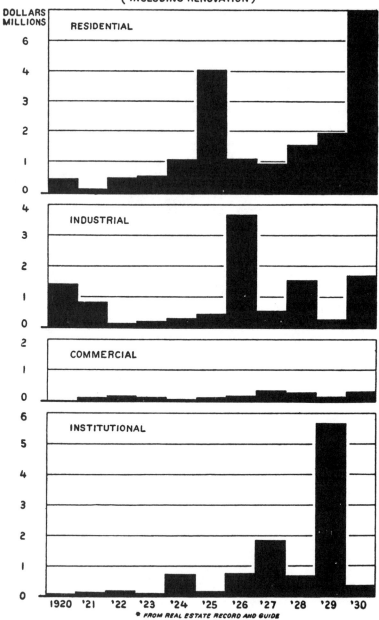

CHART-XI

TYPES OF BUILDING ACTIVITY,* 1920-1930
(INCLUDING RENOVATION)

DOLLARS
MILLIONS

RESIDENTIAL

6
4
3
2
1
0

4

INDUSTRIAL

3
2
1
0

2

COMMERCIAL

1
0

6

INSTITUTIONAL

5
4
3
2
1
0

1920 '21 '22 '23 '24 '25 '26 '27 '28 '29 '30

* FROM REAL ESTATE RECORD AND GUIDE

1920. Approximately a thousand new property-owners had acquired local real estate by purchase or bequest during the decade as against only some five hundred who remained as owners from the beginning to the end of the period. Even with due allowance for the inevitable changes in private ownership in a period of ten years through death, it is clear that the local real estate market was an active one in these years.

TABLE XXVI. TYPE OF PROPERTY OWNERSHIP

AMOUNT OF PROPERTY, MEASURED ACCORDING TO IMPROVED VALUE, HELD BY
TYPES OF OWNERS [1]

	1920		1930	
	AMOUNT IN MILLIONS	PER CENT	AMOUNT IN MILLIONS	PER CENT
Real estate corporations...............	$ 3.0	5%	$ 25.6	22%
Business companies....................	6.7	11	12.8	11
Institutions				
Income-producing..................	4.2	7	8.1	7
Used by institution [2]...............	6.1	10	13.9	12
Individuals				
Italians..........................	4.9	8	15.1	13
Others...........................	35.8	59	40.7	35
	60.7	100	116.2	100

Most distinctive among the new owners were real estate corporations. Between 1920 and 1930, 17 per cent of the real estate in the area passed out of the hands of private individuals and into the hands of 217 corporations, only 14 of which had had local holdings in 1920. By 1930, corporate holdings amounted to 22 per cent of the property in the locality.[3]

Among the individuals who acquired property, an increasingly large

[1] Compiled from Tax Assessors' lists, 1920, 1930, as published in the *City Record*. Classification based on names as here recorded. Subject to serious error because: (1) spelling of names by assessor not consistent and some individual may be counted twice or not found on succeeding list; (2) classification 'Italian' on the basis of name unsatisfactory; (3) properties actually held as a unit are sometimes listed in the names of several members of a family; (4) business companies, unless incorporated, cannot always be distinguished from individuals; (5) real estate corporations frequently incorporate each property which they hold separately, giving an appearance of more companies with smaller holdings than is actually the case; (6) private owners may incorporate, giving the appearance that their holding has changed hands. This and following tables showing ownership must be accepted as only an approximation to the actual situation.

[2] Exempt from city taxes.

[3] Cf. Table XXV, p. 446.

proportion had Italian names and were, presumably, local Italian residents who had put their savings into tenement buildings or bought the sites of their stores. A handful were in the real estate business, but the rest — numbering more than 300 — had made small investments only. In 1920, only 12 per cent of the private individuals owning property were Italians by name; in 1930, 29 per cent appeared to be of Italian extraction. They held some 13 per cent of the property of the district in 1930 as against 8 per cent in 1920.[1]

TABLE XXVII. SIZE OF HOLDINGS

AVERAGE IMPROVED VALUE OF PROPERTY HELD BY TYPES OF OWNERS [2]

	1920	1930	1930	
	AVERAGE HOLDING	AVERAGE HOLDING	AVERAGE HOLDING OF THOSE WHO WERE OWNERS IN 1920	AVERAGE HOLDING OF THOSE NOT OWNERS IN 1920
Real estate corporations..	$ 51,700	$121,500	$204,000	$116,000
Business companies......	70,700	165,400	322,000	109,700
Institutions				
Income-producing[3] ..	120,000	197,800	266,000	43,200
Institutional use....	160,000	328,000		
Individuals				
Italian.............	24,200	45,000	55,000	40,000
Other.............	26,300	50,000	57,800	44,200
Total income-producing..	$ 35,700	$ 78,000		
Total all property.......	32,000	69,000	$ 83,400	$ 61,600

Apart from these changes, the real estate developments of these years did not bring any striking alteration in ownership. In spite of the advent of real estate corporations, the district remained principally in the hands of small individual investors. Although the total number of holders decreased by 10 per cent, the average size of holding increased no more than was accounted for by the general rise in values, and the number of large holdings was no greater in 1930 than in 1920. Average holdings of $35,700

[1] Cf. Table XXVI, p. 447.
[2] Compiled from Tax Assessors' lists, 1920, 1930, as published in the *City Record*. See Table XXVI, p. 447, note 1, for accuracy of data.
[3] Average distorted by holdings of Trinity Church Corporation which constituted 62 per cent of income-producing property held by institutions in 1920 and 71 per cent in 1930.

and $77,000 for 1920 and 1930 respectively and the fact that 91.5 per cent of the holdings were under $50,000 in 1920 and 89 per cent were under $100,000 in 1930 clearly indicate the absence of concentration in local land-ownership.[1] Apart from the City of New York itself and the railroad engaged in building tracks and a freight terminal, the only three really large holders dated their claims by some hundred years — Trinity Church whose glebe lands had lain partly within the bounds of the Village, the estate owned by one of the original suburbanites when the Village was a fashionable suburb, and the brewery which had taken over the property of the State Prison when the latter moved to Sing Sing in 1829.

[1] Cf. Table XXVII, p. 448.   Source of error in fact that large corporations frequently incorporated each property separately, so that they would appear as many small holders rather than as one large holder.

APPENDIX D

GREENWICH VILLAGE INDUSTRY

ON THE whole, industrial developments in Greenwich Village illustrated the generalizations made by the Regional Plan of New York in 1922 and confirmed its predictions as to the future trends of economic activity on lower Manhattan.[1] The industries which moved out of the Village corresponded to the type said by the Regional Plan to be ill-fitted for survival upon lower Manhattan; namely, those where space was at a premium and time was not, where labor demands were large, constant, and for relatively unskilled, and where nuisance features were conspicuous. Those which remained partially fitted the pattern of small plants engaged in lines where the labor demand was specialized and fluctuating, but the space needed was unspecialized and small in relation to the number of workers. Most especially, the prediction that the processes involving distribution, management, or facilitation would be more likely to remain than actual fabrication was amply borne out by the relative strength of maintenance and service functions among the industrial activities which survived in the Village. Where contact with customers, time, style, and market accessibility were of relatively great importance, sections of Manhattan other than the Village offered greater advantages.

The Greenwich section of lower Manhattan was never a great industrial region. The plants actually within the confines of the Village represented a miscellaneous collection rather than one or more localized industries. As such, their comings and goings would be more likely to be determined by those 'irrational' and 'personal' factors [2] which tend to interfere with the most favorable location of industry, rather than by economic considerations causing industrial establishments to migrate as a group. Many were clearly held in their Village location by inertia. A canvass in 1930 showed that all the local industrial establishments had been in the Village for an average of thirteen and one-half years. In the western part of the district, which was a long-established industrial section, with the advantages of proximity to the waterfront, no zoning restrictions, and low land values, the average time at the location was twenty years. Along the eastern edge, which was the boundary of the garment trade section, largely abandoned by 1930, where land values were low and buildings decrepit, the average was eighteen years. At the

[1] *Regional Survey of New York and its Environs*, vol. I, 'Major Economic Factors in Metropolitan Growth and Arrangement,' by R. M. Haig, New York, 1927, pp. 104–07.

[2] *Ibid.*, p. 26.

northern edge of the Village, industry was interspersed with low-priced retail stores and the plants in this section had been there on the average of twelve years. In the center of the Village, individual factory and loft buildings were scattered here and there through residential blocks and had housed the same concerns for an average of fourteen years. The new lofts in the southern section housed the firms which had newly come into the Village and which averaged a life in the locality of two years.

Relatively short leases, however, indicated either that, in spite of their length of life, local industries were unstable or that the owners of industrial properties expected a change in land usage and would not give long leases. Less than a third either owned their premises or held more than a five-year lease. Nine per cent rented on a yearly or monthly basis.

Certain of the factors likely to hold industry on Manhattan were present in the area. For the fabrication of water-borne raw material, the waterfront section was favorably situated. Railway tracks passed along the edge of the Village and a freight terminal was located a short distance to the south. For an easy and fluctuating supply of workers, rapid-transit facilities were ample. A generous supply of obsolete buildings had been left by the rapid changes in the character of the district and these offered cheap industrial quarters until still further developments made their replacement economic. The district, however, was not immediately accessible to the retail district, the passenger railway terminals, or the financial center, and was not, therefore, favorably placed for selling or style-setting. The city's zoning ordinance partly determined what sorts of industry should be carried on locally. Along the waterfront there were no restrictions, but from the rest of the district, except for isolated streets, 'nuisance' industries were excluded, and only those were permitted which fell within the city's definition of a 'business district.'

On the whole, it was the larger plants which had gone out and the smaller which remained in 1930.[1] Only 8 out of 218 manufacturing establishments in the Village in 1930 employed over 100 workers. Only 3 of these employed over 200. Three quarters of all the plants employed less than 20 workers.

The departure of the 'heavy' industries had been quite general. Where metal, wood, or chemical plants of any size remained, either they were engaged in the fabrication of small articles, they needed access to their market, or they were long established, conservative firms. Among the metal products, the four largest plants in 1930 — employing from

[1] Unless otherwise noted, all data on Village industries in 1930 were drawn from a canvass of the district in October, 1930. The managers of 178 firms were interviewed. Supplementary information was secured for most of the remaining firms either by mail or in the course of an investigation of labor conditions.

75 to 130 workers — were producers of jewelry, watches, or articles made of precious metals. The 10 plants producing bulky light metal products — presumably owing their location to the difficulty of transporting such space-consuming products as showcases or tin cans — all employed less than 60 workers and averaged only 25. Of a similar size were the 9 plants producing such heavy metal products as electric hoists and ventilating systems, whose average number of employees was 30. The large wood products — planing mills, piano factories, furniture shops — had all left the locality by 1930. Only half a dozen small shops remained employing a total of less than 50 workers and making such miscellaneous products as toys, signs, boxes, and accordions.

In the chemical industry, 2 relatively large plants making soap and asbestos respectively, and employing over 100 workers, still remained in 1930. One had a continuous history at the same location of 83 years, the other of 30 years. The former occupied a dilapidated building from which it refused to move, even when a railroad tried to buy the property for its tracks and terminal development. The rest of the chemical plants were small affairs, only 3 others employing more than 40 workers.

The survival of some heavy industry in the locality seemed to be due to negative reasons of inertia and the use of obsolete buildings rather than to positively favorable factors which held them to the center of the metropolis.

In respect to the lighter industries, size appeared to have been the principal selective factor in determining the removal of local plants from the area. In such industries as food, upholstery, needle trades, and novelties, the larger plants had almost all gone by 1930. With the exception of one large candy factory, none of the 67 plants employed more than 25 workers. In 1922, there had been 13 food factories and 12 needle trade establishments with over 20 workers.

The needle trades and artificial-flower shops in particular were not only the smaller, but the weaker, shops in the industry. These were the only industries which had been massed in the vicinity of the Village, in what had been, before the War, the principal industrial section of Manhattan immediately to the east. The mass migration of the fur, needle, millinery, and artificial-flower trades to the mid-town area was already in progress in 1920.[1] The completion of this movement in the next ten years, combined with the style changes which broke the artificial-flower industry, transformed this section from a thriving industrial center to a region of empty and dilapidated lofts, and left only the dregs of these industries behind. The 33 artificial-flower establishments in the Village in

[1] *Regional Survey of New York and its Environs*, vol. I, pp. 86, 92, 93, 99.

1930 were the most precarious of any local industries and contained the worst working conditions of any plants in the area.

The three industries which increased locally in these years showed the effect of the positive influences which kept some manufacturing on Manhattan. Printing and electrical apparatus necessary to maintain telephone service both provided functions of maintenance and service. Small cosmetics firms were chiefly concerned with problems of marketing.

The largest single plant that moved into the district in this decade was engaged in assembling and maintaining telephone equipment. Its location in the Village was clearly not a matter of accident, for there were three other large establishments engaged in different branches of the same activity in the immediate vicinity. Although the main center of job printing remained close to the old newspaper section and the financial district, a tendency for printing to concentrate in and about the area was also apparent. Most of the printing shops were job printers rather than book printers and as such came within the category of service industries, but the largest printer in the section — the second largest plant of any sort — printed periodicals upon which pressure of time was not so great as to preclude the location of the plant outside of the city. Its continued presence in the area was probably attributable to inertia. Bookbinding also, the branch of the printing industry regarded as the least likely to remain near the center of the city,[1] was located in 1930 in an up-to-date loft building immediately to the south of the district. Out of the 55 printing establishments in the Village in 1930, 20 did general job printing, 15 specialized in bookbinding and magazine set-ups, and 15 in advertising work. Seventy per cent of the shops, employing 41 per cent of the workers, had come in since 1920. These were all small shops, averaging 20 workers per shop. The average of all the printing establishments in 1930, exclusive of the one plant with 860 workers, was 21 workers. Forty-one per cent had less than 10 employees.

The cosmetics industry had expanded rapidly in Manhattan from 1914 to 1922. In the latter year it was described as 'a mushroom growth; most of the companies are not firmly established; and there is every indication that as the industry becomes more stable, many of the larger plants will move out of Manhattan.'[2] In 1930, the 14 Village plants manufacturing patent medicines and cosmetics were small, occupied lofts unsuitable for heavy industry, and employed chiefly unskilled girls. They presumably owed their Village location to the desire to be near their market, since, with one exception, they were not nationally known firms with elaborate selling and advertising methods.

[1] *Regional Survey of New York and Environs*, vol. I, p. 73.
[2] *Regional Plan of New York*, Monograph 1, the Chemical Industry, p. 16.

The firms operating in Greenwich Village were far from typical of the trend in industrial organization in these years. Although the largest and newest plant belonged to a subsidiary of the American Telephone and Telegraph Company, the largest corporation in the country, only 3.5 per cent of all the plants in the area in 1930 were owned by large corporations. The bulk were individually owned and had been in the hands of the same family throughout their existence. The average business life of the firms was 22 years. Out of 165 businesses for which information was available, 33 per cent were carried on under individual or partnership names and 63 per cent by individuals or partners operating under a corporate name but furnishing capital and management themselves. A large proportion of the shops which remained in the Village depended chiefly on hand labor. Twelve per cent reported that they used practically no machinery and another 50 per cent used little. Only 38 per cent used machinery to a large extent in their production. Clearly big business and mass production had not come to the Village to an important extent.

TABLE XXVIII

NUMBER OF PLANTS AND EMPLOYEES IN GREENWICH VILLAGE BY INDUSTRIES, SHOWN BY CANVASS OF MANUFACTURING ESTABLISHMENTS, OCTOBER, 1930

INDUSTRY	NO. OF PLANTS	PER CENT	NO. OF EMPLOYEES	PER CENT
Printing	55	25.2	2,000	29.6
Electrical	13	6.0	1,800	26.7
Chemical	28	12.8	850	12.6
Metal	23	10.6	850	12.6
Flower	33	15.1	250	3.7
Needle	24	11.0	100	1.5
Food	15	6.9	300	4.4
Wood and upholstery	11	5.1	100	1.5
Paper	4	1.8	300	4.4
Miscellaneous [1]	12	5.5	200	3.0
Total	218	100.0	6,750	100.0

[1] Four glass products, three cigars, one mica, four art products.

APPENDIX E

THE PUBLIC SCHOOL'S CONTRIBUTION TO THE MALADAPTATION OF THE ITALIAN BOY [1]

By Archie Bromsen

THE outside observer is too apt to lose sight of the prime fact that the boy of the Italian tenement district is just essentially 'boy.' The problem of being of foreign stock, of suffering from grueling poverty, of being involved in ethnic conflict, are not for him in the early years of his life. All of the environmental conditions which are sufficiently different to be noted by an observer from the outer group are simply taken for granted by the boy.

Trouble originating from differences in the culture pattern of the boy and the pattern of the outer group does not directly affect him during the early childhood period in which his activities are limited to his own group. It is when he enters the school that this period of more or less contented adjustment is brought abruptly to an end. There, to his bewilderment, he finds his home and the bulk of the customs which he has made his mode of life under fire from the teachers of the school, and even after school hours from all the other institutions into which the State and irresistible conditions force him.

At home, the criticism which he receives is of a personal nature — for those violations of the rules of conduct set down for him by his parents. He is punished for failure to obey definite orders and for laxity in observance of commonly assumed habits. His offense lies in his own conduct and its failure to conform to standards made clear to him, and which he understands. Whereas at home he is censured, this censure is no greater than any other boy of any other position receives. And he is censured for very much the same things — for refusing to eat what is distasteful to him, or for failure to go to bed on time.

In the school, however, the boy is subjected to criticism, not for his misdemeanors, but because he acts as he has been taught to act. It is not that the child disobeys, but that the very mode of conduct which he naturally follows is objected to. The world in which he has been

[1] The author of this article, Mr. Bromsen, grew up in the Italian community and attended the school of which he writes. At the time when the article was written, he was attending college and assisting in the research for this study. His account was supported by the experience of a number of Italian boys — both those who had gone on to high school and those who had left school as soon as possible. The article is appearing in a Polish translation in the *Polish Sociological Review*.

trained is condemned by the new world into which he has moved. In the school, the child finds, with practically no warning or preparation, that those things which are taken for granted as the proper procedure in his home and immediate environment are not only undesirable but severely forbidden. It is in the school that the child first learns with any degree of definiteness that he is not an American, but an Italian child of the slums; it is in the school that the one institution which is an integral part of his nature and devotion — his home — is constantly subjected to objections which tend to become expressive of real displeasure.

The natural reaction to such treatment is bound to be unfavorable to the school authorities, and it is small wonder that the child's response is often one of indiscriminate rebellion. The boy, in protest against sweeping denunciations, sets himself against the ways of those in charge, and in so doing he fails to distinguish between the teacher and what she is trying to teach him. His teachers retaliate with as little discrimination as the boy, and neither will make concessions to the viewpoint of the other. In consequence, the boy's school life is a period of inescapable subjection and defiance — from the time when as a child he scrawls words on the wall, long before he comprehends their significance, to the time when, as a boy in the graduating term, he masturbates in the classroom during an admonitory lecture on the evils of self-abuse. The teachers, however, are unaware for the most part of the correlation between the conflict with the boy's home environment and his objectionable conduct in the school.

A major consideration in assimilation into any group is that one speak the language of that group, and such is not true of the Italian child of the slums, whose language at home is, from earliest years, an Italian dialect. The school likewise finds that the Italian immigrant home, which is representative for the most part of the peasant class of Italy, is to a very large extent illiterate — a condition which the school assumes to be synonymous with ignorance and unintelligence. The school objects to the practice of a great many families, of taking the children out of school at as early an age as the law will permit, not merely because of the necessity of augmenting the family income, but as a result of an undisguised disregard for book learning.

Another disturbing trait of the home is the difference within the family group itself — not in the outer structure of the group, but in the relative importance and relationships of the different members. A primary difficulty in dealing with the Italian family group is that the position of the father is too despotic — that his power of position and command is entirely inconsistent with his knowledge and understanding of the surrounding circumstances which determine in a large degree the fate of his family. This difficulty is emphasized whenever the father attempts to maintain his own judgment against the decisions of the school in regard to any specific problem involving the child.

The other problem arising from dealing with the Italian family is the impenetrable solidarity which the group possesses as a unit. Any of the most important interests and programs of the community are lightly ignored by members of the family for the benefit of the entire family or any single member. It is this devotion to what are termed 'smaller loyalties' which reconditely serves to baffle the most intense efforts of the agencies of the community in all lines of endeavor.

The basic habits of food, shelter, hygiene, etc., of the family all come in for their share of criticism and complaint. The teachers of the school make it miserably clear to the child that it is not sufficient for him to 'take a bath twice a month, whether he needs it or not,' nor are they sparing in their remarks on his clothes. The usual meals likewise are preached against, since the breakfast is seldom likely to be exactly as recommended by the pink-faced cherub of the cereal advertisements; as a substitute for the piping hot lunch which is so strongly recommended to him in the class, the boy buys instead a sandwich of Gargantuan proportions, and hot dogs, ice cream, candy, pie, or cigarettes — which last item generally is a token of defiance of his teacher, and the utterly incomprehensible, undesirable totality she represents and teaches, rather than a means of satisfying a powerful craving.

More perhaps than for anything else, the Italian boy is resented because of what is regarded as his inevitable future 'lack of morality,' as forecast by his boyhood 'filthiness,' which is, on analysis, only another form of the boy's adaptation to local conditions. The conduct of the boy, which is regarded by his compatriots as a preparation for his adult life of license, is regarded by the teacher as expressive of an outlook which is destructive of moral fiber and integrity.

All these faults the school surveys from the high vantage-point of its own standards, and tries in consequence to supplant these objectionable traits with ways and modes of conduct which are 'characteristically American.' One of the first attempts at this correction is made on the most apparent distinction between the way of the Italian boy and the American, the tainted speech of the boy, but very little is accomplished in regard to this because the class as a unit suffers from this defect.

Without being fully aware of the fundamental significance of the boy's intense loyalty to his family, the school attempts to instill in him, not as a complementary attribute, but as an exclusive substitute, the 'broader loyalty' of allegiance to the community. In place of the laxer codes of the Italian home, the school attempts to substitute the ideals of the American boy — to be trustworthy, courteous, and polite to all; to act with self-control and regard for civic welfare; to be truthful, not merely because of the consequences, but because of an intrinsic, inviolable sacredness which truth possesses; and above all to keep clean in body and thought.

It will be readily seen that to attempt to effect a replacement of the habits of the boy, which are so firmly ingrained in him from the earliest days of his training, by these new ideals, requires a method of approach which abandons the school's emphasis on punishment. Since it happens, however, that the teacher is often unaware of the existence of two patterns, she treats every fault of the boy as willful disobedience. Starting with the assumption that her ways and traditions are the only desirable and possible modes of conduct, she interprets any and every departure from her ways as personal defiance and disobedience. The boy to her is not 'different' — he is 'bad.' This approach, which puts the boy in a position of perpetual misbehavior, engenders an almost universal hatred for the teacher and contempt for her and her ways. In sullen resentment he takes every opportunity to vex her, and to subject her, as far as is consistent with safety, to every possible annoyance and inconvenience.

But the dislike is, at least, mutual. It is no small task to come downtown each morning to try to pound learning into a bunch of little, garlic-eating greasers. Maybe they do not actually smell of garlic, but somehow they do seem greasy. Rather the word is slimy, like eels, with their minds in the mud and filth. The way they talk — and what little pigs they are in general! It is clearly evident that the waterline on Tony's neck will never, never recede, and it would not be such a bad idea to make an example of him by scrubbing him in front of the class. Or would it be better to take him out and thrash him in the hallway? Not too hard, of course — nothing like any of the boys get whom she manages to catch running their hands along her in the press of the passageways. What a bunch of little animals they are, one and all! If one could only get transferred! They are so dirty!

Smuttiness is the growing pain of childhood, but the school of the Italian district is characterized by a degree of sexiness that is far out of proportion to the usual rôle this subject plays in childhood. To attempt an explanation of the group mind which follows so extremely this line of thought on a mere basis of boyhood obscenity is to miss a very significant point in the study of the failure of the school to cope with the problem of education of the Latin second generation of the slum. Because the boy knows how extremely repugnant to the teachers his sexual attitude or behavior is, he makes use of it so that it serves, in addition to its usual rôle as an emotional outlet, as a gratifying defiance of the oppression of those in charge. Teachers are subjected to muttered revilements throughout the day. On every occasion they are discussed by the boys in terms of their probable sexual experiences and irregularities. It is the common assumption that every female teacher augments her official salary in the evening by her heavy schedule in some house of prostitution. The men teachers are reputed to be all addicted to diverse forms of homosexuality, or else to devote their time to orgies of perversion after hours in the classrooms. These quaint qualities of the instructors are not fully believed in, but rather hoped for, as a sort of internal reassurance that there must be something wrong with these tight-lipped, superior persons who crack the whip from nine to three o'clock.

As a counter-force against this resentful, angry submission, the teachers strive for some semblance of order by walloping boys in general and mauling ringleaders in particular. It generally is sufficient for female instructors to beat a heavy ruler on a disobedient boy's shoulder, to pull his hair until his eyes water, or to knock his head against the blackboard. But should the enraged boy offer resistance, or should his offense have been severe enough, any of the gym teachers may be summoned to render forceful assistance. This action is generally reserved for those cases in which the teacher has been struck by an inflamed boy, or the equally frequent cases in which the boy is directly concerned in some sexual misconduct.

Surprisingly enough, some of the women maintain better discipline than the men, who have a tendency to overlook some of the petty misdeeds which prove so exasperating to a mere woman. The effort of a young instructor to continue his lessons at the blackboard while a lad in a back seat was making an exhibition of his masturbation — until he finally gave up and punched the boy around the room — was in crude contrast to the equally ineffectual method of the women instructors who generally deliver lectures to the classes embellished with vivid descriptions of the tertiary stages of syphilis.

It is in this atmosphere of bitter opposition and intense conflict that the school tries in unconscious irony to inculcate into the boy a spirit of co-operative participation in the programs of the community. For a certain number of hours each week, the boy is drilled in the teacher's conception of the principles and functions of the municipal government, and in the rôle which he will occupy in this community which she so casually frees from all the crudities and unpleasantnesses of reality. When the boy has memorized this lesson, the teacher proceeds, with equal aloofness, to the hour of arithmetic.

And so school goes on; the boy waiting for graduation so that he can get just any kind of job; the teacher thrashing her way through the years to her pension. All the time there is this cordial dislike and antipathy, till the day when the teacher affixes her signature in the album to the sentiment which she has used for years. 'In the golden chain of friendship, may I ever remain a link.' And the boy leaves, frames his diploma, and goes for his job. The world lies invitingly before him.

What does he find his position in the world to be? To what extent has the school succeeded in its avowed purpose of fitting him for his future life? In place of the culture which has been scraped off the boy, what has he been given?

The school has drilled him for his part in a democratic paradise, but instead, he finds himself assigned to no enviable position in a blue-eyed aristocracy. The most intense emphasis of the school's teaching has been in condemning the home the boy comes from, and in teaching him to desire instead a home which conforms to the 'American standard of living.' In the world of severely limited incomes in which the Italian boy finds himself confined, however, this home can never be more than a longing, and as an unattainable goal only further darkens the sordidness of the cold-water flat in which he actually lives.

In the world, the boy finds, as he had long suspected, that the teacher spoke of conditions which were ideal rather than real. The virtues of honesty and courtesy which he recited so dutifully in the classroom are of necessity forgotten as soon as he realized that his existence depends on his ability to be more skillfully crooked than his neighbor. To the school teacher the officer at the street crossing may have been a 'gentleman hero of the peace': to the boy he is, without hesitation, 'a big, fat Irish bastard' who guzzles from speakeasy to speakeasy.

The mockery of preaching to the boy of American equality and of excluding him and damning him because he is a 'Wop' is a bitter potion that thoroughly purges the mind of all traces of community allegiance. It is difficult to accept a rôle of inferiority because of superficial habits and characteristics which have been acquired as assets and absolute necessities in the smaller boyhood community. The severe handicap imposed upon anybody exhibiting any traces of the objectionable characteristics of the boy of Italian descent gives the direct lie to the fervent insistence of the authorities that anyone can rise from the masses.

What the pressure of the school has accomplished has been to drive him from the security of the family group, but it has failed in its effort to draw him into the circle of community loyalty. As a concession to the ways of the outer group, the new generation gets 'stewed' with the rest and the best on Saturday night. His home, instead of being a source of comfort, rich with the warmth of family friendship, has become a place to which he returns reluctantly, even to eat and sleep. In exchange for this, the community has given him the street corner and poolroom, where he finds solace in the company of his friends who are sympathetically maladjusted.

For the sake of a better job, which he seldom obtains, he undergoes his confinement in the public school and the tribulations which a break with the customs of the home must of necessity occasion. And for what? Those whom he loves and who love him are spiritually estranged; those with whom he seeks familiarity greet his advances with embittering contempt and disparagement. He longs at moments for the happiness of the old, and he dare not take it; he yearns for the elusive newness, and fails miserably to attain it. Instead of education, he has been disciplined into irremediable maladjustment to both the conflicting cultures. He has been educated for the Presidency, and he becomes a truck-driver.

APPENDIX F

TABLE I. GREENWICH VILLAGE POPULATION BY AGE GROUPS
1910, 1920, 1930 [1]

	1910	1920	1930
Under 5...............................	6,650	5,391	2,048
5–9..................................	5,669	5,180	2,488
10–14................................	5,244	4,632	2,702
15–20................................	7,465	5,057	3,672
21–44................................	not available	23,455	18,158
45 plus..............................	not available	10,861	8,977
Total under 21.......................	25,028	20,260	10,910
21 plus..............................	42,691	34,383 [2]	27,135 [3]
Total, all ages......................	67,719	54,643	38,045

[1] *U.S. Census, 1910, 1920,* reported in Cities Census Committee, *Materials for Demographic Studies of New York City.* Special tabulation furnished by Census Bureau for 1930.

[2] Including 67 whose age was unknown.

[3] Including 73 whose age was unknown.

TABLE II. SCALE OF RENTS, 1930

PER CENT OF DWELLINGS ACCORDING TO MONTHLY RENTAL [1]

MONTHLY RENTAL	GREEN-WICH VILLAGE	MANHAT-TAN	NEW YORK CITY	LOWER [2] EAST SIDE	UPPER [3] WEST SIDE	BRONX
Under $15......	1.9	4.3	2.1	17.4	.9	.3
$15–29.........	34.1 [4]	28.3 [4]	19.0 [4]	60.1	13.9	5.3
$30–49.........	24.9	25.5	35.0	18.7	11.2	41.0
$50–99.........	30.0 [5]	26.4 [5]	36.5 [5]	3.5	19.4	50.3
Over $100......	9.1	15.5	7.4	.3	54.6	3.1
	100.0	100.0	100.0	100.0	100.0	100.0

[1] *U.S. Census, Fifteenth Census, 1930.* Population Bulletin, *Families,* New York, pp. 13, 14, 54; MSS. reports for Greenwich Village. Percentages based on number reporting rents. Proportion unknown ranges from 1.6 to 10.7 per cent.

[2] Statistical Area M2B.

[3] Statistical Area M5A.

[4] $15–19...........Greenwich Village........... 6.9 per cent
                 Manhattan................. 8.4
                 New York City.............. 4.3
    $20–29...........Greenwich Village...........27.2
                 Manhattan.................19.9
                 New York City..............14.7

[5] $50–74...........Greenwich Village...........18.6
                 Manhattan.................18.8
                 New York City..............29.4
    $75–99...........Greenwich Village...........11.4
                 Manhattan................. 7.6
                 New York City.............. 7.1

TABLE III. NATIVITY, 1910, 1920, AND 1930 [1]
PER CENT OF THE TOTAL POPULATION IN EACH NATIVITY GROUP

NATIVITY GROUP	GREENWICH VILLAGE	MANHATTAN	NEW YORK CITY
Native white, native parents			
1910................	18.9	14.8	19.3
1920................	17.7	17.0	20.7
1930................	28.4	21.0	21.7
Native white, foreign parents			
1910................	35.4	35.1	38.2
1920................	40.7	37.5	41.0
1930................	36.5	32.6	40.2
Foreign-born white			
1910................	43.8	47.4	40.4
1920................	40.5	40.4	35.4
1930................	33.7	34.4	33.1
Negro and other races			
1910................	1.9	2.6	1.9
1920................	1.1	4.8	2.7
1930................	1.4	12.0	4.9
Total population			
1910................	100.0	100.0	100.0
1920................	100.0	100.0	100.0
1930................	100.0	100.0	100.0

[1] *U.S. Census, 1910, 1920, 1930.*

TABLE V. AGE DISTRIBUTION OF GREENWICH VILLAGE,
1910, 1920, AND 1930 [1]

PER CENT DISTRIBUTION OF POPULATION OF CERTAIN AGES IN EACH NATIVITY GROUP

YEARS	NATIVE WHITE NATIVE PARENTS			NATIVE WHITE FOREIGN PARENTS			FOREIGN-BORN WHITE			NEGRO AND OTHER RACES			TOTAL POPULATION		
	1910	1920	1930	1910	1920	1930	1910	1920	1930	1910	1920	1930	1910	1920	1930
0–5	11.6[2]	11.8	7.2	19.7[2]	18.6	8.8	0.9[2]	0.3	0.2	5.5[2]	5.8	2.0	9.8[2]	9.9	5.4
5–9	9.2	9.2	6.9	15.8	17.9	11.7	2.4	1.2	0.7	4.8	5.9	3.1	8.4	9.5	6.5
10–14	9.2	8.8	6.6	12.1	14.2	13.5	3.7	2.6	0.9	5.1	5.9	1.3	7.7	8.5	7.1
15–20	11.5	10.3	8.9	12.8	12.6	16.7	9.5	5.5	3.0	8.9	6.6	4.9	11.0	9.2	9.7
21–44	..	42.0	53.2	..	26.7	36.7	..	59.6	54.1	..	45.6	70.6	..	42.9	47.7
45+	..	17.5	17.2	..	9.9	12.6	..	30.6	41.2	..	29.4	18.1	..	19.9	23.6
21+	58.4	59.5	70.4	39.5	36.6	48.3	83.5	90.2	95.3	75.6	75.0	88.7	63.0	62.8	71.3

[1] U.S. Census, 1910, 1920, 1930.
[2] Secured by adjusting reported figure for under 6 by the percentage difference in 1920 between figures reported for under 5 and under 6.

TABLE VI. MARITAL CONDITION, 1930

PER CENT OF THE POPULATION OF GREENWICH VILLAGE 15 YEARS AND OVER WHO
WERE MARRIED, SINGLE, WIDOWED, DIVORCED, BY SEX AND NATIVITY [1]

	SINGLE		MARRIED		WIDOWED		DIVORCED	
	Male	Female	Male	Female	Male	Female	Male	Female
Native white, native parents	54.0	52.2	41.0	37.5	3.5	8.2	1.3	1.7
Native white, foreign parents	65.3	55.4	30.6	35.7	3.2	7.5	0.5	0.7
Foreign-born, white	34.5	17.0	59.3	65.6	5.4	16.5	0.5	0.6
Negro and other races	41.0	25.7	53.9	52.5	3.6	19.8	1.4	2.0
Total population	48.2	40.0	46.5	47.4	4.2	11.2	0.7	1.0

[1] U.S. Census, 1930. Small remainder, unknown marital condition, omitted.

TABLE VII. GAINFUL EMPLOYMENT, 1930, BY TYPE OF INDUSTRY AND SEX [1]

	MALES				FEMALES				TOTAL MALES AND FEMALES			
	NUMBER Gr. V.	PER CENT Gr. V.	PER CENT Manh.	PER CENT N.Y.C.	NUMBER Gr. V.	PER CENT Gr. V.	PER CENT Manh.	PER CENT N.Y.C.	NUMBER Gr. V.	PER CENT Gr. V.	PER CENT Manh.	PER CENT N.Y.C.
Manufacturing [2]	2610	17.7	18.1	24.4	1638	25.8	19.1	24.2	4248	20.1	18.3	24.4
Transportation communication	2691	18.2	12.5	11.3	301	4.7	3.4	5.6	2992	14.2	9.6	9.4
Wholesale and retail trade	2246	15.2	18.2	20.2	644	10.2	12.1	15.1	2890	13.7	16.3	18.9
Service [3]	3206	21.6	25.5	17.6	1383	21.8	43.7	28.8	4589	21.7	31.4	20.5
Professional and semi-professional	1426	9.6	6.2	4.9	1639	25.8	13.7	12.6	3065	14.5	8.7	6.7
Finance [4]	908	6.2	6.0	6.4	415	6.5	3.7	6.7	1323	6.3	5.3	6.5
Construction	1060	7.2	9.4	12.1	31	.5	.4	.5	1091	5.2	6.5	8.9
Mining, agriculture, fishing	30	.2	.2	.3	4	.1	.0	.0	34	.1	.0	.2
Not specified	604	4.1	3.9	2.8	291	4.6	3.9	6.5	895	4.2	3.9	4.5
Total	14781	100.0	100.0	100.0	6346	100.0	100.0	100.0	21127	100.0	100.0	100.0
Per cent of total men and women over 15 years of age		91.6	89.7	88.7		43.3	43.1	33.0				

[1] U.S. Census, 1930.

[2] Principal types of manufacturing:

	NUMBER MALES	NUMBER FEMALES
Printing	536	253
Clothing	514	707
Iron and steel	257	24
Textiles	130	115

[3] Principal forms of service:

	NUMBER MALES	NUMBER FEMALES
Hotels, restaurants, boarding houses	1367	317
Other domestic and personal service	723	565
Public service	386	53
Recreation and amusement	248	231
Laundry, cleaning	86	63

[4]

	NUMBER MALES	NUMBER FEMALES
Banking and brokerage	542	209
Real estate and insurance	366	206

TABLE IX. THE EIGHT PROTESTANT CHURCHES WITHIN GREENWICH VILLAGE [1]

	CHURCH MEMBERSHIP	SUNDAY SCHOOL MEMBERSHIP	EXPENDITURES OF 5 CHURCHES [2]
1901	3706 [5]	2734 [5]	$34,599 [4]
1905	3356 [4]	2224 [4]	25,593
1910	3800 [4]	1926 [3]	43,203 [3]
1915	3497 [5]	1752 [5]	37,117
1920	3231 [3]	1438 [3]	59,136 [3]
1925	2198 [4]	1340 [4]	68,880 [3]
1929	2136	793	71,318

[1] From *Annual Reports* of churches.   [2] Figures available for only 5 of 8 churches.

[3] In case of one church, estimates, or figures for following or preceding year (nearest available) used.

[4] In case of two churches, estimates or figures for following or preceding years used.

[5] In case of three churches, estimates or figures for following or preceding years used.

TABLE X. SCHOOL ENROLLMENT, 1920, 1930

	1920	1930
Number in school [1]		
Aged 5	296	123
Aged 6–15 [2]	8,264	4,853
Aged 16–20	454	874
Number enrolled in: [3]		
Kindergarten: Boys	281	270
Girls	256	260
Total	537	530
Grades 1–8: Boys	3,859	2,159
Girls	4,229	2,430
Total	8,088	4,589
Grade 9	45	215
Ungraded classes	83	56
Classes for physically handicapped	126	116
Per cent of those in grades 1–8 attending each type of school: [3]		
Public	66.0%	62.6%
Parochial	32.5%	33.1%
Private	1.5%	4.3%
Per cent of total population aged 16–20 in school [1]	10.6%	28.2%

[1] *U.S. Census, 1920, 1930.*   [2] 9000 in school in 1910.

[3] New York City Board of Education, *Monthly School Reports*, for public schools; *Catholic Directory*, for parochial schools; *Annual Reports*, for private schools. Totals for each school adjusted on basis of samples of discharge cards used to furnish an estimate of proportion of each school's enrollment resident within the district.

TABLE XI. DESTINATION OF THOSE LEAVING BOYS' PUBLIC SCHOOL [1]

	1924	1928	1930
Per cent graduating from 8B who:			
Went to work from 8B	16%	6%	7%
Went to high school from 8B	2%	2%	0
Left because over age before end of 9B	20%	15%	6%
Went to work from 9B	11%	19%	28%
Declared intention of entering senior high school from 9B	51%	58%	59%
Per cent leaving school (excluding transfers) who left because they were over age without completing a grade	40%	32%	25%

[1] From school discharge cards; records for earlier years and for other schools too incomplete to use.

TABLE XII. MAGAZINES AND NEWSPAPERS READ BY VILLAGERS AND LOCAL PEOPLE

MAGAZINES

	Number sold weekly or monthly on Village newsstands [1]	Number of readers in sample of 75 Villagers [2]
New Yorker	1,013	42
Liberty	1,012	2
Saturday Evening Post	402	14
Cosmopolitan	395	3
Colliers	306	15
True Story	275	0
Woman's Home Companion	264	0
True Detectives	256	0
Red Book	200	0
Vogue	160	1
Ladies Home Journal	157	0
McCalls	152	0
Vanity Fair	148	3
Photoplay	143	0
Screen Play	111	0
Delineator	105	2
Harper's [3]		23
Atlantic Monthly [5]		19
Nation [4]		12
Scribner's [5]		11

[1] Canvassed, 1930. Numbers estimated by news dealers as their average sales. These sales appear from comparison with sample of Villagers to reflect chiefly the reading of the local people.

[2] Moshier, *op. cit.*

[3] A few sales reported on 4 out of 48 stands.

[4] Sales reported on 7 stands.

[5] Not reported on any stand.

TABLE XII. — *Continued*

NEWSPAPERS

	Number sold daily on Village newsstands	Number of readers in sample of 75 Villagers
Daily News	2,300	5
Times	1,393	48
Journal	1,247	0
Sun	1,217	1
Mirror	1,011	0
Graphic	1,005	0
World Telegram	978	11
Herald Tribune	861	13
American	562	6
Il Progresso	536	0
Post	517	6
Corriere d'America	353	0
Bolletino della Sera	234	0

TABLE XIII. MORTALITY RATES PER 1000 OF THE POPULATION BY PRINCIPAL CAUSES OF DEATH FOR SECTIONS OF GREENWICH VILLAGE 1920–22, 1928–30 [1]

	CONTAGION	T.B.	PNEUMONIA	DIGESTIVE	CANCER	HEART	OTHER DEGENERATIVE	PUERPERAL	ACCIDENT	OTHER	TOTAL
Italian tenement section [2]											
1920–22......	.8	1.5	1.9	.4	.8	2.1	1.7	.1	.7	3.8	13.8
1928–30......	.3	.9	1.5	.1	1.2	2.3	1.4	.1	.7	3.3	11.7
Remodeled section [3]											
1920–22......	.7	1.6	2.6	.5	1.8	3.0	2.2	.0	1.0	5.0	18.5
1928–30......	.4	1.0	2.1	.3	1.9	3.5	2.1	.1	1.4	5.1	17.9
Waterfront section [4]											
1920–22......	1.4	2.7	3.0	.7	1.0	1.9	2.4	.1	1.9	5.0	20.1
1928–30......	.6	1.5	2.8	.4	1.2	3.8	2.4	.1	1.9	6.0	20.7
Greenwich Village											
1920–22......	.8	1.6	2.2	.5	1.0	2.1	1.9	.1	1.0	4.5	15.7
1928–30......	.4	1.0	1.9	.2	1.5	3.0	1.8	.1	1.1	4.2	15.1

[1] Figures supplied by New York City Department of Health; population estimated on a straight line trend.
[2] Sanitary Areas 65 and 67.
[3] Sanitary Areas 71 and 73.
[4] Sanitary Areas 69 and 75.

Table XIV. Mortality Rates per 1000 of the Population by Age Groups for Sections of Greenwich Village, 1920-22, 1928-30 [1]

Age	−1	1-4	5-14	15-44	45+	All Ages
Italian tenement section [2]						
1920-22	93.0	12.5	2.6	7.1	34.8	13.8
1928-30	46.4	7.8	2.2	5.0	32.7	11.7
Remodeled section [3]						
1920-22	93.7	15.0	4.0	7.8	39.5	18.5
1928-30	69.2	12.7	3.9	7.5	46.3	17.9
Waterfront section [4]						
1920-22	167.0	14.6	2.6	12.5	42.8	20.1
1928-30	122.0	15.2	2.4	11.2	51.1	20.7
Greenwich Village						
1920-22	102.4	13.5	3.0	8.1	37.8	15.7
1928-30	65.6	10.1	2.7	6.7	40.0	15.1

[1] Figures supplied by New York City Department of Health; population estimated on a straight line trend.   [2] Sanitary Areas 65 and 67.

[3] Sanitary Areas 71 and 73.   [4] Sanitary Areas 69 and 75.

Table XV. Infant Mortality Rates per 1000 of Live Births [1]

	Under One Year	Under One Month
Italian tenement section [2]		
1920-22	96	37
1927-29	55	29
Remodeled section [3]		
1920-22	97	41
1927-29	73	40
Waterfront section [4]		
1920-22	144	40
1927-29	119	34
Greenwich Village		
1920-22	103	40
1927-29	71	34
Manhattan		
1920-22	83	[5]
1927-29	81	
New York City		
1920-22	77	[5]
1927-29	60	

[1] Figures supplied by New York City Department of Health; population estimated on a straight line trend.   [2] Sanitary Areas 65 and 67.

[3] Sanitary Areas 71 and 73.   [4] Sanitary Areas 69 and 75.   [5] Not available.

TABLE XVI. TYPE OF CLINICAL SERVICES PROVIDED IN GREENWICH VILLAGE, 1920, 1925, 1929 [1]

	NUMBER OF AGENCIES			NUMBER OF PERSONS SERVED [2]	
	1920	1925	1929	1925	1929
General medical [3]	2	3	3	14,333 [4]	11,051
General surgical	1	1	1	12,615	13,827
Child health: baby and pre-school	0	2	2	2,764 [4]	2,954
Dental	2 [5]	3	3	12,050 [4]	11,662
Ear, Nose, Throat	2	3	2	3,375 [4]	3,297
Eye	2	3	3	2,050 [4]	1,449
Cardiac	0	2	1	226	150
Gynecological	1	2	2	1,265	1,574
Genito-Urinary	1	1	1	697	326
Mental	0	0	1	0	131

Cases carried by visiting nurses....................................2,947 [6]   3,152

	1920	1925	1929
Estimate of total patients from Greenwich Village [7] served by local health centers	7,900	11,200	12,500
Per cent of total population	14%	23%	32%

[1] Compiled from reports or records of local clinics. Covers only those clinics or services located within the Village, i.e., 1 hospital, 1 dispensary, 1 health center, 1 visiting nurse service, 1 settlement, 1 welfare school. Excludes services of nurses and doctors at all public and parochial schools, at two private kindergartens and at four day nurseries. Excludes services available at city hospital, tuberculosis service from city clinic and from a city-wide case-work agency, hospitalization for contagious diseases, and many other hospital and clinic services available to people of this community.

[2] All patients served by local agencies whether residents of Greenwich Village or not. Figures derived by adding total of new cases during year to old cases of first month. Information for 1920 too incomplete to tabulate.

[3] Surgical included at one clinic.

[4] For one clinic, 1927 figures nearest available.

[5] Volume of dental service in 1920 very small.

[6] Figure for 1926.

[7] Estimated by applying to the totals reported the proportion between those residing within and those outside of the Village found in a sample of cases from the various agencies. A rough approximation only.

TABLE XVII. GREENWICH VILLAGE FAMILIES UNDER CARE OF
FAMILY CASE-WORK AGENCIES, 1920–1930 [1]

NUMBER OF NEW CASES [2] ACCORDING TO NATIONALITY AND AGENCY

	CHARITY ORGANIZATION SOCIETY	ASSOCIATION FOR IMPROVING THE CONDITION OF THE POOR	CATHOLIC CHARITIES [3]
American			
1920–22	21	56	
1923–26	9	36	
1927–30	21	26	24
Irish			
1920–22	13	13	
1923–26	29	14	
1927–30	31	5	65
Italian			
1920–22	83	102	
1923–26	104	50	
1927–30	80	33	90
Others			
1920–22	13	24	
1923–26	30	22	
1927–30	39	15	16
Total			
American	193		
Irish	170		
Italian	542		
Others	159		
	1064		

[1] Compiled from case records of each agency.

[2] For 1920, both old and new cases; Charity Organization Society 1920 cases include fall of 1919.

[3] Catholic Charities cases reported for 1927–30 only.

TABLE XVIII

Problems Presented in Cases of Family Welfare Agencies [1]
Per Cent of Cases Presenting Each Problem [2]

	1920–1930				All Groups			
	Amer-ican	Irish	Ital-ian	Other	1920–22	1923–26	1927–30	Total
Health								
Tuberculosis............	2.4	4.0	3.1	1.7	4.0	2.7	1.5	3.0
Venerial disease.........	0	.2	1.8	1.5	1.1	1.3	.7	1.2
Tonsils, dental, eyes.....	3.2	4.7	3.3	5.2	.8	2.7	4.5	3.8
Other health............	19.9	21.8	22.7	19.5	21.9	20.4	20.3	25.2
Economic								
Insufficient income......	7.0	7.3	6.2	3.8	6.4	3.7	5.4	6.1
Underemployment.......	3.0	6.8	2.9	5.8	1.6	3.4	5.5	4.9
Unemployment..........	21.8	13.8	15.4	16.0	16.7	11.3	13.2	16.2
Family								
Neglect of children......	1.9	2.3	2.3	1.7	.3	2.8	1.7	2.2
Old age...............	4.8	5.9	2.8	5.2	3.2	2.1	4.2	4.0
Widows and widowers....	2.2	2.0	3.6	2.4	4.2	2.6	1.7	3.0
Maternity.............	3.2	2.0	3.7	2.9	3.7	2.1	2.5	3.2
Illegitimacy............	1.3	1.2	.8	.9	.3	.9	1.0	1.0
Desertion..............	4.5	2.3	4.7	6.1	4.8	3.8	3.0	4.5
Non-support...........	2.7	2.3	4.1	3.4	.6	4.7	2.6	3.5
Mental and behavior.......	5.7	4.7	5.3	6.8	5.6	4.5	3.9	5.5
Moral								
Intemperance...........	6.0	6.3	2.1	3.4	3.4	3.5	2.4	3.6
Sex immorality.........	.3	1.9	1.0	.3	.5	1.3	.5	.9
Begging tendency.......	1.1	1.4	2.4	2.7	1.0	1.7	2.0	2.0
Bad management								
Bad housing............	1.6	3.0	3.0	4.7	4.2	1.7	2.3	3.1
Bad housekeeping.......	2.4	3.0	2.7	2.7	.2	2.5	2.6	2.5
Other								
Death.................	1.9	2.6	3.0	1.7	2.6	2.5	1.7	2.6
Imprisonment..........	3.0	1.4	1.5	1.5	2.3	.9	1.4	1.7

[1] Compiled from case records of three family welfare agencies.

[2] More than one problem recorded for some cases; records do not usually show other problems which may be discovered after the agency has started working on a case.

TABLE XIX. SERVICES RENDERED IN CASES OF FAMILY WELFARE AGENCIES

PER CENT OF CASES RECEIVING EACH SERVICE [1]

	1920–1930				ALL GROUPS				AGENCIES		
	AMERICAN	IRISH	ITALIAN	OTHER	1920–22	1923–26	1927–30	TOTAL	CHARITY ORGANIZATION SOCIETY	ASSOCIATION FOR IMPROVING THE CONDITION OF THE POOR	CATHOLIC CHARITIES
Health services......	37.2	31.2	37.0	29.6	38.1	46.3	29.7	34.7	37.1	48.2	22.9
Economic adjustment..	16.2	11.1	14.1	19.2	15.5	12.3	14.8	14.1	14.1	17.7	12.9
Child aid...........	10.9	13.2	12.9	13.8	12.7	17.5	10.5	12.5	12.4	17.6	9.8
Maternal aid........	4.7	8.5	4.9	2.8	1.1	1.8	8.6	5.4	1.2	2.6	13.5
Aged cared for......	1.5	2.3	1.0	0	1.1	.4	1.5	1.2	.8	.2	2.5
Family unit strengthened...	1.5	.6	2.7	3.4	1.7	4.8	1.2	2.1	3.5	.7	.9
Mental treatment....	4.7	6.4	4.8	2.8	2.2	4.2	6.3	4.8	5.0	2.9	5.8
Loan................	2.0	3.8	2.6	.7	2.5	.7	4.0	3.0	3.6	.5	3.6
Housing or housekeeping improved..	1.8	2.8	2.7	3.6	4.0	1.3	2.6	2.7	2.9	.9	3.5
Legal contact........	2.9	2.3	2.1	3.0	2.5	2.9	2.2	2.4	2.5	2.4	2.3
Church contact.......	6.4	12.0	7.7	7.3	11.0	.9	9.9	8.2	6.5	.5	16.0
Miscellaneous........	9.9	7.3	7.8	10.4	7.5	6.1	9.7	8.3	10.7	5.9	6.3

[1] Compiled from case records of three family welfare agencies, more than one service reported in some cases.

TABLE XXI. SIZE OF FAMILY, 1930 [1]

NUMBER OF PERSONS PER FAMILY	GREENWICH VILLAGE	MANHATTAN	NEW YORK CITY
1	25.8%	17.2%	8.3%
2	25.5	26.8	23.0
3	17.3	19.7	21.7
4	13.0	15.4	19.5
5	8.3	9.5	12.6
6	4.7	5.5	7.2
7	2.6	2.9	3.8
8	1.5	1.5	2.0
9	1.3	1.5	1.9
Total	100.0	100.0	100.0

	ITALIAN SECTION	REMODELED SECTION	WATER-FRONT SECTION
1 and 2	45.6%	60.7%	41.3%
3 and 4	33.0	26.8	31.3
5 and 6	14.9	9.5	18.5
7 and over	6.5	3.0	8.9
Total	100.0	100.0	100.0

[1] *U.S. Census, 1930.*

TABLE XXII. NUMBER OF CHILDREN IN SAMPLE ITALIAN FAMILIES, 1925, 1930 (EXCLUDING SINGLE PEOPLE, I.E., 'FAMILIES OF ONE') [1]

NUMBER OF CHILDREN	1925 SAMPLE [2]	1930 ITALIAN SECTION [3]
0–2	63.3	72.7
3–4	24.3	19.0
5–6	10.0	6.4
7 and over	2.4	1.9
Total	100.0	100.0

[1] The average number in the families of the sample of Italian women studied by Odencrantz in 1919 was 6.2 persons (4.2 children), Odencrantz, *op. cit.*, p. 16.

[2] 1221 Italian families listed in *New York State Census, 1925*, on local Italian blocks.

[3] *U.S. Census, 1930*, Sanitary Areas 65, 67.

TABLE XXIII. PROPORTION OF CHILDREN TO WOMEN OF CHILD-BEARING AGE, 1920, 1930 [1]

NUMBER OF CHILDREN UNDER TEN PER 1000 WOMEN AGED 15–44 YRS.	ITALIAN SECTION	REMOD-ELED SECTION	WATER-FRONT SECTION	GREEN-WICH VILLAGE	MAN-HATTAN	NEW YORK CITY
Native-born women [2]						
1920.................	187.8	290.0	483.9	285.3	266.3	355.0
1930.................	172.7	199.9	414.5	209.9	223.2	334.8
Foreign-born women [3]						
1920.................	1431.8	915.5	1645.5	1299.2	1059.8	1261.6
1930.................	1060.6	640.4	1301.0	1046.0	778.4	1038.0

[1] *U.S. Census, 1920, 1930.*
[2] Children reported as native-born of native parents.
[3] Children reported as foreign-born and as native-born of foreign parents.

APPENDIX G

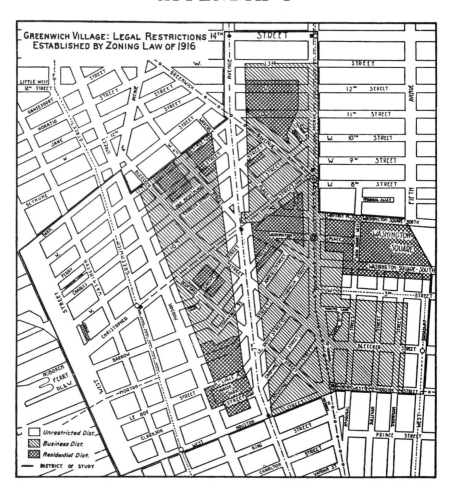

GREENWICH VILLAGE: LEGAL RESTRICTIONS ESTABLISHED BY ZONING LAW OF 1916

LAND VALUE · GREENWICH VILLAGE, 1920

Land Value in
Dollars per
Front Foot

250 - 499
500 - 749
750 - 999
1,000 - 1,249
1,250 - 1,499

FROM TENTATIVE LAND VALUE MAPS, 1920
DEPT. OF TAXES AND ASSESSMENTS

— DISTRICT OF STUDY

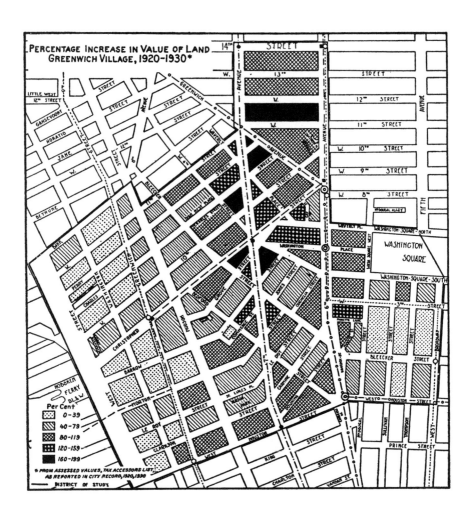

PERCENTAGE INCREASE IN VALUE OF LAND
GREENWICH VILLAGE, 1920-1930*

Per Cent
0-39
40-79
80-119
120-159
160-199

* FROM ASSESSED VALUES, TAX ACCESSORS LIST,
AS REPORTED IN CITY RECORD, 1920,1930.

DISTRICT OF STUDY

LAND VALUE: GREENWICH VILLAGE, 1930

Land Value in
Dollars per
Front Foot

250 – 499
500 – 749
750 – 999
1,000 – 1,249
1,250 – 1,499
1,500 – 1,749
1,750 and over

FROM TENTATIVE LAND VALUE MAPS, 1930
DEPT. OF TAXES AND ASSESSMENTS.

DISTRICT OF STUDY

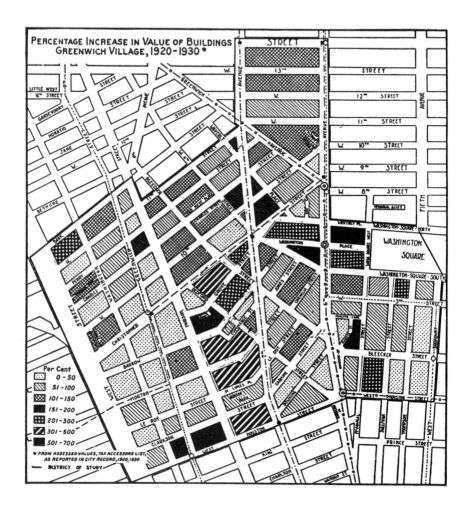

PERCENTAGE INCREASE IN VALUE OF BUILDINGS
GREENWICH VILLAGE, 1920-1930 *

Per Cent
0 - 50
51 - 100
101 - 150
151 - 200
201 - 300
301 - 500
501 - 700

* FROM ASSESSED VALUES, TAX ACCESSORS LIST,
AS REPORTED IN CITY RECORD, 1920, 1930
DISTRICT OF STUDY

INDEX

INDEX

The abbreviations 'f.' and 'ff.' indicate that the reference is to the page designated and, respectively, to that next following or to the two next following.

ABOUT THE AUTHOR

CAROLINE F. WARE (1899–1990) taught at Vassar College, Sarah Lawrence, American University, University of Puerto Rico and Howard University School of Social Work.

Dr. Ware was consultant on community development to the Organization of American States, with technical assistance and visiting-professor missions to Colombia, El Salvador, Chile. She was a United Nations Technical Assistance expert on community development, with missions to evaluate rural development and community development programs in Ceylon and Venezuela, with studies in other Latin American countries and participation in regional Latin American seminars.

Dr. Ware was the author of manuals in Spanish on community study, organization and development, published by the Pan American Union and widely used and republished in Latin America. She was the author-editor of the volume on the Twentieth Century of the UNESCO-sponsored *History of Mankind*.